MEMORIAL

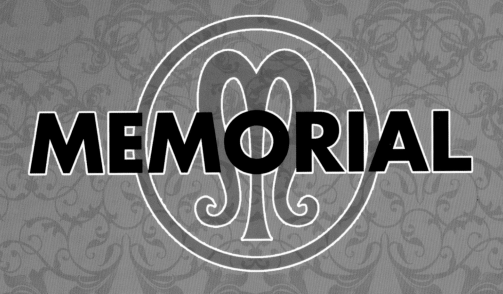

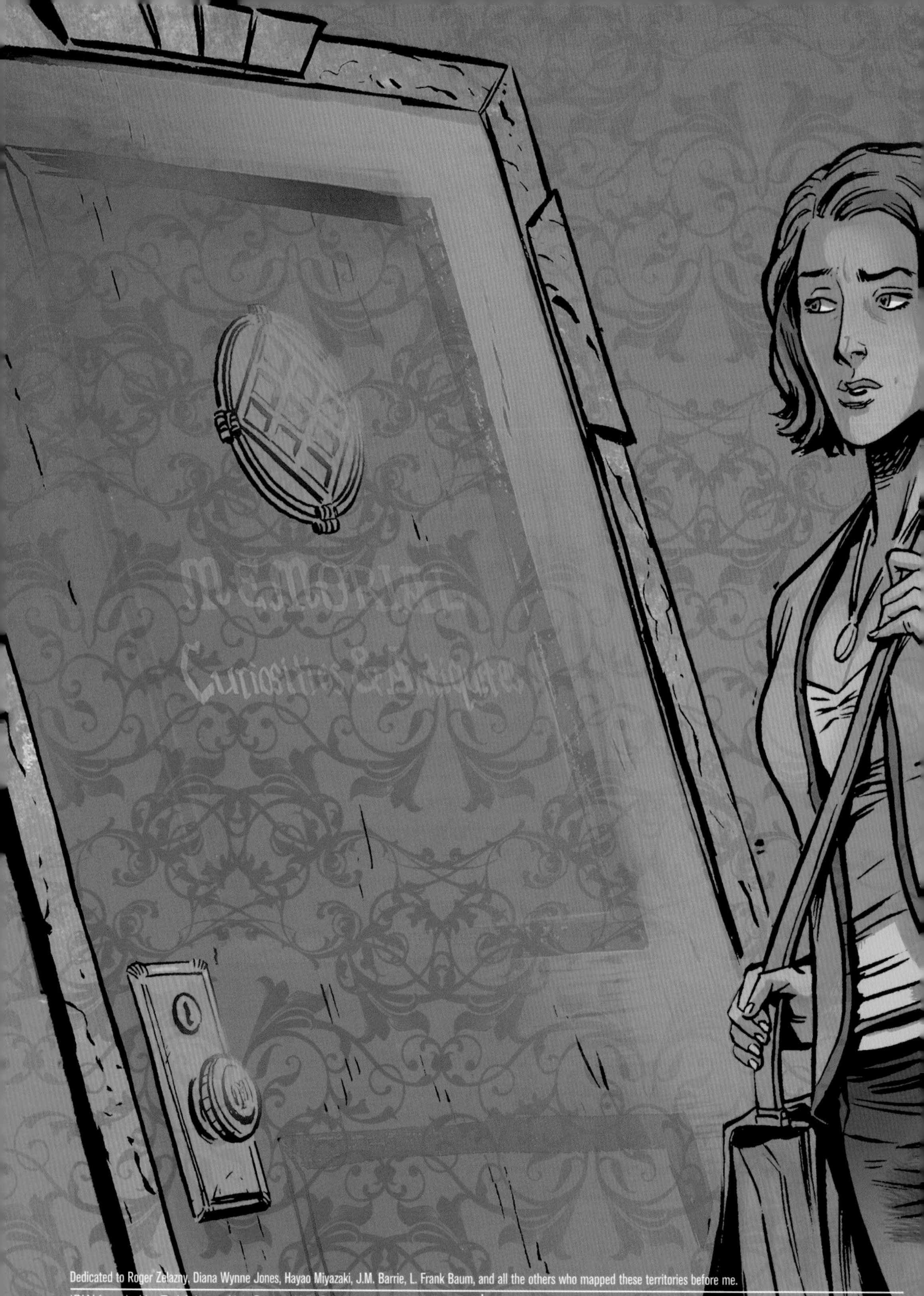

Dedicated to Roger Zelazny, Diana Wynne Jones, Hayao Miyazaki, J.M. Barrie, L. Frank Baum, and all the others who mapped these territories before me.

IDW founded by Ted Adams, Alex Garner, Kris Oprisko, and Robbie Robbins

ISBN: 978-1-61377-354-3

15 14 13 12 1 2 3 4

IDW®

Ted Adams, CEO & Publisher
Greg Goldstein, President & COO
Robbie Robbins, EVP/Sr. Graphic Artist
Chris Ryall, Chief Creative Officer/Editor-in-Chief
Matthew Ruzicka, CPA, Chief Financial Officer
Alan Payne, VP of Sales
Dirk Wood, VP of Marketing
Lorelei Bunjes, VP of Digital Services

Become our fan on Facebook **facebook.com/idwpublishing**
Follow us on Twitter **@idwpublishing**
Check us out on YouTube **youtube.com/idwpublishing**
www.IDWPUBLISHING.com

Originally published as MEMORIAL Issues #1-6.

MEMORIAL

Written by Chris Roberson

Art by Rich Ellis

Colors by Grace Allison

Letters by Neil Uyetake, Robbie Robbins, and Shawn Lee

Edits by Mariah Huehner

Cover by Michael WM Kaluta

Collection Edits by Justin Eisinger & Alonzo Simon

Design by Neil Uyetake & Robbie Robbins

I would like to gratefully acknowledge Grace Allison and Rich Ellis for their fantastic contributions (and Paul Tobin for suggesting Rich in the first place!); Michael Kaluta for his masterful covers; Ted Adams, Mariah Huehner, and Chris Ryall for the faith they demonstrated in the project; Bill Willingham and Kurt Busiek for their kind words and support; Ruiz Moreno and scores of readers like him for tirelessly promoting the book; and my favorite ladies, Allison and Georgia, for providing an endless source of encouragement and inspiration. —Chris Roberson

Heroes, Dastards, and the Ashes of Alexandria

I've known Chris Roberson's work longer than I've known him (only by about two days, but reading one of his stories is why I had to meet him right away), and here's what I know about his storytelling: He doesn't screw around when important stories need to be told. So, when he sets out to write a new fantasy comic series about a woman who's lost her memory, one of my all time favorite tropes in fantasy fiction, and chooses to call the series *Memorial*, I know something big is up.

You see, a memorial isn't just something to do with memory, it's much more focused. A memorial is a thing or event whose sole purpose is to activate memories about very specific things or events. Its job is to command memories--to demand them with authority. So, when Chris names a story about lost memories after a memorial, I know something profound and huge is on the way. Our heroine is going to be well and truly gobsmacked by great and terrible revelation. And because he's such a deft storyteller, we readers are going to be as well.

At least that's my theory, based on past experience and a wee bit of insider knowledge.

I don't want to talk much about what you're going to find in the pages that follow this introduction, since the story should be explored unspoiled. I won't talk about the magical shop in the alley, which was never there before and only appears sometimes for the right people (another fantasy standard that always works for me). Nor will I talk about the gardens of stone and the living marionette. Beg though you might, I won't mention the floating castle, the talking cat, the sinister, possibly moving, statuary, and the magic doors to--well, read and find out.

Here's something Roberson has said about the story: "Memorial is a catalogue of all the cool stuff I want to do." You may not realize what a huge statement that is. I've known him long enough to get an extended glimpse or two inside that mysterious darkened warehouse wherein he stores "all the cool stuff" of his dreams, imaginings, and personal mythology. It's vast. Think of that Indiana Jones warehouse and then multiply it times the individual particles of ash of Alexandria's lost library. "All the cool stuff" is a big promise. I hope you'll help me force him to keep it. You already know how we can do that, but I'll ask you formally at the end of this note.

Let me tell you about Rich Ellis, the artist for these tales. I don't know him. I never heard of the fellow before these pages began to land on my electronic desktop. But, without knowing him, I know he spent years honing his craft, working long hard hours in solitude, at the expense of advancement in other careers and sacrificing what most of us would insist on as a minimally adequate social life. I know this because it's the only way a comic artist this good gets this good. No one in our trade gets to leap fully formed from the forehead of Zeus. We toil and scratch through weary days for every increment of improvement. I don't know Rich, but I can see the years of his life as if I'd lived them myself. Rich Ellis tells this story with a sure hand and clarity of vision that is unfortunately all too rare in our profession. I know I'll be looking out for whatever else he chooses to turn his hand to in the future (while at the same time hoping that new issues of *Memorial* will always head up that list).

In one public forum or another, I've been testifying for some time that we're in the midst of a new movement in comic books, as powerful as the one that caused our industry to be dominated by superhero stories for more than half a century. Our new movement's early pioneers might be books like *Sandman*, *Castle Waiting*, and *League of Extraordinary Gentlemen* (It's too soon to be sure yet, since we're still at the beginning, and we'll need some perspective to really chart the movement's history). It includes hit series such as *Mouse Guard*, *Mice Templar*, *The Stuff of Legend*, and, at the unpardonable expense of tooting my own horn, my own *Fables*. A little bit deeper into the batting order comes *Kill Shakespeare* and *The Unwritten* (a lovely paradox of a title, that one). And always there are others on the horizon.

This new movement might be a bit harder to recognize, because it defies being boiled down to a single captivating word like superheroes. Call it the "folklore, stories-made-flesh, talking animal, fantasy adventure alliance."

Call it grand adventure, or magic adventure? Kurt Busiek, another epic comic book storyteller of note, wants us to call it mythic fiction and he has compelling arguments to support his proposition. So, yes, let's call it that.

But please, I beg of you, don't call it metafiction, a term I've come to despise for many reasons, but mostly since it doesn't do its job. It labels without describing. It's most often used dismissively as it wraps wonderful ideas in safety packaging that prevents actual examination and appreciation. It's an overused tool of academics, because academics and their ilk always need to be made safe from their literature.

Sorry, got off on a bit of a tangent there.

But here's my point: *Memorial* is a strong and exciting addition to our new comics movement (whatever we end up calling it). You'll encounter heroes and dastardly villains in the pages to come, some of whom you already know, and others who're tantalizingly familiar but remain just out of memory's fickle grasp. Don't worry. This is *Memorial* and those elusive memories will be recaptured and illuminated with drama and elán. If I may be forgiven the rhetorical excess, let me put it to you with maximum candor: Roberson and Ellis' new series is required reading. As long as *Memorial* continues to grace our comic shop shelves, once a month you can find me in line, impatient for every issue. I ask that you join me in this undertaking.

Bill Willingham
Just a turn or two down the misty forest road

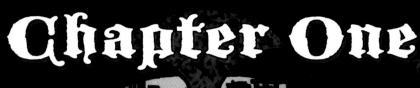

Chapter One

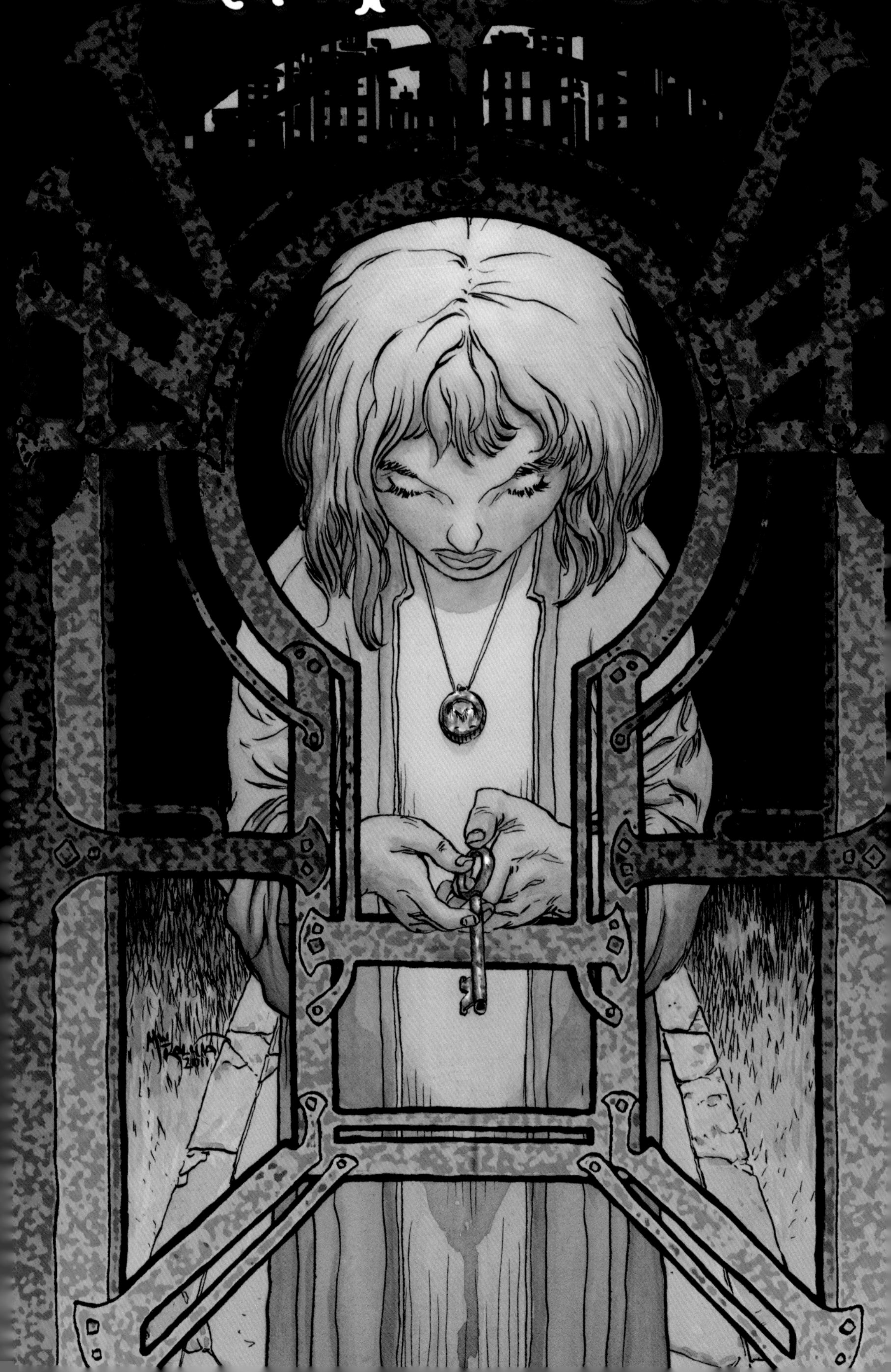

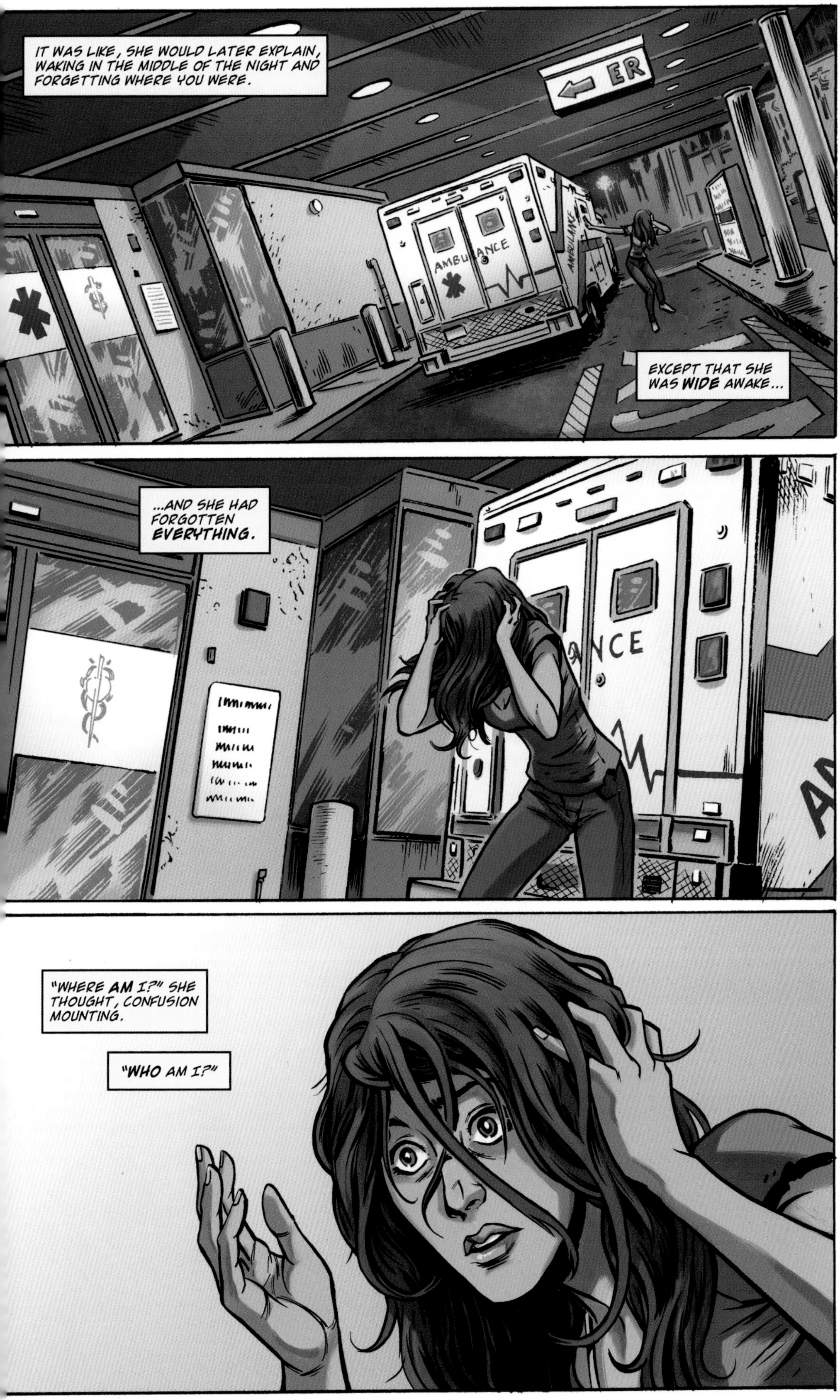
IT WAS LIKE, SHE WOULD LATER EXPLAIN, WAKING IN THE MIDDLE OF THE NIGHT AND FORGETTING WHERE YOU WERE.
ER
AMBULANCE
AMBULANCE
EXCEPT THAT SHE WAS WIDE AWAKE...
...AND SHE HAD FORGOTTEN EVERYTHING.
"WHERE AM I?" SHE THOUGHT, CONFUSION MOUNTING.
"WHO AM I?"

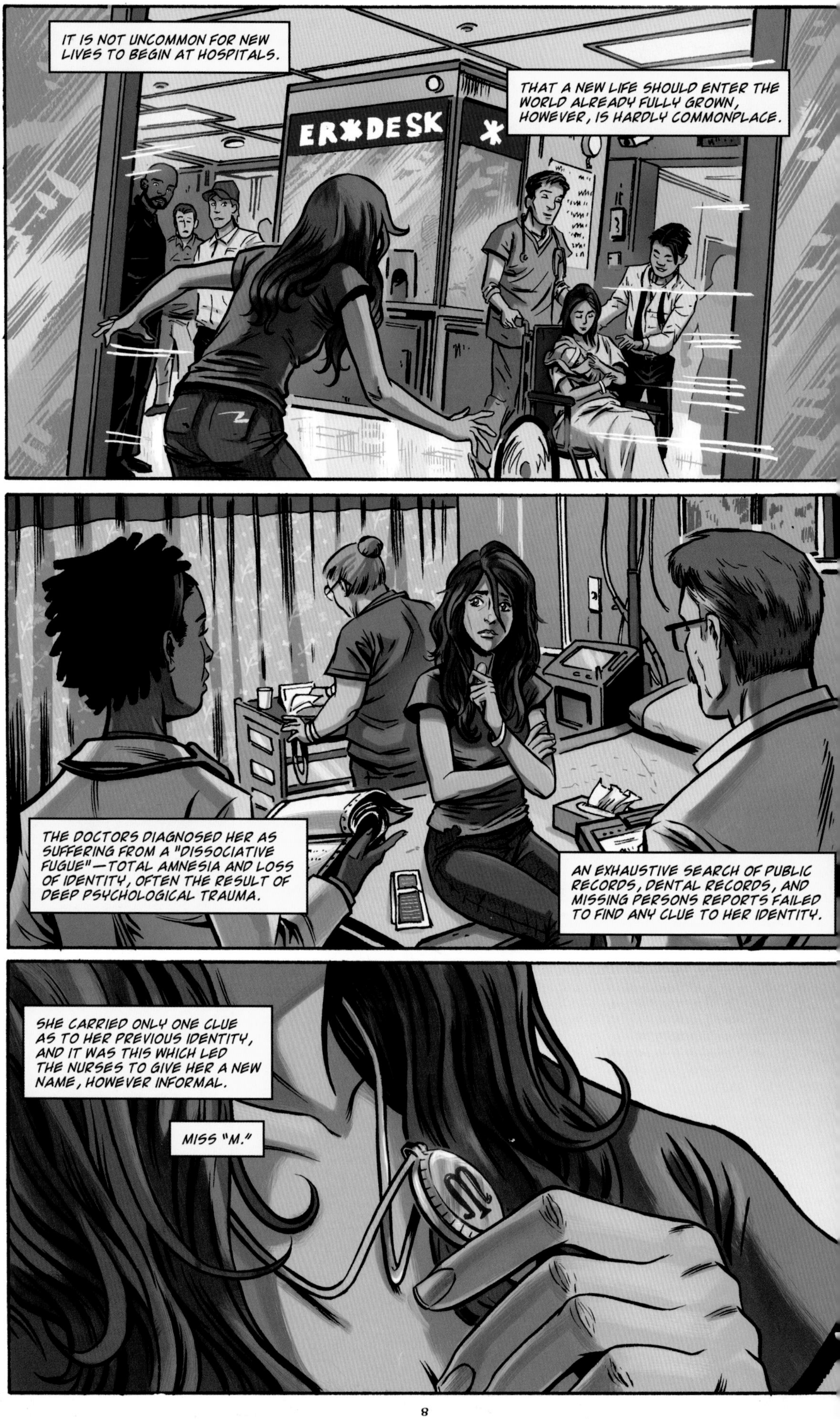
IT IS NOT UNCOMMON FOR NEW LIVES TO BEGIN AT HOSPITALS.
THAT A NEW LIFE SHOULD ENTER THE WORLD ALREADY FULLY GROWN, HOWEVER, IS HARDLY COMMONPLACE.
ER DESK
THE DOCTORS DIAGNOSED HER AS SUFFERING FROM A "DISSOCIATIVE FUGUE"—TOTAL AMNESIA AND LOSS OF IDENTITY, OFTEN THE RESULT OF DEEP PSYCHOLOGICAL TRAUMA.
AN EXHAUSTIVE SEARCH OF PUBLIC RECORDS, DENTAL RECORDS, AND MISSING PERSONS REPORTS FAILED TO FIND ANY CLUE TO HER IDENTITY.
SHE CARRIED ONLY ONE CLUE AS TO HER PREVIOUS IDENTITY, AND IT WAS THIS WHICH LED THE NURSES TO GIVE HER A NEW NAME, HOWEVER INFORMAL.
MISS "M."

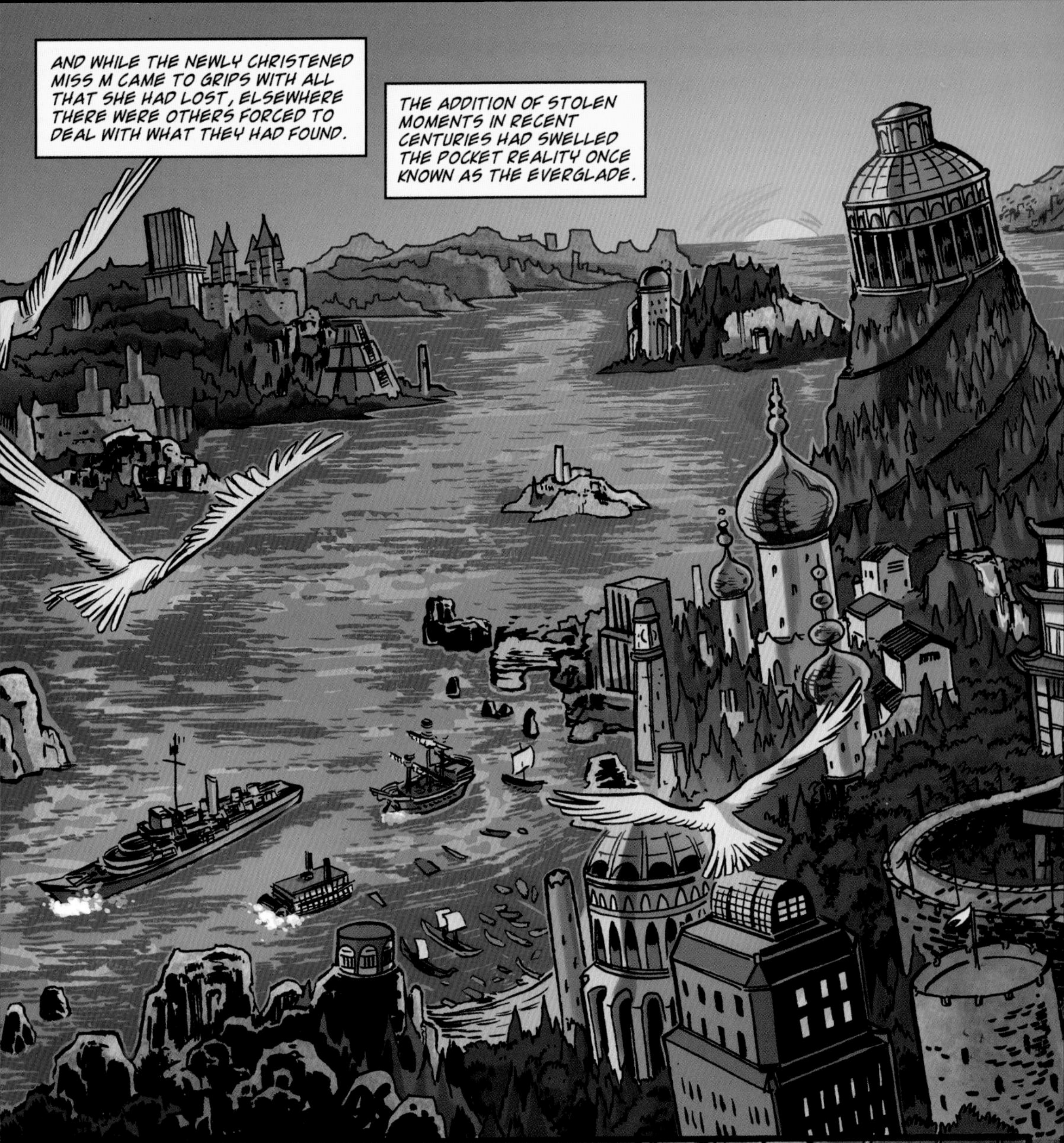
AND WHILE THE NEWLY CHRISTENED MISS M CAME TO GRIPS WITH ALL THAT SHE HAD LOST, ELSEWHERE THERE WERE OTHERS FORCED TO DEAL WITH WHAT THEY HAD FOUND.
THE ADDITION OF STOLEN MOMENTS IN RECENT CENTURIES HAD SWELLED THE POCKET REALITY ONCE KNOWN AS THE EVERGLADE.

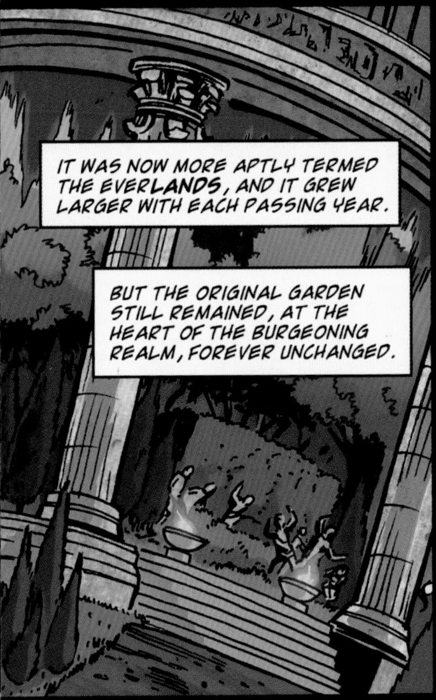
IT WAS NOW MORE APTLY TERMED THE EVERLANDS, AND IT GREW LARGER WITH EACH PASSING YEAR.
BUT THE ORIGINAL GARDEN STILL REMAINED, AT THE HEART OF THE BURGEONING REALM, FOREVER UNCHANGED.

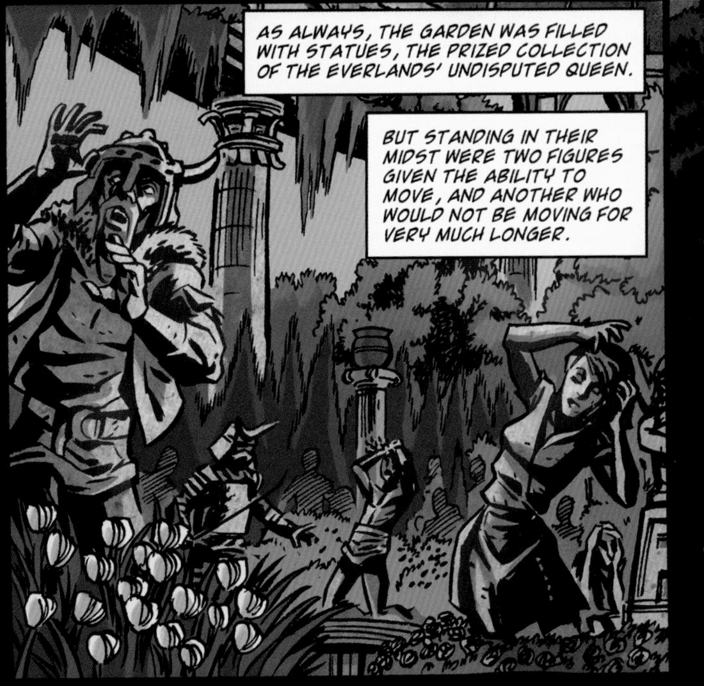
AS ALWAYS, THE GARDEN WAS FILLED WITH STATUES, THE PRIZED COLLECTION OF THE EVERLANDS' UNDISPUTED QUEEN.
BUT STANDING IN THEIR MIDST WERE TWO FIGURES GIVEN THE ABILITY TO MOVE, AND ANOTHER WHO WOULD NOT BE MOVING FOR VERY MUCH LONGER.

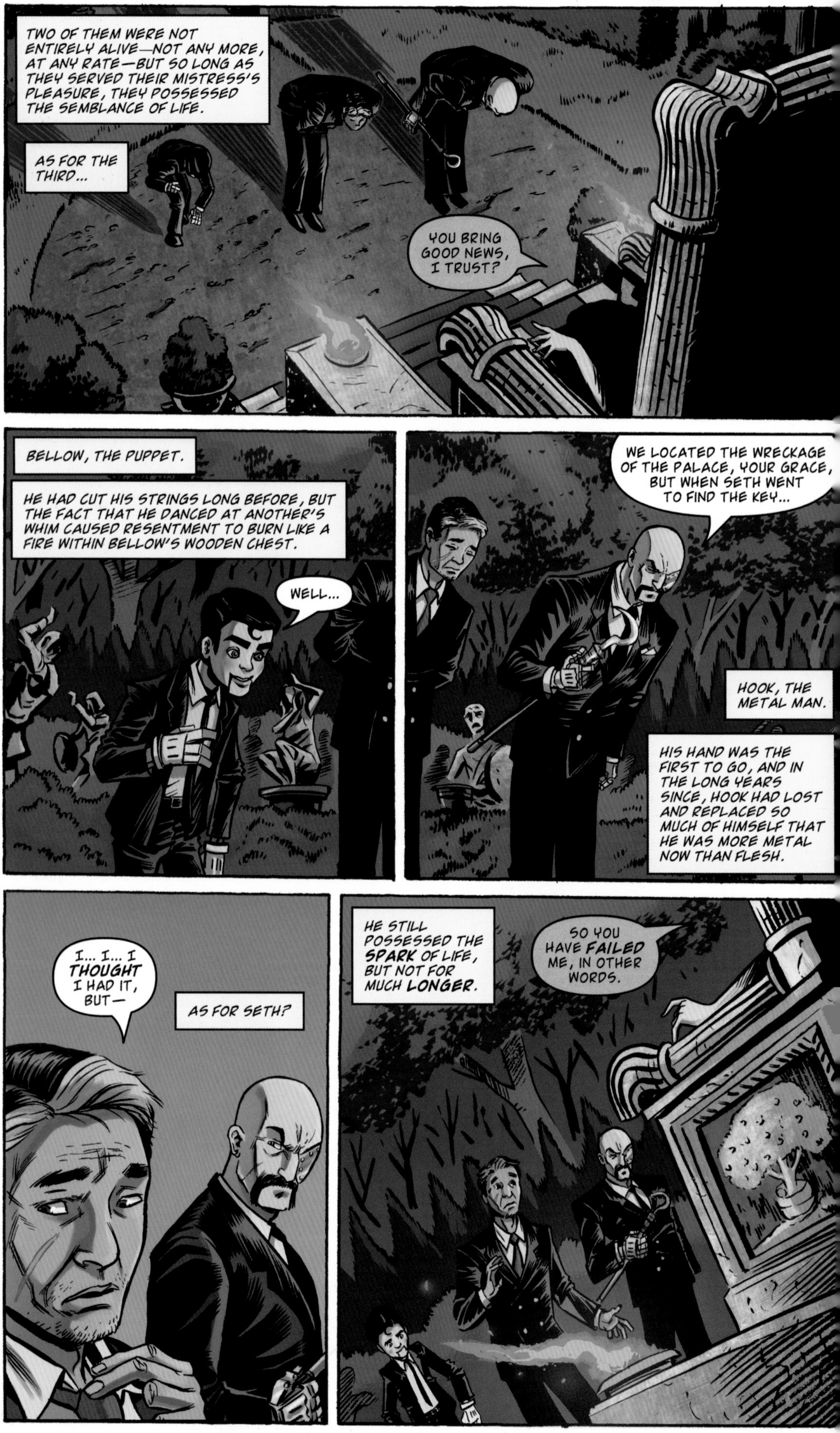
TWO OF THEM WERE NOT ENTIRELY ALIVE—NOT ANY MORE, AT ANY RATE—BUT SO LONG AS THEY SERVED THEIR MISTRESS'S PLEASURE, THEY POSSESSED THE SEMBLANCE OF LIFE.
AS FOR THE THIRD...
YOU BRING GOOD NEWS, I TRUST?
BELLOW, THE PUPPET.
HE HAD CUT HIS STRINGS LONG BEFORE, BUT THE FACT THAT HE DANCED AT ANOTHER'S WHIM CAUSED RESENTMENT TO BURN LIKE A FIRE WITHIN BELLOW'S WOODEN CHEST.
WELL...
WE LOCATED THE WRECKAGE OF THE PALACE, YOUR GRACE, BUT WHEN SETH WENT TO FIND THE KEY...
HOOK, THE METAL MAN.
HIS HAND WAS THE FIRST TO GO, AND IN THE LONG YEARS SINCE, HOOK HAD LOST AND REPLACED SO MUCH OF HIMSELF THAT HE WAS MORE METAL NOW THAN FLESH.
I... I... I THOUGHT I HAD IT, BUT—
AS FOR SETH?
HE STILL POSSESSED THE SPARK OF LIFE, BUT NOT FOR MUCH LONGER.
SO YOU HAVE FAILED ME, IN OTHER WORDS.

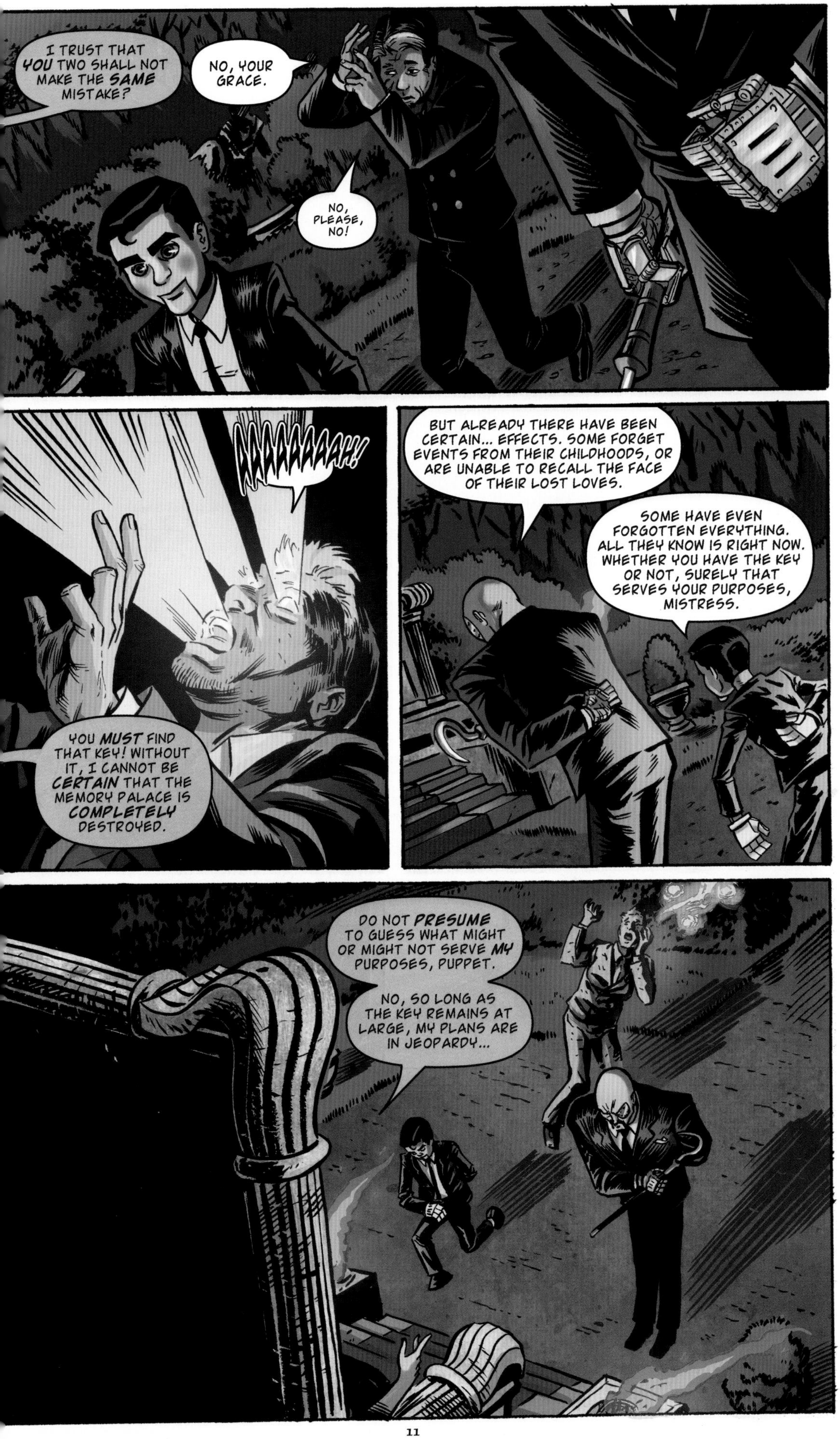
I TRUST THAT YOU TWO SHALL NOT MAKE THE SAME MISTAKE?
NO, YOUR GRACE.
NO, PLEASE, NO!
AAAAAAAAAH!
YOU MUST FIND THAT KEY! WITHOUT IT, I CANNOT BE CERTAIN THAT THE MEMORY PALACE IS COMPLETELY DESTROYED.
BUT ALREADY THERE HAVE BEEN CERTAIN... EFFECTS. SOME FORGET EVENTS FROM THEIR CHILDHOODS, OR ARE UNABLE TO RECALL THE FACE OF THEIR LOST LOVES.
SOME HAVE EVEN FORGOTTEN EVERYTHING. ALL THEY KNOW IS RIGHT NOW. WHETHER YOU HAVE THE KEY OR NOT, SURELY THAT SERVES YOUR PURPOSES, MISTRESS.
DO NOT PRESUME TO GUESS WHAT MIGHT OR MIGHT NOT SERVE MY PURPOSES, PUPPET.
NO, SO LONG AS THE KEY REMAINS AT LARGE, MY PLANS ARE IN JEOPARDY...

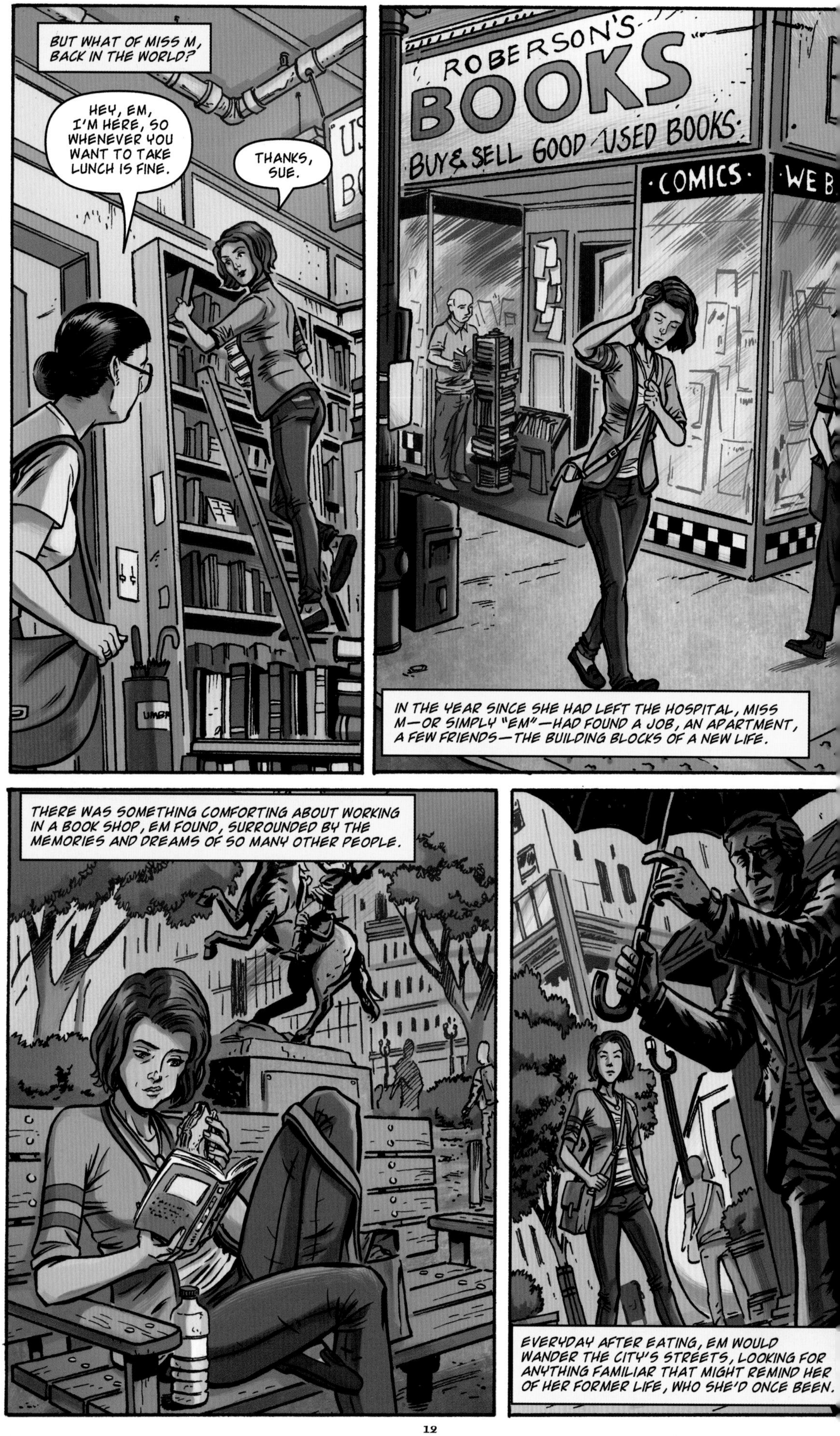
BUT WHAT OF MISS M, BACK IN THE WORLD?
HEY, EM, I'M HERE, SO WHENEVER YOU WANT TO TAKE LUNCH IS FINE.
THANKS, SUE.
ROBERSON'S BOOKS
BUY & SELL GOOD USED BOOKS
COMICS
IN THE YEAR SINCE SHE HAD LEFT THE HOSPITAL, MISS M—OR SIMPLY "EM"—HAD FOUND A JOB, AN APARTMENT, A FEW FRIENDS—THE BUILDING BLOCKS OF A NEW LIFE.
THERE WAS SOMETHING COMFORTING ABOUT WORKING IN A BOOK SHOP, EM FOUND, SURROUNDED BY THE MEMORIES AND DREAMS OF SO MANY OTHER PEOPLE.
EVERYDAY AFTER EATING, EM WOULD WANDER THE CITY'S STREETS, LOOKING FOR ANYTHING FAMILIAR THAT MIGHT REMIND HER OF HER FORMER LIFE, WHO SHE'D ONCE BEEN.

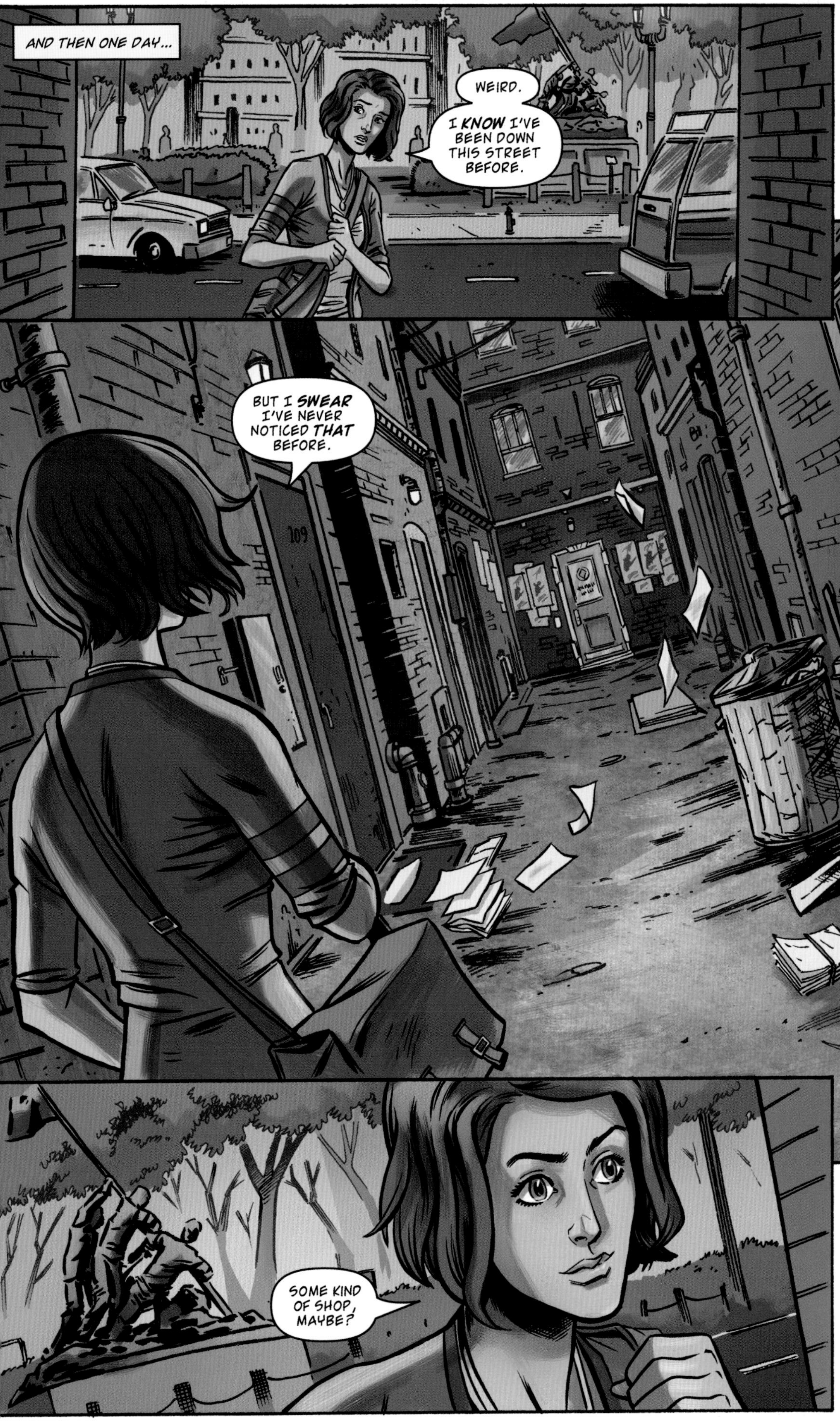
AND THEN ONE DAY...
WEIRD.
I KNOW I'VE BEEN DOWN THIS STREET BEFORE.
BUT I SWEAR I'VE NEVER NOTICED THAT BEFORE.
SOME KIND OF SHOP, MAYBE?

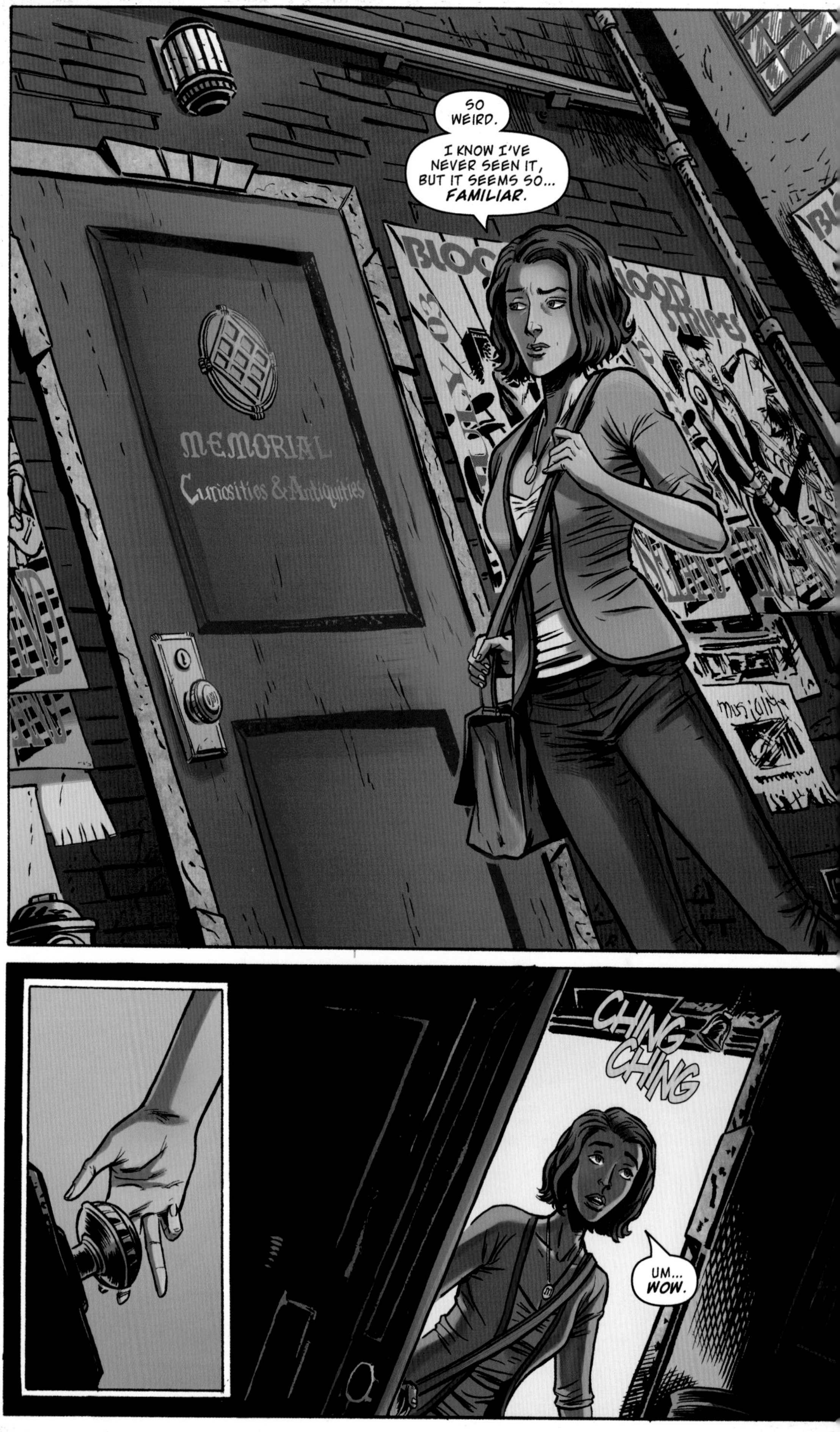
SO WEIRD.
I KNOW I'VE NEVER SEEN IT, BUT IT SEEMS SO... FAMILIAR.
MEMORIAL
Curiosities & Antiquities
BLOOD STRIPES
CHING CHING
UM... WOW.

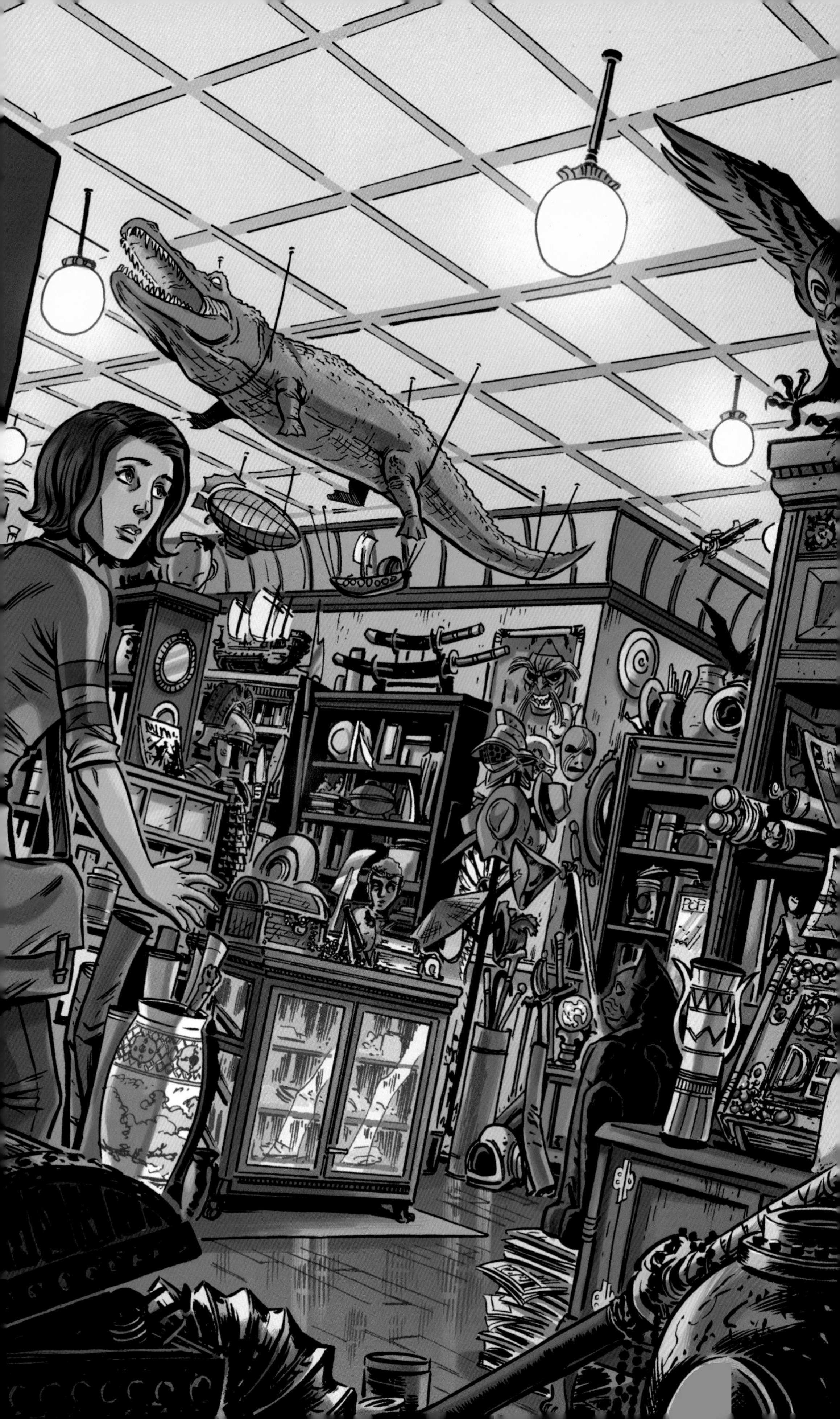

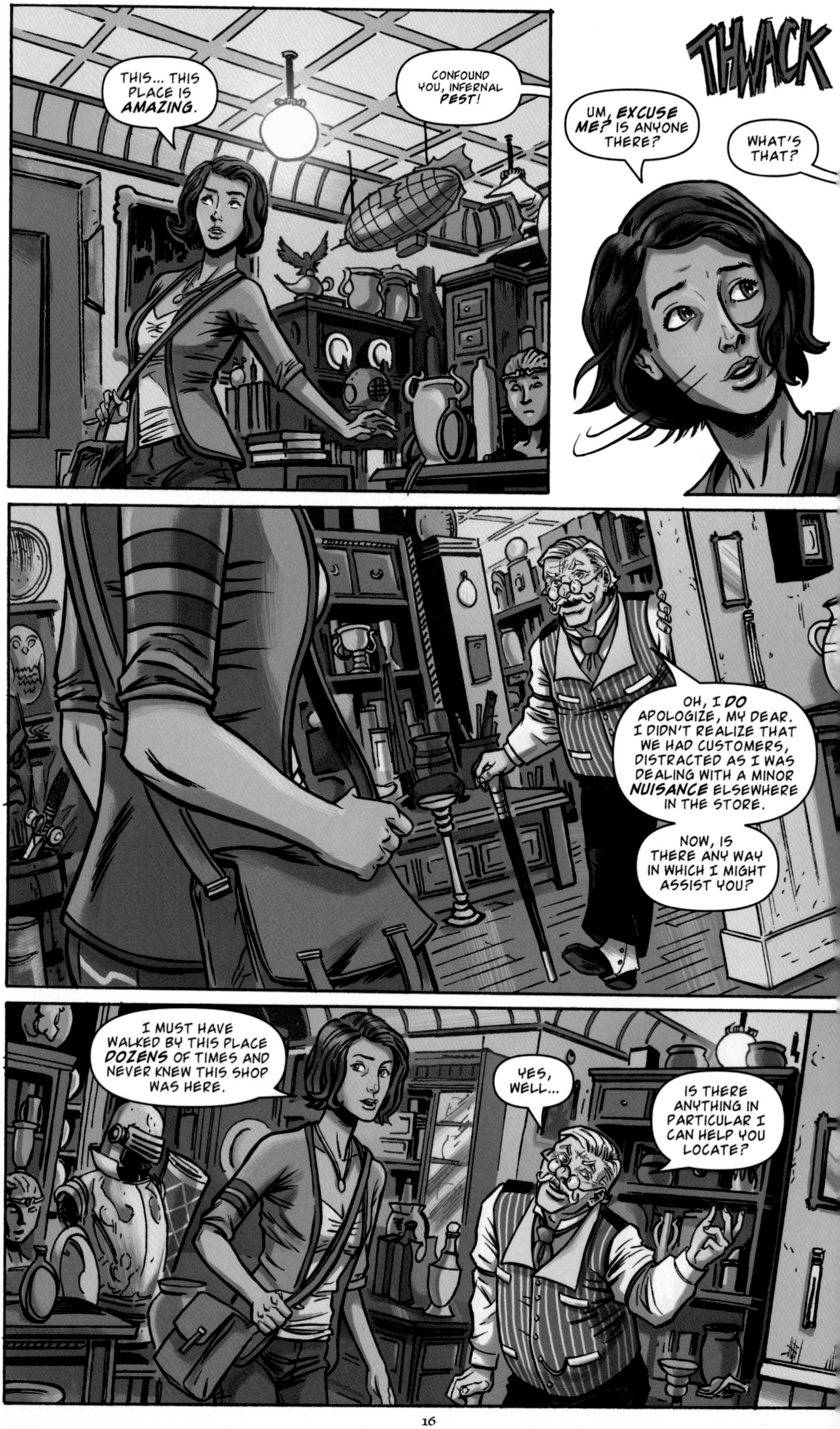
THIS... THIS PLACE IS AMAZING.
CONFOUND YOU, INFERNAL PEST!
THWACK
UM, EXCUSE ME? IS ANYONE THERE?
WHAT'S THAT?
OH, I DO APOLOGIZE, MY DEAR. I DIDN'T REALIZE THAT WE HAD CUSTOMERS, DISTRACTED AS I WAS DEALING WITH A MINOR NUISANCE ELSEWHERE IN THE STORE.
NOW, IS THERE ANY WAY IN WHICH I MIGHT ASSIST YOU?
I MUST HAVE WALKED BY THIS PLACE DOZENS OF TIMES AND NEVER KNEW THIS SHOP WAS HERE.
YES, WELL...
IS THERE ANYTHING IN PARTICULAR I CAN HELP YOU LOCATE?

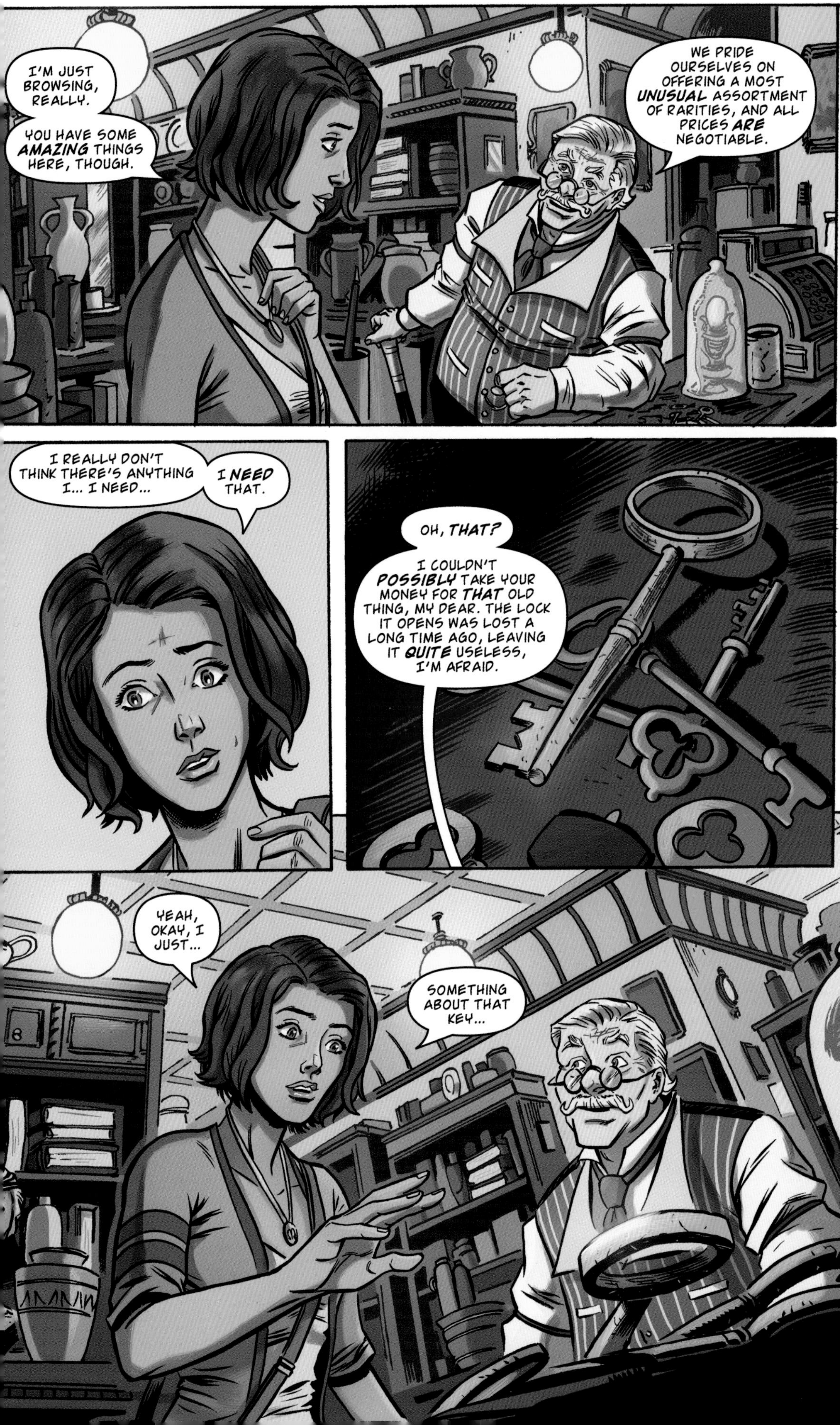
I'M JUST BROWSING, REALLY.
YOU HAVE SOME AMAZING THINGS HERE, THOUGH.
WE PRIDE OURSELVES ON OFFERING A MOST UNUSUAL ASSORTMENT OF RARITIES, AND ALL PRICES ARE NEGOTIABLE.
I REALLY DON'T THINK THERE'S ANYTHING I... I NEED...
I NEED THAT.
OH, THAT?
I COULDN'T POSSIBLY TAKE YOUR MONEY FOR THAT OLD THING, MY DEAR. THE LOCK IT OPENS WAS LOST A LONG TIME AGO, LEAVING IT QUITE USELESS, I'M AFRAID.
YEAH, OKAY, I JUST...
SOMETHING ABOUT THAT KEY...

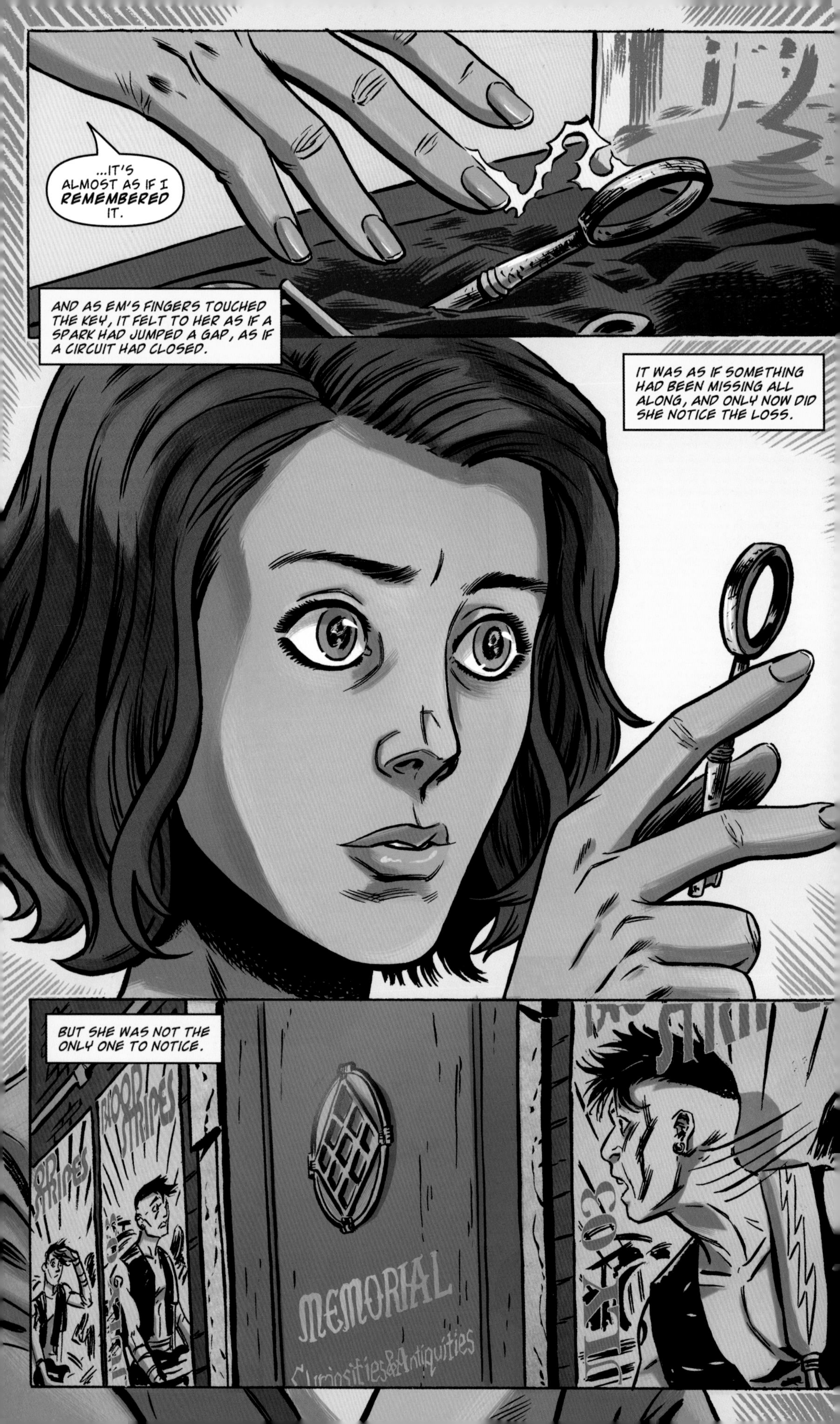
...IT'S ALMOST AS IF I **REMEMBERED** IT.
AND AS EM'S FINGERS TOUCHED THE KEY, IT FELT TO HER AS IF A SPARK HAD JUMPED A GAP, AS IF A CIRCUIT HAD CLOSED.
IT WAS AS IF SOMETHING HAD BEEN MISSING ALL ALONG, AND ONLY NOW DID SHE NOTICE THE LOSS.
BUT SHE WAS NOT THE ONLY ONE TO NOTICE.
MEMORIAL
Curiosities&Antiquities

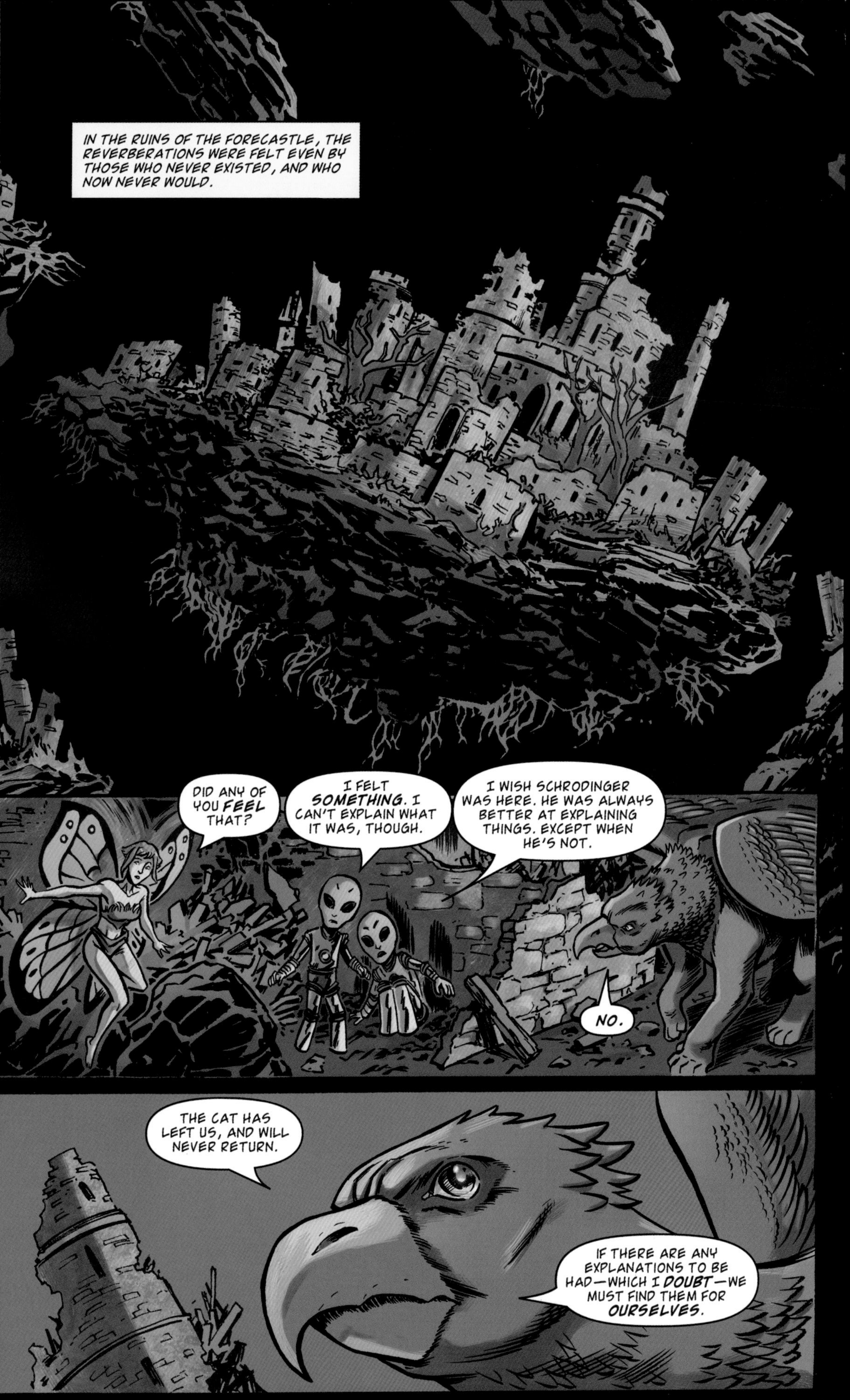
IN THE RUINS OF THE FORECASTLE, THE REVERBERATIONS WERE FELT EVEN BY THOSE WHO NEVER EXISTED, AND WHO NOW NEVER WOULD.
DID ANY OF YOU FEEL THAT?
I FELT SOMETHING. I CAN'T EXPLAIN WHAT IT WAS, THOUGH.
I WISH SCHRODINGER WAS HERE. HE WAS ALWAYS BETTER AT EXPLAINING THINGS. EXCEPT WHEN HE'S NOT.
NO.
THE CAT HAS LEFT US, AND WILL NEVER RETURN.
IF THERE ARE ANY EXPLANATIONS TO BE HAD—WHICH I DOUBT—WE MUST FIND THEM FOR OURSELVES.

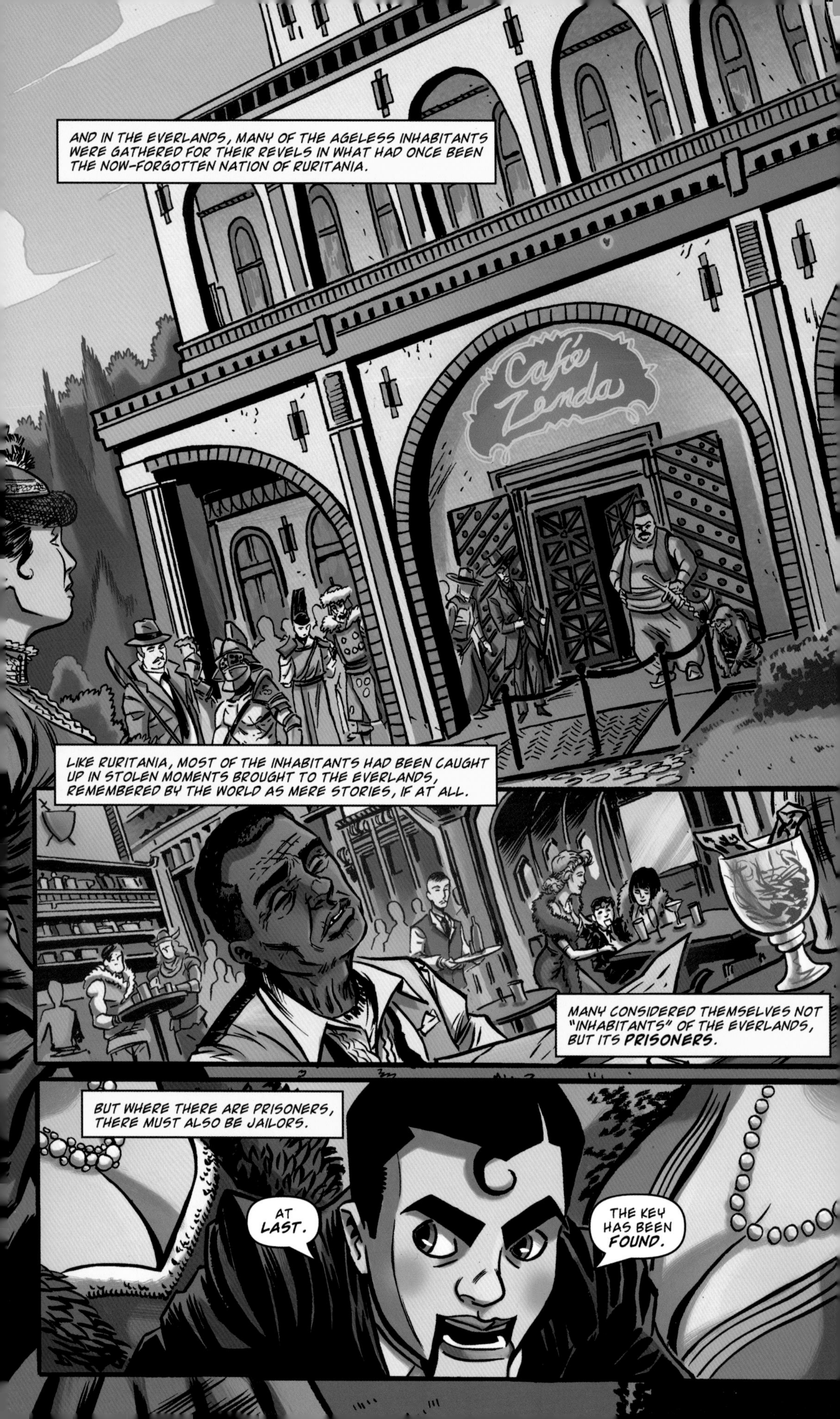
AND IN THE EVERLANDS, MANY OF THE AGELESS INHABITANTS WERE GATHERED FOR THEIR REVELS IN WHAT HAD ONCE BEEN THE NOW-FORGOTTEN NATION OF RURITANIA.
Café Zenda
LIKE RURITANIA, MOST OF THE INHABITANTS HAD BEEN CAUGHT UP IN STOLEN MOMENTS BROUGHT TO THE EVERLANDS, REMEMBERED BY THE WORLD AS MERE STORIES, IF AT ALL.
MANY CONSIDERED THEMSELVES NOT "INHABITANTS" OF THE EVERLANDS, BUT ITS PRISONERS.
BUT WHERE THERE ARE PRISONERS, THERE MUST ALSO BE JAILORS.
AT LAST.
THE KEY HAS BEEN FOUND.

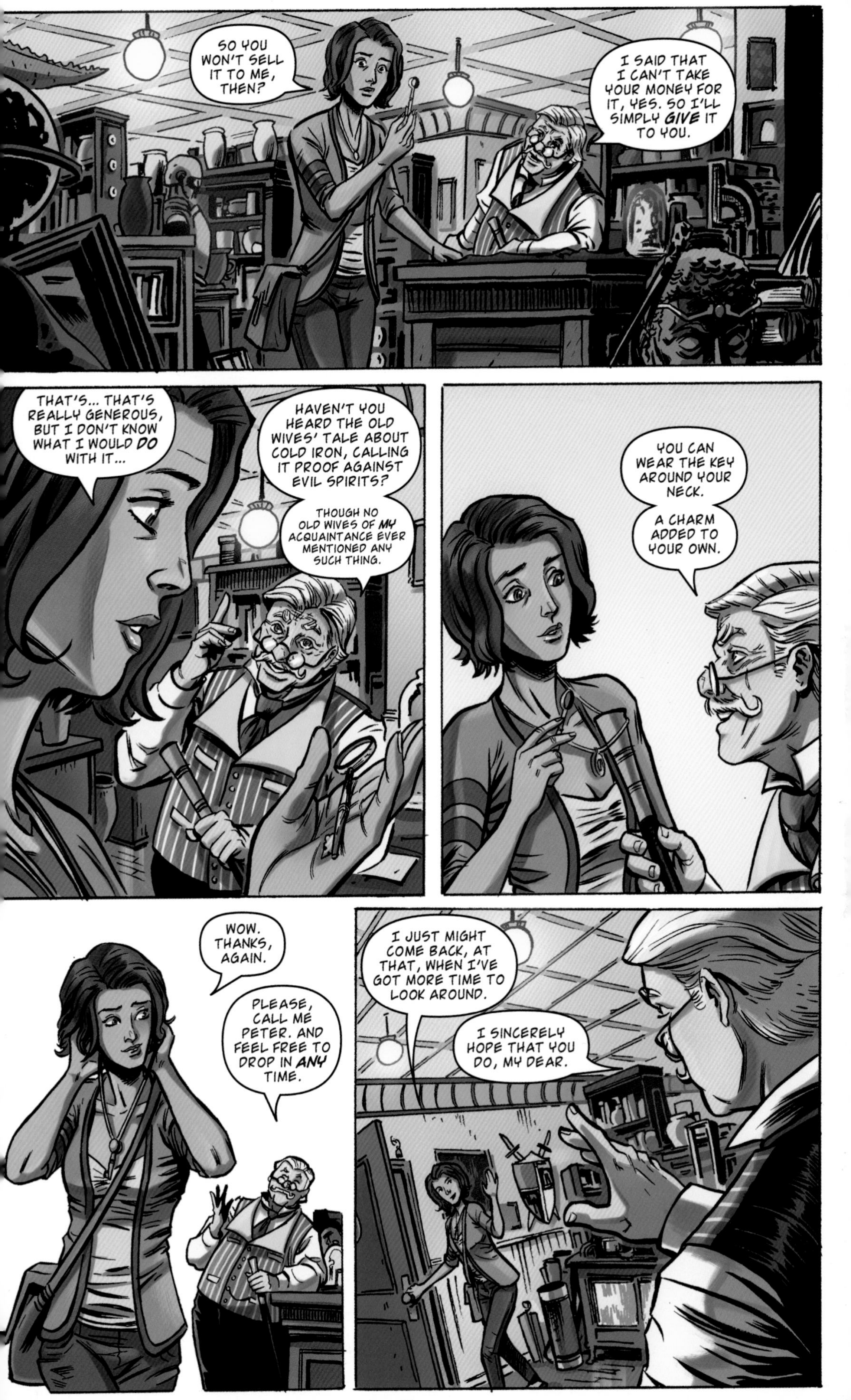
SO YOU WON'T SELL IT TO ME, THEN?
I SAID THAT I CAN'T TAKE YOUR MONEY FOR IT, YES. SO I'LL SIMPLY GIVE IT TO YOU.
THAT'S... THAT'S REALLY GENEROUS, BUT I DON'T KNOW WHAT I WOULD DO WITH IT...
HAVEN'T YOU HEARD THE OLD WIVES' TALE ABOUT COLD IRON, CALLING IT PROOF AGAINST EVIL SPIRITS?
THOUGH NO OLD WIVES OF MY ACQUAINTANCE EVER MENTIONED ANY SUCH THING.
YOU CAN WEAR THE KEY AROUND YOUR NECK.
A CHARM ADDED TO YOUR OWN.
WOW. THANKS, AGAIN.
PLEASE, CALL ME PETER. AND FEEL FREE TO DROP IN ANY TIME.
I JUST MIGHT COME BACK, AT THAT, WHEN I'VE GOT MORE TIME TO LOOK AROUND.
I SINCERELY HOPE THAT YOU DO, MY DEAR.

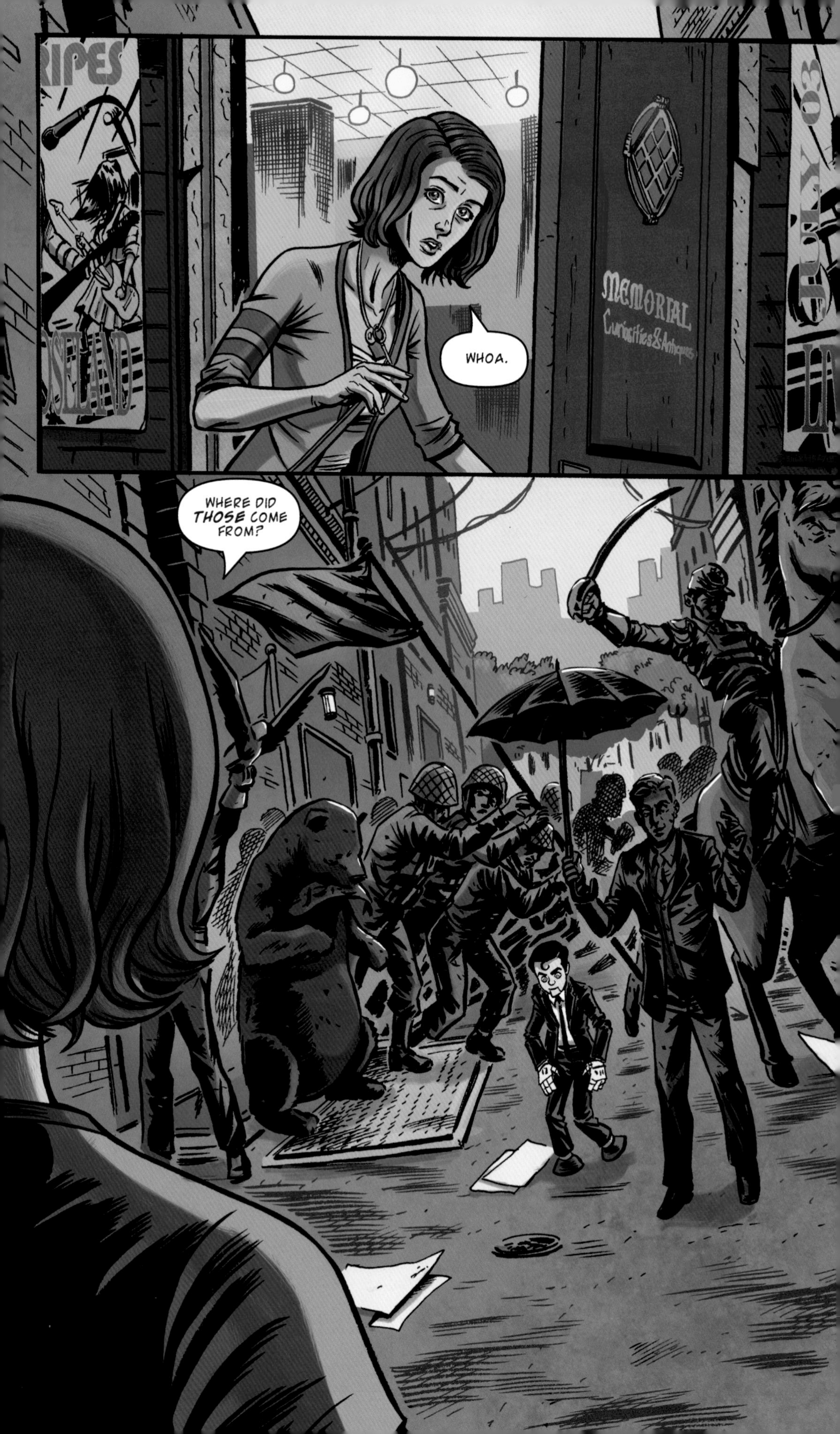
RIPES
MEMORIAL
Curiosities & Antiques
WHOA.
WHERE DID THOSE COME FROM?

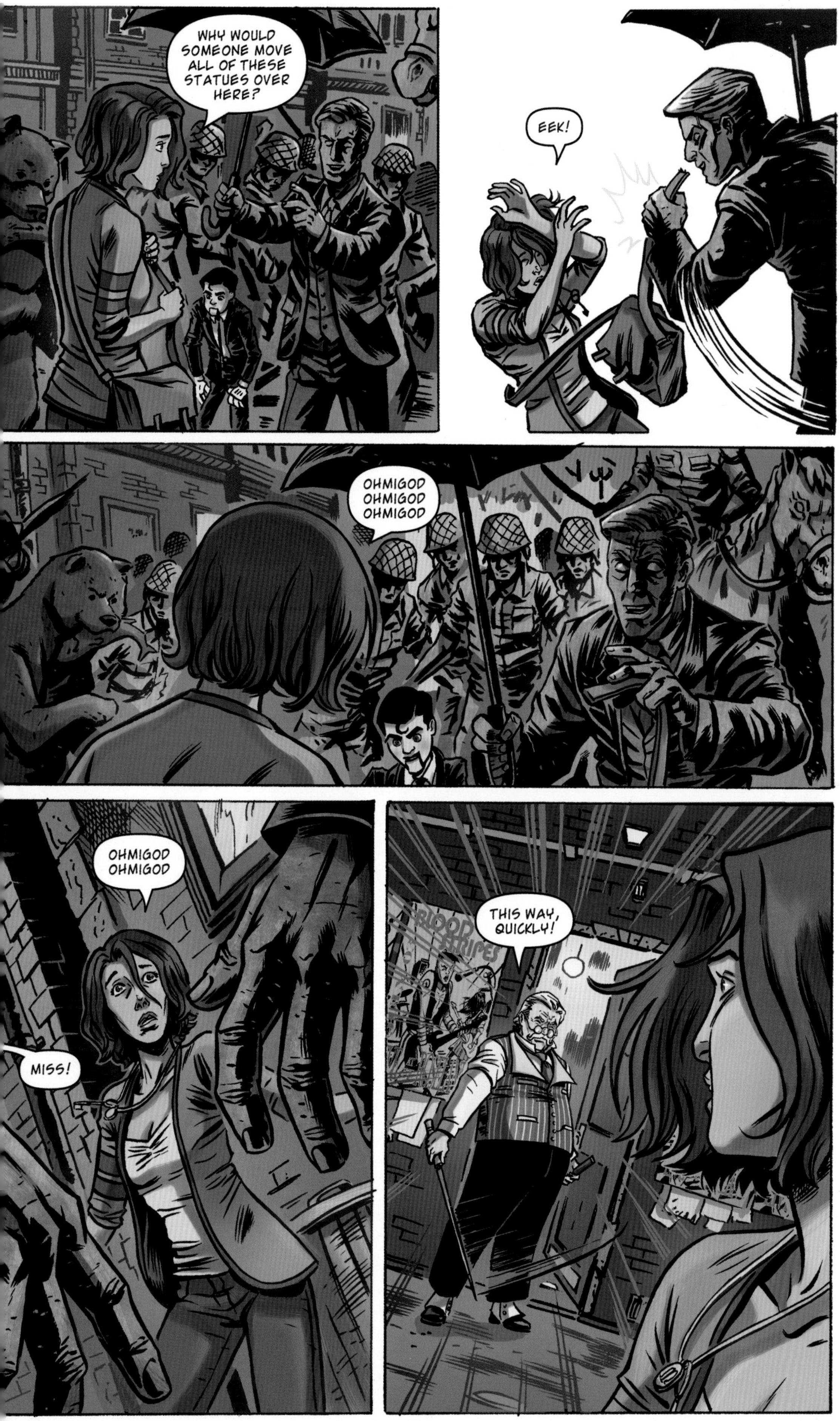
WHY WOULD SOMEONE MOVE ALL OF THESE STATUES OVER HERE?
EEK!
OHMIGOD OHMIGOD OHMIGOD
OHMIGOD OHMIGOD
MISS!
THIS WAY, QUICKLY!
BLOOD STRIPES

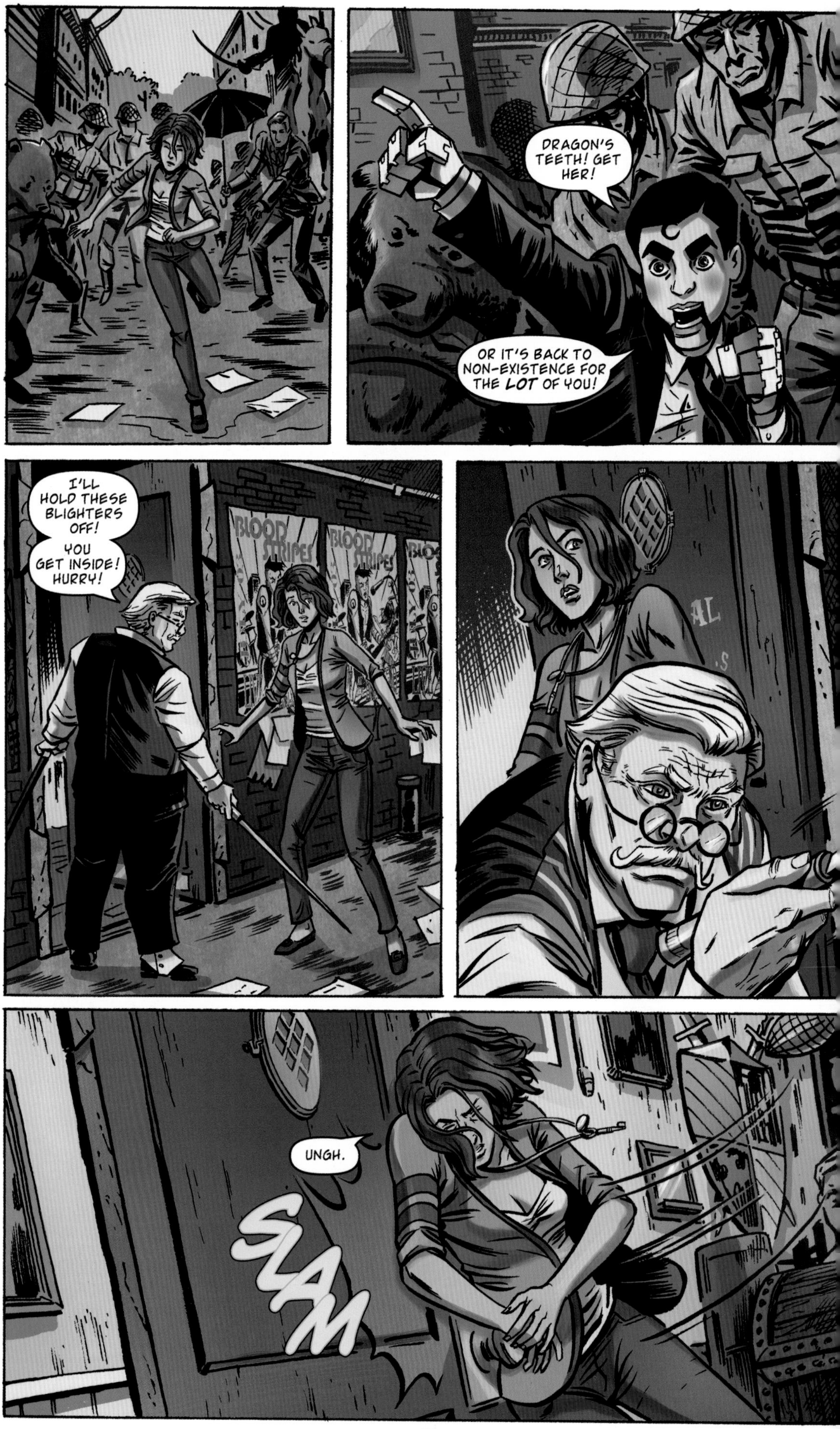
DRAGON'S TEETH! GET HER!
OR IT'S BACK TO NON-EXISTENCE FOR THE LOT OF YOU!
I'LL HOLD THESE BLIGHTERS OFF!
YOU GET INSIDE! HURRY!
BLOOD STRIPES
BLOOD STRIPES
UNGH.
SLAM

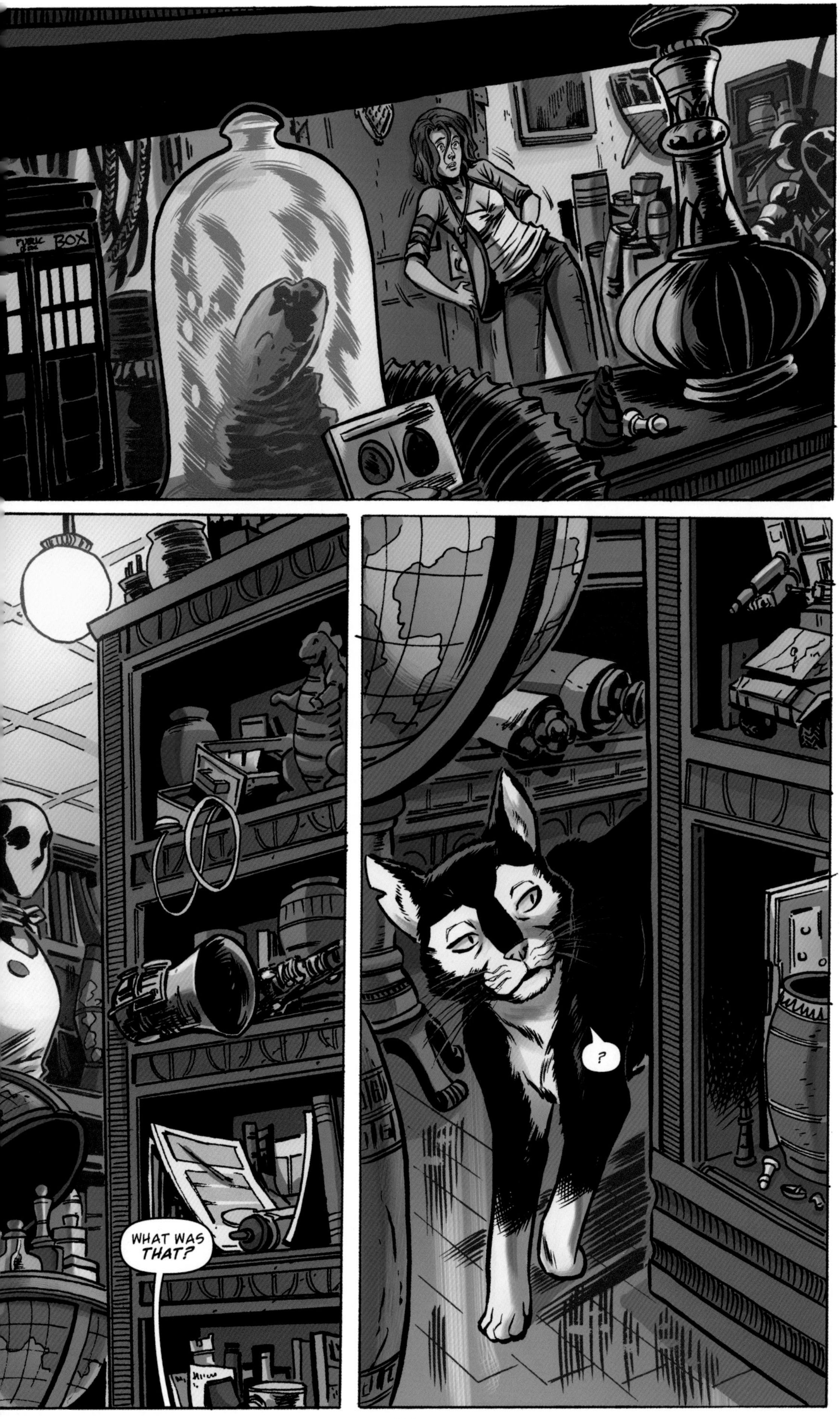

PUBLIC BOX
WHAT WAS THAT?
?

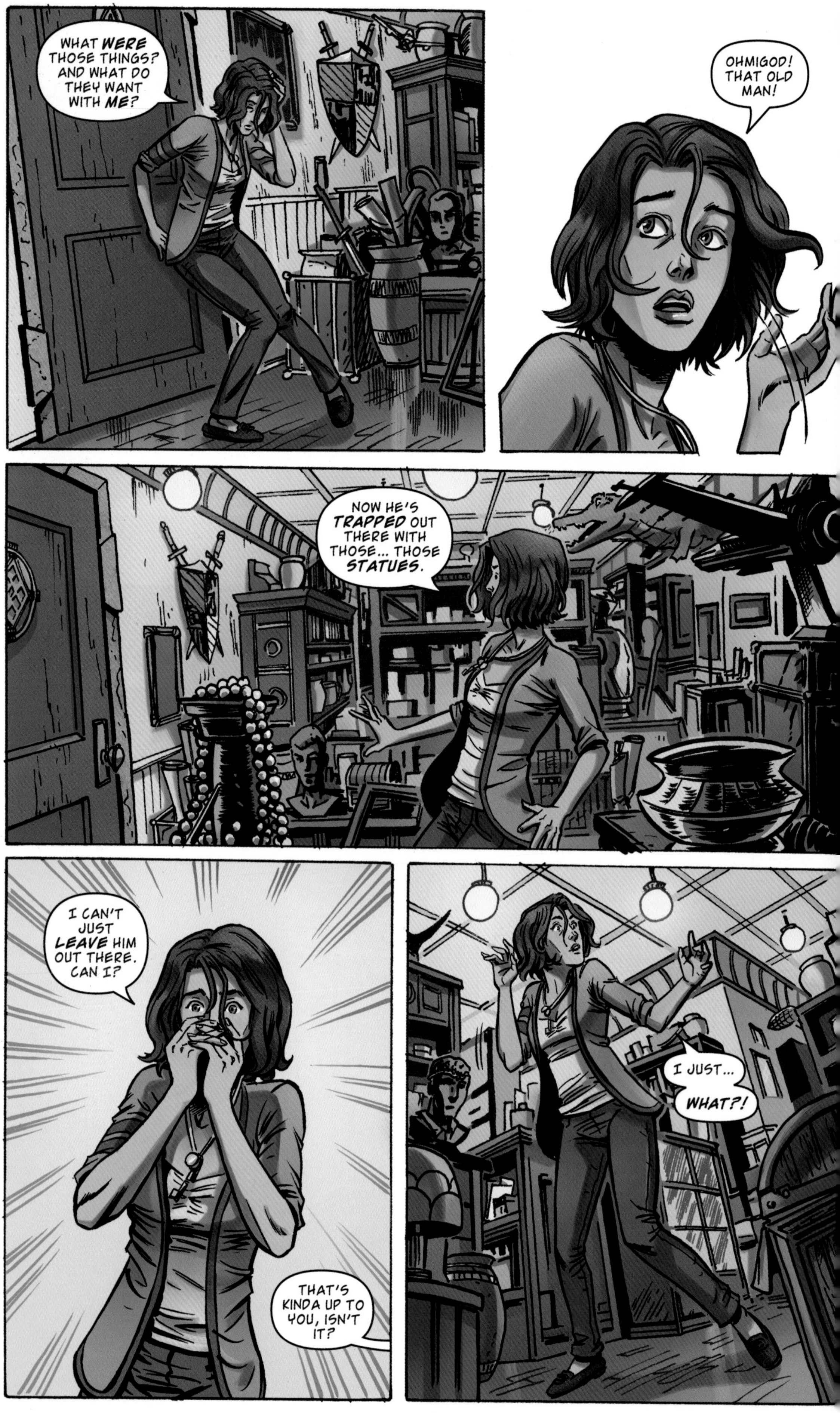
WHAT WERE THOSE THINGS? AND WHAT DO THEY WANT WITH ME?
OHMIGOD! THAT OLD MAN!
NOW HE'S TRAPPED OUT THERE WITH THOSE... THOSE STATUES.
I CAN'T JUST LEAVE HIM OUT THERE. CAN I?
THAT'S KINDA UP TO YOU, ISN'T IT?
I JUST...
WHAT?!

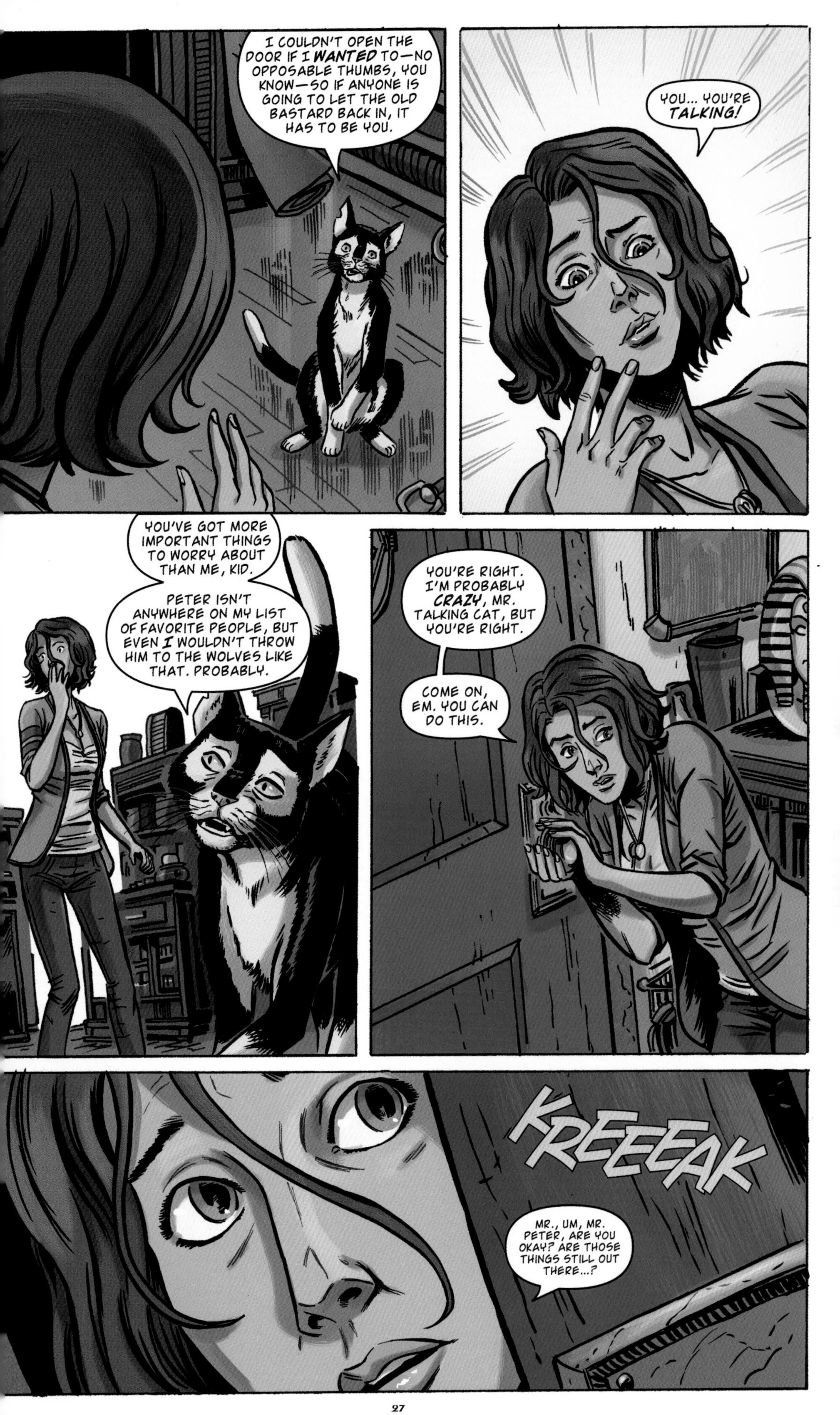
I COULDN'T OPEN THE DOOR IF I WANTED TO—NO OPPOSABLE THUMBS, YOU KNOW—SO IF ANYONE IS GOING TO LET THE OLD BASTARD BACK IN, IT HAS TO BE YOU.
YOU... YOU'RE TALKING!
YOU'VE GOT MORE IMPORTANT THINGS TO WORRY ABOUT THAN ME, KID.
PETER ISN'T ANYWHERE ON MY LIST OF FAVORITE PEOPLE, BUT EVEN I WOULDN'T THROW HIM TO THE WOLVES LIKE THAT. PROBABLY.
YOU'RE RIGHT. I'M PROBABLY CRAZY, MR. TALKING CAT, BUT YOU'RE RIGHT.
COME ON, EM. YOU CAN DO THIS.
KREEEAK
MR., UM, MR. PETER, ARE YOU OKAY? ARE THOSE THINGS STILL OUT THERE...?

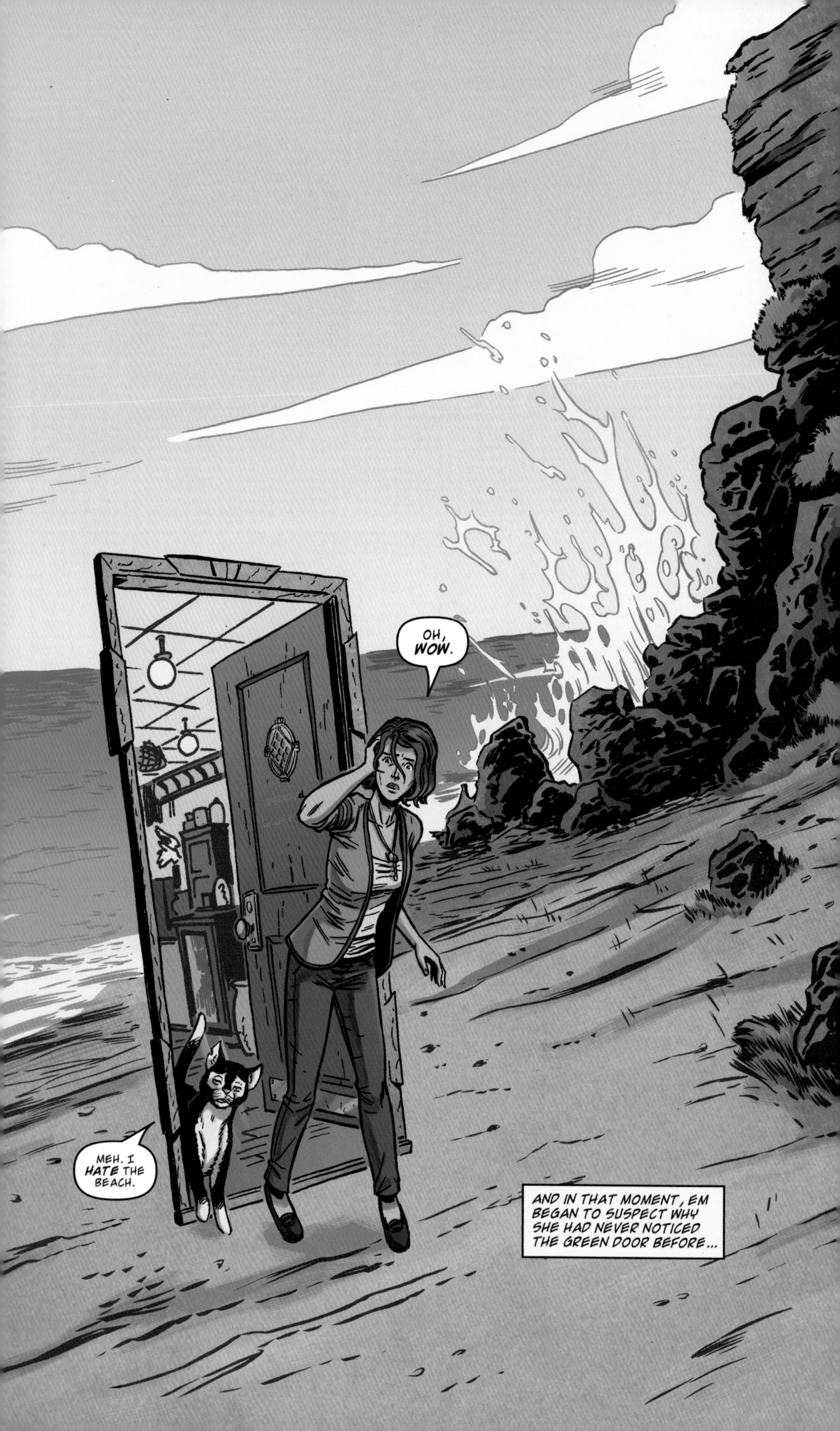
OH, WOW.
MEH. I HATE THE BEACH.
AND IN THAT MOMENT, EM BEGAN TO SUSPECT WHY SHE HAD NEVER NOTICED THE GREEN DOOR BEFORE...

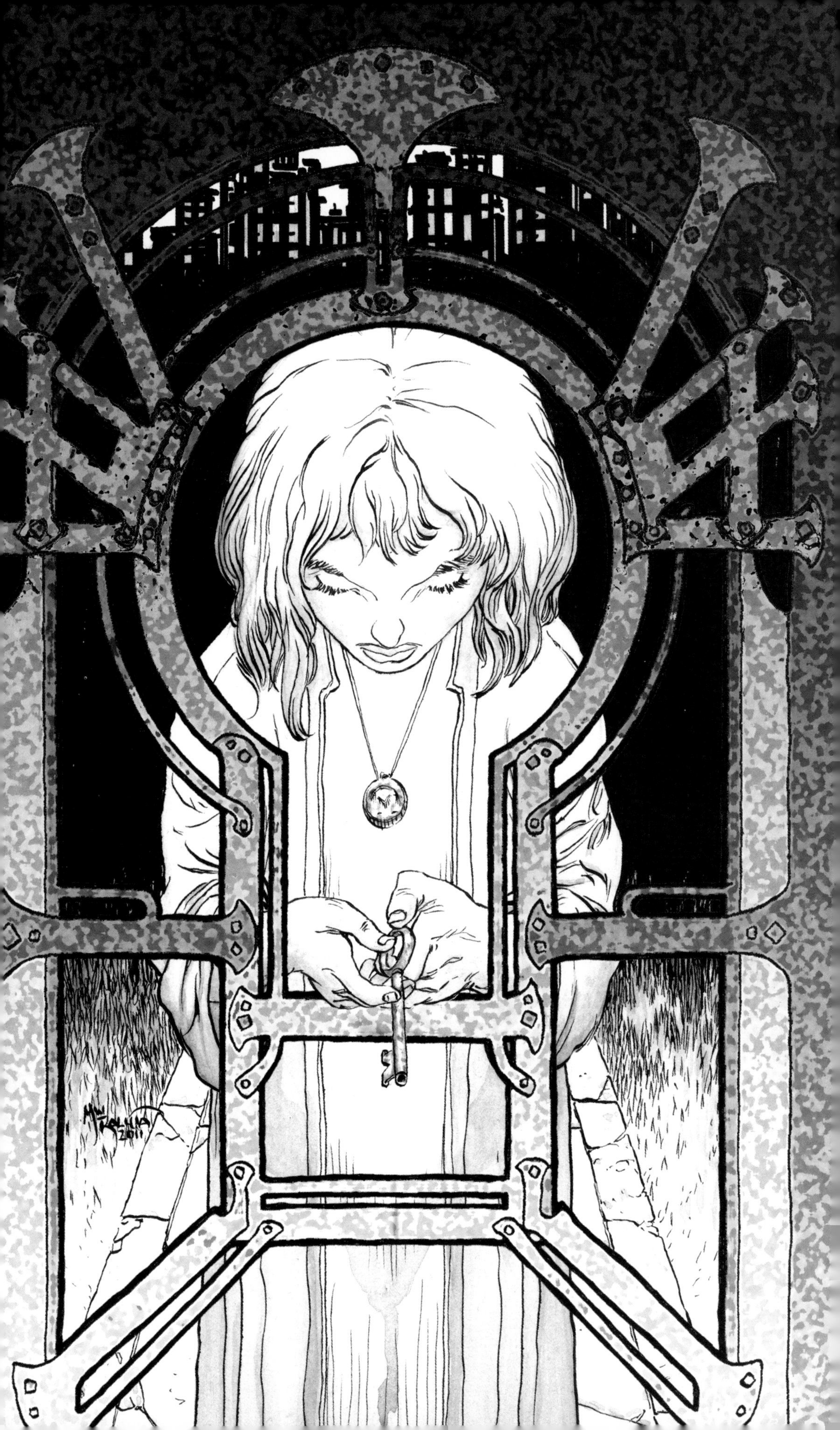

Chapter Two

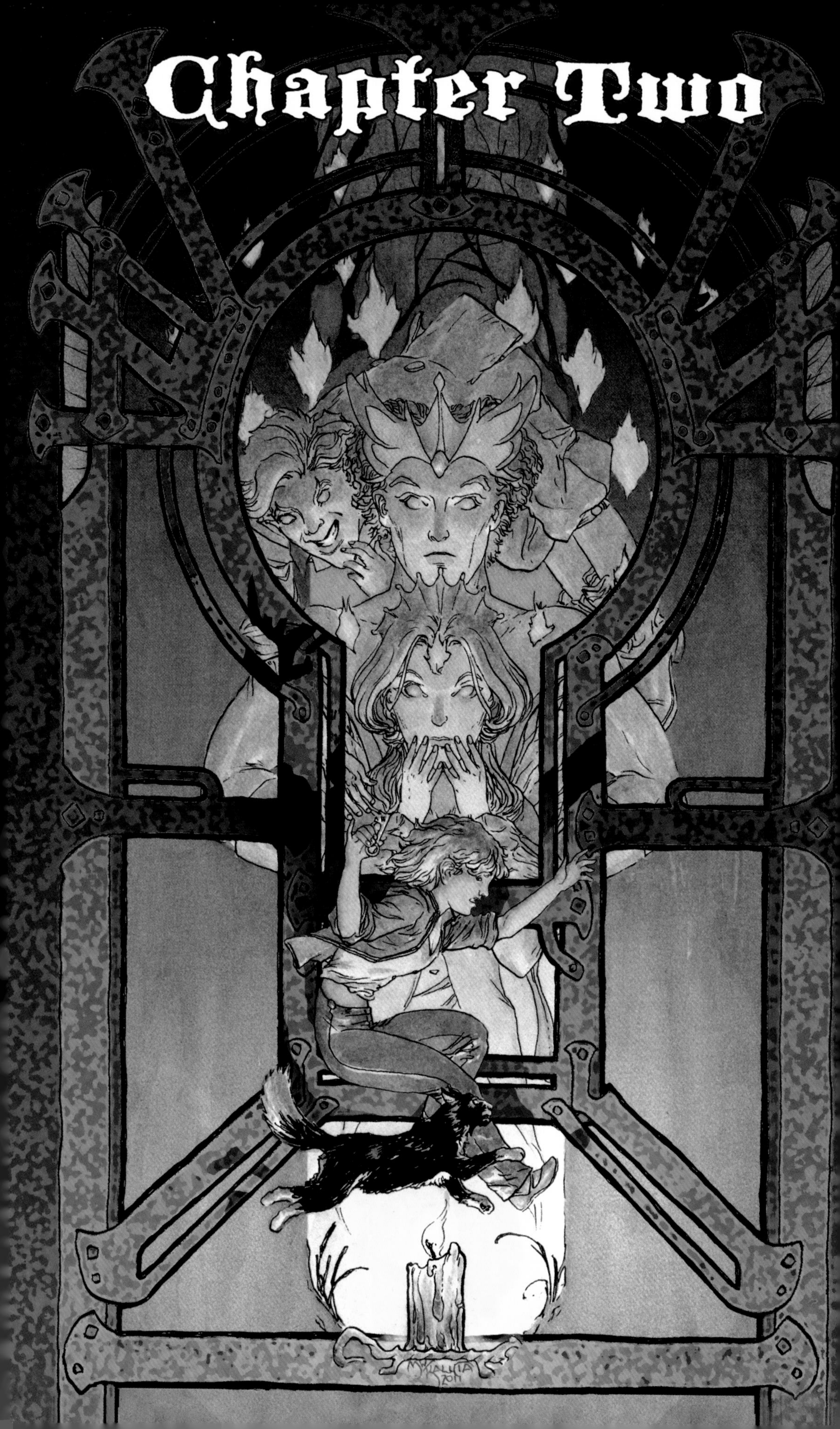

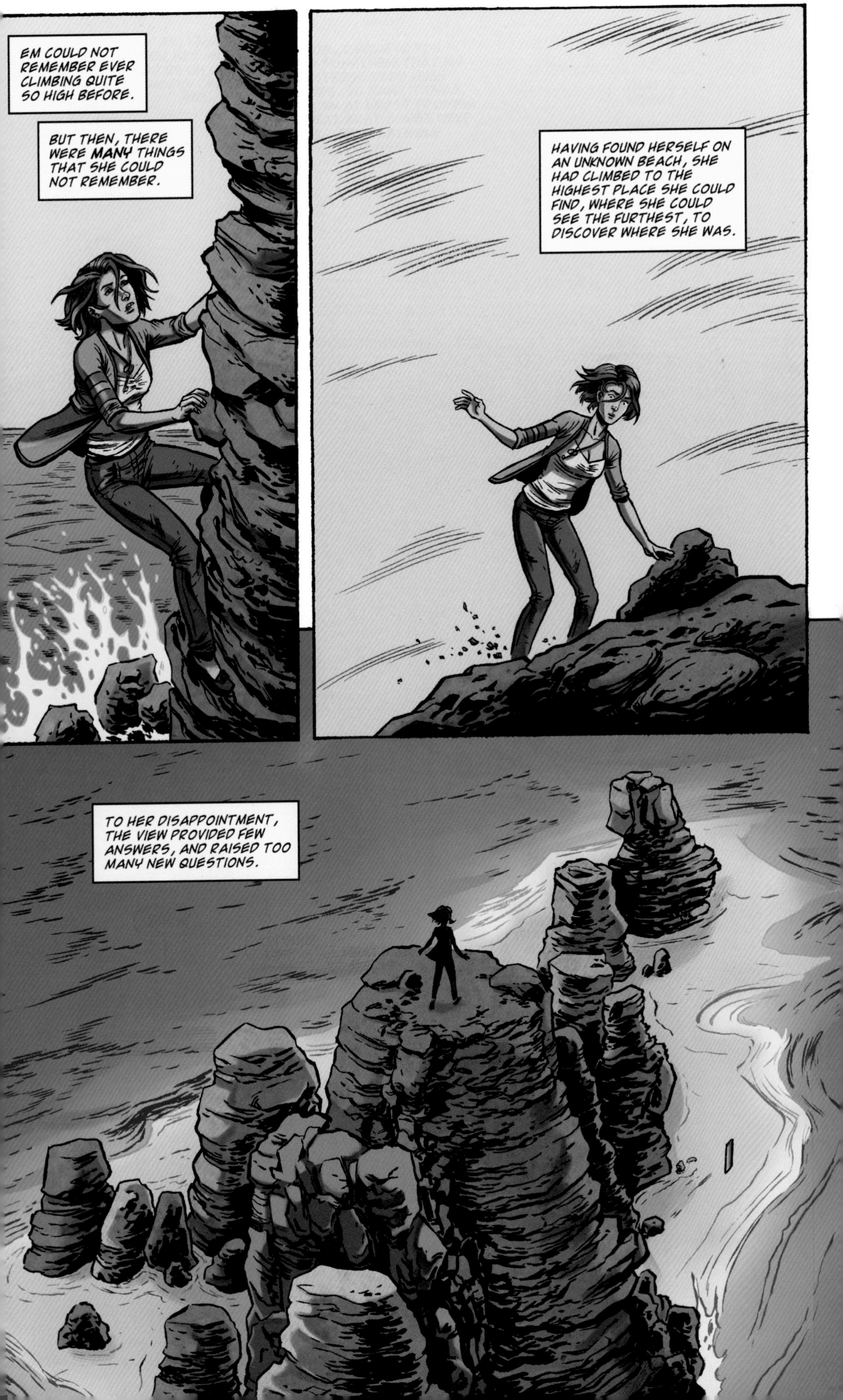
EM COULD NOT REMEMBER EVER CLIMBING QUITE SO HIGH BEFORE.
BUT THEN, THERE WERE **MANY** THINGS THAT SHE COULD NOT REMEMBER.
HAVING FOUND HERSELF ON AN UNKNOWN BEACH, SHE HAD CLIMBED TO THE HIGHEST PLACE SHE COULD FIND, WHERE SHE COULD SEE THE FURTHEST, TO DISCOVER WHERE SHE WAS.
TO HER DISAPPOINTMENT, THE VIEW PROVIDED FEW ANSWERS, AND RAISED TOO MANY NEW QUESTIONS.

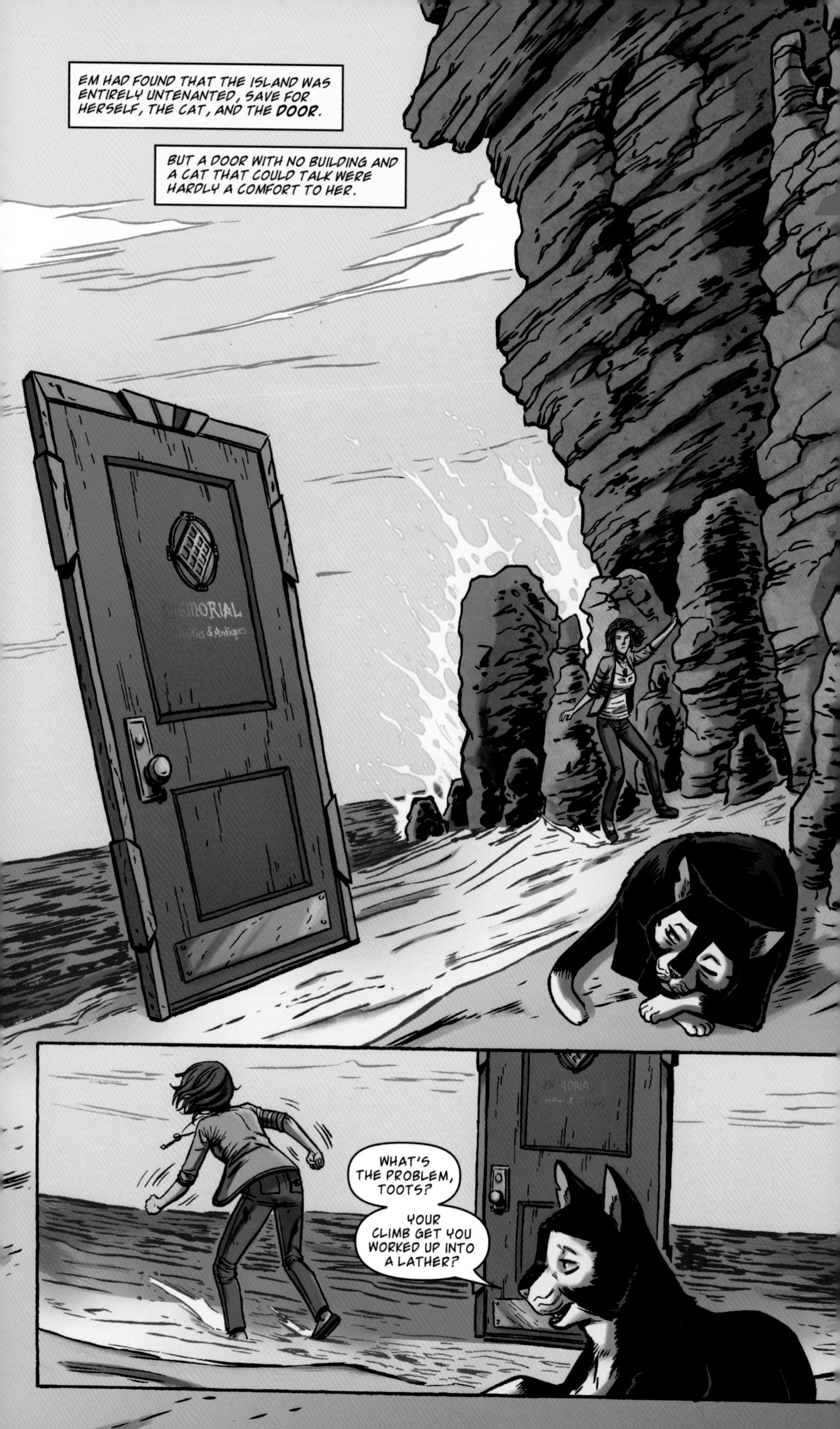
EM HAD FOUND THAT THE ISLAND WAS ENTIRELY UNTENANTED, SAVE FOR HERSELF, THE CAT, AND THE DOOR.
BUT A DOOR WITH NO BUILDING AND A CAT THAT COULD TALK WERE HARDLY A COMFORT TO HER.
WHAT'S THE PROBLEM, TOOTS?
YOUR CLIMB GET YOU WORKED UP INTO A LATHER?

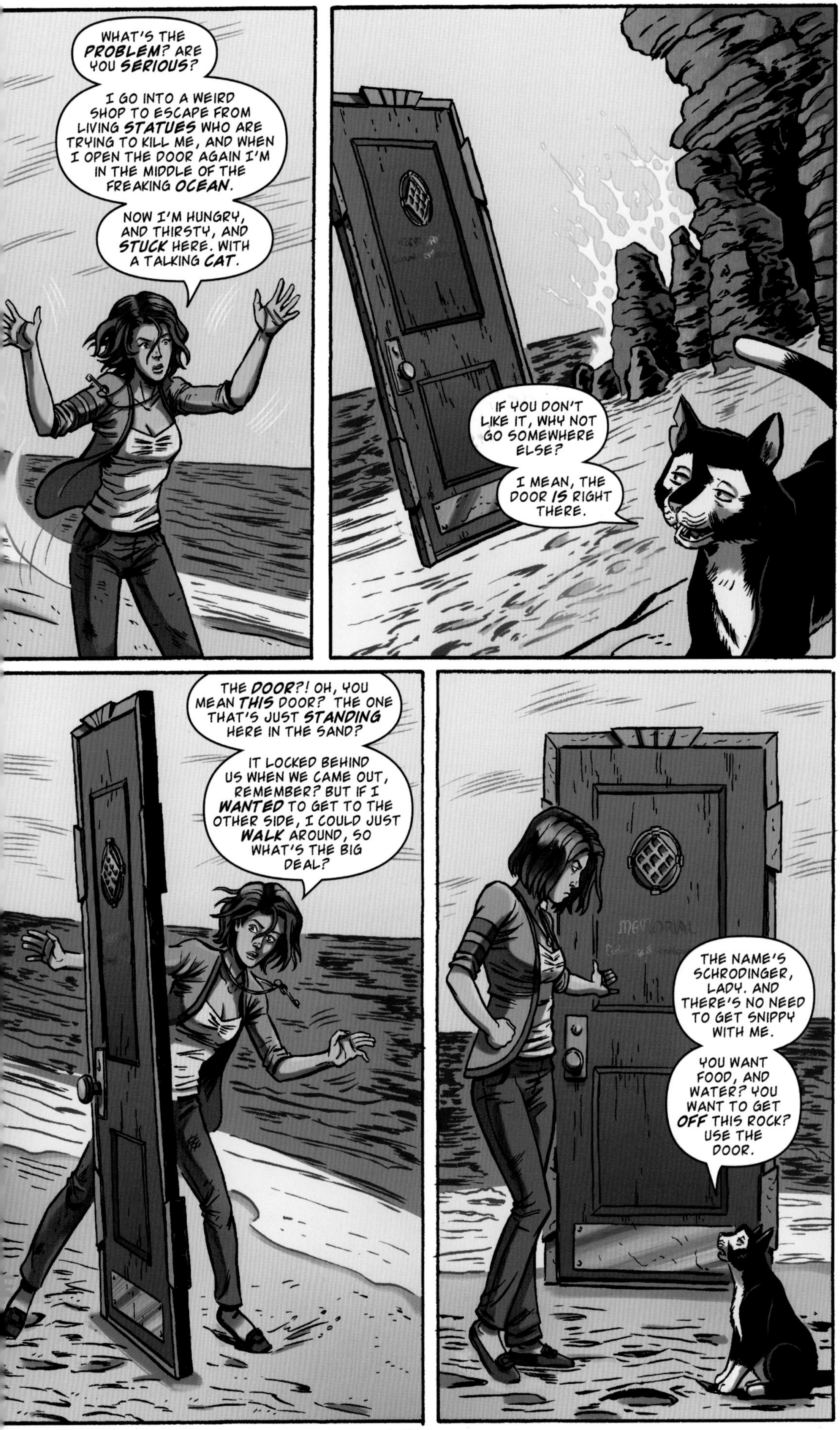
WHAT'S THE PROBLEM? ARE YOU SERIOUS?
I GO INTO A WEIRD SHOP TO ESCAPE FROM LIVING STATUES WHO ARE TRYING TO KILL ME, AND WHEN I OPEN THE DOOR AGAIN I'M IN THE MIDDLE OF THE FREAKING OCEAN.
NOW I'M HUNGRY, AND THIRSTY, AND STUCK HERE. WITH A TALKING CAT.
IF YOU DON'T LIKE IT, WHY NOT GO SOMEWHERE ELSE?
I MEAN, THE DOOR IS RIGHT THERE.
THE DOOR?! OH, YOU MEAN THIS DOOR? THE ONE THAT'S JUST STANDING HERE IN THE SAND?
IT LOCKED BEHIND US WHEN WE CAME OUT, REMEMBER? BUT IF I WANTED TO GET TO THE OTHER SIDE, I COULD JUST WALK AROUND, SO WHAT'S THE BIG DEAL?
THE NAME'S SCHRODINGER, LADY. AND THERE'S NO NEED TO GET SNIPPY WITH ME.
YOU WANT FOOD, AND WATER? YOU WANT TO GET OFF THIS ROCK? USE THE DOOR.

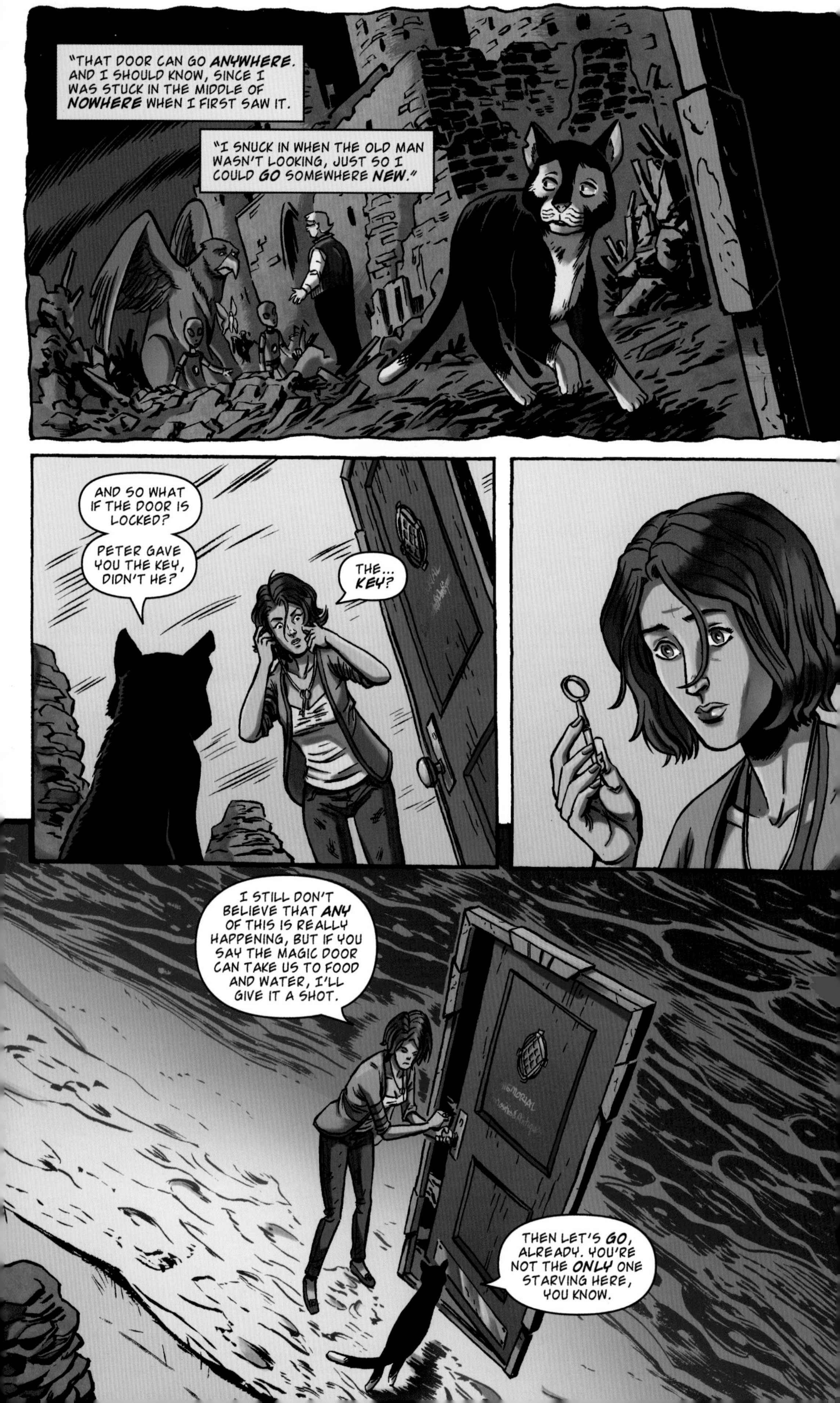
"THAT DOOR CAN GO *ANYWHERE*. AND I SHOULD KNOW, SINCE I WAS STUCK IN THE MIDDLE OF *NOWHERE* WHEN I FIRST SAW IT.
"I SNUCK IN WHEN THE OLD MAN WASN'T LOOKING, JUST SO I COULD *GO* SOMEWHERE *NEW*."
AND SO WHAT IF THE DOOR IS LOCKED?
PETER GAVE YOU THE KEY, DIDN'T HE?
THE... *KEY*?
I STILL DON'T BELIEVE THAT *ANY* OF THIS IS REALLY HAPPENING, BUT IF YOU SAY THE MAGIC DOOR CAN TAKE US TO FOOD AND WATER, I'LL GIVE IT A SHOT.
THEN LET'S *GO*, ALREADY. YOU'RE NOT THE *ONLY* ONE STARVING HERE, YOU KNOW.

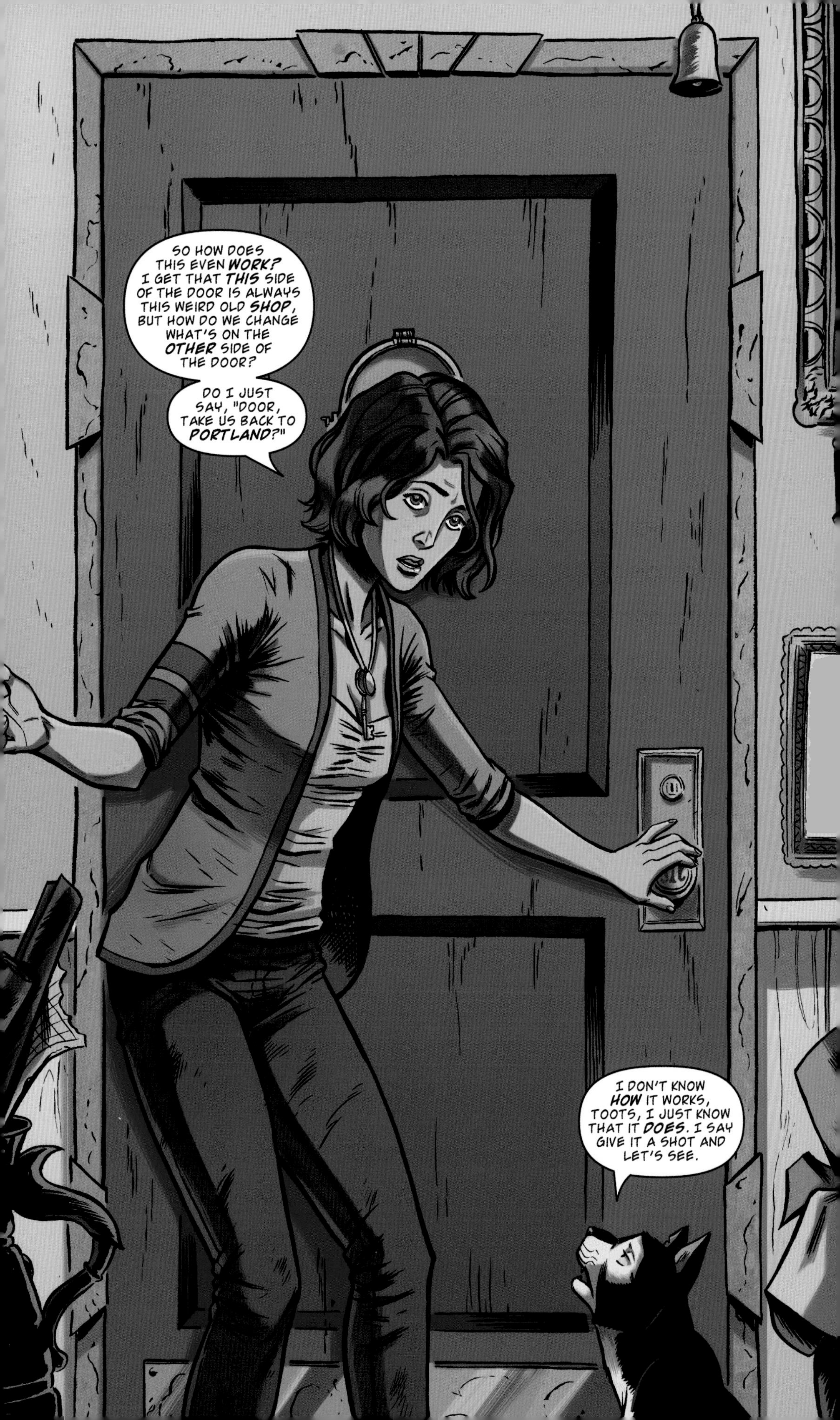
SO HOW DOES THIS EVEN WORK? I GET THAT THIS SIDE OF THE DOOR IS ALWAYS THIS WEIRD OLD SHOP, BUT HOW DO WE CHANGE WHAT'S ON THE OTHER SIDE OF THE DOOR?
DO I JUST SAY, "DOOR, TAKE US BACK TO PORTLAND?"
I DON'T KNOW HOW IT WORKS, TOOTS, I JUST KNOW THAT IT DOES. I SAY GIVE IT A SHOT AND LET'S SEE.

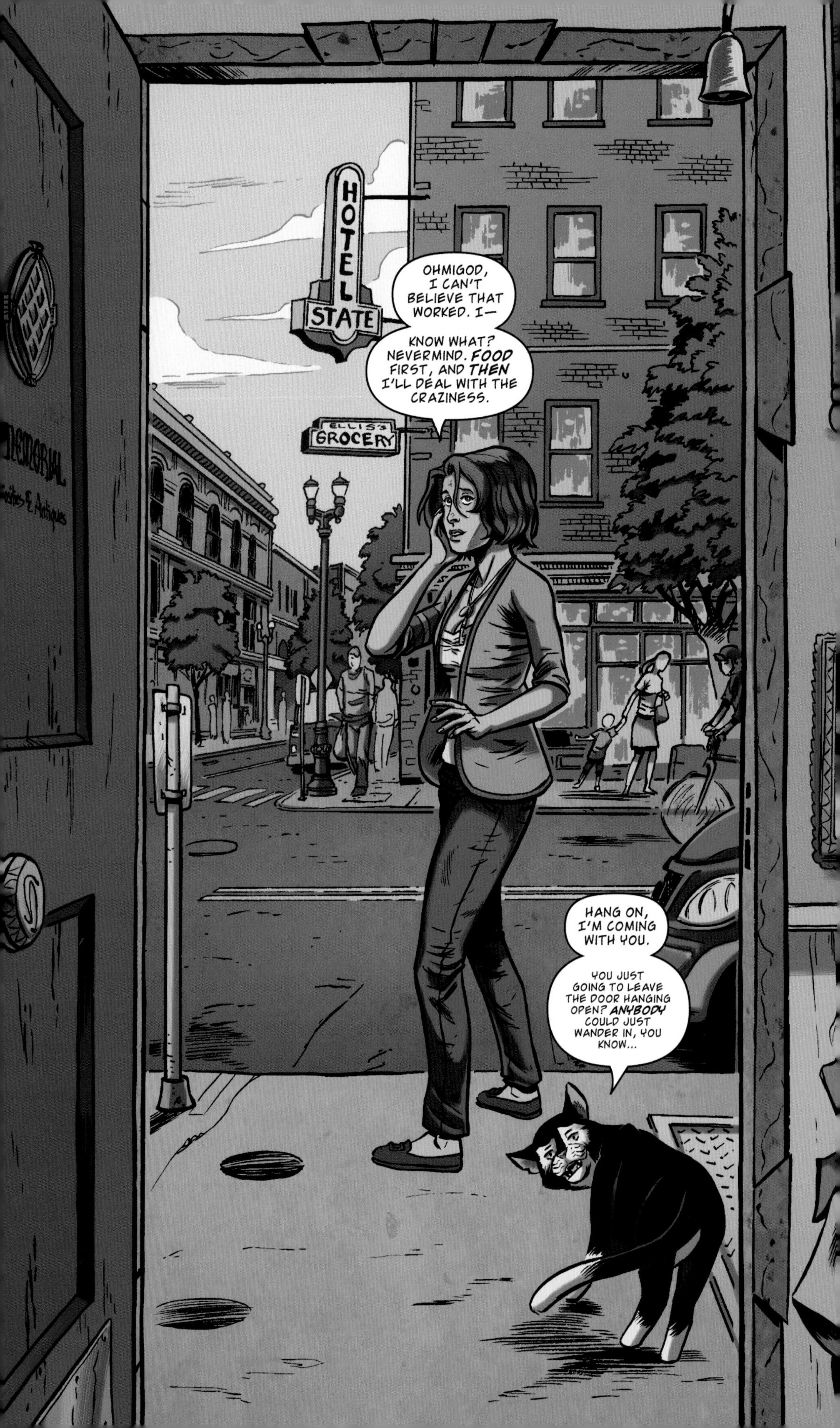
HOTEL
STATE
ELLIS'S
GROCERY
OHMIGOD, I CAN'T BELIEVE THAT WORKED. I—
KNOW WHAT? NEVERMIND. **FOOD** FIRST, AND **THEN** I'LL DEAL WITH THE CRAZINESS.
HANG ON, I'M COMING WITH YOU.
YOU JUST GOING TO LEAVE THE DOOR HANGING OPEN? **ANYBODY** COULD JUST WANDER IN, YOU KNOW...

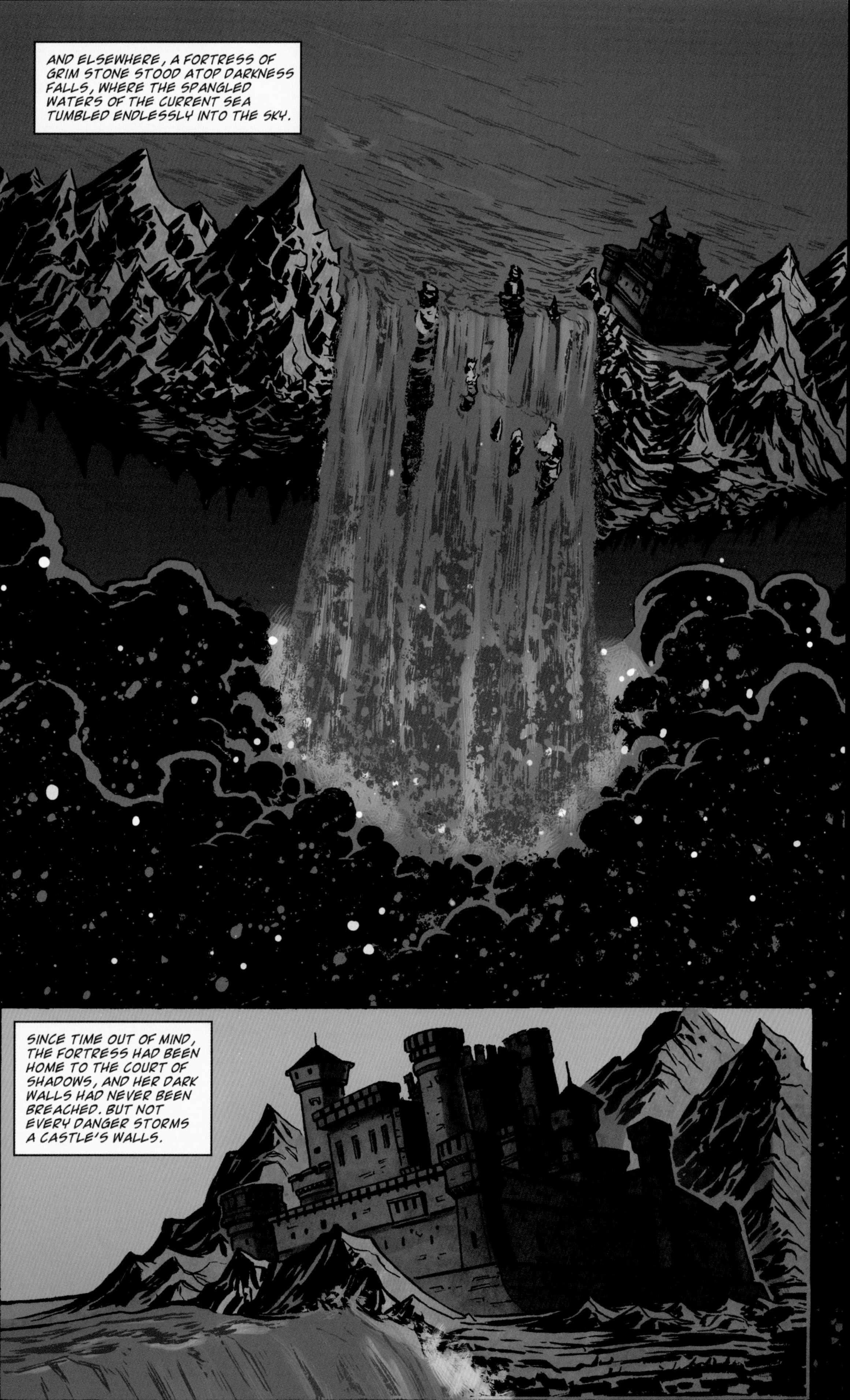
AND ELSEWHERE, A FORTRESS OF GRIM STONE STOOD ATOP DARKNESS FALLS, WHERE THE SPANGLED WATERS OF THE CURRENT SEA TUMBLED ENDLESSLY INTO THE SKY.
SINCE TIME OUT OF MIND, THE FORTRESS HAD BEEN HOME TO THE COURT OF SHADOWS, AND HER DARK WALLS HAD NEVER BEEN BREACHED. BUT NOT EVERY DANGER STORMS A CASTLE'S WALLS.

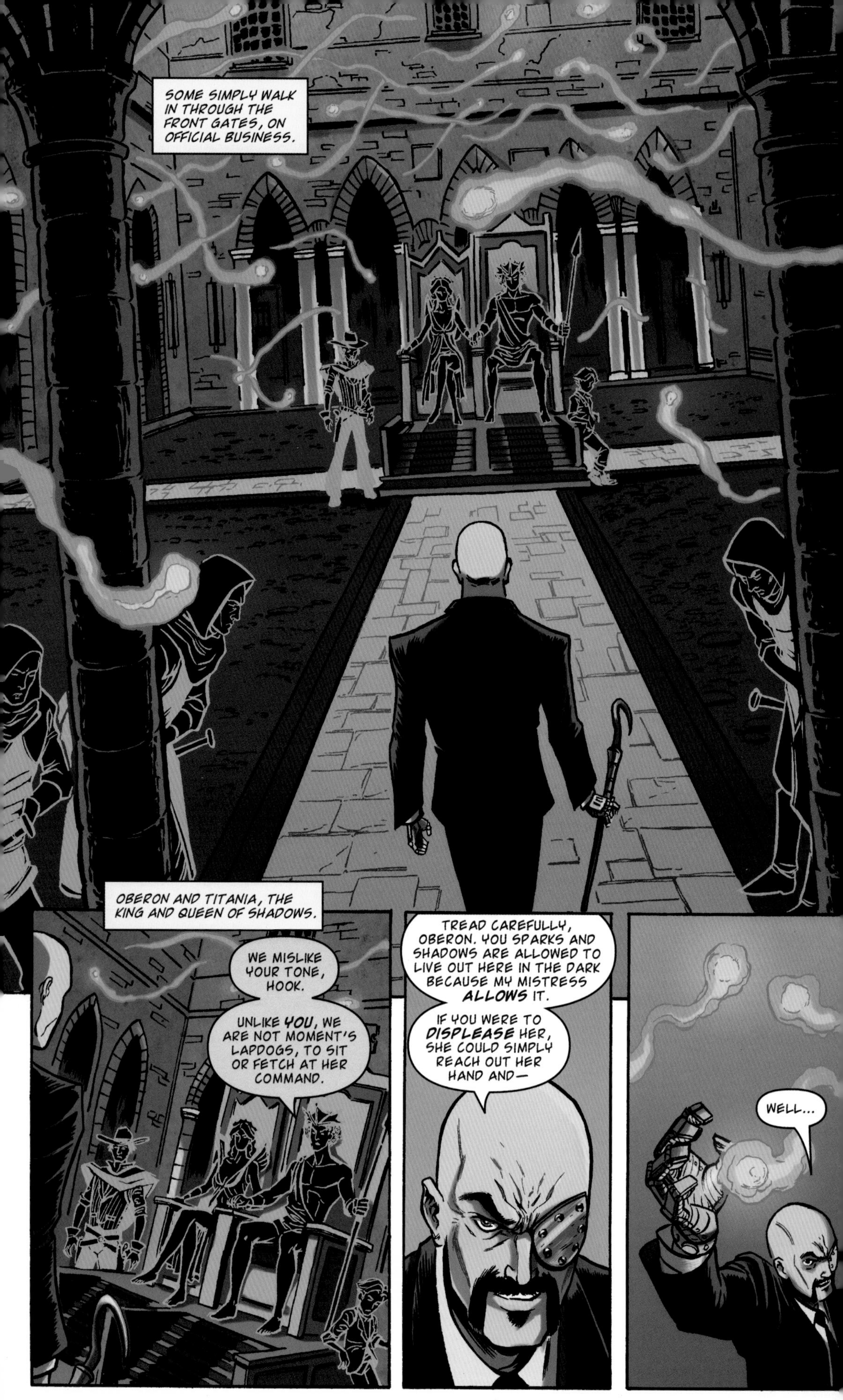
SOME SIMPLY WALK IN THROUGH THE FRONT GATES, ON OFFICIAL BUSINESS.
OBERON AND TITANIA, THE KING AND QUEEN OF SHADOWS.
WE MISLIKE YOUR TONE, HOOK.
UNLIKE YOU, WE ARE NOT MOMENT'S LAPDOGS, TO SIT OR FETCH AT HER COMMAND.
TREAD CAREFULLY, OBERON. YOU SPARKS AND SHADOWS ARE ALLOWED TO LIVE OUT HERE IN THE DARK BECAUSE MY MISTRESS ALLOWS IT.
IF YOU WERE TO DISPLEASE HER, SHE COULD SIMPLY REACH OUT HER HAND AND—
WELL...

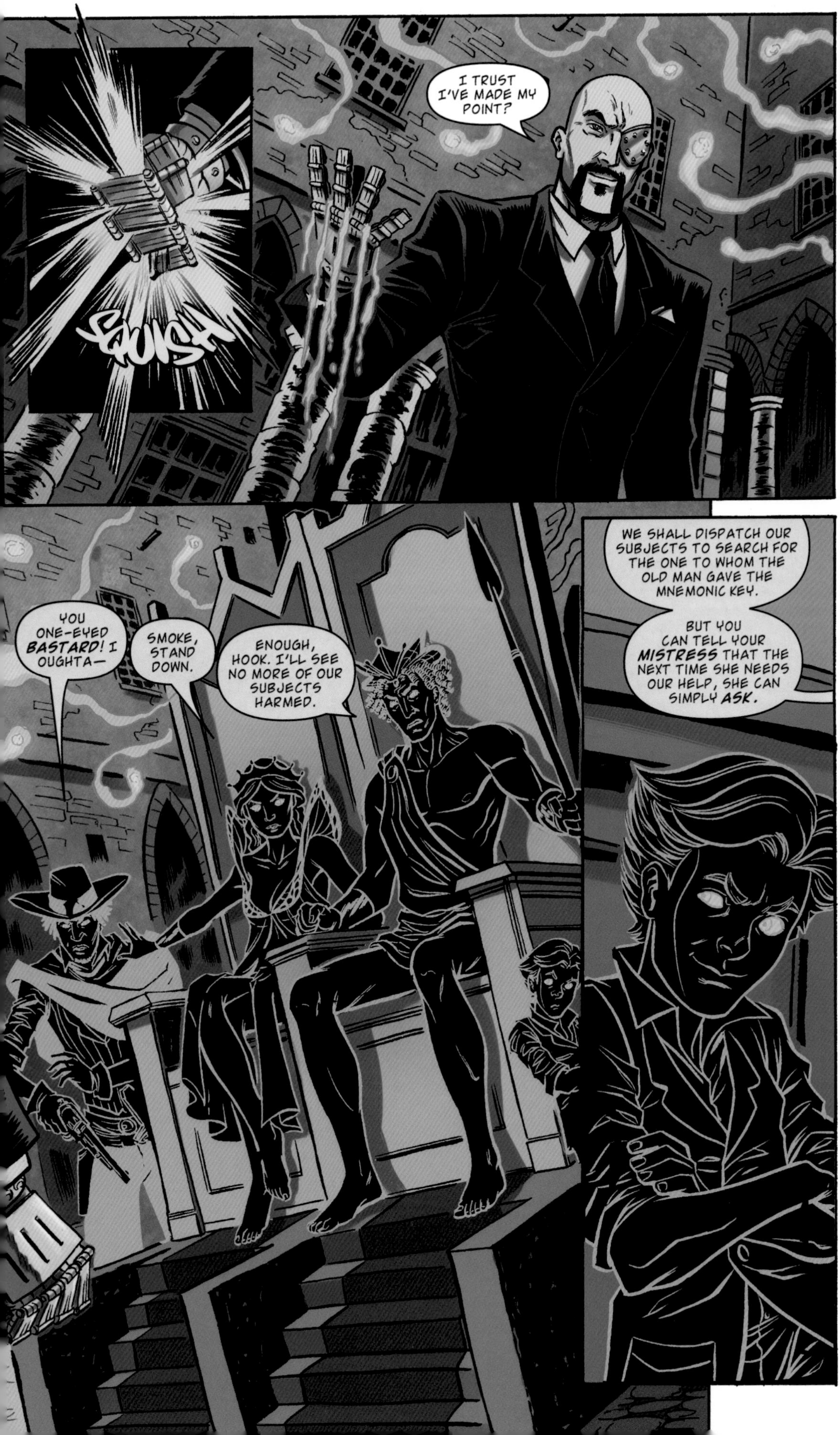
SQUISH
I TRUST I'VE MADE MY POINT?
YOU ONE-EYED BASTARD! I OUGHTA—
SMOKE, STAND DOWN.
ENOUGH, HOOK. I'LL SEE NO MORE OF OUR SUBJECTS HARMED.
WE SHALL DISPATCH OUR SUBJECTS TO SEARCH FOR THE ONE TO WHOM THE OLD MAN GAVE THE MNEMONIC KEY.
BUT YOU CAN TELL YOUR MISTRESS THAT THE NEXT TIME SHE NEEDS OUR HELP, SHE CAN SIMPLY ASK.

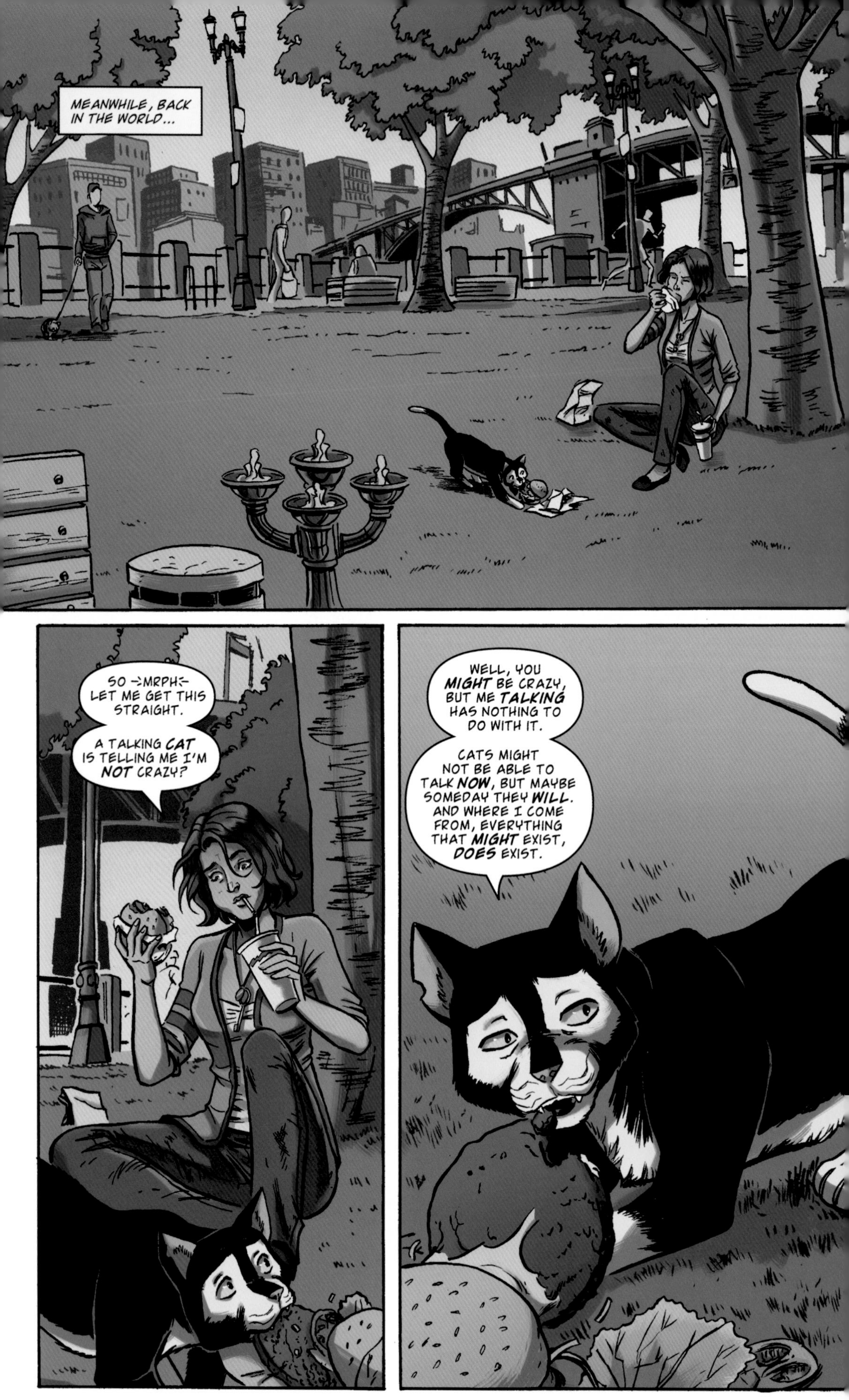
MEANWHILE, BACK IN THE WORLD...
SO -MRPH- LET ME GET THIS STRAIGHT.
A TALKING CAT IS TELLING ME I'M NOT CRAZY?
WELL, YOU MIGHT BE CRAZY, BUT ME TALKING HAS NOTHING TO DO WITH IT.
CATS MIGHT NOT BE ABLE TO TALK NOW, BUT MAYBE SOMEDAY THEY WILL. AND WHERE I COME FROM, EVERYTHING THAT MIGHT EXIST, DOES EXIST.

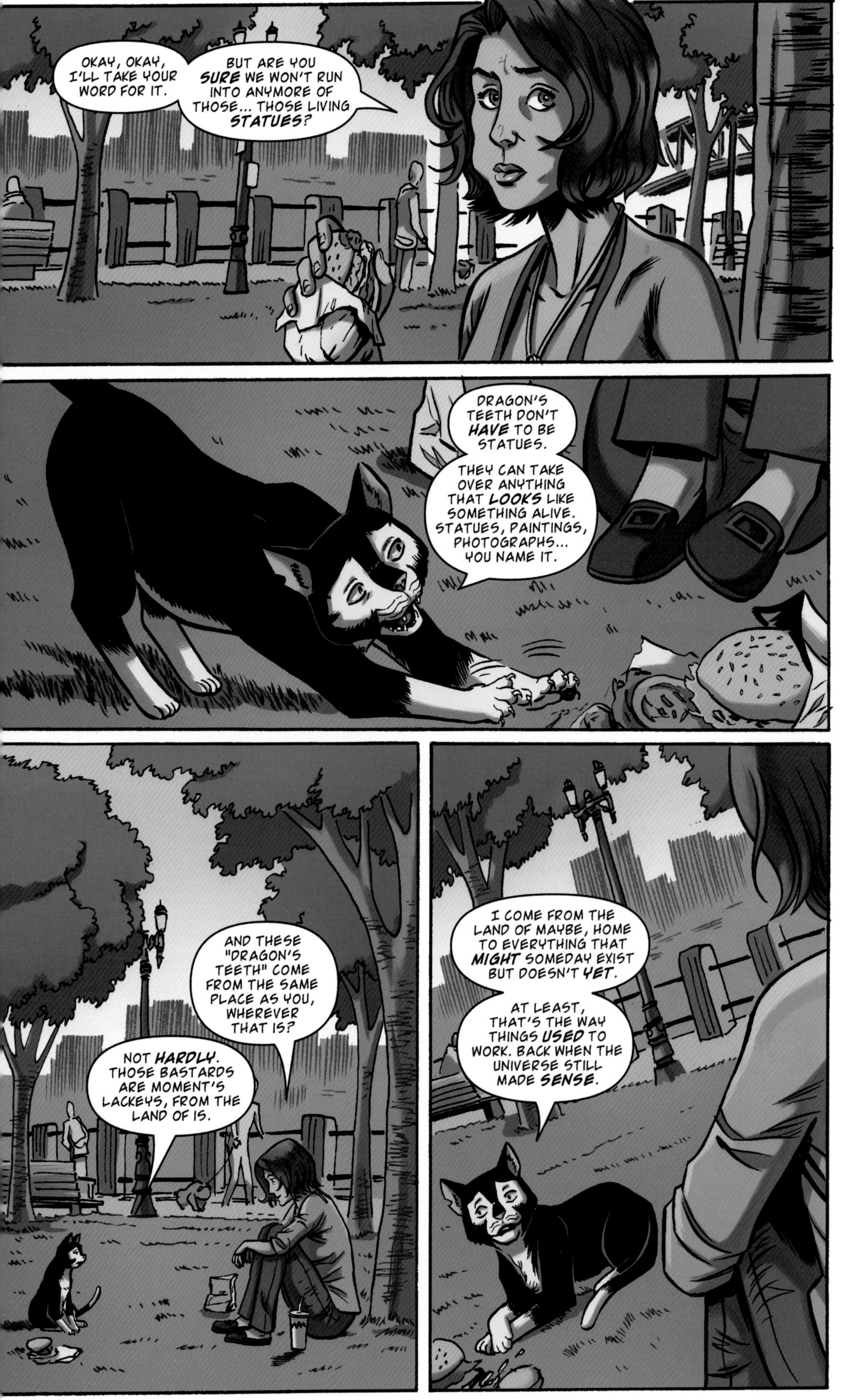
OKAY, OKAY, I'LL TAKE YOUR WORD FOR IT.
BUT ARE YOU SURE WE WON'T RUN INTO ANYMORE OF THOSE... THOSE LIVING STATUES?
DRAGON'S TEETH DON'T HAVE TO BE STATUES.
THEY CAN TAKE OVER ANYTHING THAT LOOKS LIKE SOMETHING ALIVE. STATUES, PAINTINGS, PHOTOGRAPHS... YOU NAME IT.
AND THESE "DRAGON'S TEETH" COME FROM THE SAME PLACE AS YOU, WHEREVER THAT IS?
NOT HARDLY. THOSE BASTARDS ARE MOMENT'S LACKEYS, FROM THE LAND OF IS.
I COME FROM THE LAND OF MAYBE, HOME TO EVERYTHING THAT MIGHT SOMEDAY EXIST BUT DOESN'T YET.
AT LEAST, THAT'S THE WAY THINGS USED TO WORK. BACK WHEN THE UNIVERSE STILL MADE SENSE.

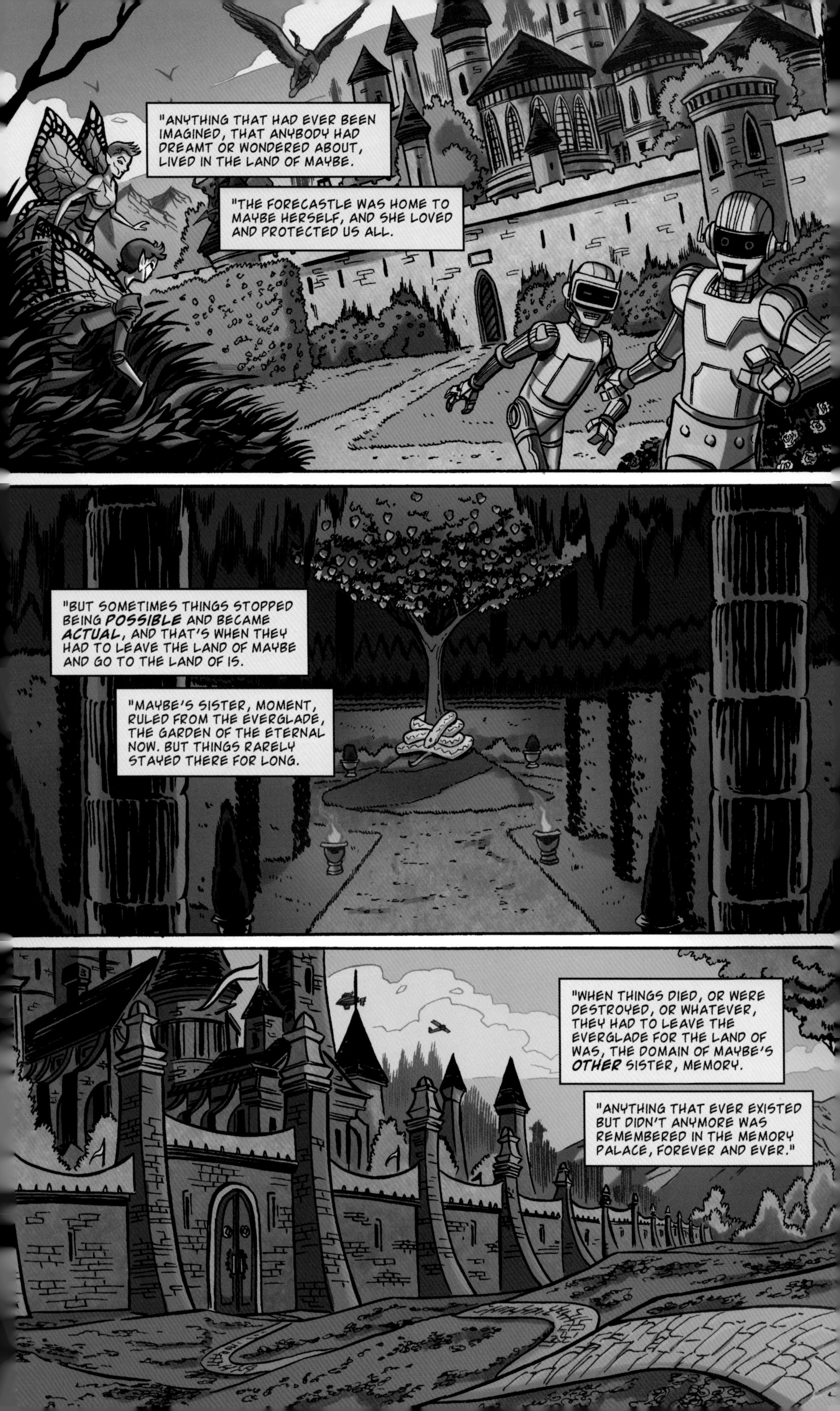
"ANYTHING THAT HAD EVER BEEN IMAGINED, THAT ANYBODY HAD DREAMT OR WONDERED ABOUT, LIVED IN THE LAND OF MAYBE.
"THE FORECASTLE WAS HOME TO MAYBE HERSELF, AND SHE LOVED AND PROTECTED US ALL.
"BUT SOMETIMES THINGS STOPPED BEING *POSSIBLE* AND BECAME *ACTUAL*, AND THAT'S WHEN THEY HAD TO LEAVE THE LAND OF MAYBE AND GO TO THE LAND OF IS.
"MAYBE'S SISTER, MOMENT, RULED FROM THE EVERGLADE, THE GARDEN OF THE ETERNAL NOW. BUT THINGS RARELY STAYED THERE FOR LONG.
"WHEN THINGS DIED, OR WERE DESTROYED, OR WHATEVER, THEY HAD TO LEAVE THE EVERGLADE FOR THE LAND OF WAS, THE DOMAIN OF MAYBE'S *OTHER* SISTER, MEMORY.
"ANYTHING THAT EVER EXISTED BUT DIDN'T ANYMORE WAS REMEMBERED IN THE MEMORY PALACE, FOREVER AND EVER."

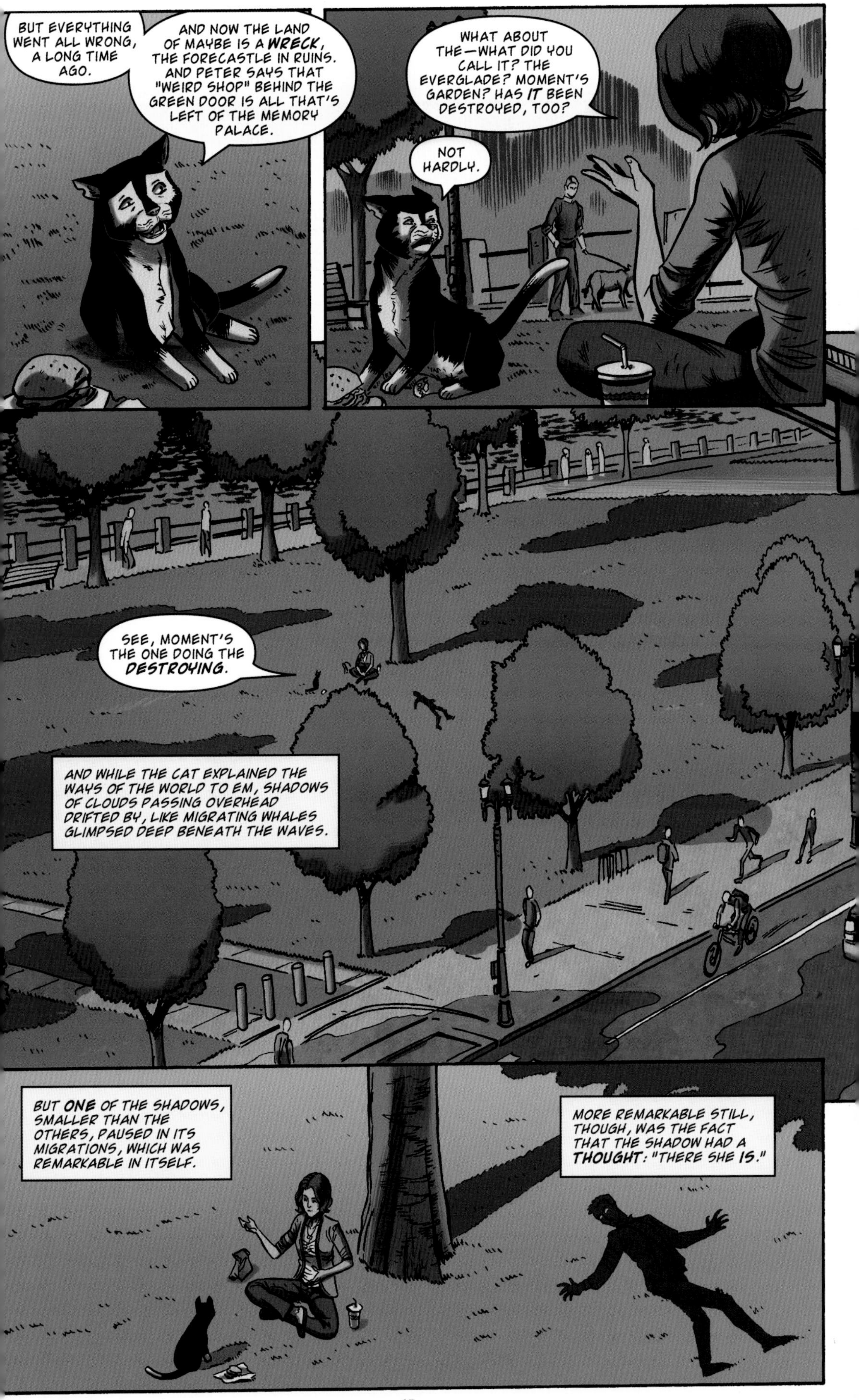
BUT EVERYTHING WENT ALL WRONG, A LONG TIME AGO.
AND NOW THE LAND OF MAYBE IS A WRECK, THE FORECASTLE IN RUINS. AND PETER SAYS THAT "WEIRD SHOP" BEHIND THE GREEN DOOR IS ALL THAT'S LEFT OF THE MEMORY PALACE.
WHAT ABOUT THE—WHAT DID YOU CALL IT? THE EVERGLADE? MOMENT'S GARDEN? HAS IT BEEN DESTROYED, TOO?
NOT HARDLY.
SEE, MOMENT'S THE ONE DOING THE DESTROYING.
AND WHILE THE CAT EXPLAINED THE WAYS OF THE WORLD TO EM, SHADOWS OF CLOUDS PASSING OVERHEAD DRIFTED BY, LIKE MIGRATING WHALES GLIMPSED DEEP BENEATH THE WAVES.
BUT ONE OF THE SHADOWS, SMALLER THAN THE OTHERS, PAUSED IN ITS MIGRATIONS, WHICH WAS REMARKABLE IN ITSELF.
MORE REMARKABLE STILL, THOUGH, WAS THE FACT THAT THE SHADOW HAD A THOUGHT: "THERE SHE IS."

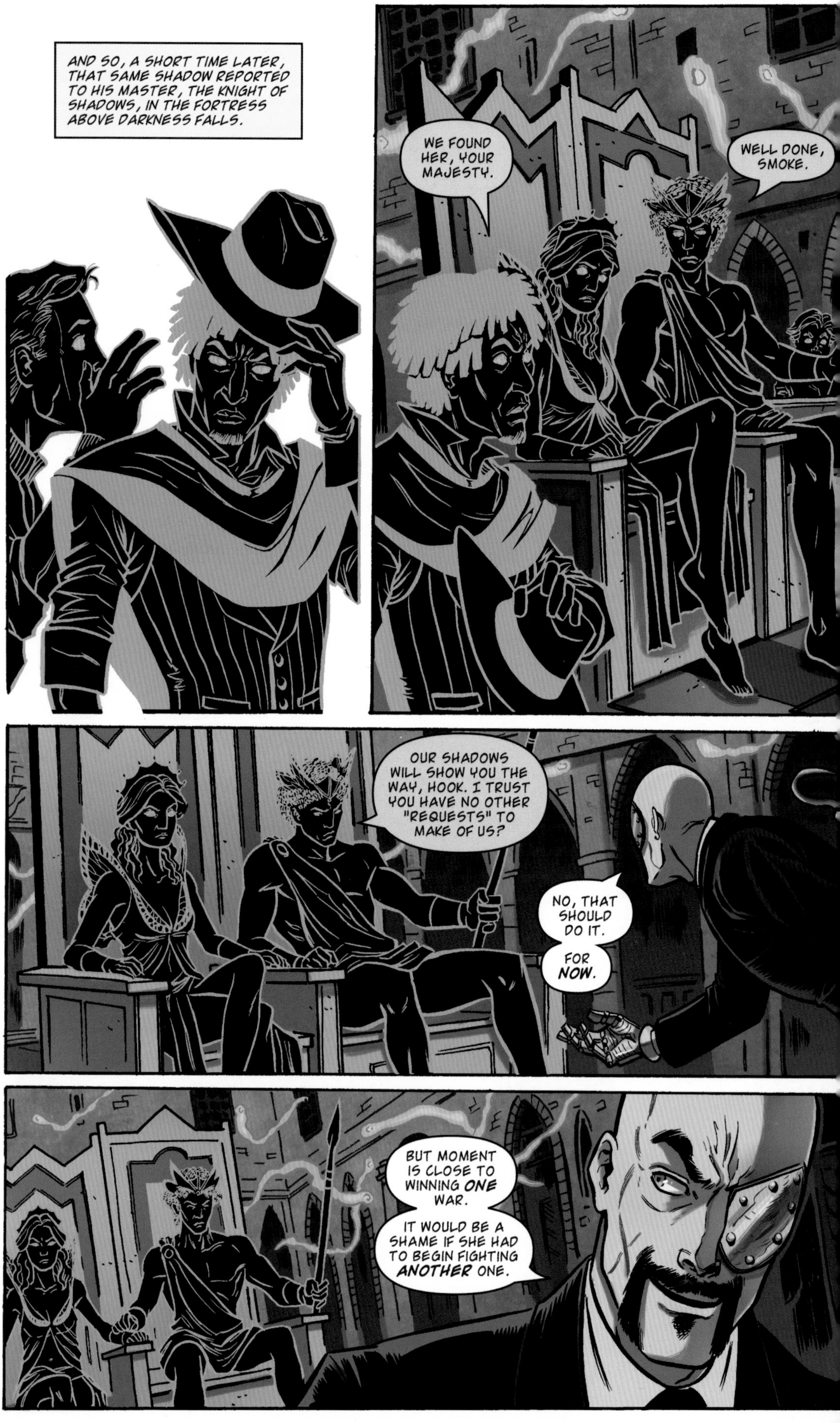
AND SO, A SHORT TIME LATER, THAT SAME SHADOW REPORTED TO HIS MASTER, THE KNIGHT OF SHADOWS, IN THE FORTRESS ABOVE DARKNESS FALLS.
WE FOUND HER, YOUR MAJESTY.
WELL DONE, SMOKE.
OUR SHADOWS WILL SHOW YOU THE WAY, HOOK. I TRUST YOU HAVE NO OTHER "REQUESTS" TO MAKE OF US?
NO, THAT SHOULD DO IT.
FOR NOW.
BUT MOMENT IS CLOSE TO WINNING ONE WAR.
IT WOULD BE A SHAME IF SHE HAD TO BEGIN FIGHTING ANOTHER ONE.

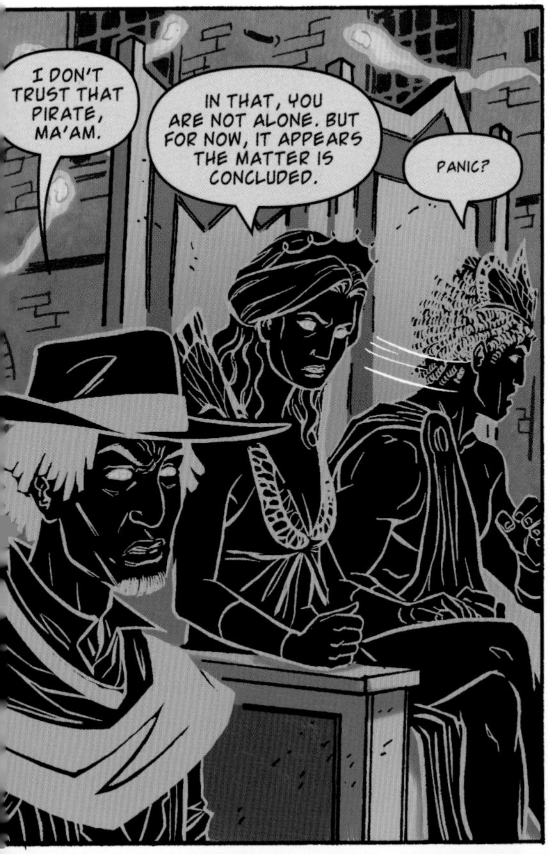
I DON'T TRUST THAT PIRATE, MA'AM.
IN THAT, YOU ARE NOT ALONE. BUT FOR NOW, IT APPEARS THE MATTER IS CONCLUDED.
PANIC?

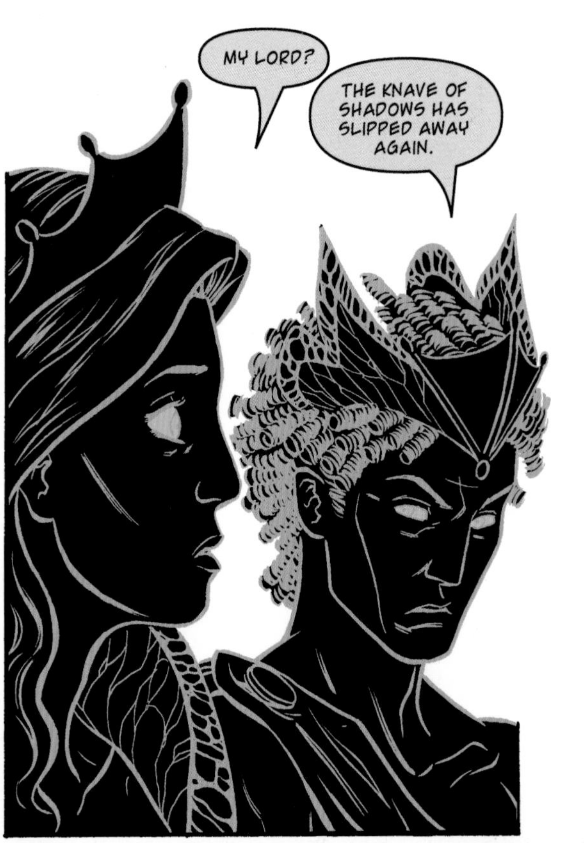
MY LORD?
THE KNAVE OF SHADOWS HAS SLIPPED AWAY AGAIN.

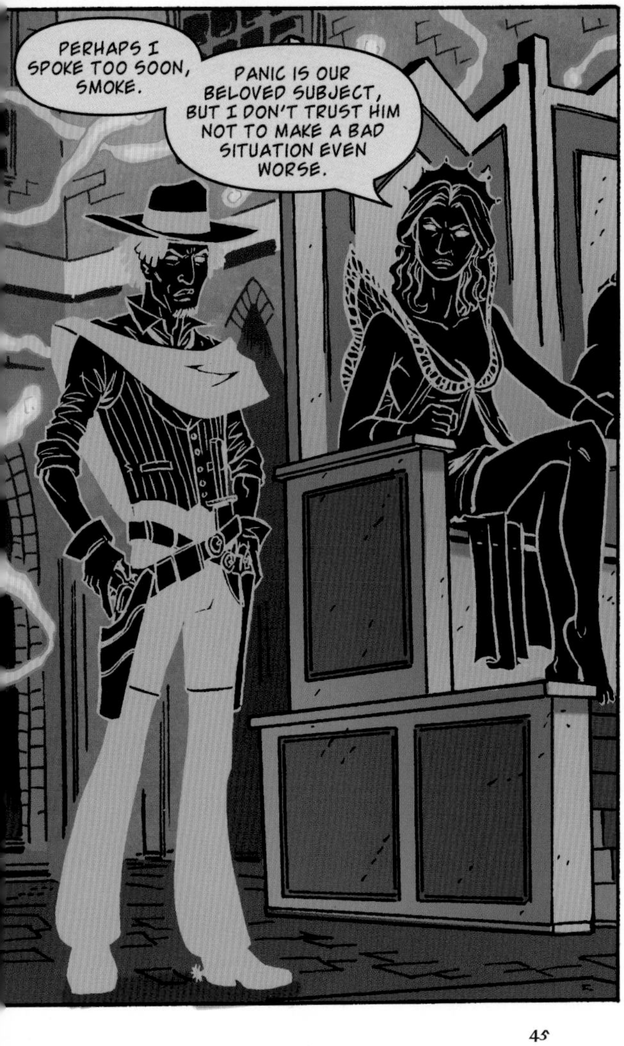
PERHAPS I SPOKE TOO SOON, SMOKE.
PANIC IS OUR BELOVED SUBJECT, BUT I DON'T TRUST HIM NOT TO MAKE A BAD SITUATION EVEN WORSE.

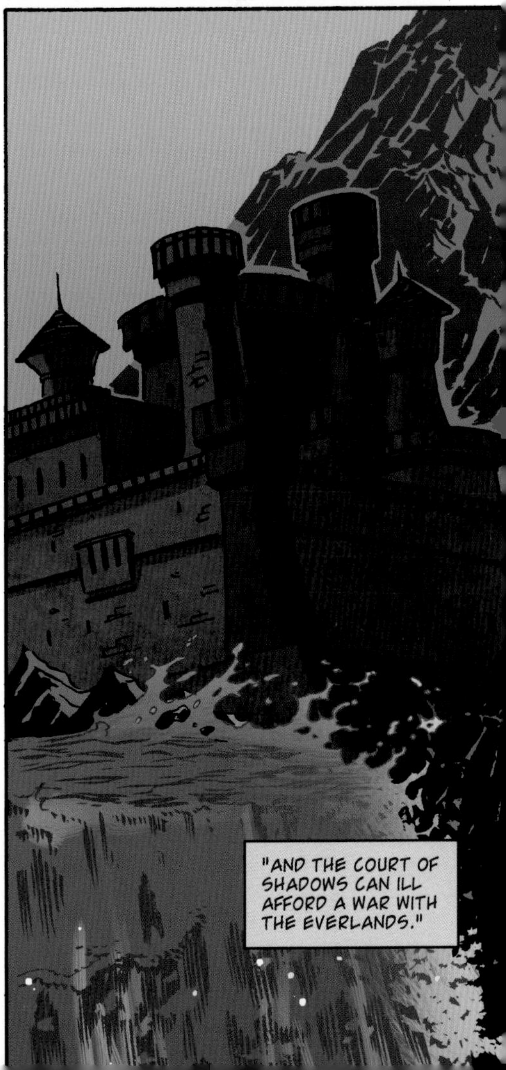
"AND THE COURT OF SHADOWS CAN ILL AFFORD A WAR WITH THE EVERLANDS."

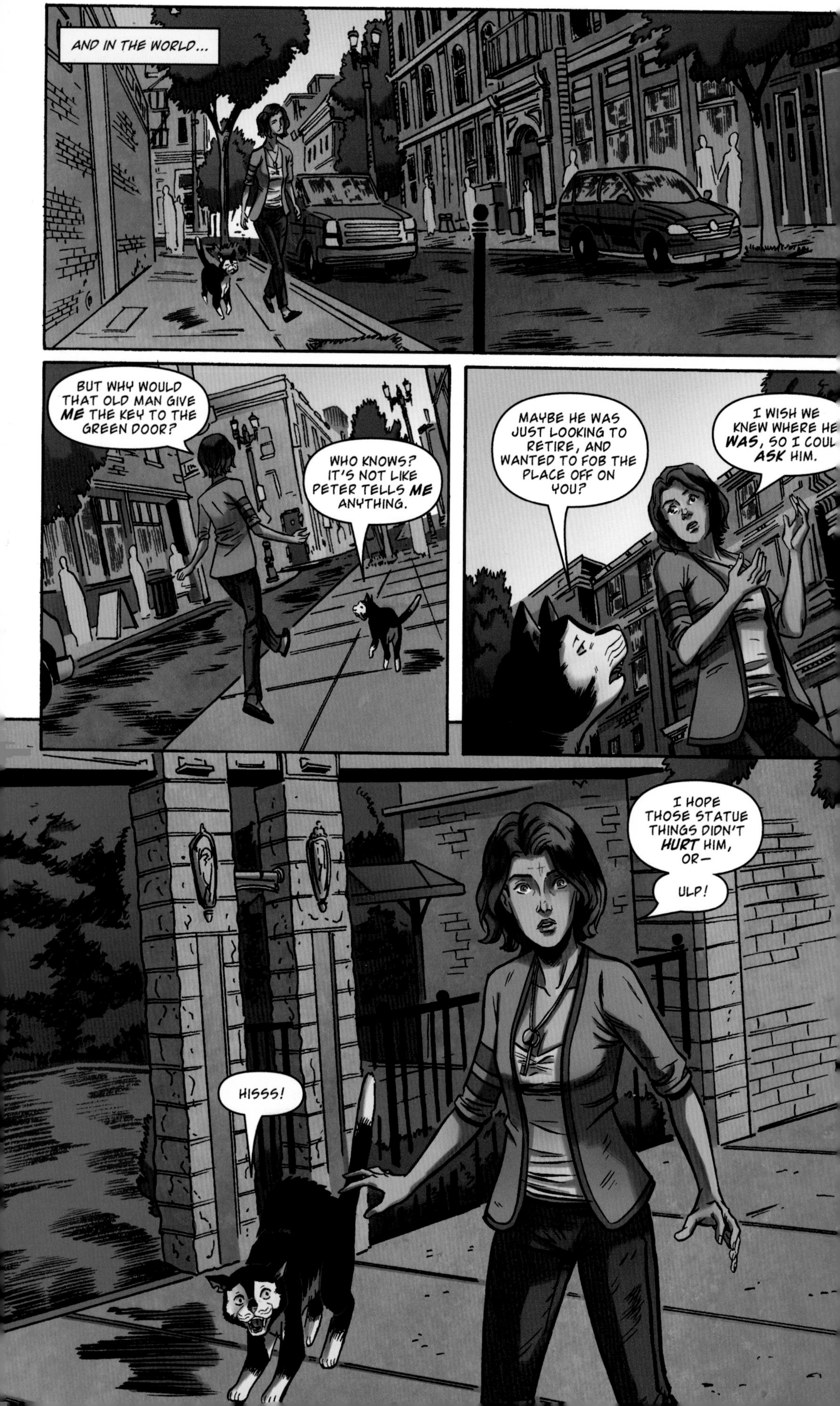
AND IN THE WORLD...
BUT WHY WOULD THAT OLD MAN GIVE ME THE KEY TO THE GREEN DOOR?
WHO KNOWS? IT'S NOT LIKE PETER TELLS ME ANYTHING.
MAYBE HE WAS JUST LOOKING TO RETIRE, AND WANTED TO FOB THE PLACE OFF ON YOU?
I WISH WE KNEW WHERE HE WAS, SO I COUL ASK HIM.
I HOPE THOSE STATUE THINGS DIDN'T HURT HIM, OR—
ULP!
HISSS!

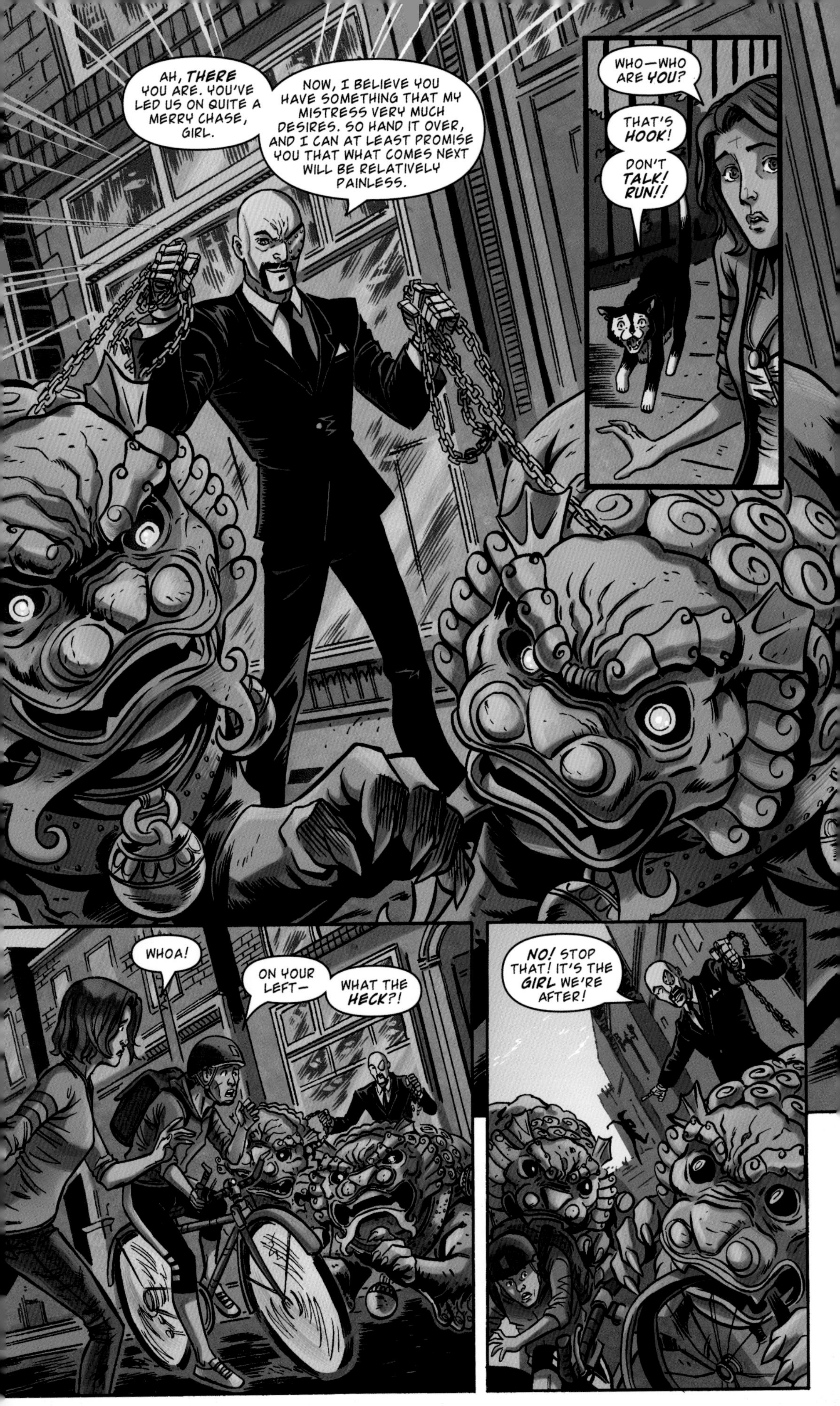
AH, THERE YOU ARE. YOU'VE LED US ON QUITE A MERRY CHASE, GIRL.
NOW, I BELIEVE YOU HAVE SOMETHING THAT MY MISTRESS VERY MUCH DESIRES. SO HAND IT OVER, AND I CAN AT LEAST PROMISE YOU THAT WHAT COMES NEXT WILL BE RELATIVELY PAINLESS.
WHO—WHO ARE YOU?
THAT'S HOOK!
DON'T TALK! RUN!!
WHOA!
ON YOUR LEFT—
WHAT THE HECK?!
NO! STOP THAT! IT'S THE GIRL WE'RE AFTER!

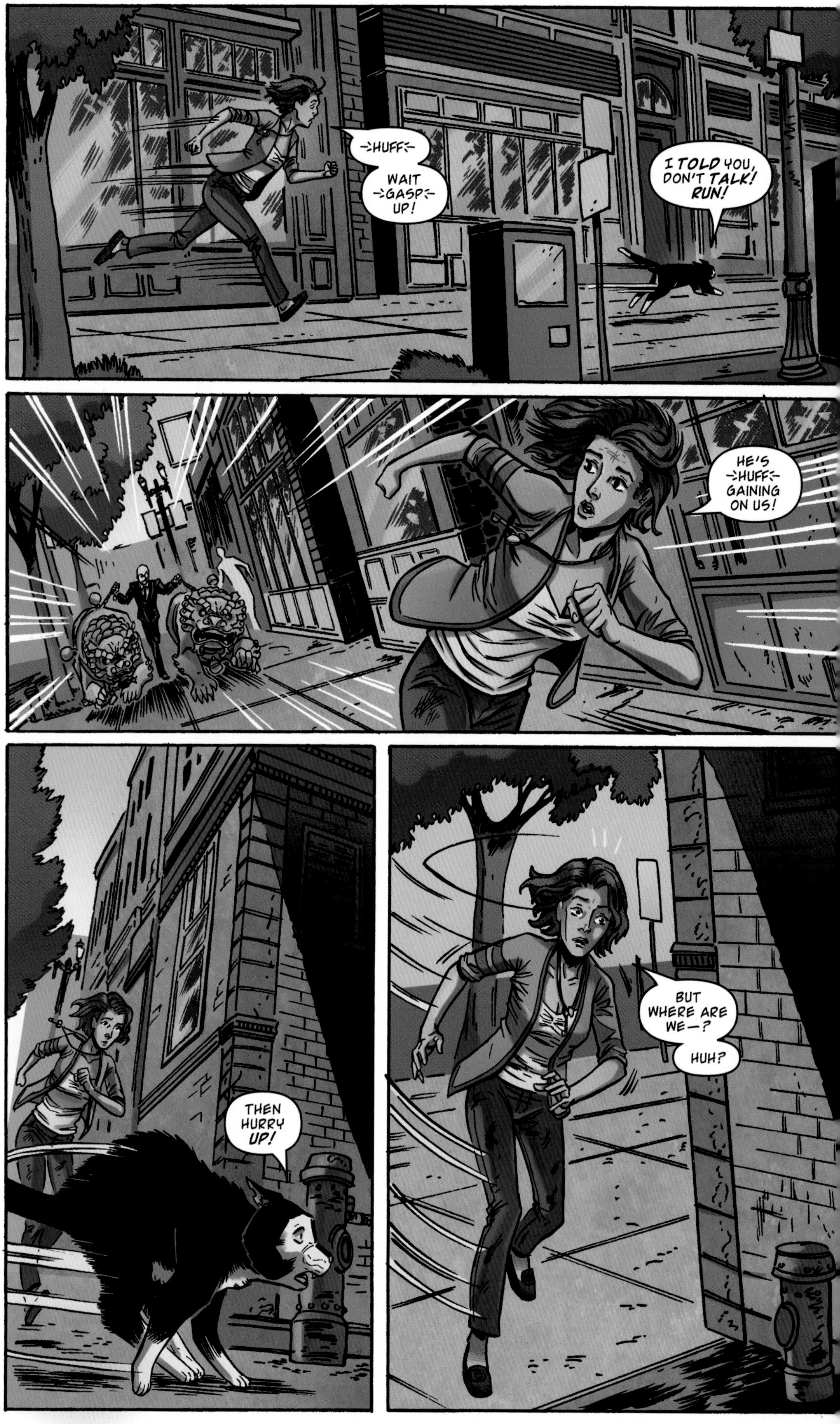

-HUFF-
WAIT -GASP- UP!
I TOLD YOU, DON'T TALK! RUN!
HE'S -HUFF- GAINING ON US!
THEN HURRY UP!
BUT WHERE ARE WE—?
HUH?

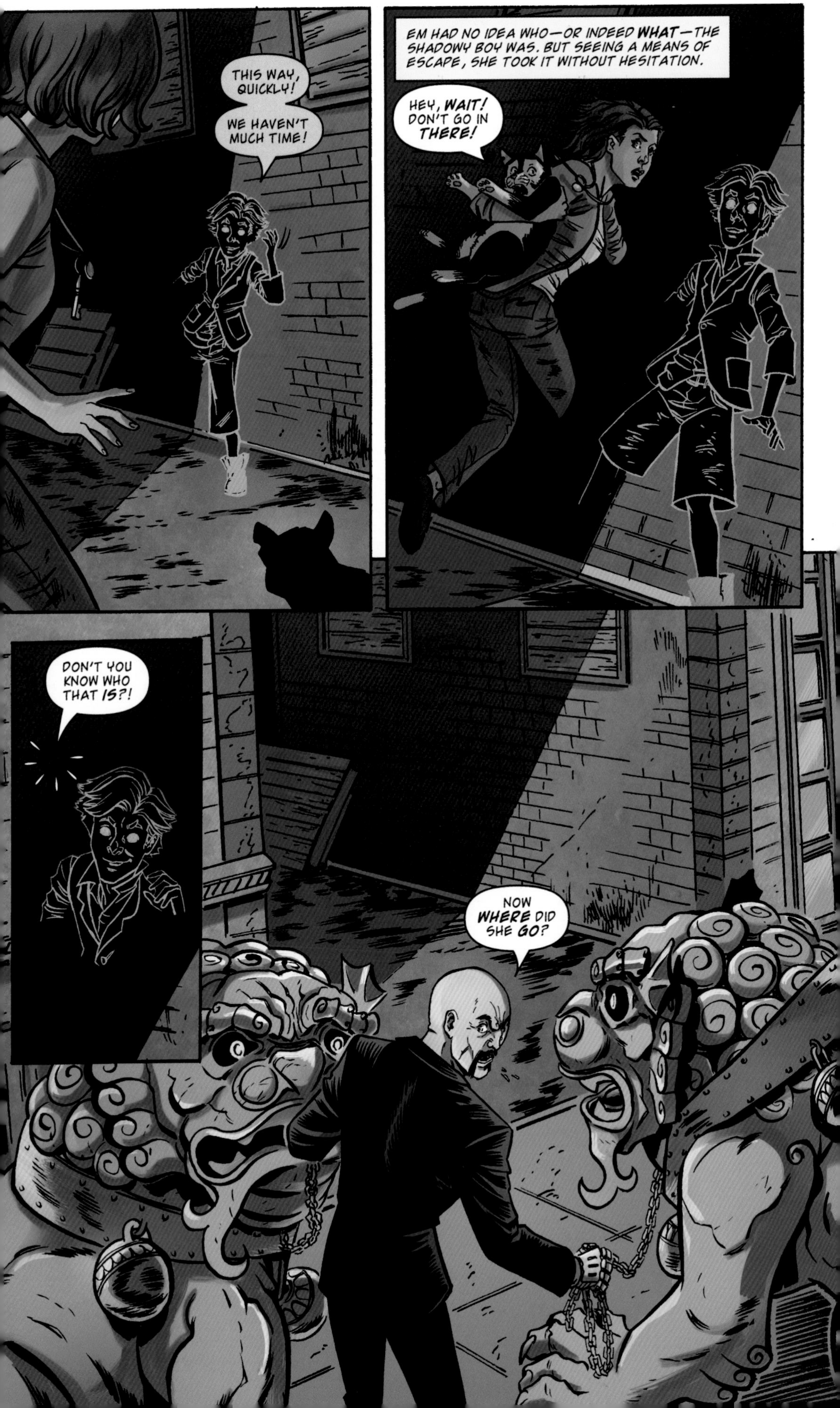
THIS WAY, QUICKLY!
WE HAVEN'T MUCH TIME!
EM HAD NO IDEA WHO—OR INDEED WHAT—THE SHADOWY BOY WAS. BUT SEEING A MEANS OF ESCAPE, SHE TOOK IT WITHOUT HESITATION.
HEY, WAIT! DON'T GO IN THERE!
DON'T YOU KNOW WHO THAT IS?!
NOW WHERE DID SHE GO?

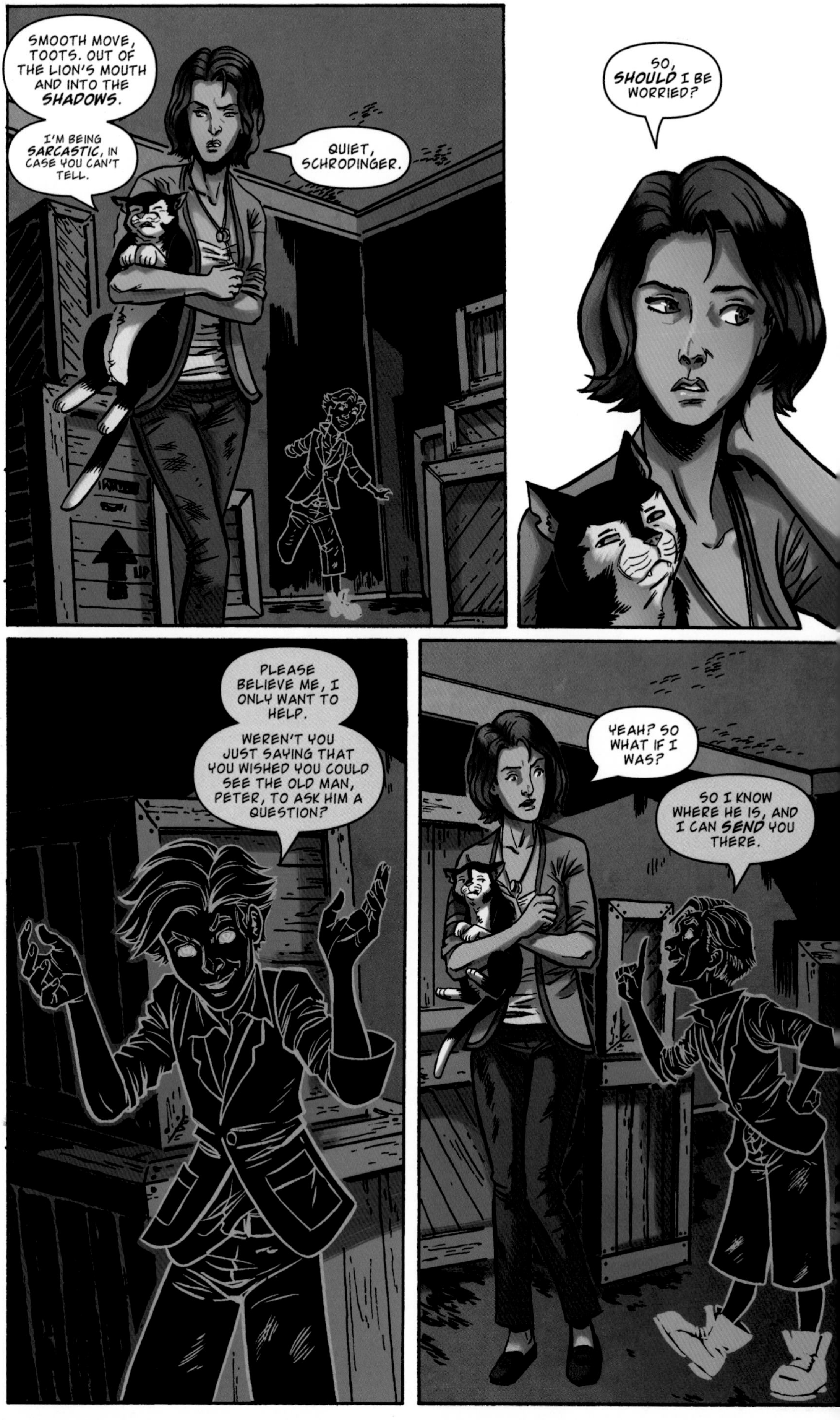
SMOOTH MOVE, TOOTS. OUT OF THE LION'S MOUTH AND INTO THE SHADOWS.
I'M BEING SARCASTIC, IN CASE YOU CAN'T TELL.
QUIET, SCHRODINGER.
SO, SHOULD I BE WORRIED?
PLEASE BELIEVE ME, I ONLY WANT TO HELP.
WEREN'T YOU JUST SAYING THAT YOU WISHED YOU COULD SEE THE OLD MAN, PETER, TO ASK HIM A QUESTION?
YEAH? SO WHAT IF I WAS?
SO I KNOW WHERE HE IS, AND I CAN SEND YOU THERE.

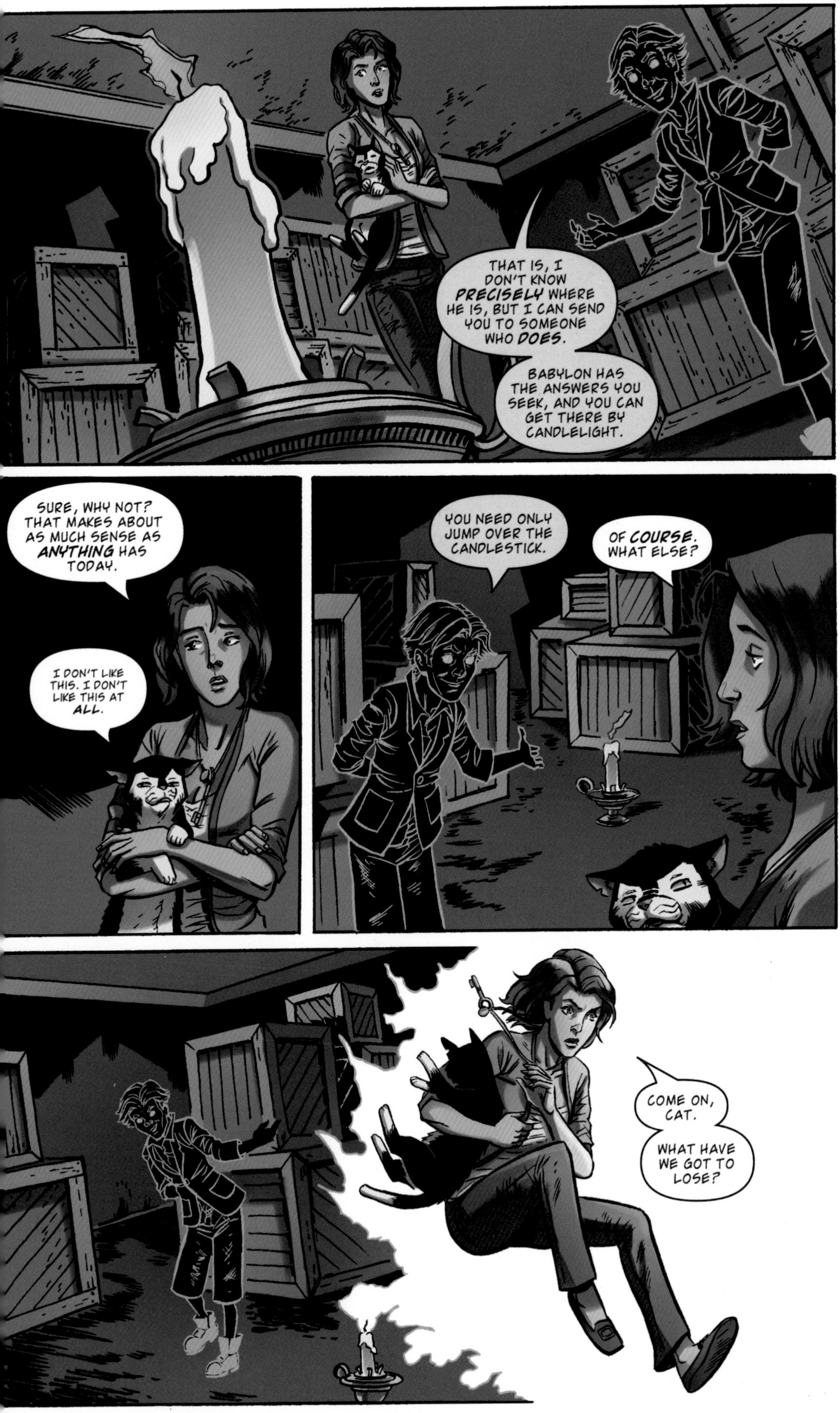
THAT IS, I DON'T KNOW PRECISELY WHERE HE IS, BUT I CAN SEND YOU TO SOMEONE WHO DOES.
BABYLON HAS THE ANSWERS YOU SEEK, AND YOU CAN GET THERE BY CANDLELIGHT.
SURE, WHY NOT? THAT MAKES ABOUT AS MUCH SENSE AS ANYTHING HAS TODAY.
I DON'T LIKE THIS. I DON'T LIKE THIS AT ALL.
YOU NEED ONLY JUMP OVER THE CANDLESTICK.
OF COURSE. WHAT ELSE?
COME ON, CAT.
WHAT HAVE WE GOT TO LOSE?

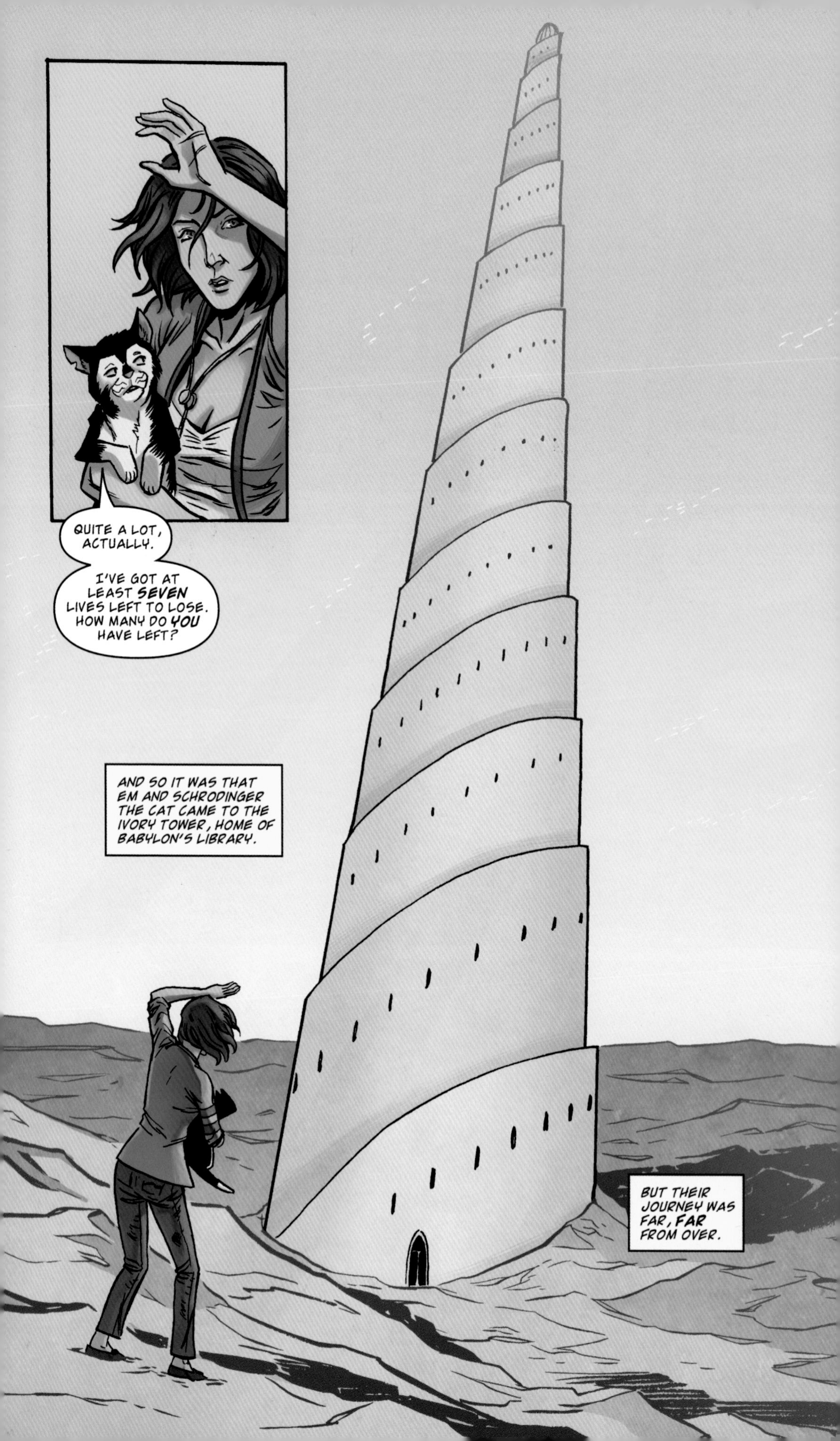
QUITE A LOT, ACTUALLY.
I'VE GOT AT LEAST SEVEN LIVES LEFT TO LOSE. HOW MANY DO YOU HAVE LEFT?
AND SO IT WAS THAT EM AND SCHRODINGER THE CAT CAME TO THE IVORY TOWER, HOME OF BABYLON'S LIBRARY.
BUT THEIR JOURNEY WAS FAR, FAR FROM OVER.

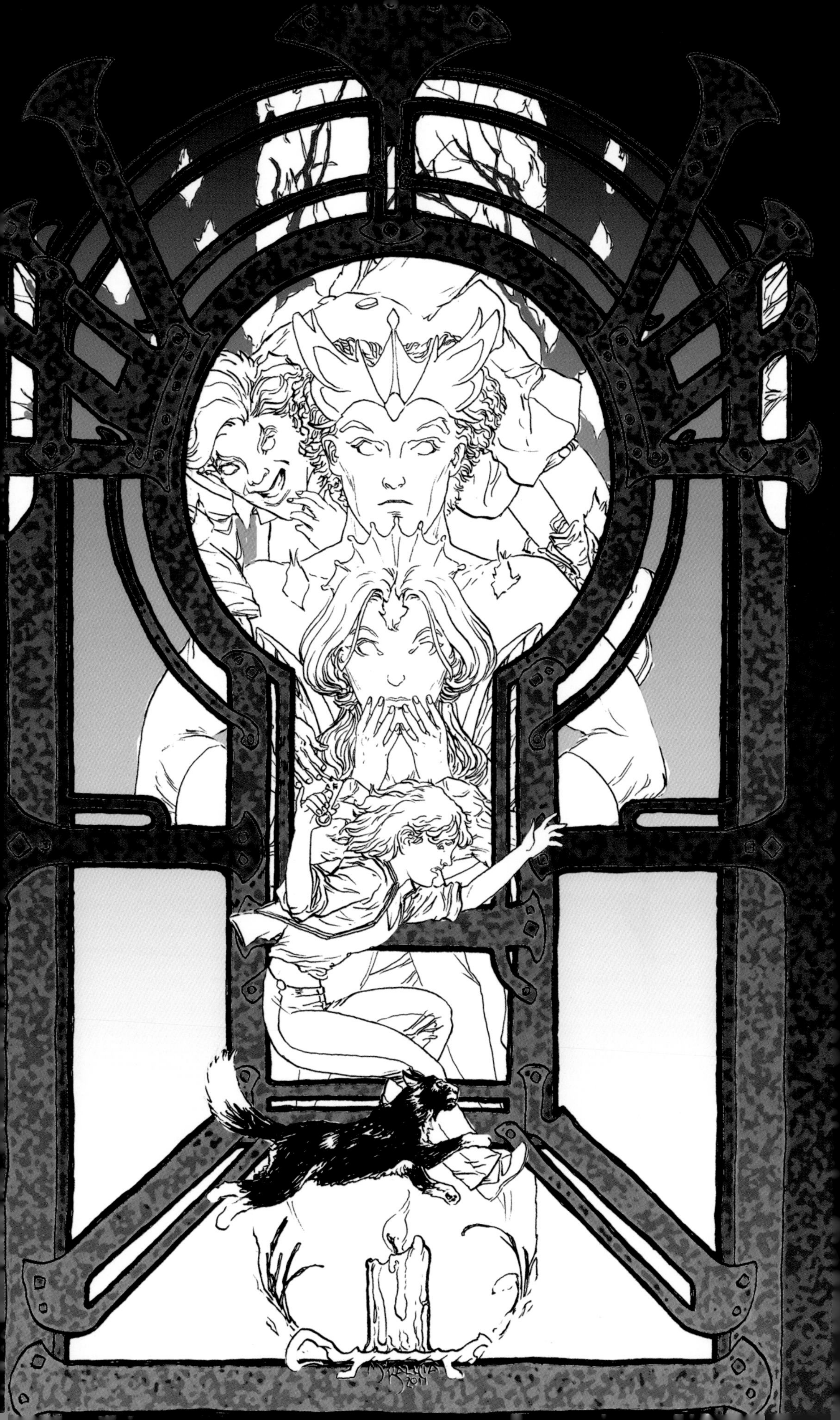

Chapter Three

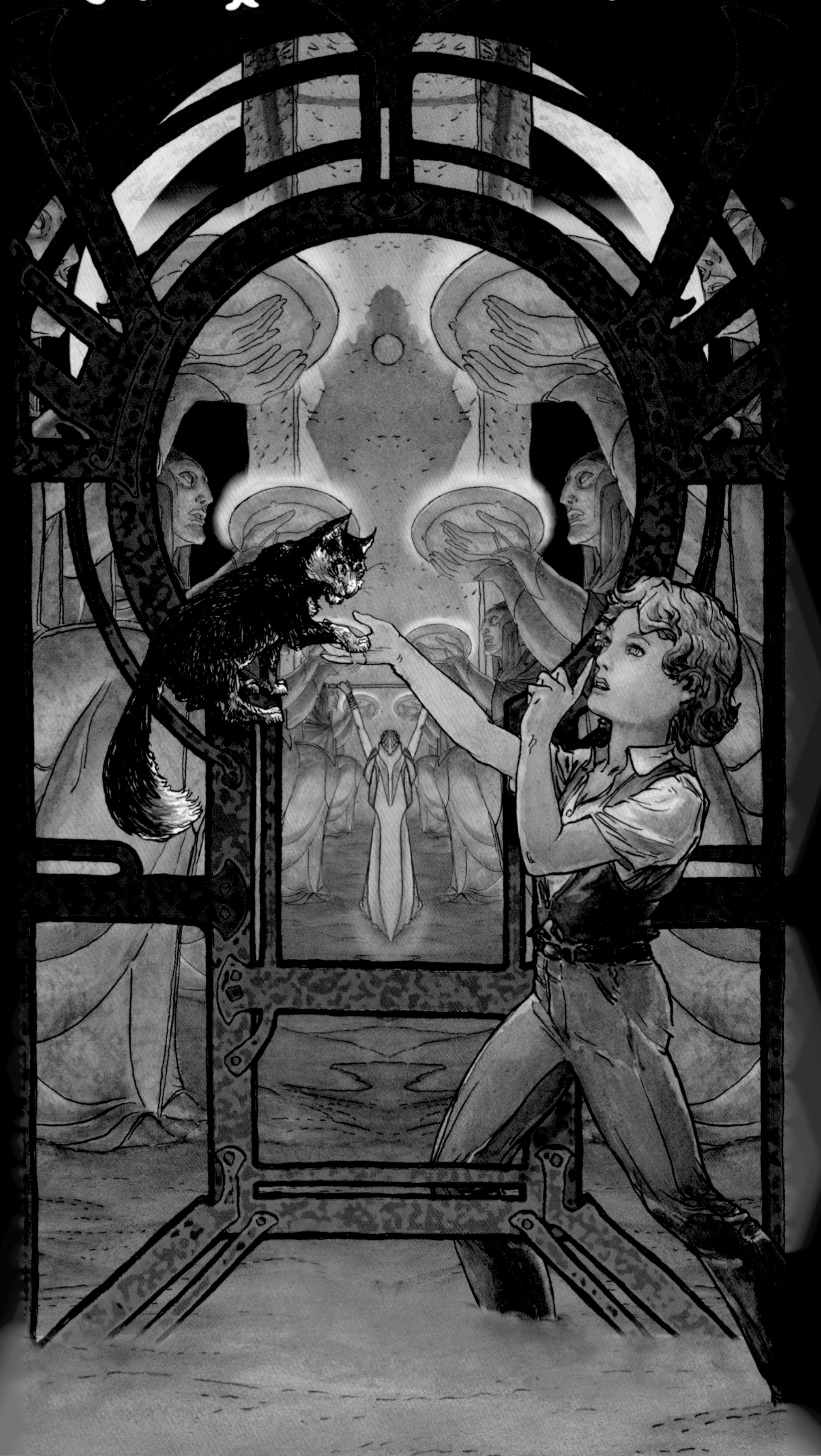

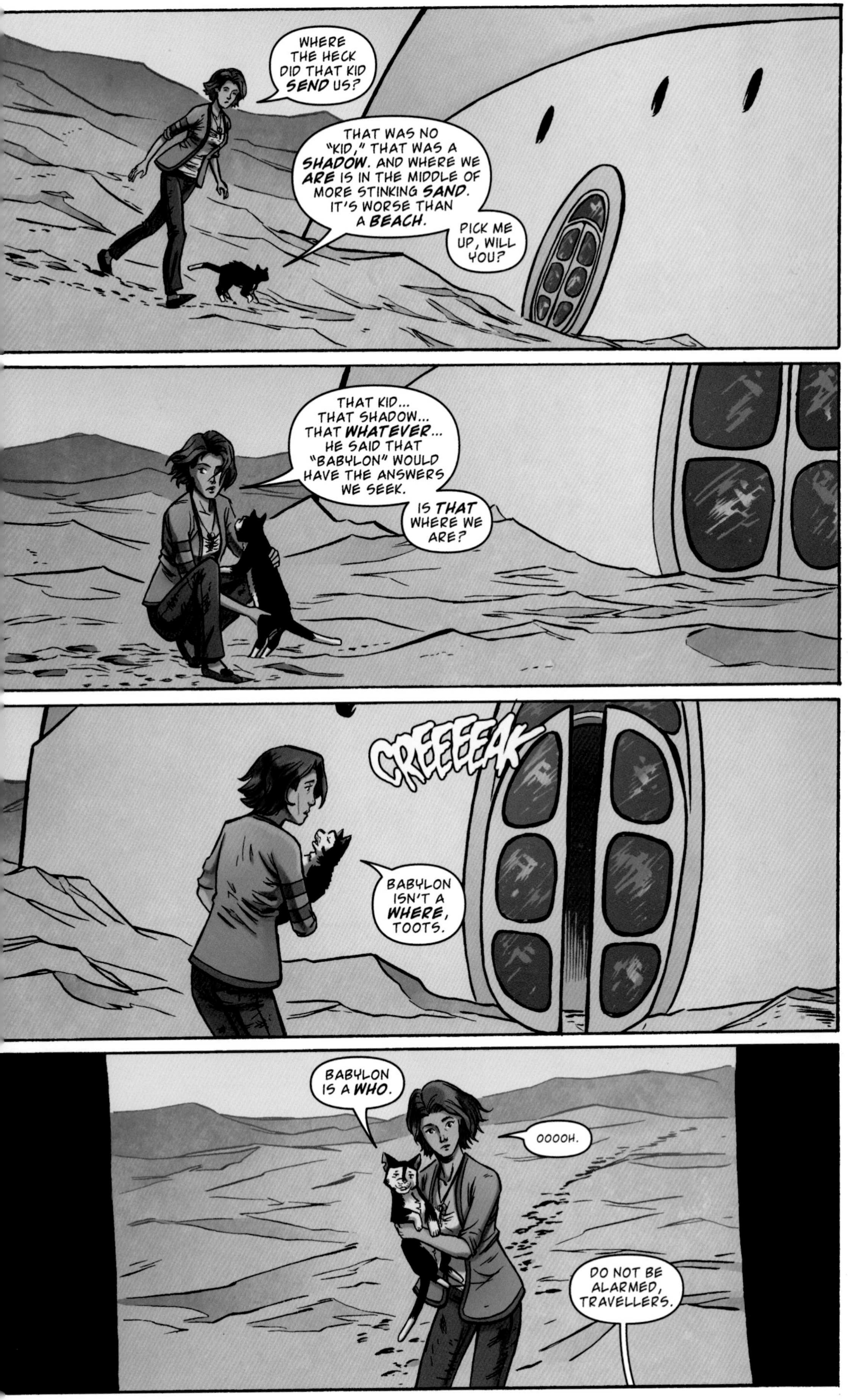
WHERE THE HECK DID THAT KID SEND US?
THAT WAS NO "KID," THAT WAS A SHADOW. AND WHERE WE ARE IS IN THE MIDDLE OF MORE STINKING SAND. IT'S WORSE THAN A BEACH.
PICK ME UP, WILL YOU?
THAT KID... THAT SHADOW... THAT WHATEVER... HE SAID THAT "BABYLON" WOULD HAVE THE ANSWERS WE SEEK.
IS THAT WHERE WE ARE?
CREEEEAK
BABYLON ISN'T A WHERE, TOOTS.
BABYLON IS A WHO.
OOOOH.
DO NOT BE ALARMED, TRAVELLERS.

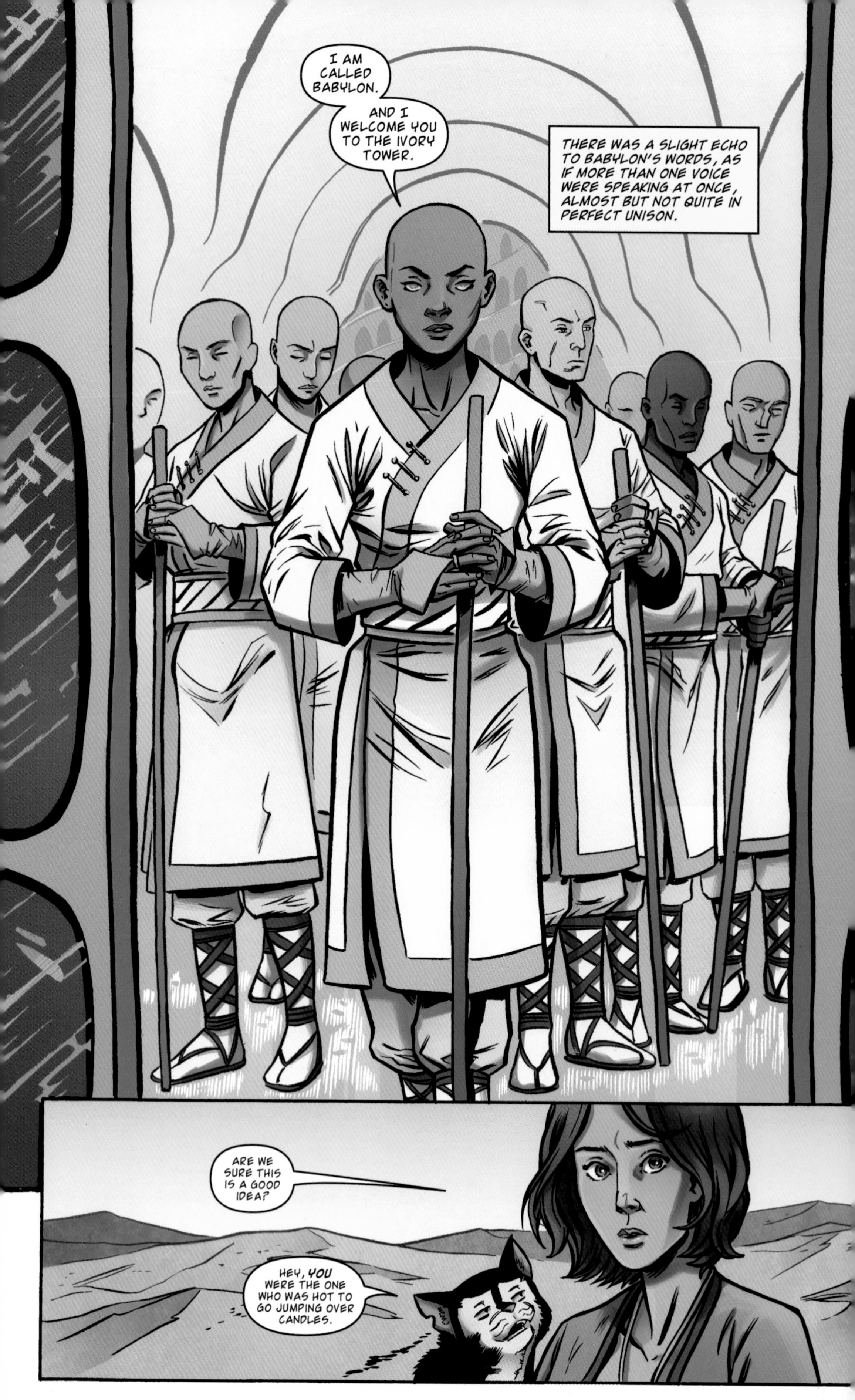
I AM CALLED BABYLON.
AND I WELCOME YOU TO THE IVORY TOWER.
THERE WAS A SLIGHT ECHO TO BABYLON'S WORDS, AS IF MORE THAN ONE VOICE WERE SPEAKING AT ONCE, ALMOST BUT NOT QUITE IN PERFECT UNISON.
ARE WE SURE THIS IS A GOOD IDEA?
HEY, YOU WERE THE ONE WHO WAS HOT TO GO JUMPING OVER CANDLES.

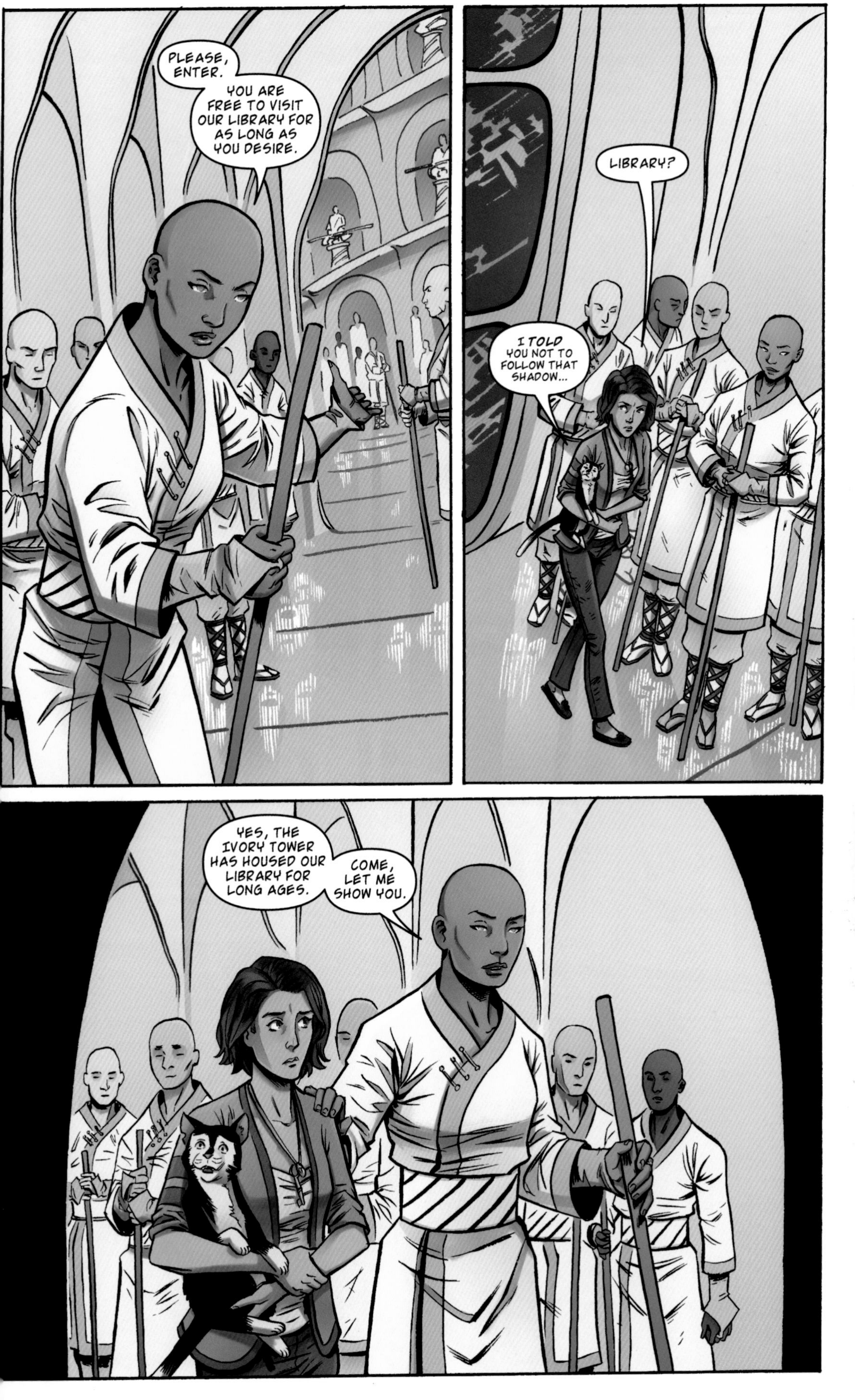
PLEASE, ENTER.
YOU ARE FREE TO VISIT OUR LIBRARY FOR AS LONG AS YOU DESIRE.
LIBRARY?
I TOLD YOU NOT TO FOLLOW THAT SHADOW...
YES, THE IVORY TOWER HAS HOUSED OUR LIBRARY FOR LONG AGES.
COME, LET ME SHOW YOU.

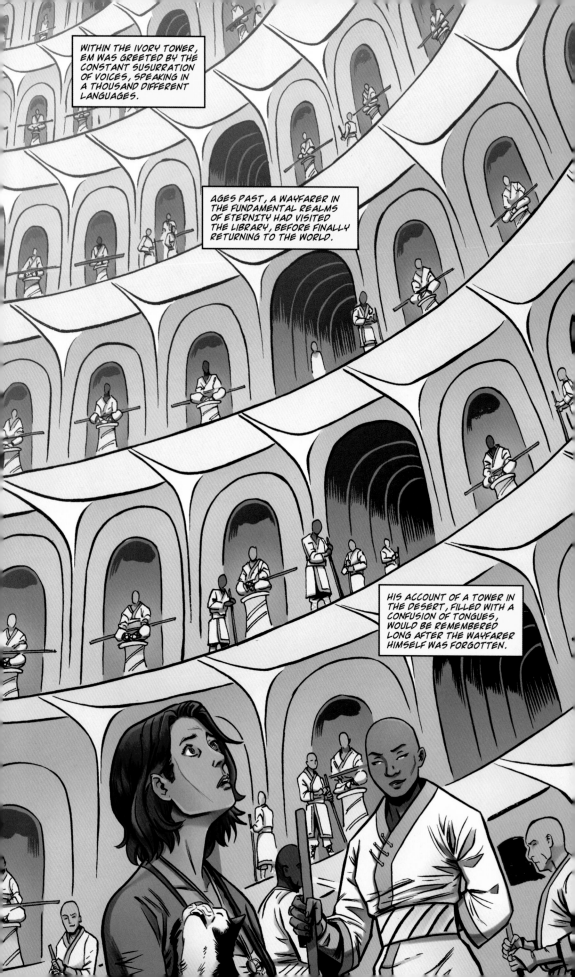

WITHIN THE IVORY TOWER, EM WAS GREETED BY THE CONSTANT SUSURRATION OF VOICES, SPEAKING IN A THOUSAND DIFFERENT LANGUAGES.

AGES PAST, A WAYFARER IN THE FUNDAMENTAL REALMS OF ETERNITY HAD VISITED THE LIBRARY, BEFORE FINALLY RETURNING TO THE WORLD.

HIS ACCOUNT OF A TOWER IN THE DESERT, FILLED WITH A CONFUSION OF TONGUES, WOULD BE REMEMBERED LONG AFTER THE WAYFARER HIMSELF WAS FORGOTTEN.

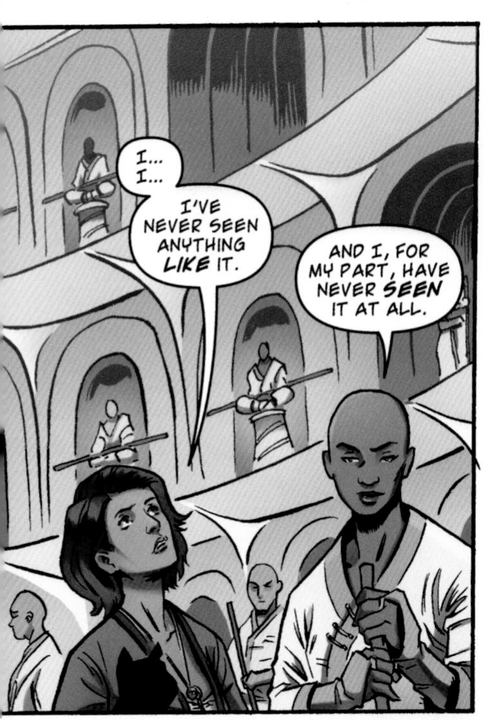
I... I...
I'VE NEVER SEEN ANYTHING LIKE IT.
AND I, FOR MY PART, HAVE NEVER SEEN IT AT ALL.

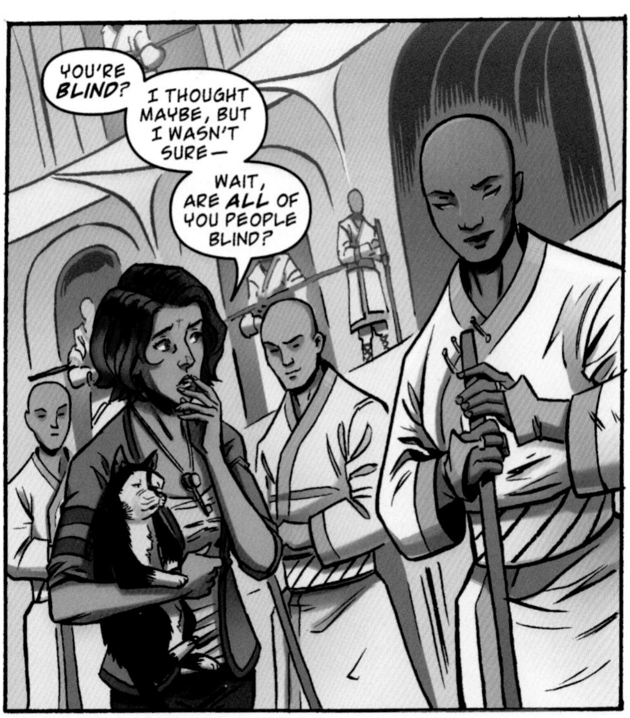
YOU'RE BLIND?
I THOUGHT MAYBE, BUT I WASN'T SURE—
WAIT, ARE ALL OF YOU PEOPLE BLIND?

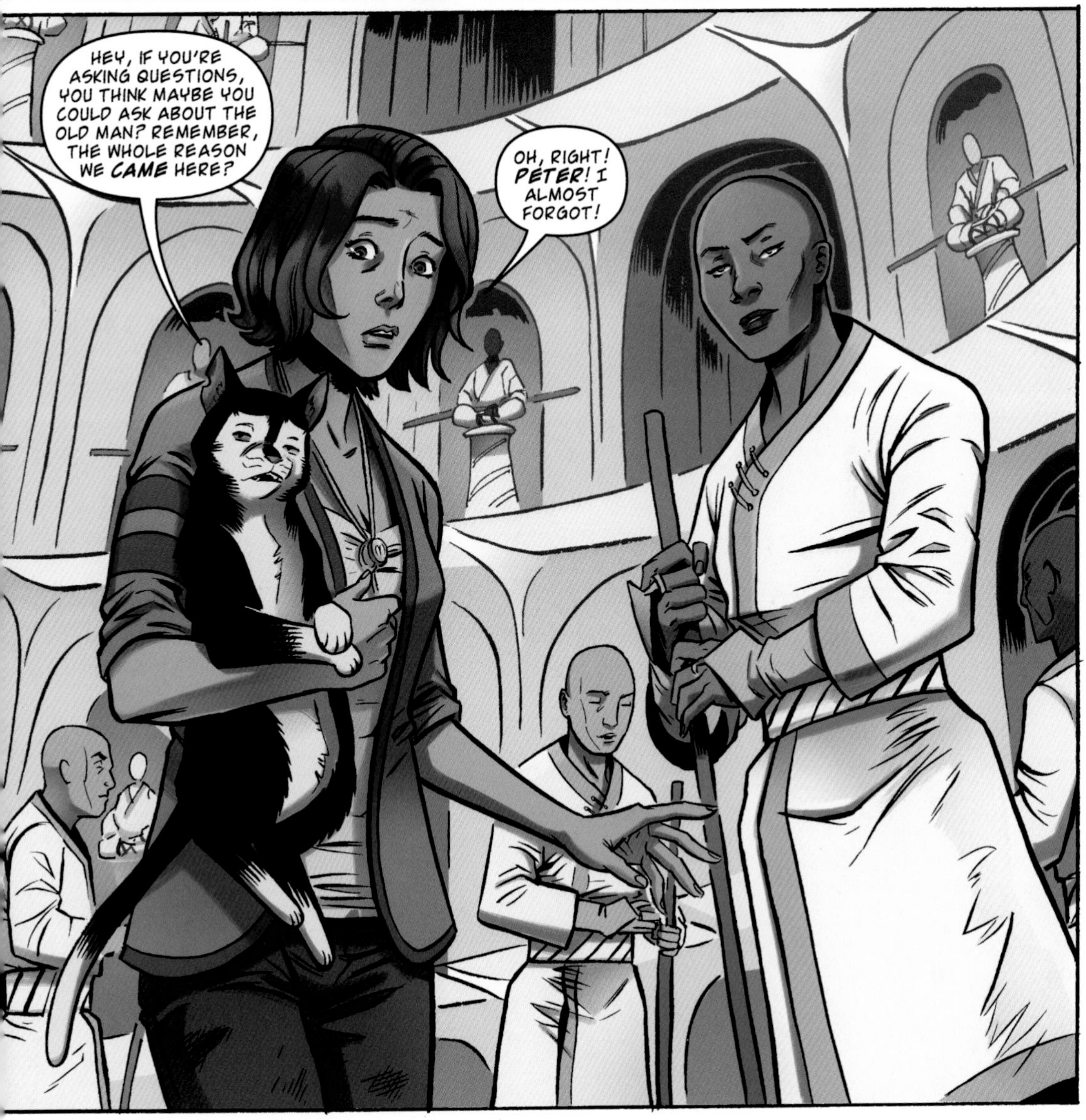
HEY, IF YOU'RE ASKING QUESTIONS, YOU THINK MAYBE YOU COULD ASK ABOUT THE OLD MAN? REMEMBER, THE WHOLE REASON WE CAME HERE?
OH, RIGHT! PETER! I ALMOST FORGOT!

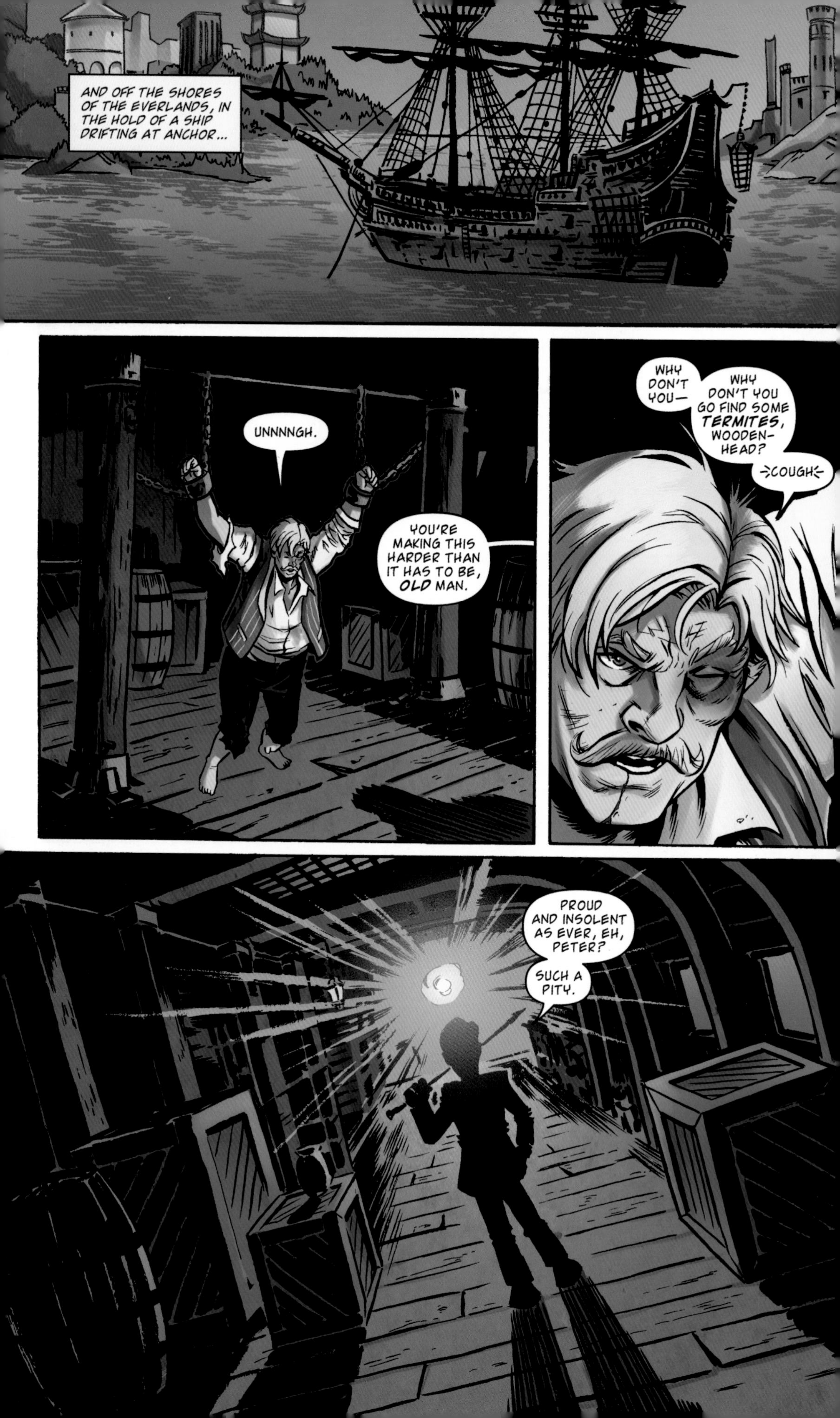

AND OFF THE SHORES OF THE EVERLANDS, IN THE HOLD OF A SHIP DRIFTING AT ANCHOR...
UNNNNGH.
YOU'RE MAKING THIS HARDER THAN IT HAS TO BE, OLD MAN.
WHY DON'T YOU—
WHY DON'T YOU GO FIND SOME TERMITES, WOODEN-HEAD?
COUGH
PROUD AND INSOLENT AS EVER, EH, PETER?
SUCH A PITY.

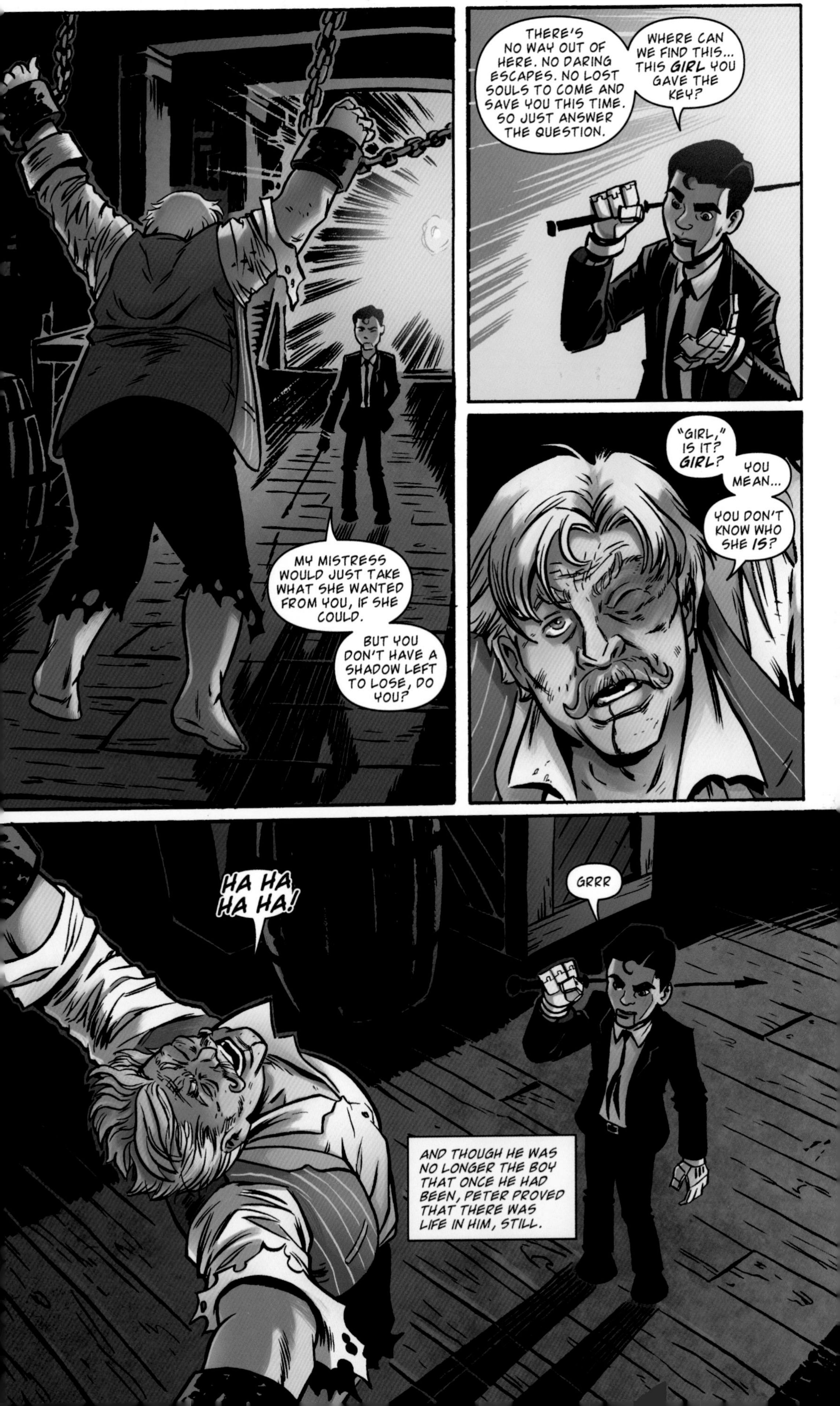
MY MISTRESS WOULD JUST TAKE WHAT SHE WANTED FROM YOU, IF SHE COULD.
BUT YOU DON'T HAVE A SHADOW LEFT TO LOSE, DO YOU?
THERE'S NO WAY OUT OF HERE. NO DARING ESCAPES. NO LOST SOULS TO COME AND SAVE YOU THIS TIME. SO JUST ANSWER THE QUESTION.
WHERE CAN WE FIND THIS... THIS GIRL YOU GAVE THE KEY?
"GIRL," IS IT? GIRL?
YOU MEAN...
YOU DON'T KNOW WHO SHE IS?
HA HA HA HA!
GRRR
AND THOUGH HE WAS NO LONGER THE BOY THAT ONCE HE HAD BEEN, PETER PROVED THAT THERE WAS LIFE IN HIM, STILL.

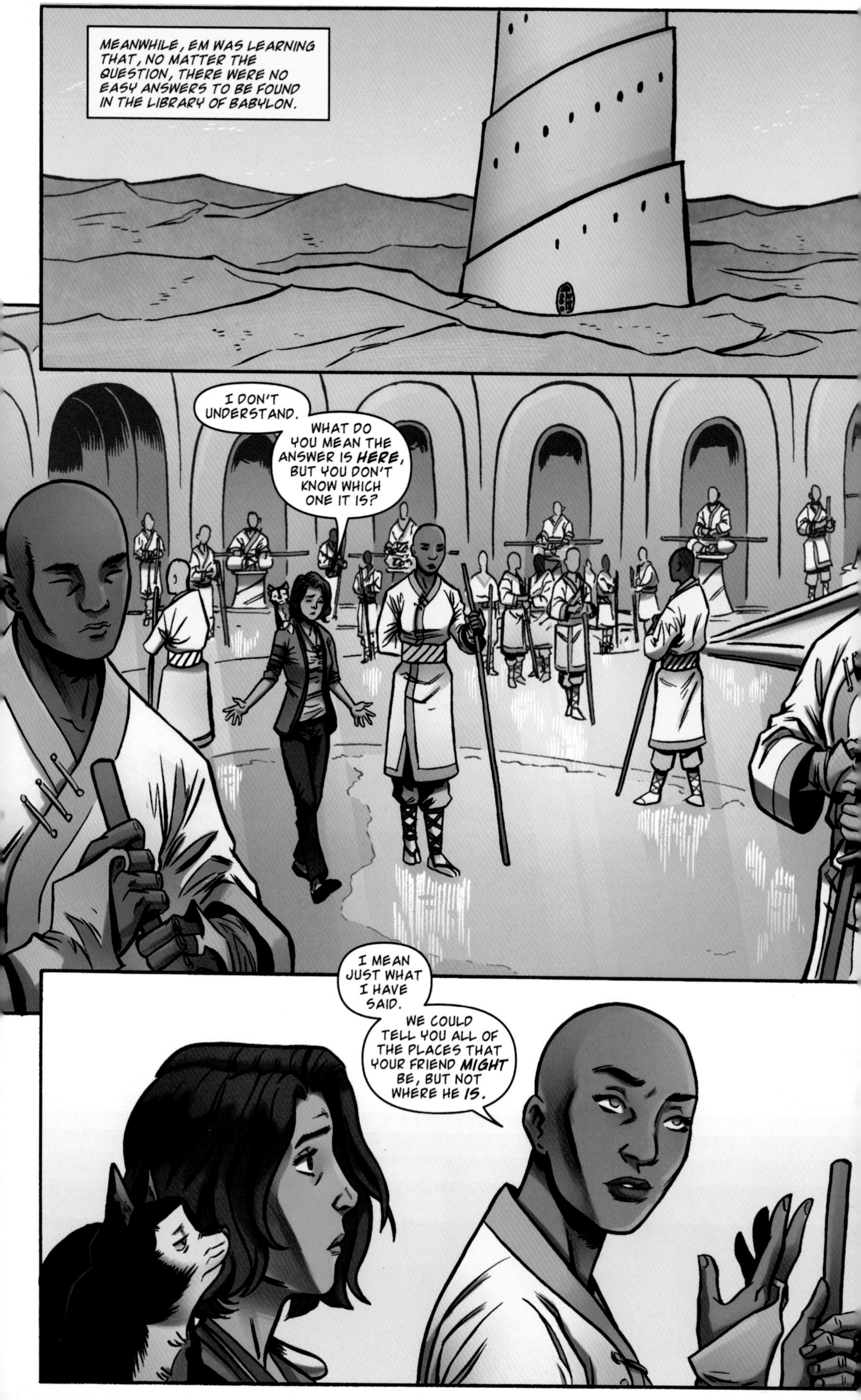

MEANWHILE, EM WAS LEARNING THAT, NO MATTER THE QUESTION, THERE WERE NO EASY ANSWERS TO BE FOUND IN THE LIBRARY OF BABYLON.
I DON'T UNDERSTAND.
WHAT DO YOU MEAN THE ANSWER IS **HERE**, BUT YOU DON'T KNOW WHICH ONE IT IS?
I MEAN JUST WHAT I HAVE SAID.
WE COULD TELL YOU ALL OF THE PLACES THAT YOUR FRIEND **MIGHT** BE, BUT NOT WHERE HE **IS**.

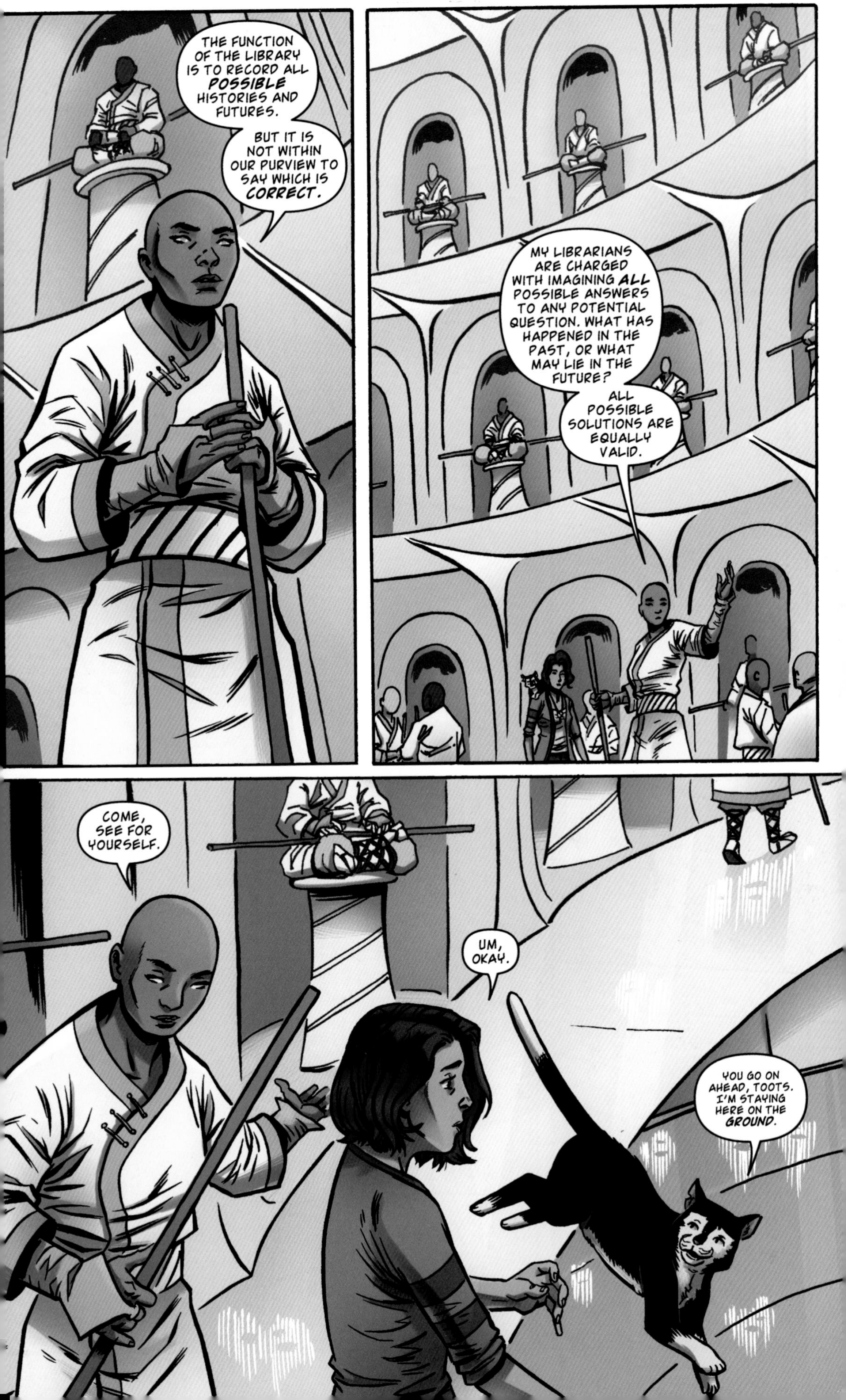
THE FUNCTION OF THE LIBRARY IS TO RECORD ALL POSSIBLE HISTORIES AND FUTURES.
BUT IT IS NOT WITHIN OUR PURVIEW TO SAY WHICH IS CORRECT.
MY LIBRARIANS ARE CHARGED WITH IMAGINING ALL POSSIBLE ANSWERS TO ANY POTENTIAL QUESTION. WHAT HAS HAPPENED IN THE PAST, OR WHAT MAY LIE IN THE FUTURE?
ALL POSSIBLE SOLUTIONS ARE EQUALLY VALID.
COME, SEE FOR YOURSELF.
UM, OKAY.
YOU GO ON AHEAD, TOOTS. I'M STAYING HERE ON THE GROUND.

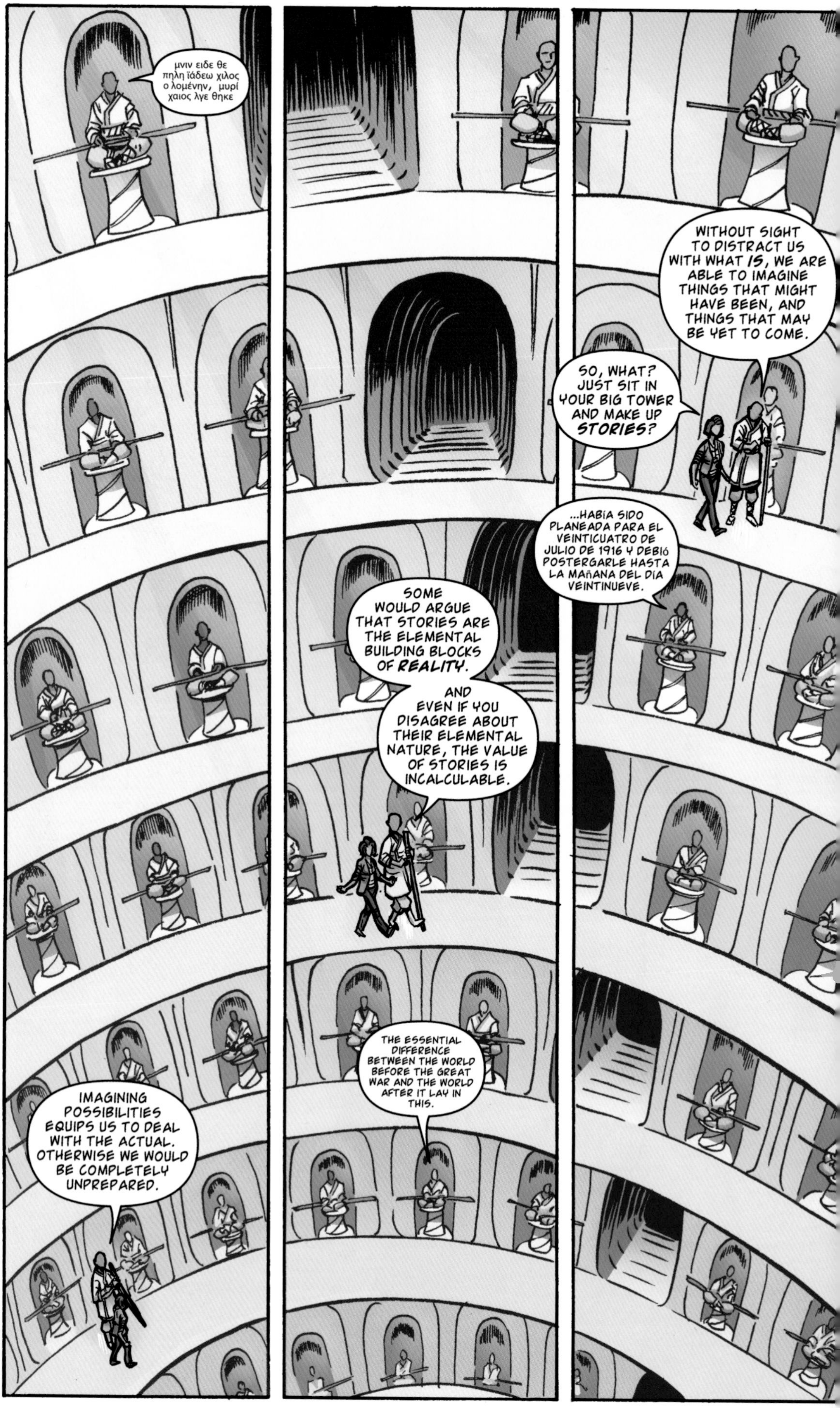
μνιν ειδε θε πηλη ϊάδεω χιλος ο λομένην, μυρί χαιος λγε θηκε
SOME WOULD ARGUE THAT STORIES ARE THE ELEMENTAL BUILDING BLOCKS OF *REALITY*.
AND EVEN IF YOU DISAGREE ABOUT THEIR ELEMENTAL NATURE, THE VALUE OF STORIES IS INCALCULABLE.
WITHOUT SIGHT TO DISTRACT US WITH WHAT *IS*, WE ARE ABLE TO IMAGINE THINGS THAT MIGHT HAVE BEEN, AND THINGS THAT MAY BE YET TO COME.
SO, WHAT? JUST SIT IN YOUR BIG TOWER AND MAKE UP *STORIES*?
...HABÍA SIDO PLANEADA PARA EL VEINTICUATRO DE JULIO DE 1916 Y DEBIó POSTERGARLE HASTA LA MAñANA DEL DÍA VEINTINUEVE.
IMAGINING POSSIBILITIES EQUIPS US TO DEAL WITH THE ACTUAL. OTHERWISE WE WOULD BE COMPLETELY UNPREPARED.
THE ESSENTIAL DIFFERENCE BETWEEN THE WORLD BEFORE THE GREAT WAR AND THE WORLD AFTER IT LAY IN THIS.

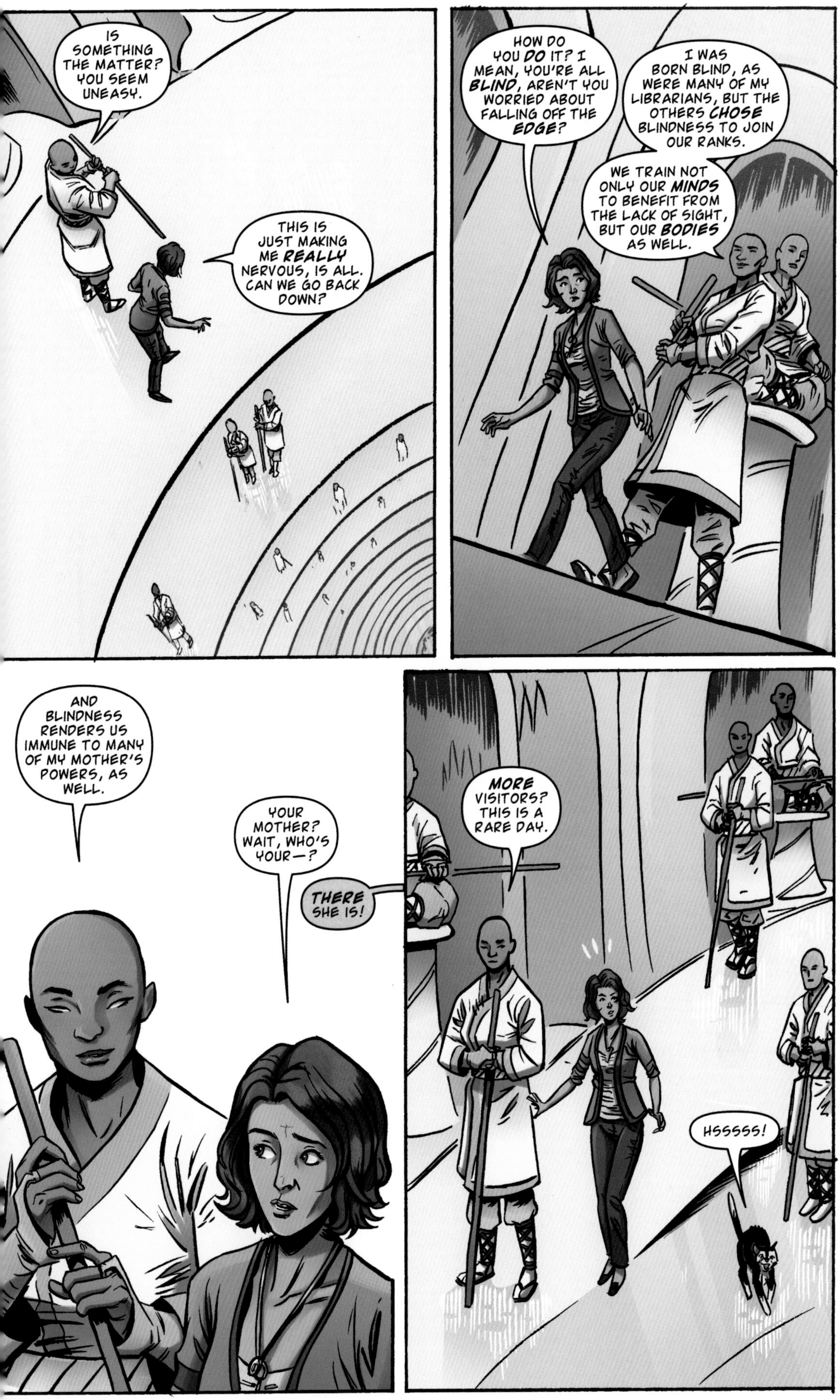
IS SOMETHING THE MATTER? YOU SEEM UNEASY.
THIS IS JUST MAKING ME REALLY NERVOUS, IS ALL. CAN WE GO BACK DOWN?
HOW DO YOU DO IT? I MEAN, YOU'RE ALL BLIND, AREN'T YOU WORRIED ABOUT FALLING OFF THE EDGE?
I WAS BORN BLIND, AS WERE MANY OF MY LIBRARIANS, BUT THE OTHERS CHOSE BLINDNESS TO JOIN OUR RANKS.
WE TRAIN NOT ONLY OUR MINDS TO BENEFIT FROM THE LACK OF SIGHT, BUT OUR BODIES AS WELL.
AND BLINDNESS RENDERS US IMMUNE TO MANY OF MY MOTHER'S POWERS, AS WELL.
YOUR MOTHER? WAIT, WHO'S YOUR—?
THERE SHE IS!
MORE VISITORS? THIS IS A RARE DAY.
HSSSSS!

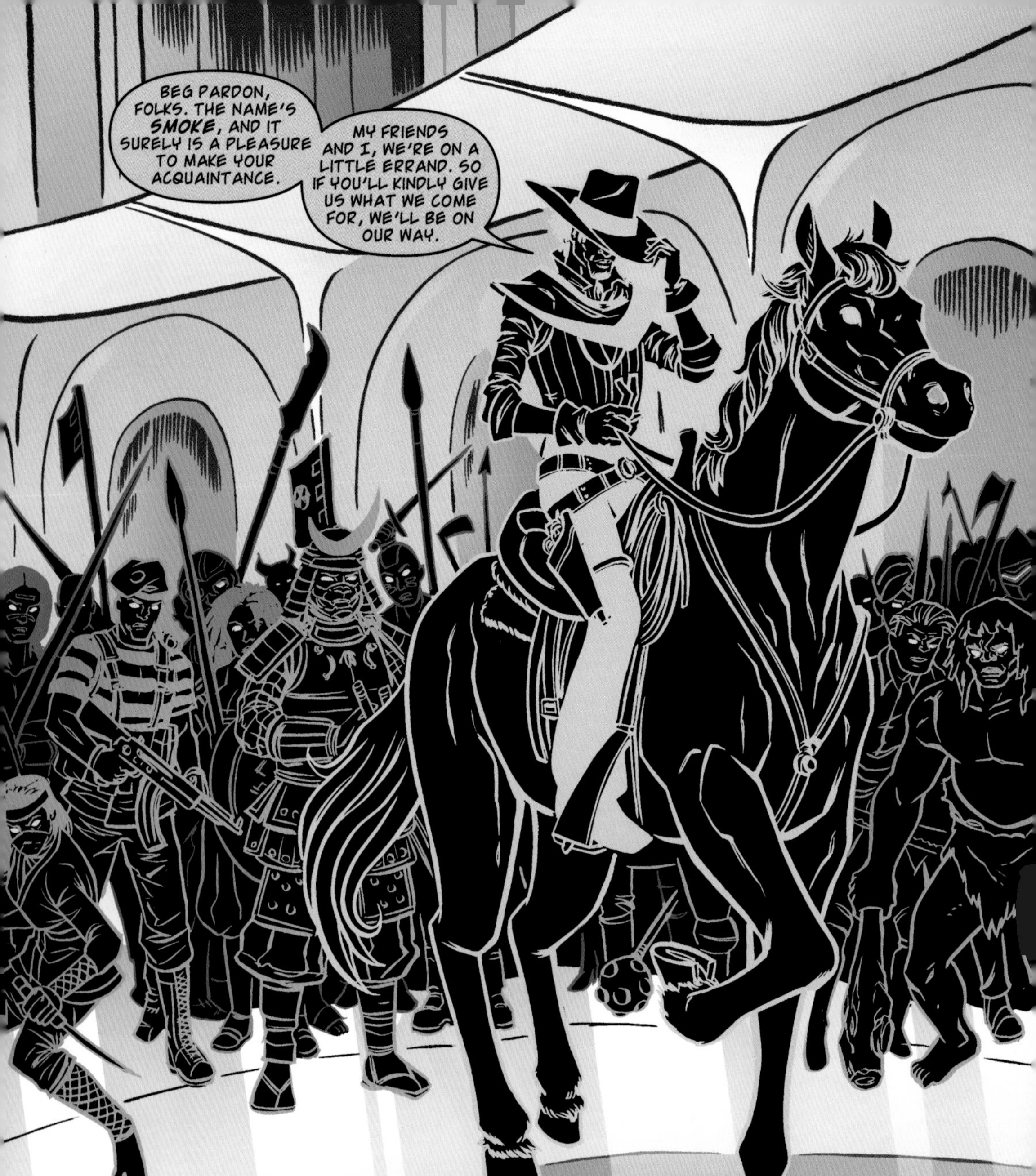
BEG PARDON, FOLKS. THE NAME'S **SMOKE**, AND IT SURELY IS A PLEASURE TO MAKE YOUR ACQUAINTANCE.
MY FRIENDS AND I, WE'RE ON A LITTLE ERRAND. SO IF YOU'LL KINDLY GIVE US WHAT WE COME FOR, WE'LL BE ON OUR WAY.

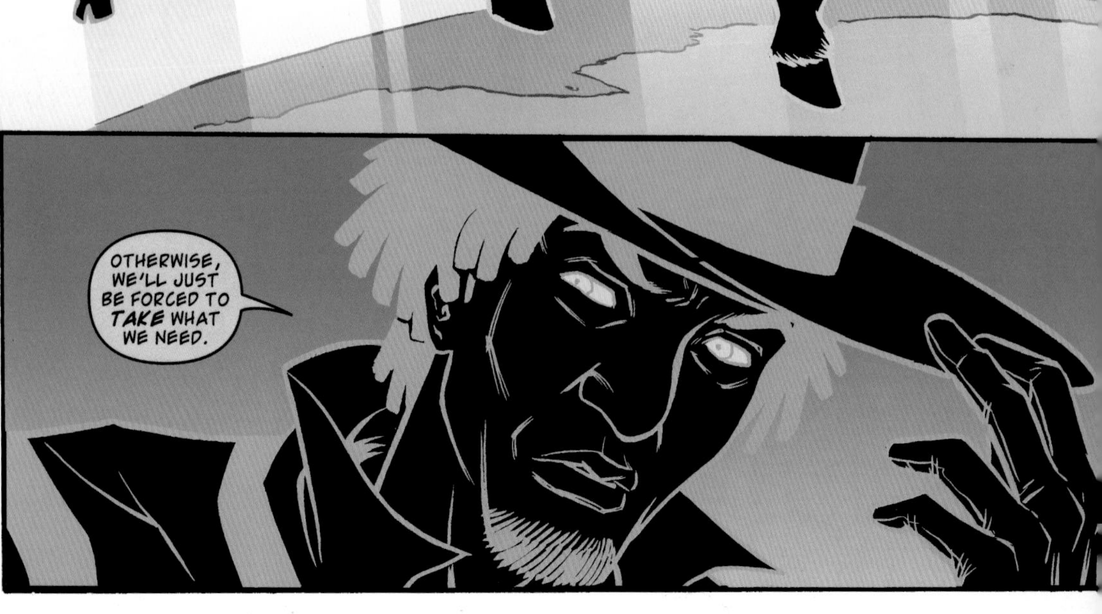
OTHERWISE, WE'LL JUST BE FORCED TO ***TAKE*** WHAT WE NEED.

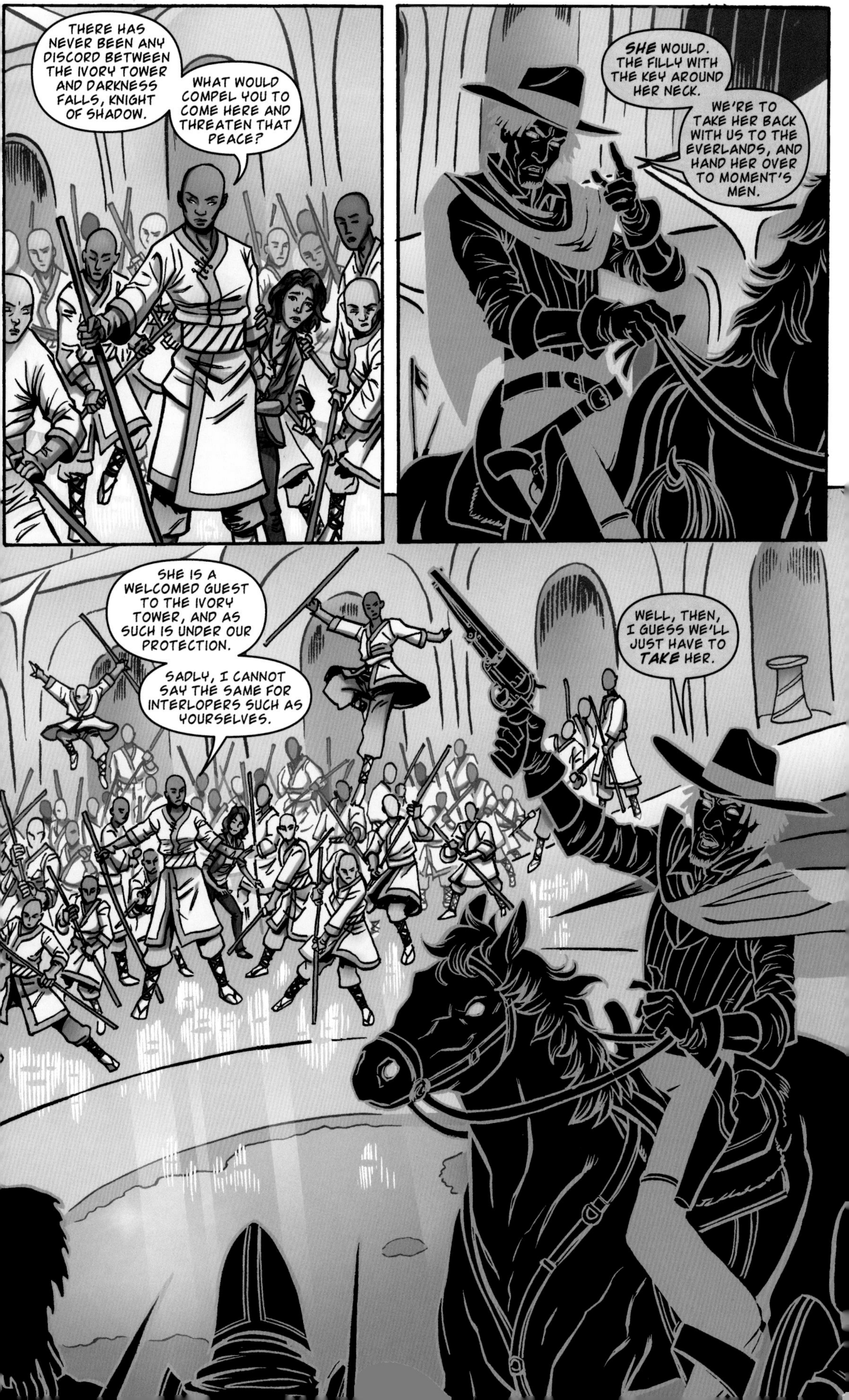
THERE HAS NEVER BEEN ANY DISCORD BETWEEN THE IVORY TOWER AND DARKNESS FALLS, KNIGHT OF SHADOW.
WHAT WOULD COMPEL YOU TO COME HERE AND THREATEN THAT PEACE?
SHE WOULD. THE FILLY WITH THE KEY AROUND HER NECK.
WE'RE TO TAKE HER BACK WITH US TO THE EVERLANDS, AND HAND HER OVER TO MOMENT'S MEN.
SHE IS A WELCOMED GUEST TO THE IVORY TOWER, AND AS SUCH IS UNDER OUR PROTECTION.
SADLY, I CANNOT SAY THE SAME FOR INTERLOPERS SUCH AS YOURSELVES.
WELL, THEN, I GUESS WE'LL JUST HAVE TO TAKE HER.

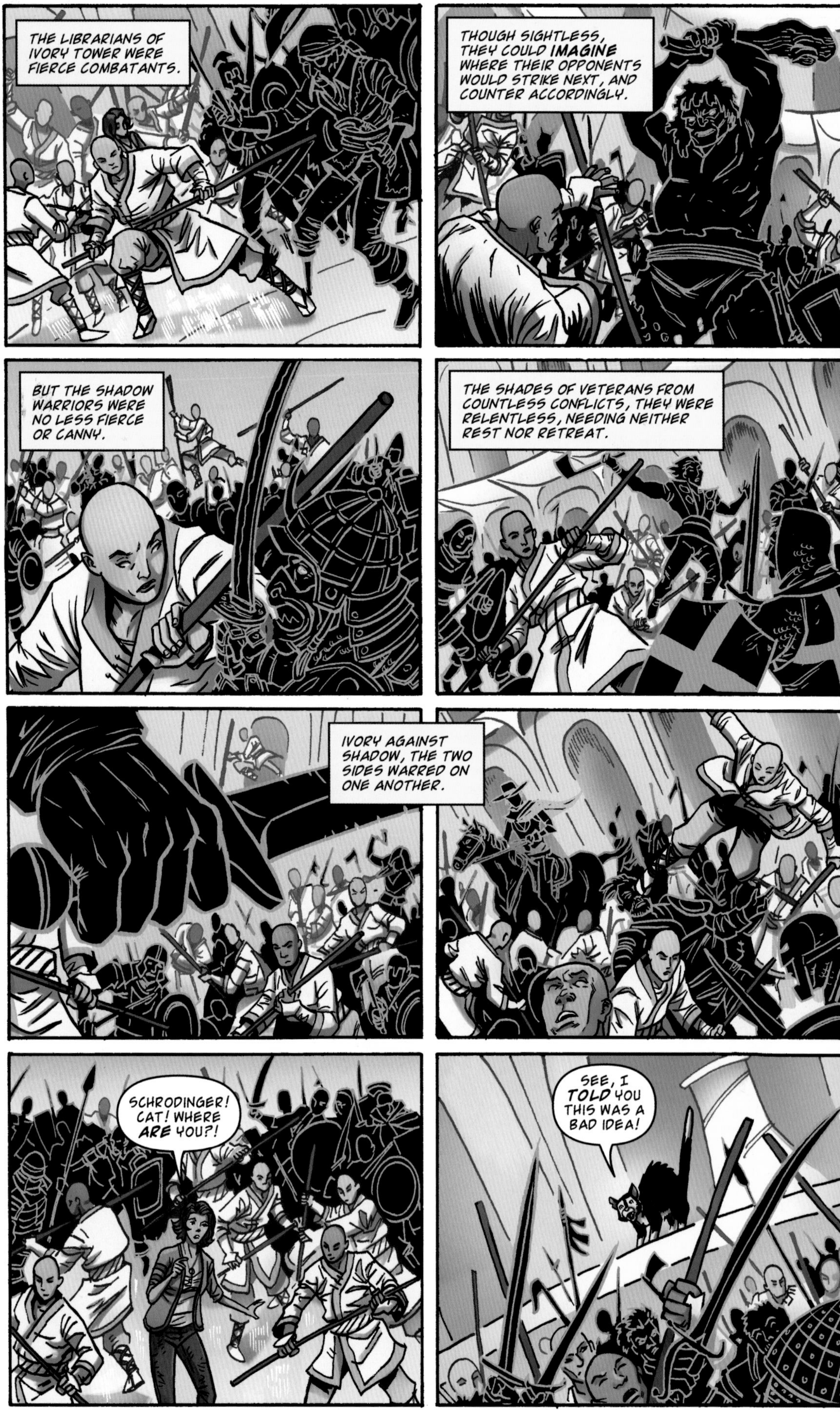
THE LIBRARIANS OF IVORY TOWER WERE FIERCE COMBATANTS.
THOUGH SIGHTLESS, THEY COULD IMAGINE WHERE THEIR OPPONENTS WOULD STRIKE NEXT, AND COUNTER ACCORDINGLY.
BUT THE SHADOW WARRIORS WERE NO LESS FIERCE OR CANNY.
THE SHADES OF VETERANS FROM COUNTLESS CONFLICTS, THEY WERE RELENTLESS, NEEDING NEITHER REST NOR RETREAT.
IVORY AGAINST SHADOW, THE TWO SIDES WARRED ON ONE ANOTHER.
SCHRODINGER! CAT! WHERE ARE YOU?!
SEE, I TOLD YOU THIS WAS A BAD IDEA!

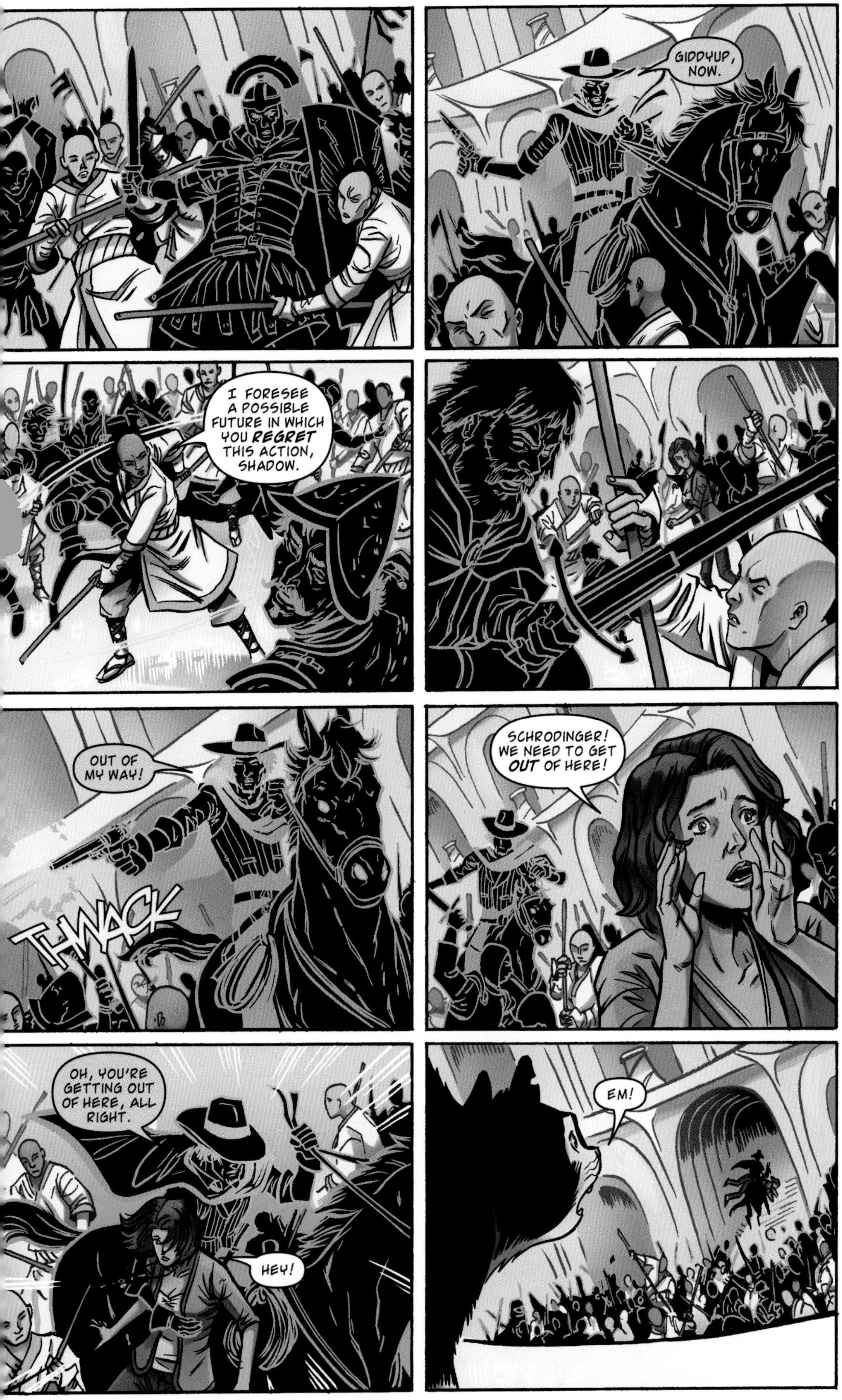
GIDDYUP, NOW.
I FORESEE A POSSIBLE FUTURE IN WHICH YOU REGRET THIS ACTION, SHADOW.
OUT OF MY WAY!
THWACK
SCHRODINGER! WE NEED TO GET OUT OF HERE!
OH, YOU'RE GETTING OUT OF HERE, ALL RIGHT.
HEY!
EM!

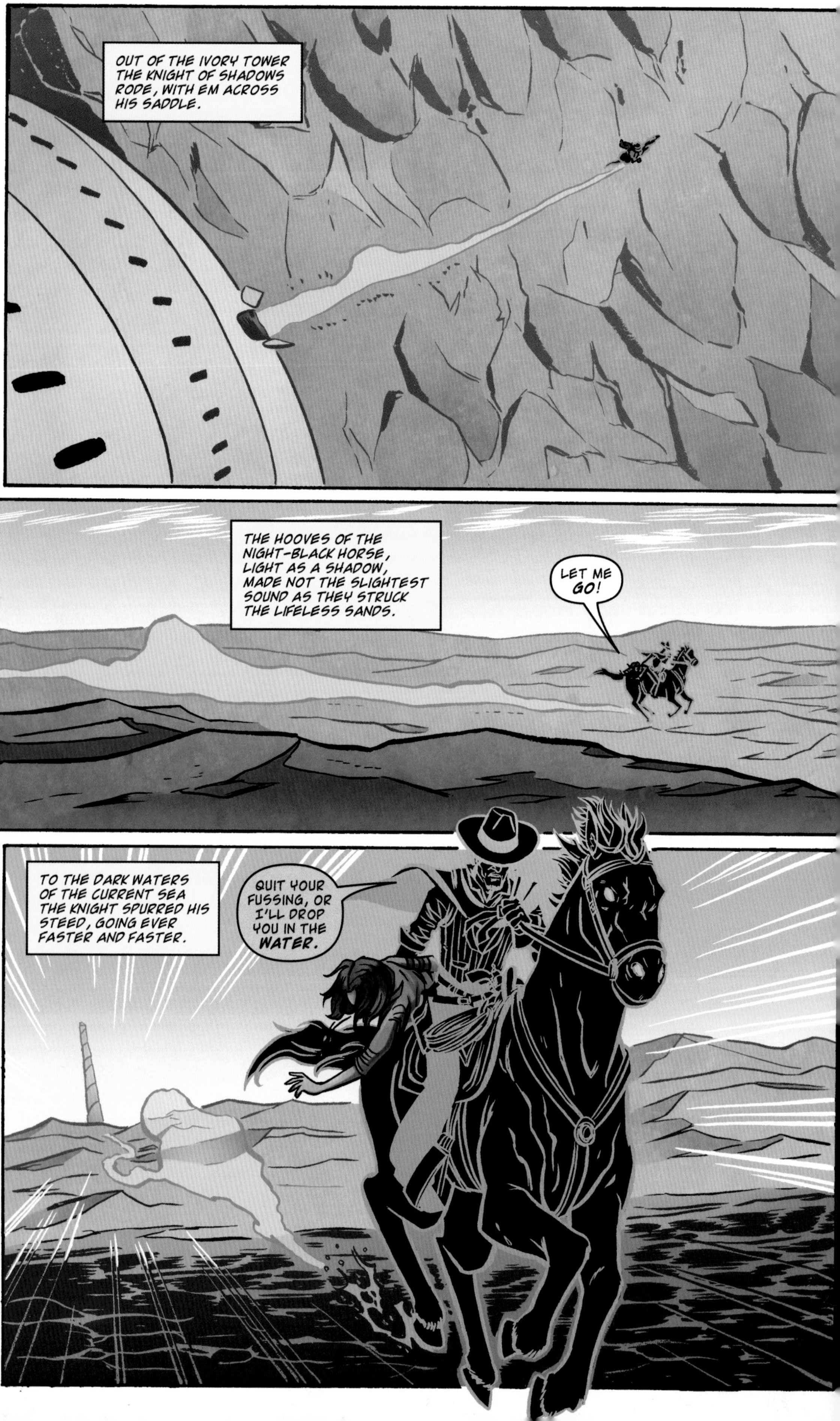
OUT OF THE IVORY TOWER THE KNIGHT OF SHADOWS RODE, WITH EM ACROSS HIS SADDLE.
THE HOOVES OF THE NIGHT-BLACK HORSE, LIGHT AS A SHADOW, MADE NOT THE SLIGHTEST SOUND AS THEY STRUCK THE LIFELESS SANDS.
LET ME GO!
TO THE DARK WATERS OF THE CURRENT SEA THE KNIGHT SPURRED HIS STEED, GOING EVER FASTER AND FASTER.
QUIT YOUR FUSSING, OR I'LL DROP YOU IN THE WATER.

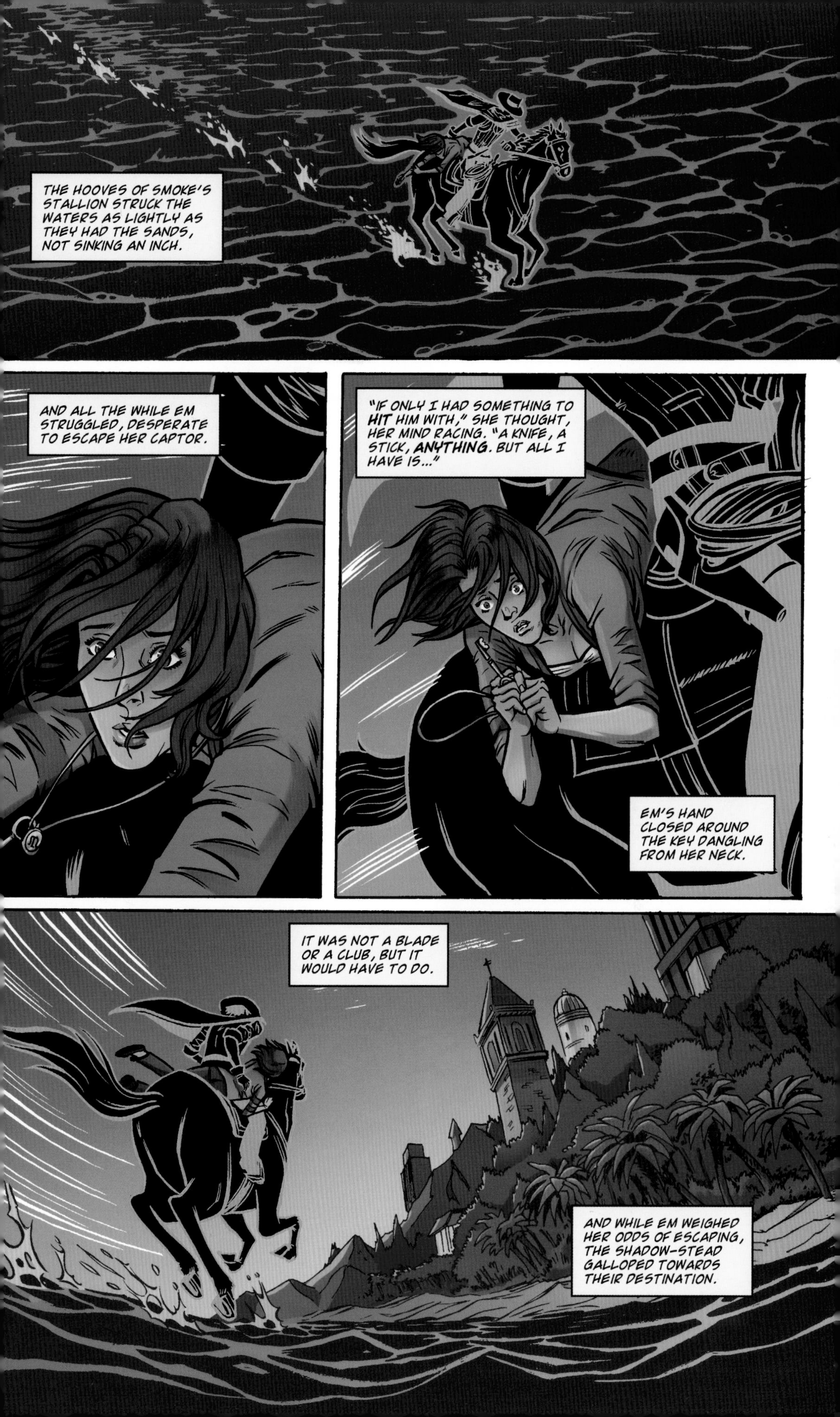
THE HOOVES OF SMOKE'S STALLION STRUCK THE WATERS AS LIGHTLY AS THEY HAD THE SANDS, NOT SINKING AN INCH.
AND ALL THE WHILE EM STRUGGLED, DESPERATE TO ESCAPE HER CAPTOR.
"IF ONLY I HAD SOMETHING TO HIT HIM WITH," SHE THOUGHT, HER MIND RACING. "A KNIFE, A STICK, ANYTHING. BUT ALL I HAVE IS..."
EM'S HAND CLOSED AROUND THE KEY DANGLING FROM HER NECK.
IT WAS NOT A BLADE OR A CLUB, BUT IT WOULD HAVE TO DO.
AND WHILE EM WEIGHED HER ODDS OF ESCAPING, THE SHADOW-STEAD GALLOPED TOWARDS THEIR DESTINATION.

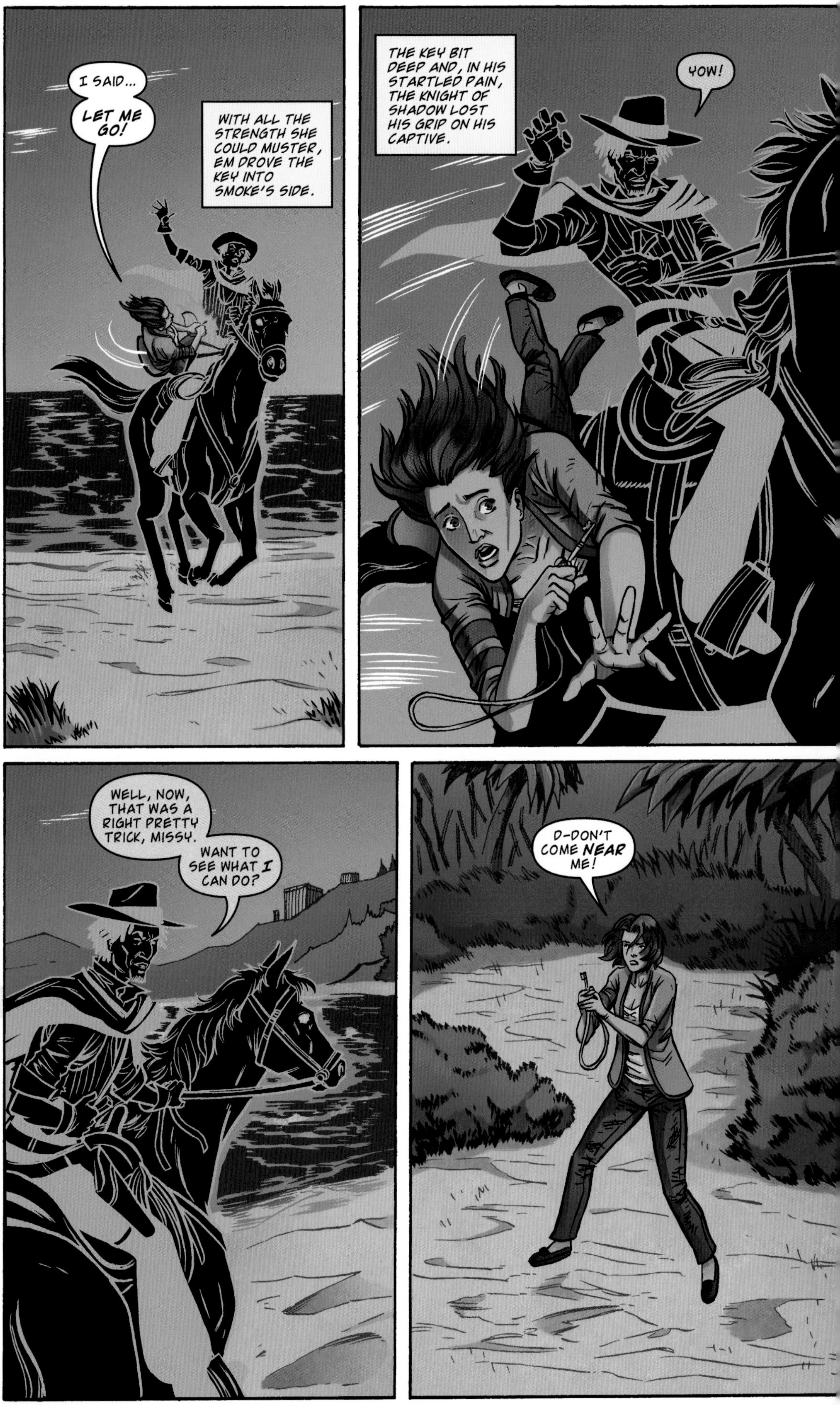
I SAID...
LET ME GO!
WITH ALL THE STRENGTH SHE COULD MUSTER, EM DROVE THE KEY INTO SMOKE'S SIDE.
THE KEY BIT DEEP AND, IN HIS STARTLED PAIN, THE KNIGHT OF SHADOW LOST HIS GRIP ON HIS CAPTIVE.
YOW!
WELL, NOW, THAT WAS A RIGHT PRETTY TRICK, MISSY.
WANT TO SEE WHAT I CAN DO?
D-DON'T COME NEAR ME!

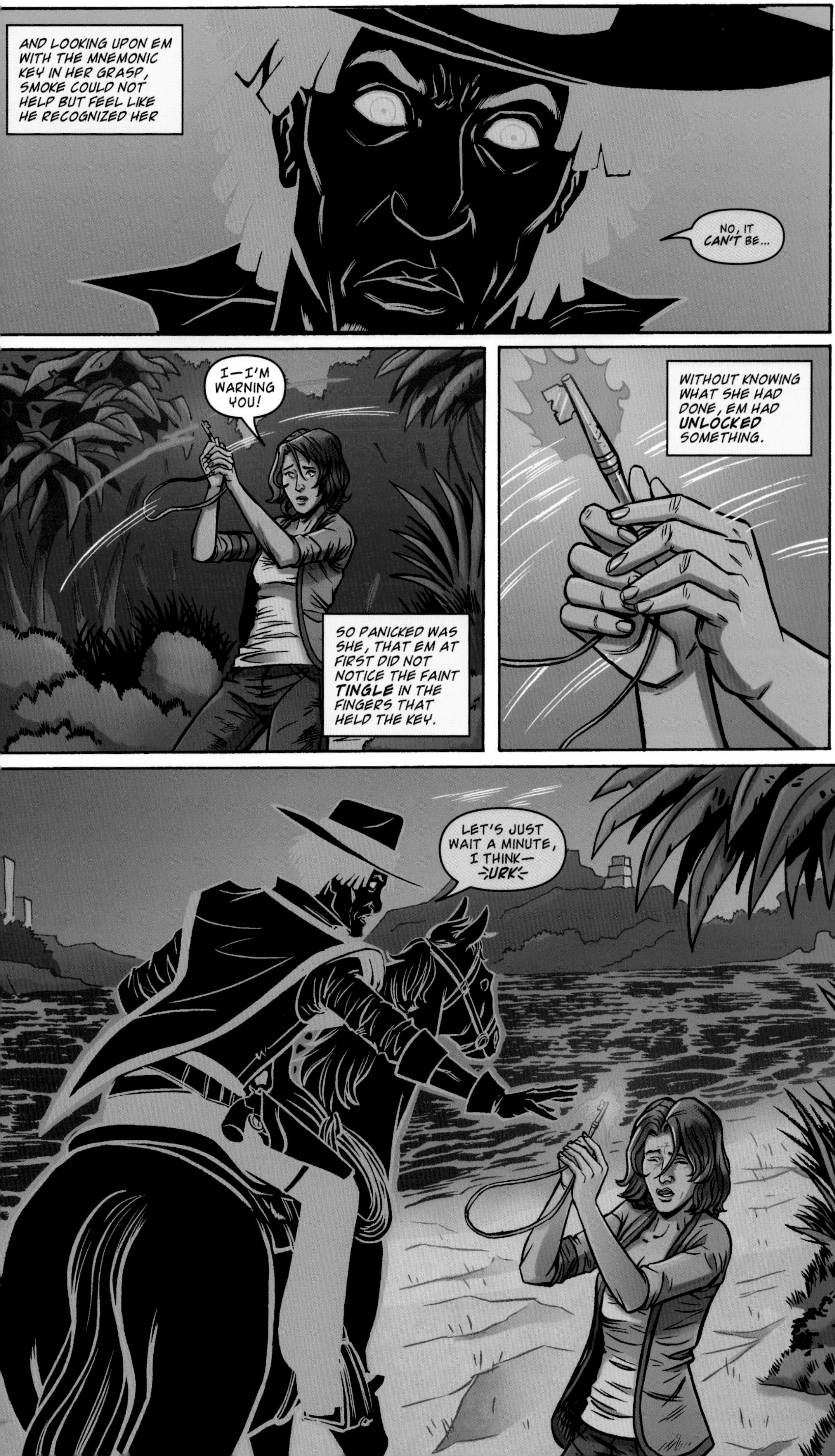
AND LOOKING UPON EM WITH THE MNEMONIC KEY IN HER GRASP, SMOKE COULD NOT HELP BUT FEEL LIKE HE RECOGNIZED HER
NO, IT CAN'T BE...
I—I'M WARNING YOU!
SO PANICKED WAS SHE, THAT EM AT FIRST DID NOT NOTICE THE FAINT TINGLE IN THE FINGERS THAT HELD THE KEY.
WITHOUT KNOWING WHAT SHE HAD DONE, EM HAD UNLOCKED SOMETHING.
LET'S JUST WAIT A MINUTE, I THINK— URK

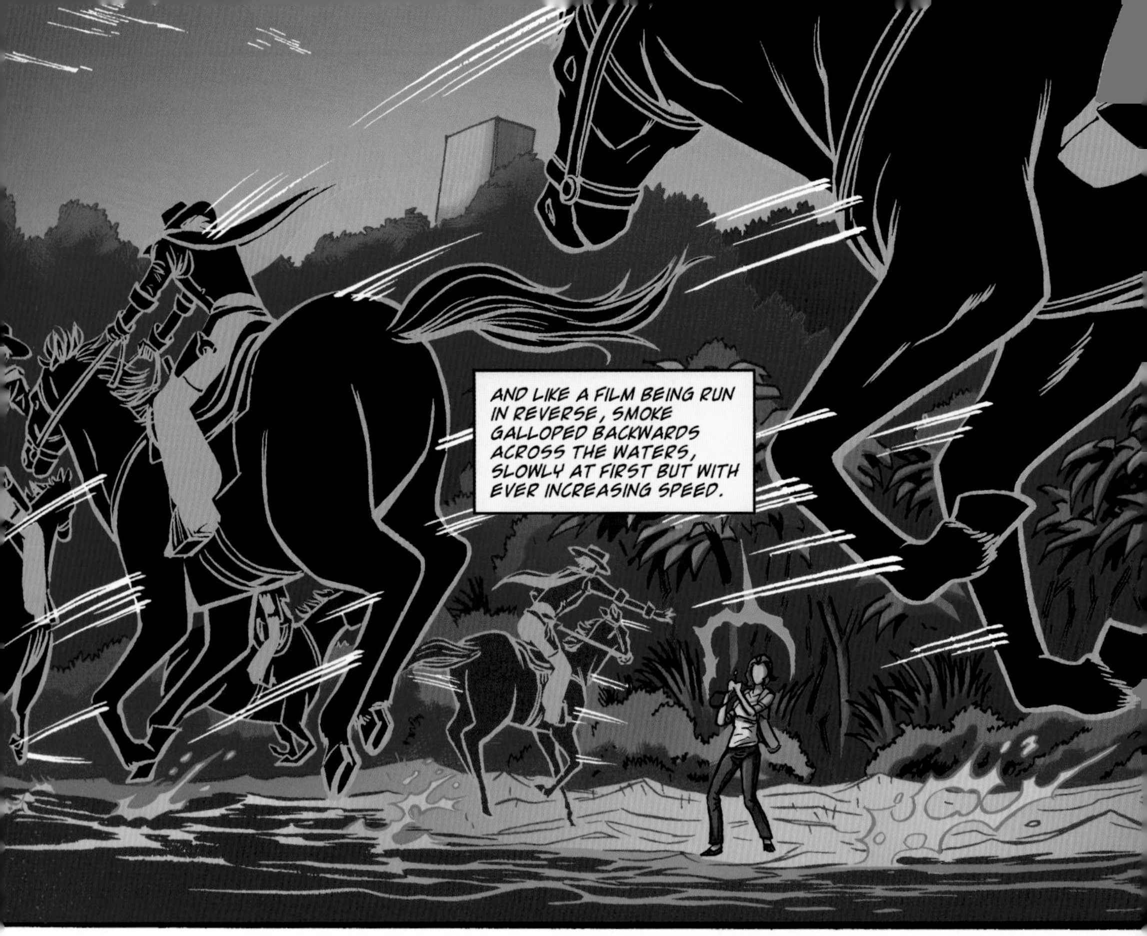
AND LIKE A FILM BEING RUN IN REVERSE, SMOKE GALLOPED BACKWARDS ACROSS THE WATERS, SLOWLY AT FIRST BUT WITH EVER INCREASING SPEED.

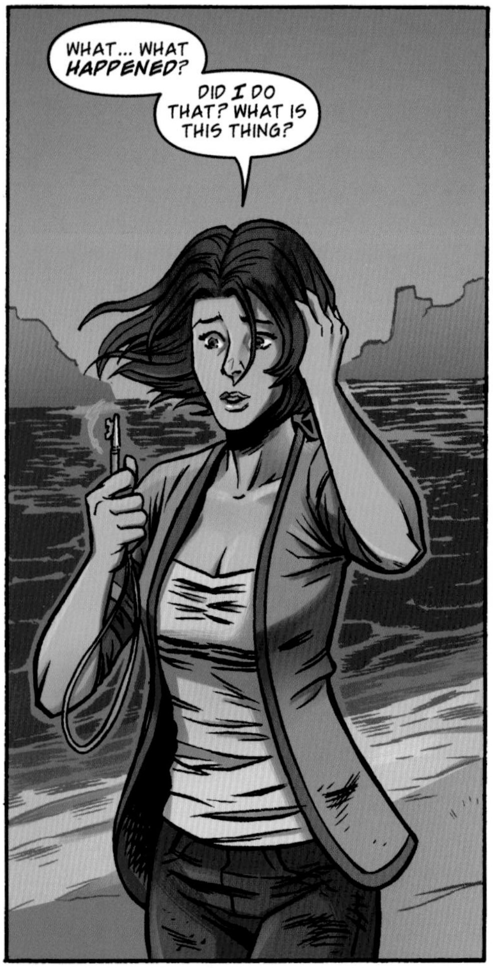
WHAT... WHAT HAPPENED?
DID I DO THAT? WHAT IS THIS THING?

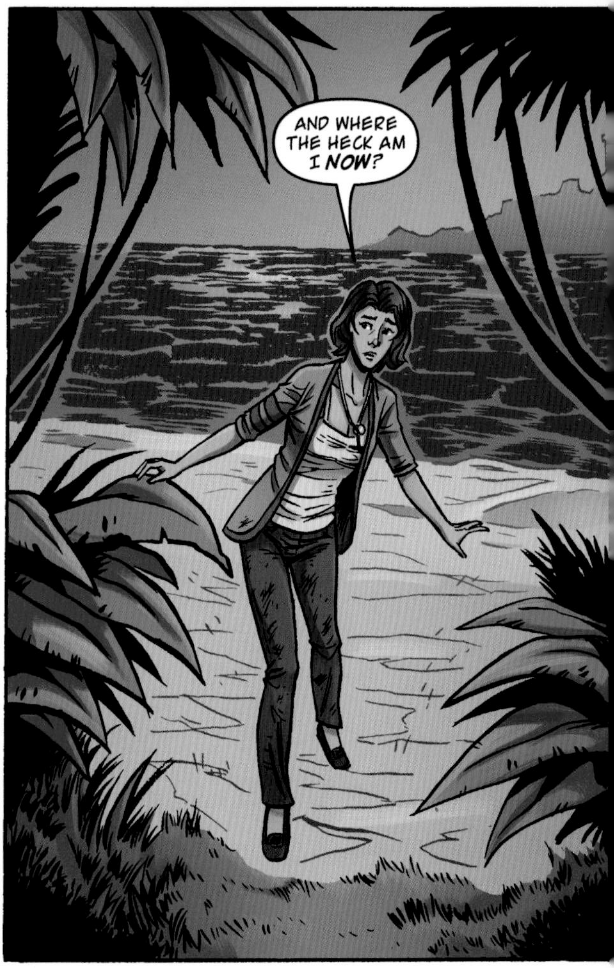
AND WHERE THE HECK AM I NOW?

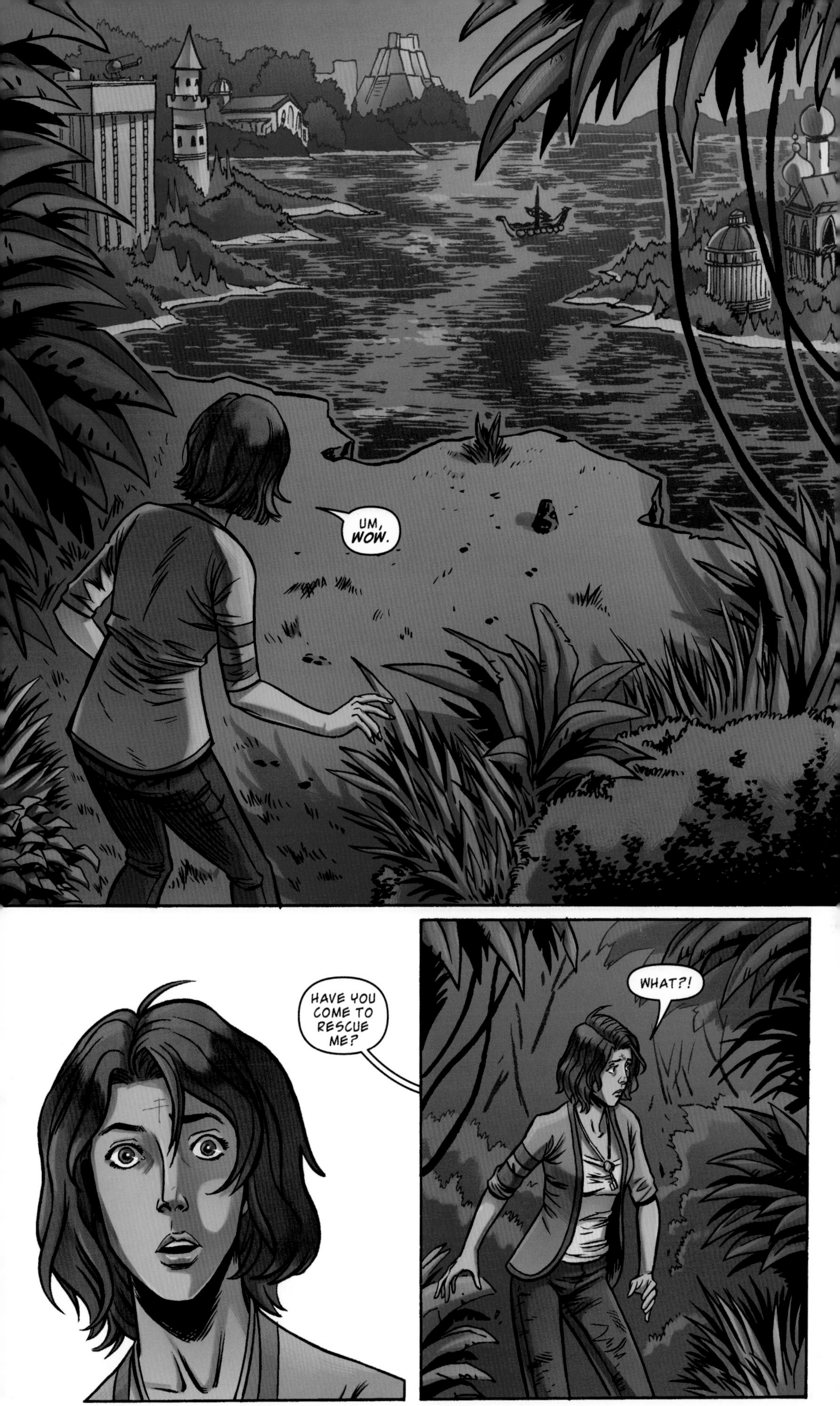
UM, WOW.
HAVE YOU COME TO RESCUE ME?
WHAT?!

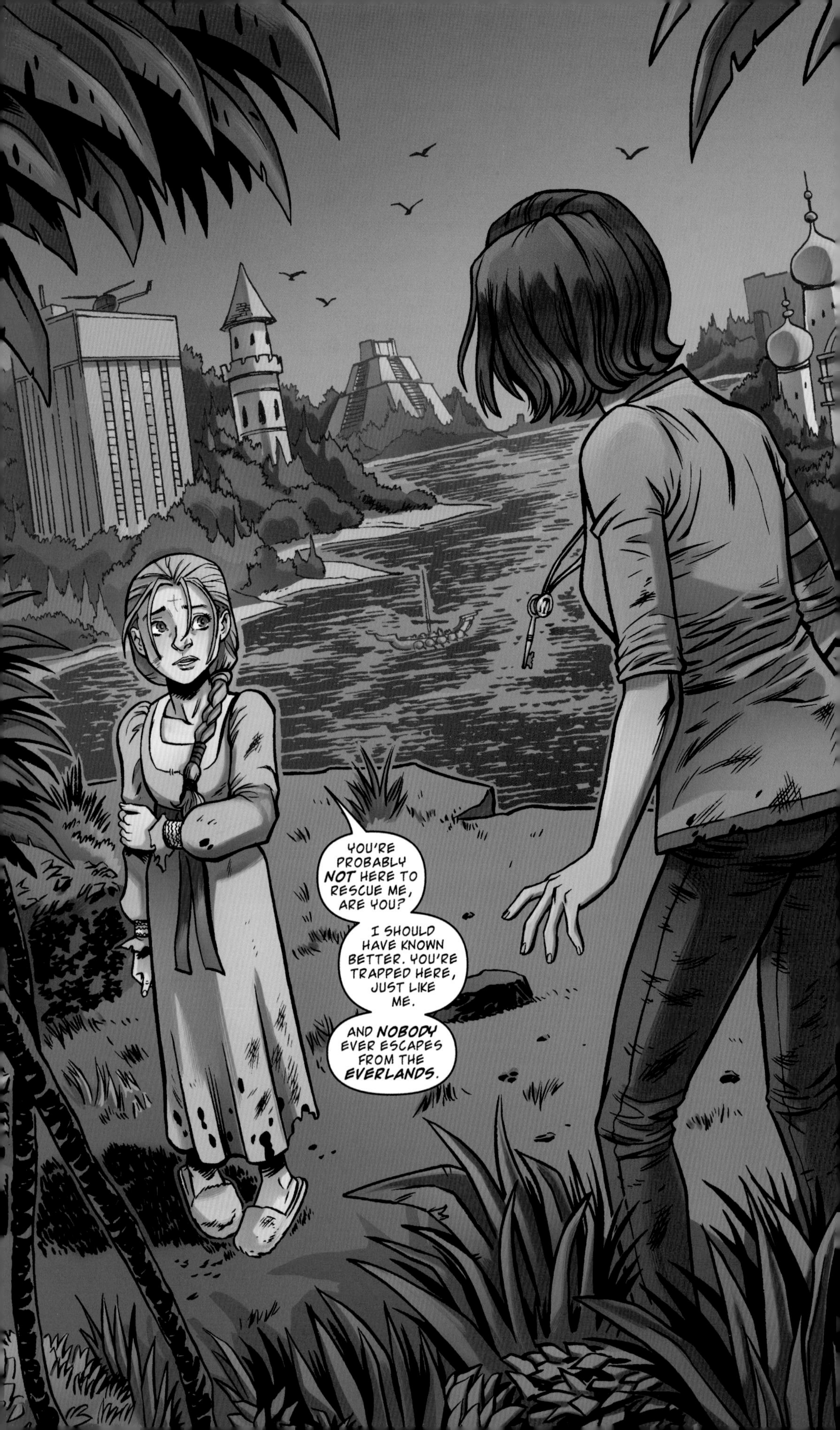
YOU'RE PROBABLY NOT HERE TO RESCUE ME, ARE YOU?
I SHOULD HAVE KNOWN BETTER. YOU'RE TRAPPED HERE, JUST LIKE ME.
AND NOBODY EVER ESCAPES FROM THE EVERLANDS.

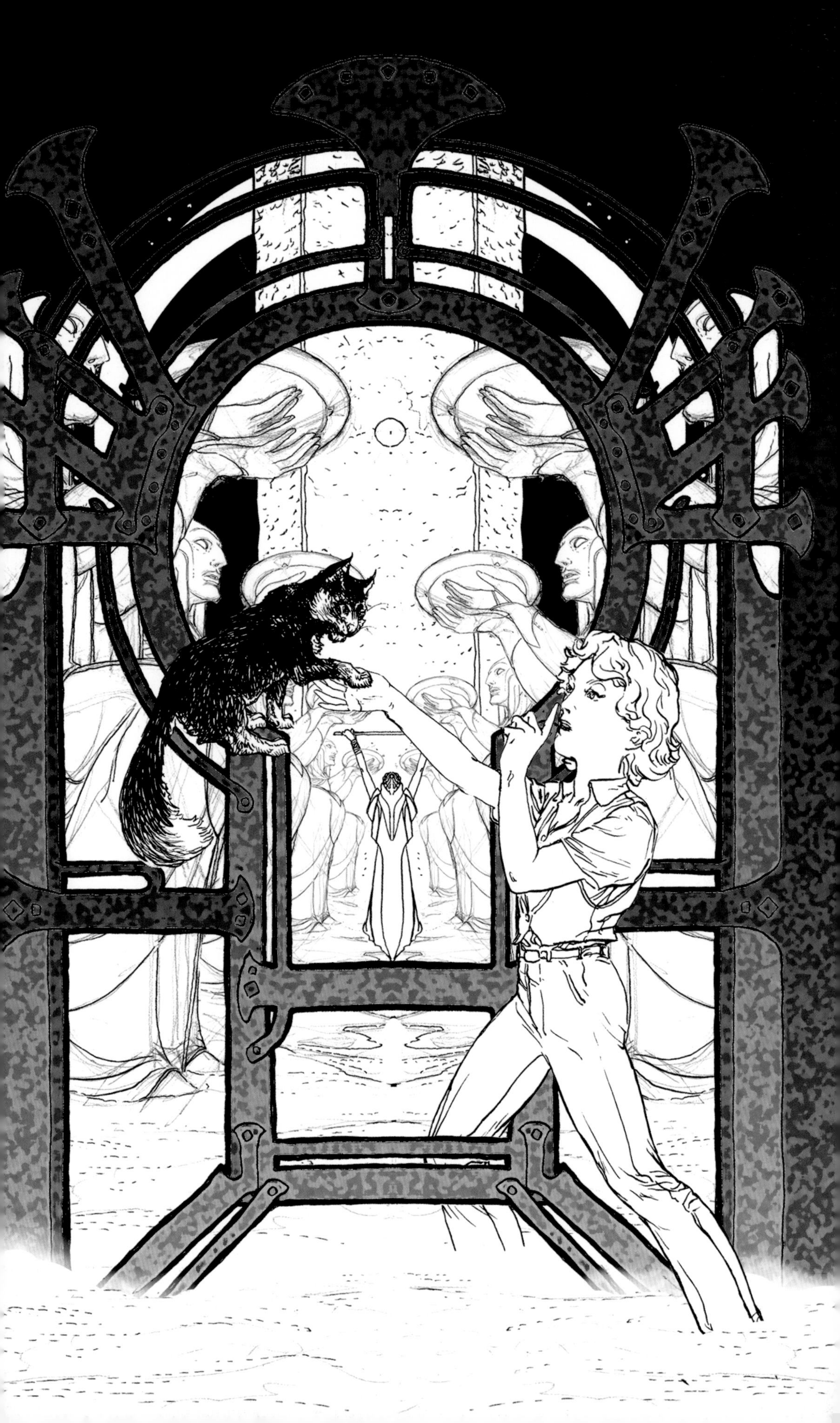

Chapter Four

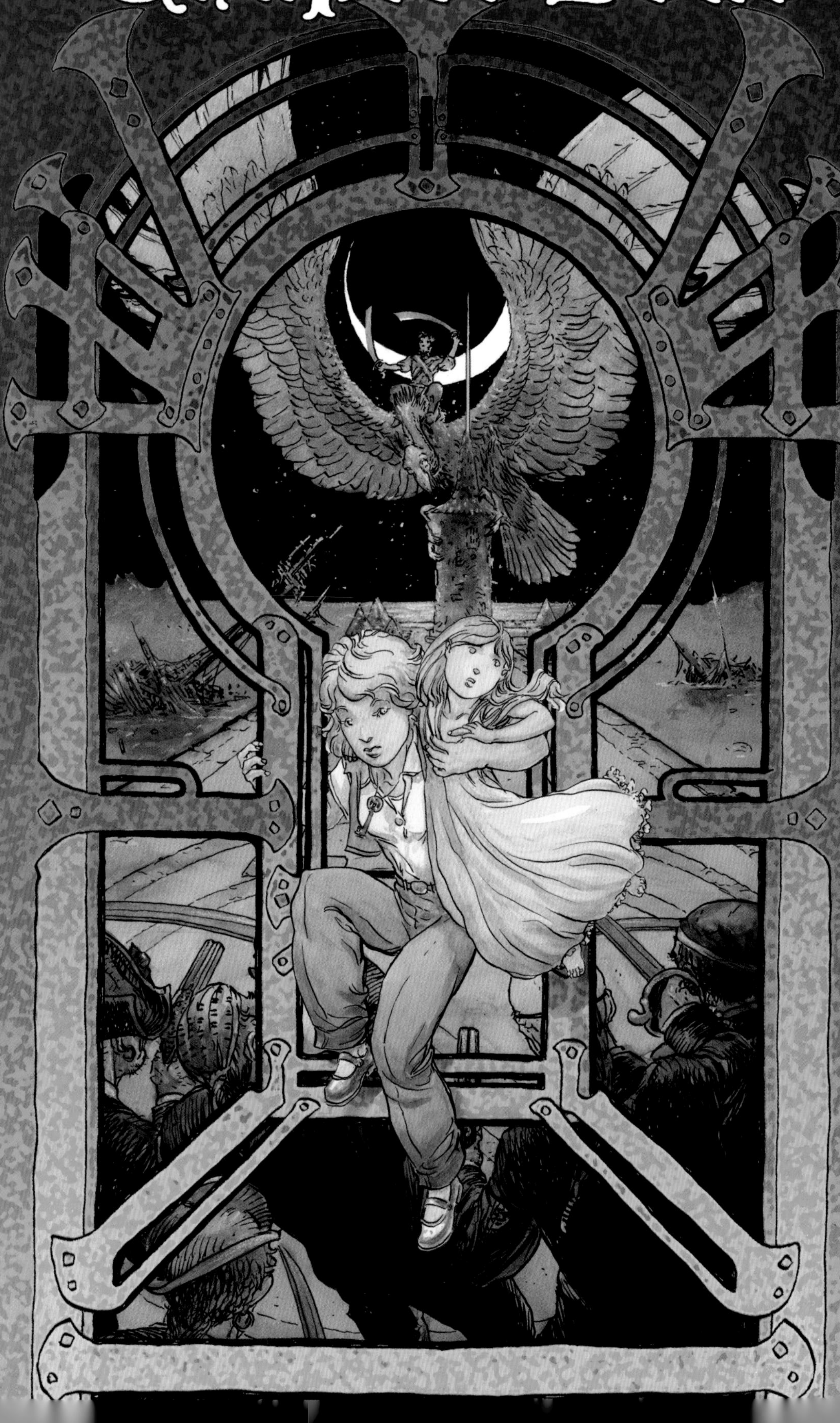

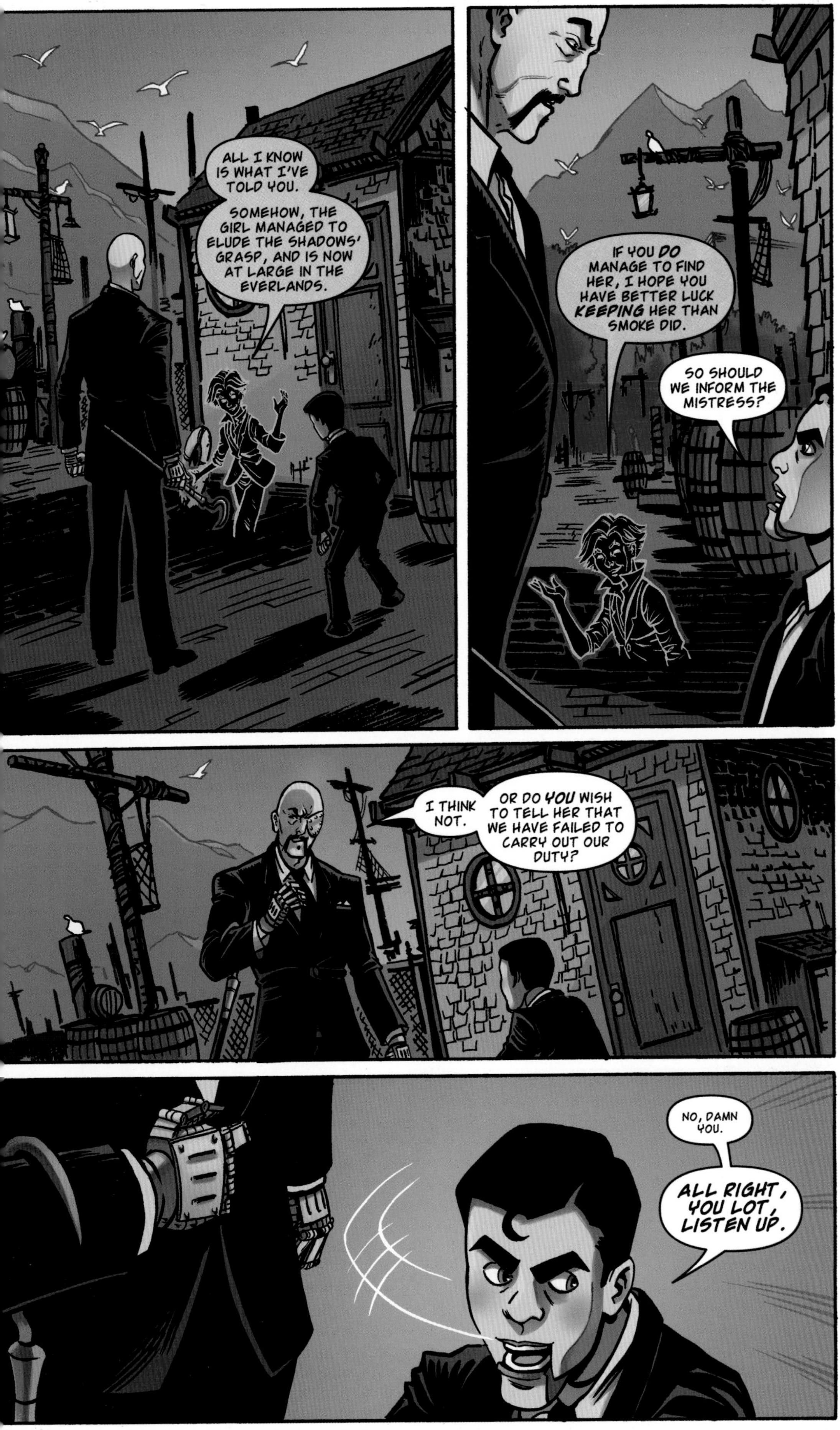
ALL I KNOW IS WHAT I'VE TOLD YOU.
SOMEHOW, THE GIRL MANAGED TO ELUDE THE SHADOWS' GRASP, AND IS NOW AT LARGE IN THE EVERLANDS.
IF YOU DO MANAGE TO FIND HER, I HOPE YOU HAVE BETTER LUCK KEEPING HER THAN SMOKE DID.
SO SHOULD WE INFORM THE MISTRESS?
I THINK NOT.
OR DO YOU WISH TO TELL HER THAT WE HAVE FAILED TO CARRY OUT OUR DUTY?
NO, DAMN YOU.
ALL RIGHT, YOU LOT, LISTEN UP.

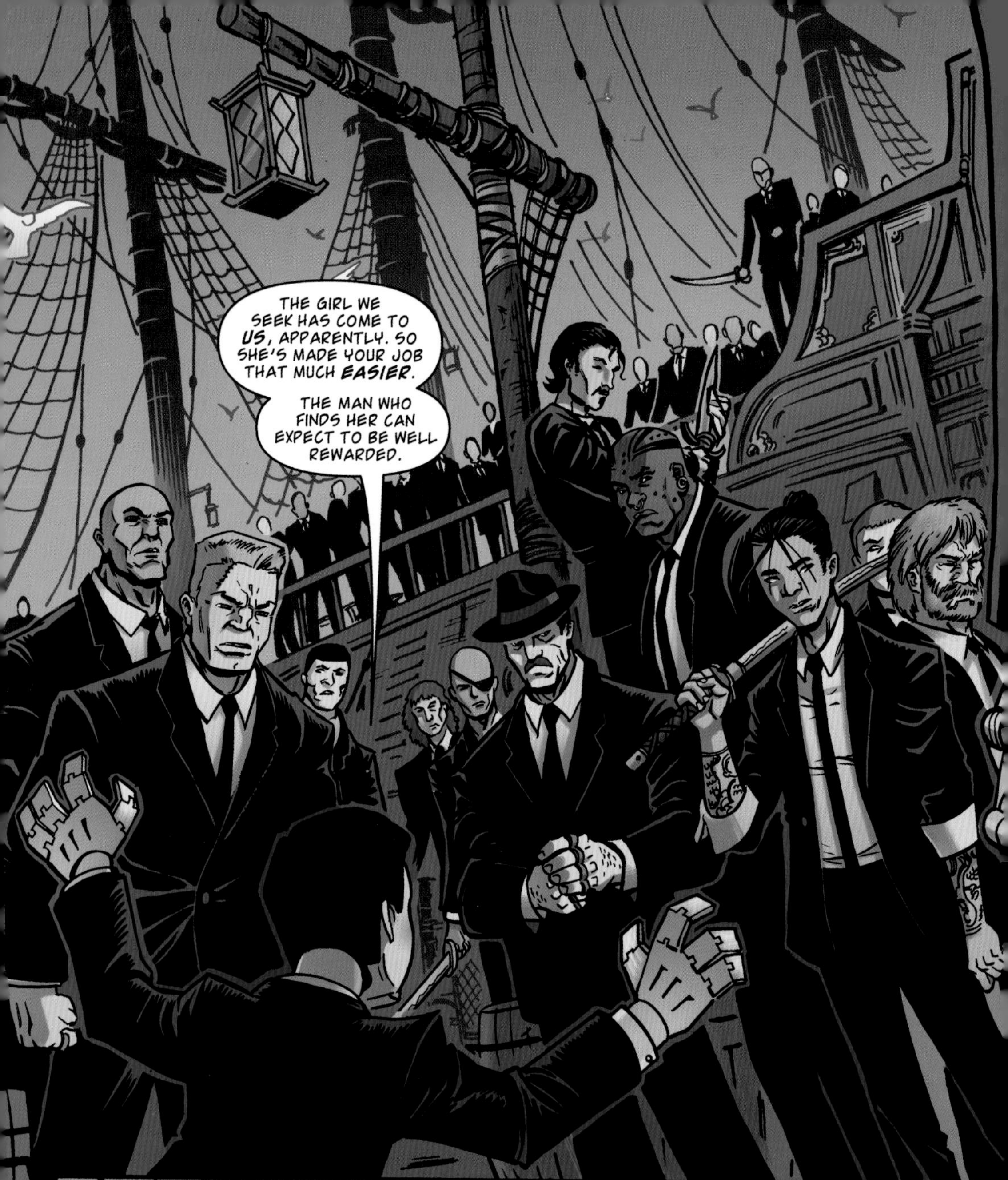
THE GIRL WE SEEK HAS COME TO US, APPARENTLY. SO SHE'S MADE YOUR JOB THAT MUCH EASIER.
THE MAN WHO FINDS HER CAN EXPECT TO BE WELL REWARDED.

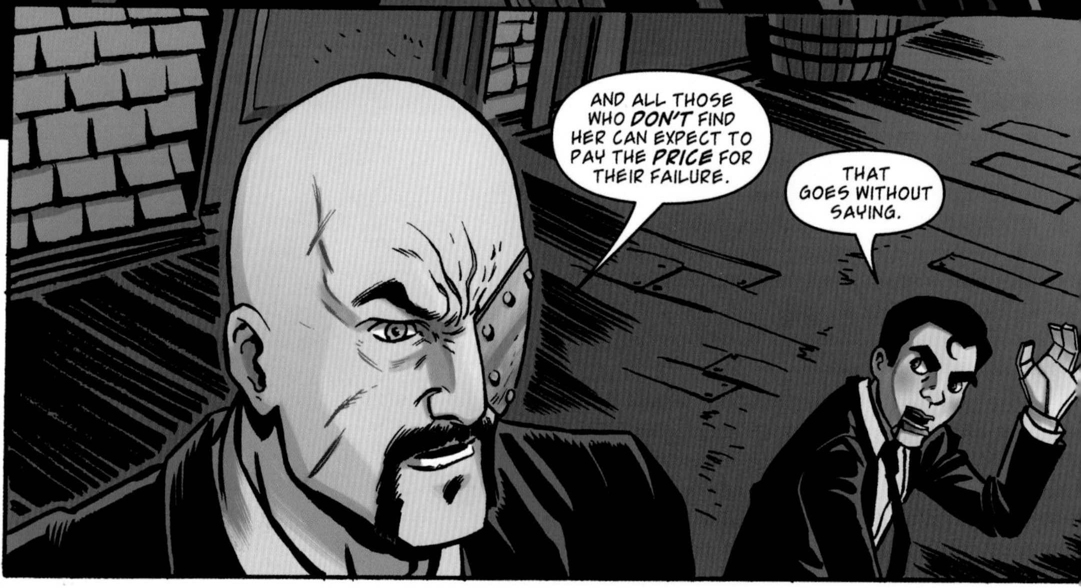
AND ALL THOSE WHO DON'T FIND HER CAN EXPECT TO PAY THE PRICE FOR THEIR FAILURE.
THAT GOES WITHOUT SAYING.

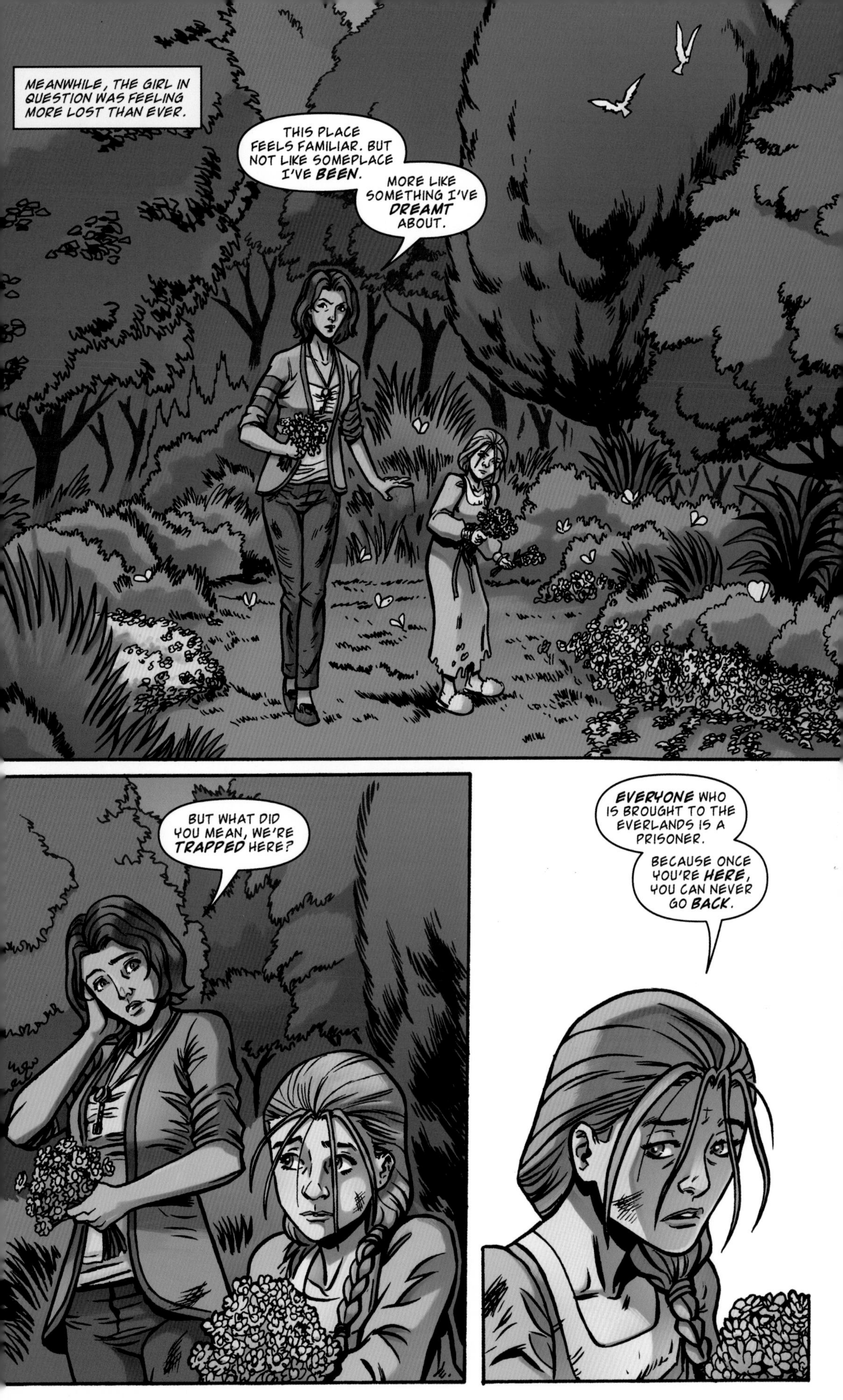
MEANWHILE, THE GIRL IN QUESTION WAS FEELING MORE LOST THAN EVER.
THIS PLACE FEELS FAMILIAR. BUT NOT LIKE SOMEPLACE I'VE BEEN.
MORE LIKE SOMETHING I'VE DREAMT ABOUT.
BUT WHAT DID YOU MEAN, WE'RE TRAPPED HERE?
EVERYONE WHO IS BROUGHT TO THE EVERLANDS IS A PRISONER.
BECAUSE ONCE YOU'RE HERE, YOU CAN NEVER GO BACK.

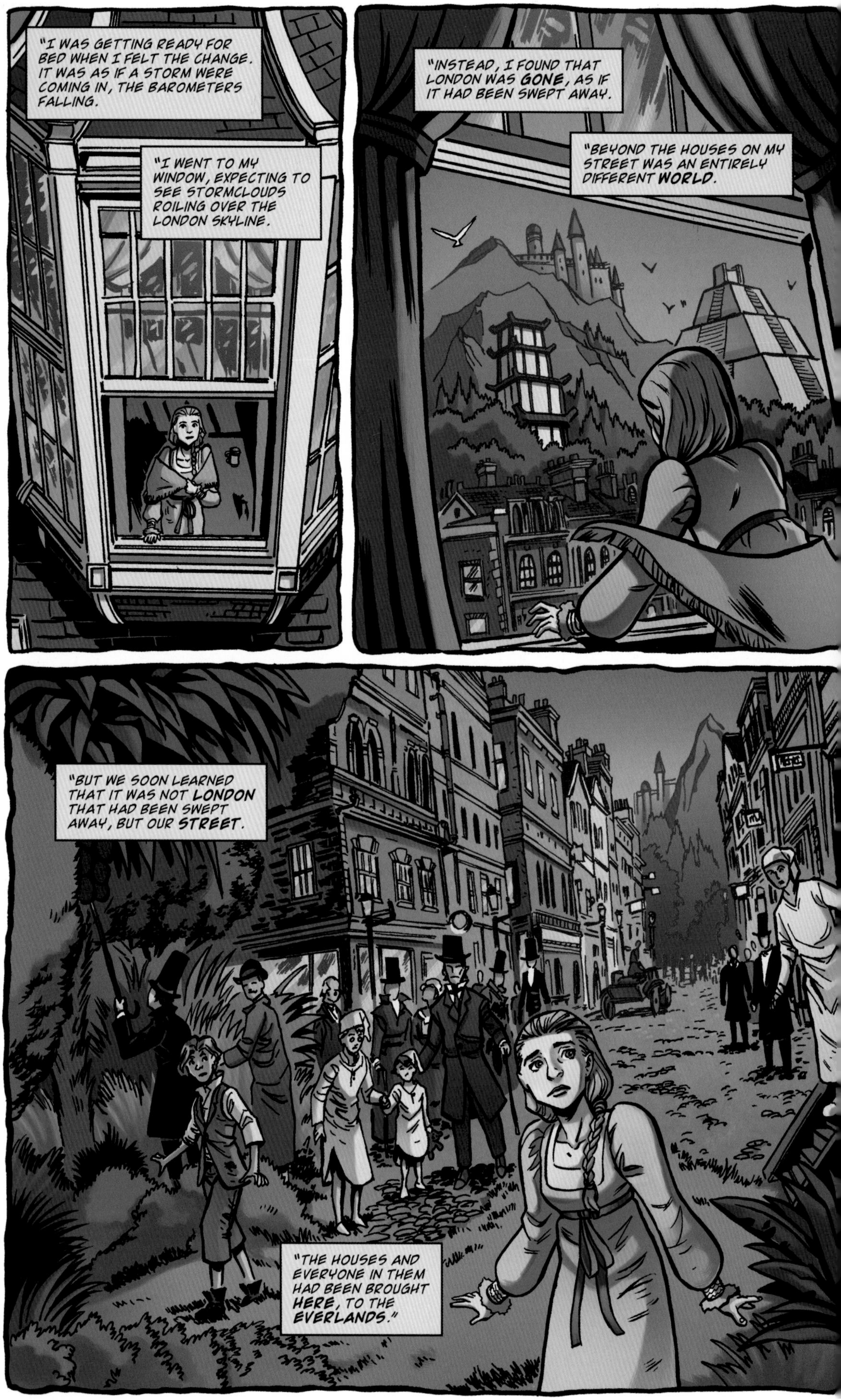
"I WAS GETTING READY FOR BED WHEN I FELT THE CHANGE. IT WAS AS IF A STORM WERE COMING IN, THE BAROMETERS FALLING.
"I WENT TO MY WINDOW, EXPECTING TO SEE STORMCLOUDS ROILING OVER THE LONDON SKYLINE.
"INSTEAD, I FOUND THAT LONDON WAS GONE, AS IF IT HAD BEEN SWEPT AWAY.
"BEYOND THE HOUSES ON MY STREET WAS AN ENTIRELY DIFFERENT WORLD.
"BUT WE SOON LEARNED THAT IT WAS NOT LONDON THAT HAD BEEN SWEPT AWAY, BUT OUR STREET.
"THE HOUSES AND EVERYONE IN THEM HAD BEEN BROUGHT HERE, TO THE EVERLANDS."

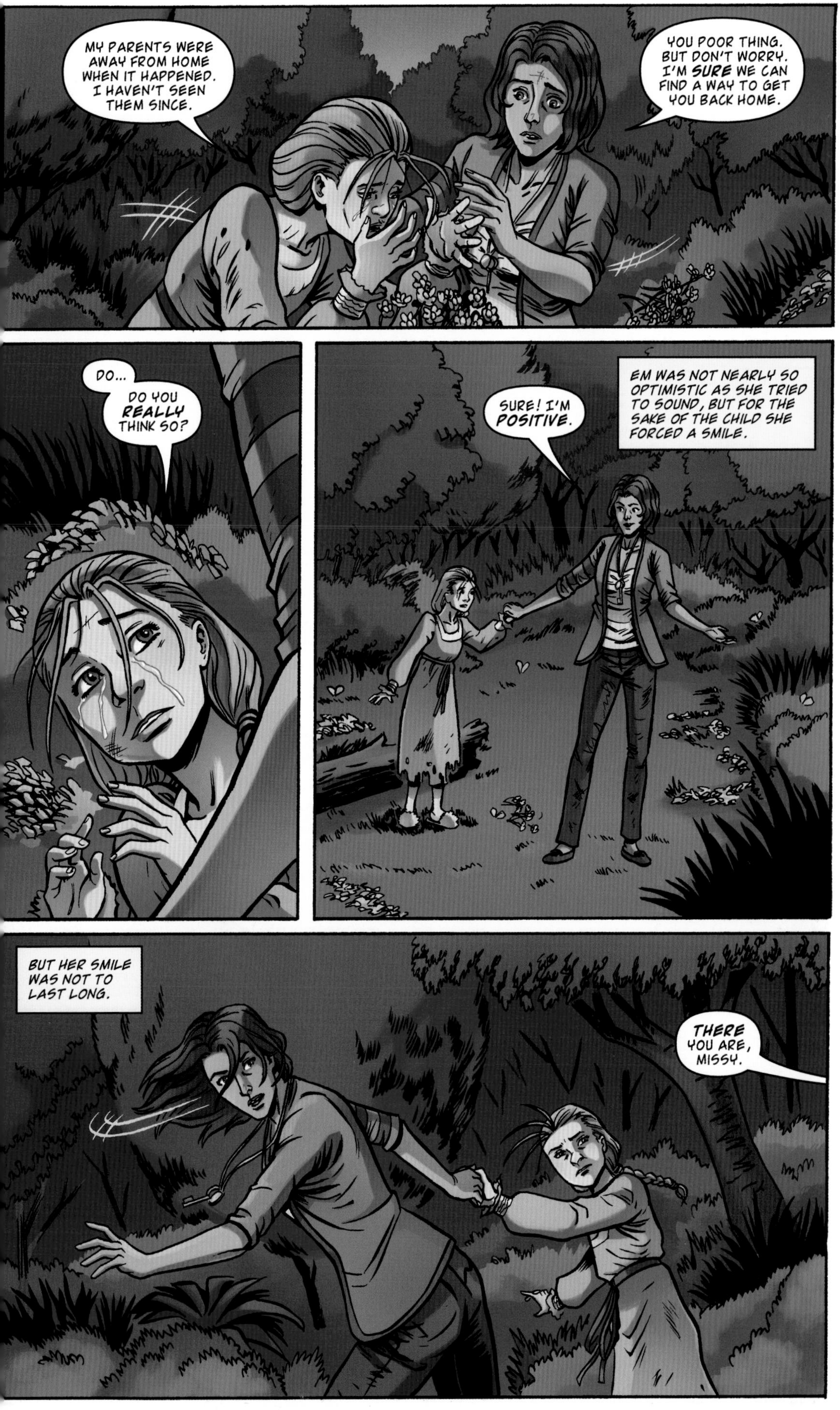
MY PARENTS WERE AWAY FROM HOME WHEN IT HAPPENED. I HAVEN'T SEEN THEM SINCE.
YOU POOR THING. BUT DON'T WORRY. I'M SURE WE CAN FIND A WAY TO GET YOU BACK HOME.
DO...
DO YOU REALLY THINK SO?
SURE! I'M POSITIVE.
EM WAS NOT NEARLY SO OPTIMISTIC AS SHE TRIED TO SOUND, BUT FOR THE SAKE OF THE CHILD SHE FORCED A SMILE.
BUT HER SMILE WAS NOT TO LAST LONG.
THERE YOU ARE, MISSY.

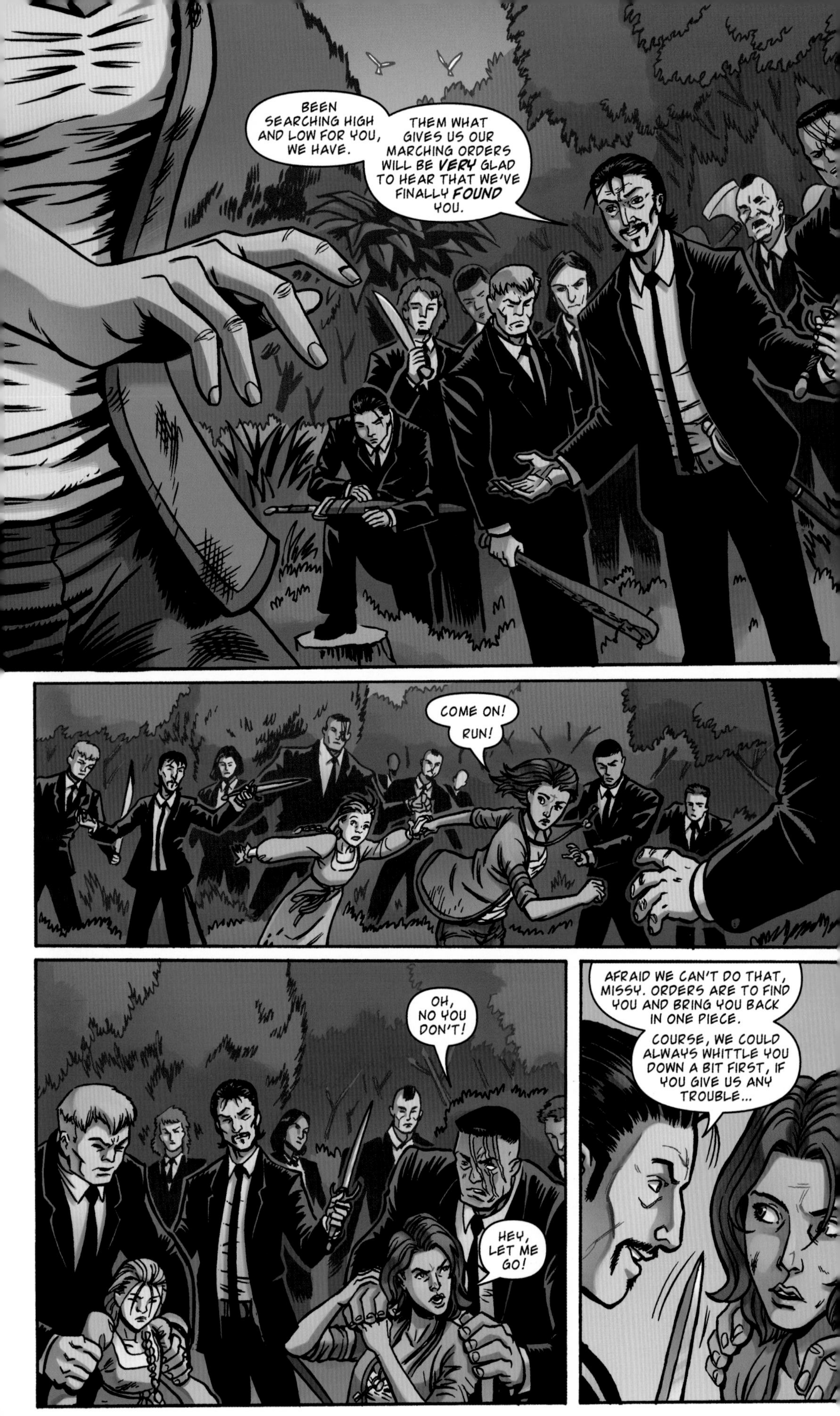

BEEN SEARCHING HIGH AND LOW FOR YOU, WE HAVE.
THEM WHAT GIVES US OUR MARCHING ORDERS WILL BE VERY GLAD TO HEAR THAT WE'VE FINALLY FOUND YOU.
COME ON!
RUN!
OH, NO YOU DON'T!
HEY, LET ME GO!
AFRAID WE CAN'T DO THAT, MISSY. ORDERS ARE TO FIND YOU AND BRING YOU BACK IN ONE PIECE.
COURSE, WE COULD ALWAYS WHITTLE YOU DOWN A BIT FIRST, IF YOU GIVE US ANY TROUBLE...

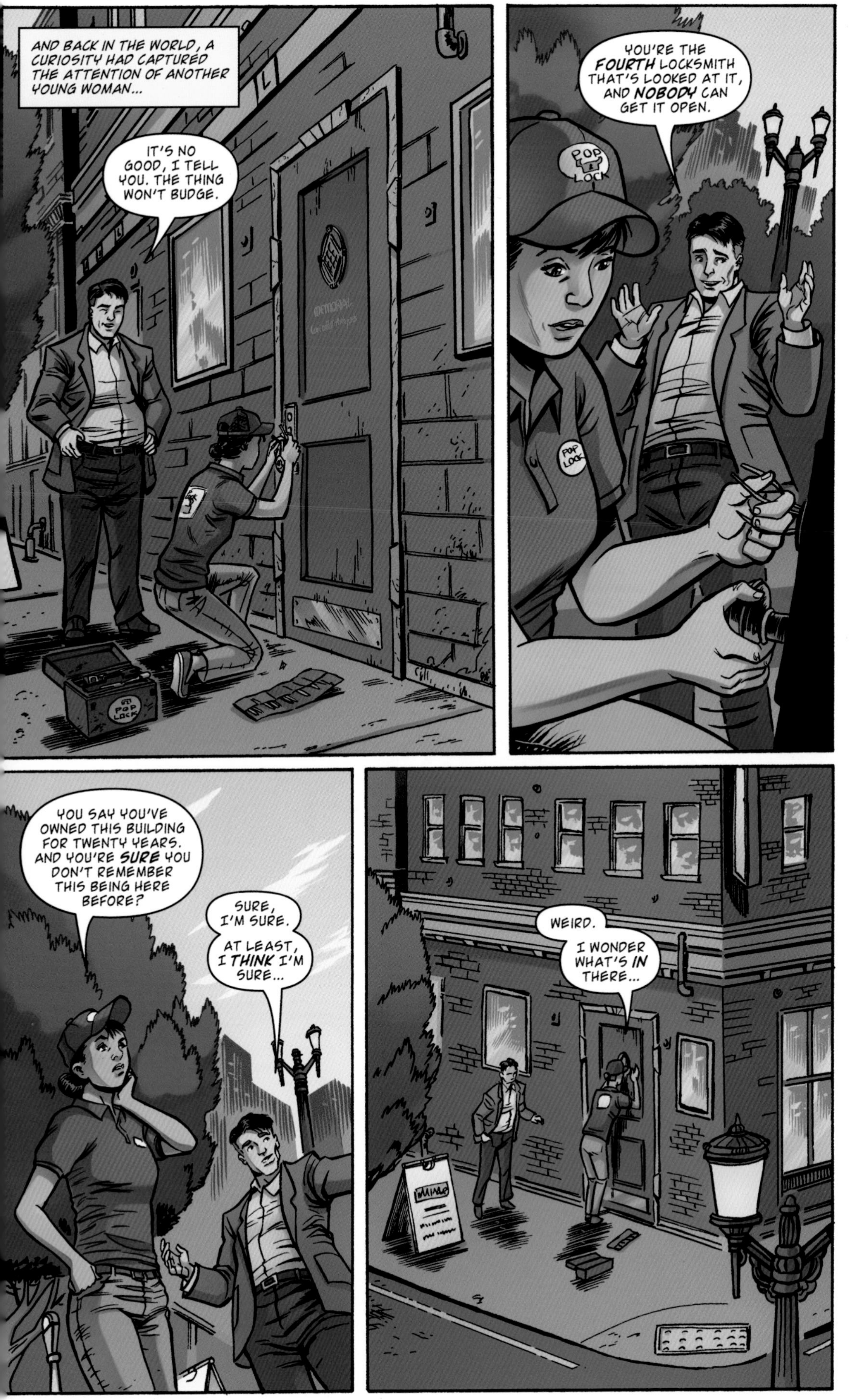
AND BACK IN THE WORLD, A CURIOSITY HAD CAPTURED THE ATTENTION OF ANOTHER YOUNG WOMAN...
IT'S NO GOOD, I TELL YOU. THE THING WON'T BUDGE.
YOU'RE THE **FOURTH** LOCKSMITH THAT'S LOOKED AT IT, AND **NOBODY** CAN GET IT OPEN.
YOU SAY YOU'VE OWNED THIS BUILDING FOR TWENTY YEARS. AND YOU'RE **SURE** YOU DON'T REMEMBER THIS BEING HERE BEFORE?
SURE, I'M SURE.
AT LEAST, I **THINK** I'M SURE...
WEIRD.
I WONDER WHAT'S **IN** THERE...

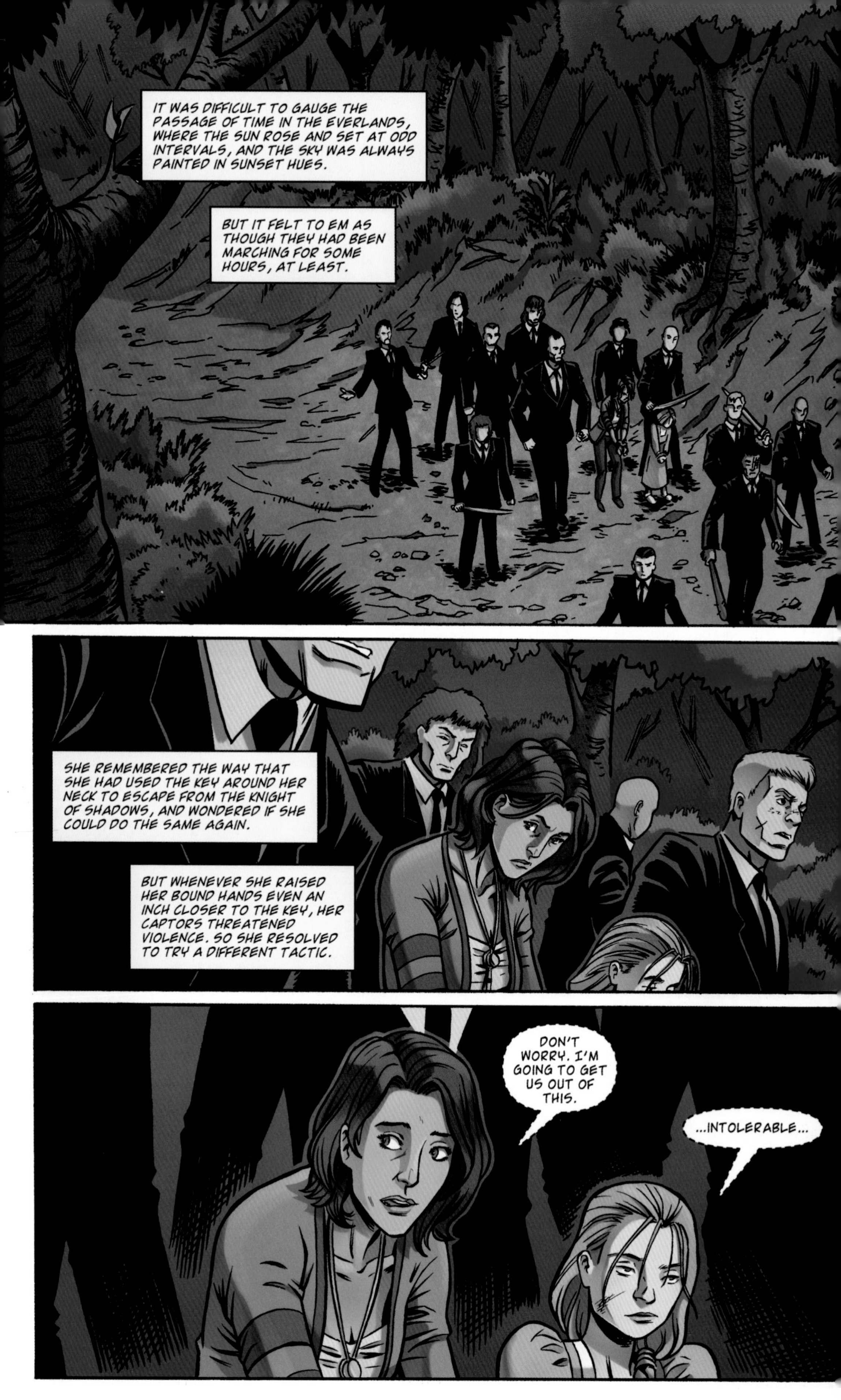
IT WAS DIFFICULT TO GAUGE THE PASSAGE OF TIME IN THE EVERLANDS, WHERE THE SUN ROSE AND SET AT ODD INTERVALS, AND THE SKY WAS ALWAYS PAINTED IN SUNSET HUES.
BUT IT FELT TO EM AS THOUGH THEY HAD BEEN MARCHING FOR SOME HOURS, AT LEAST.
SHE REMEMBERED THE WAY THAT SHE HAD USED THE KEY AROUND HER NECK TO ESCAPE FROM THE KNIGHT OF SHADOWS, AND WONDERED IF SHE COULD DO THE SAME AGAIN.
BUT WHENEVER SHE RAISED HER BOUND HANDS EVEN AN INCH CLOSER TO THE KEY, HER CAPTORS THREATENED VIOLENCE. SO SHE RESOLVED TO TRY A DIFFERENT TACTIC.
DON'T WORRY. I'M GOING TO GET US OUT OF THIS.
...INTOLERABLE...

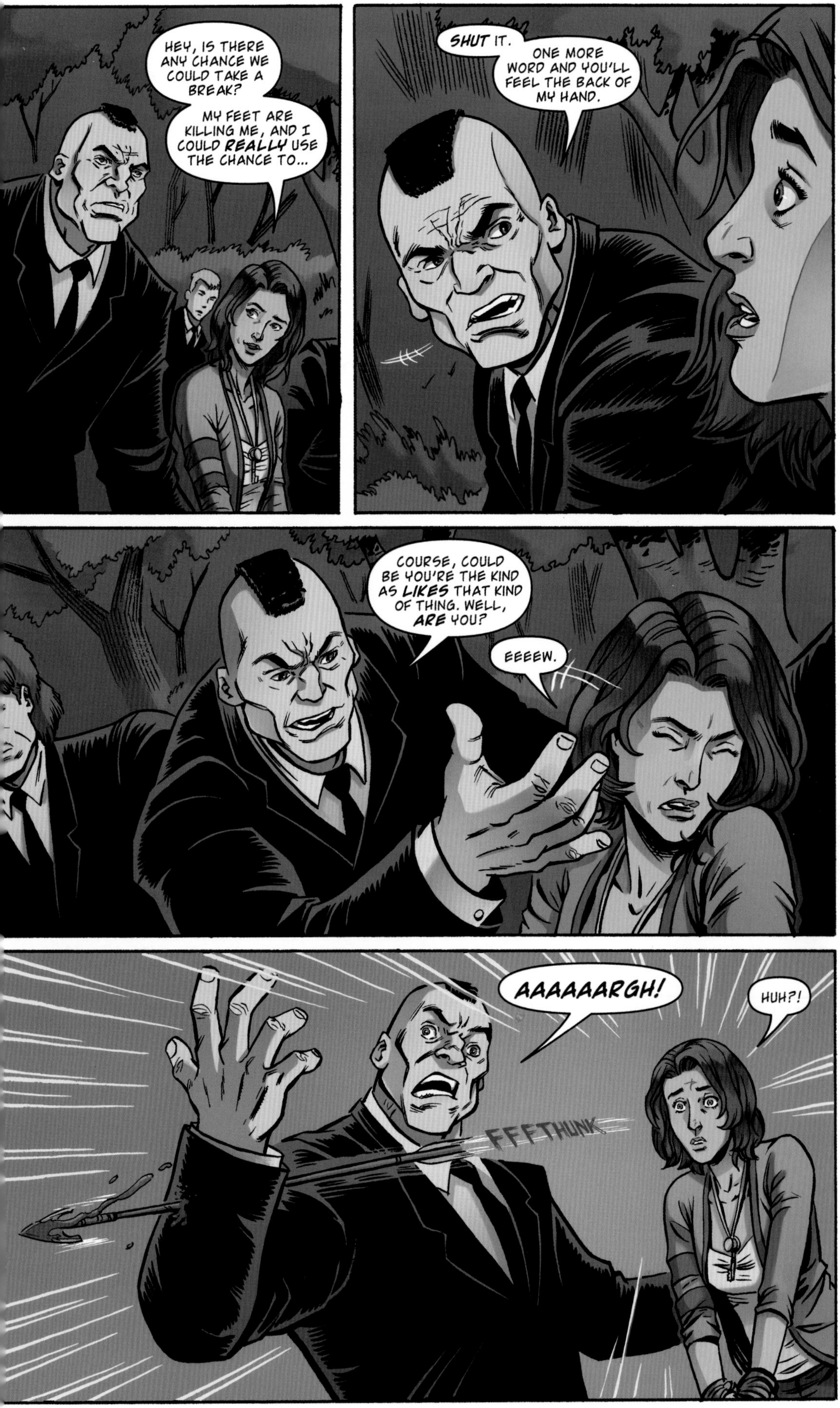
HEY, IS THERE ANY CHANCE WE COULD TAKE A BREAK?
MY FEET ARE KILLING ME, AND I COULD REALLY USE THE CHANCE TO...
SHUT IT.
ONE MORE WORD AND YOU'LL FEEL THE BACK OF MY HAND.
COURSE, COULD BE YOU'RE THE KIND AS LIKES THAT KIND OF THING. WELL, ARE YOU?
EEEEW.
AAAAAARGH!
HUH?!
FFFTHUNK

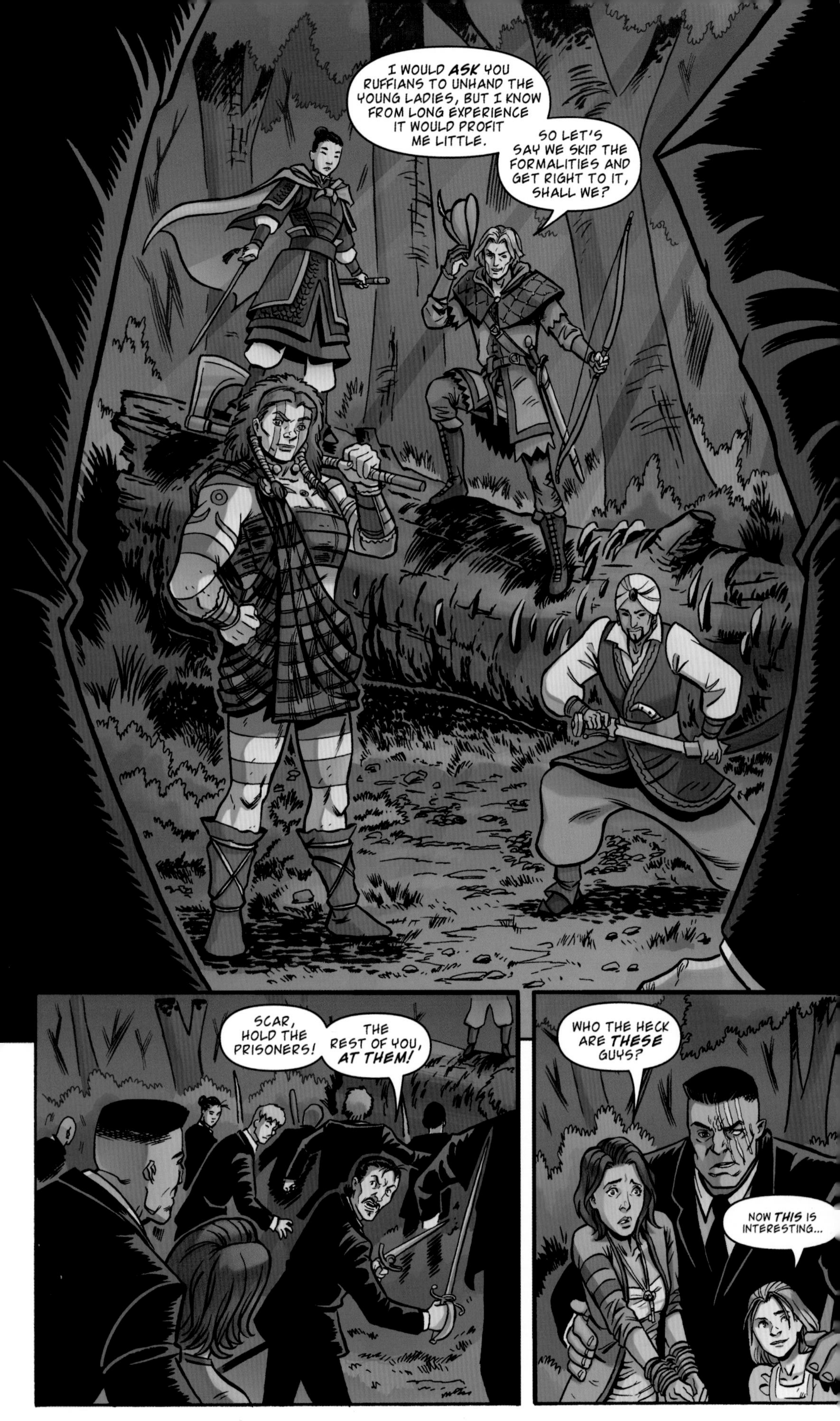
I WOULD ASK YOU RUFFIANS TO UNHAND THE YOUNG LADIES, BUT I KNOW FROM LONG EXPERIENCE IT WOULD PROFIT ME LITTLE.
SO LET'S SAY WE SKIP THE FORMALITIES AND GET RIGHT TO IT, SHALL WE?
SCAR, HOLD THE PRISONERS!
THE REST OF YOU, AT THEM!
WHO THE HECK ARE THESE GUYS?
NOW THIS IS INTERESTING...

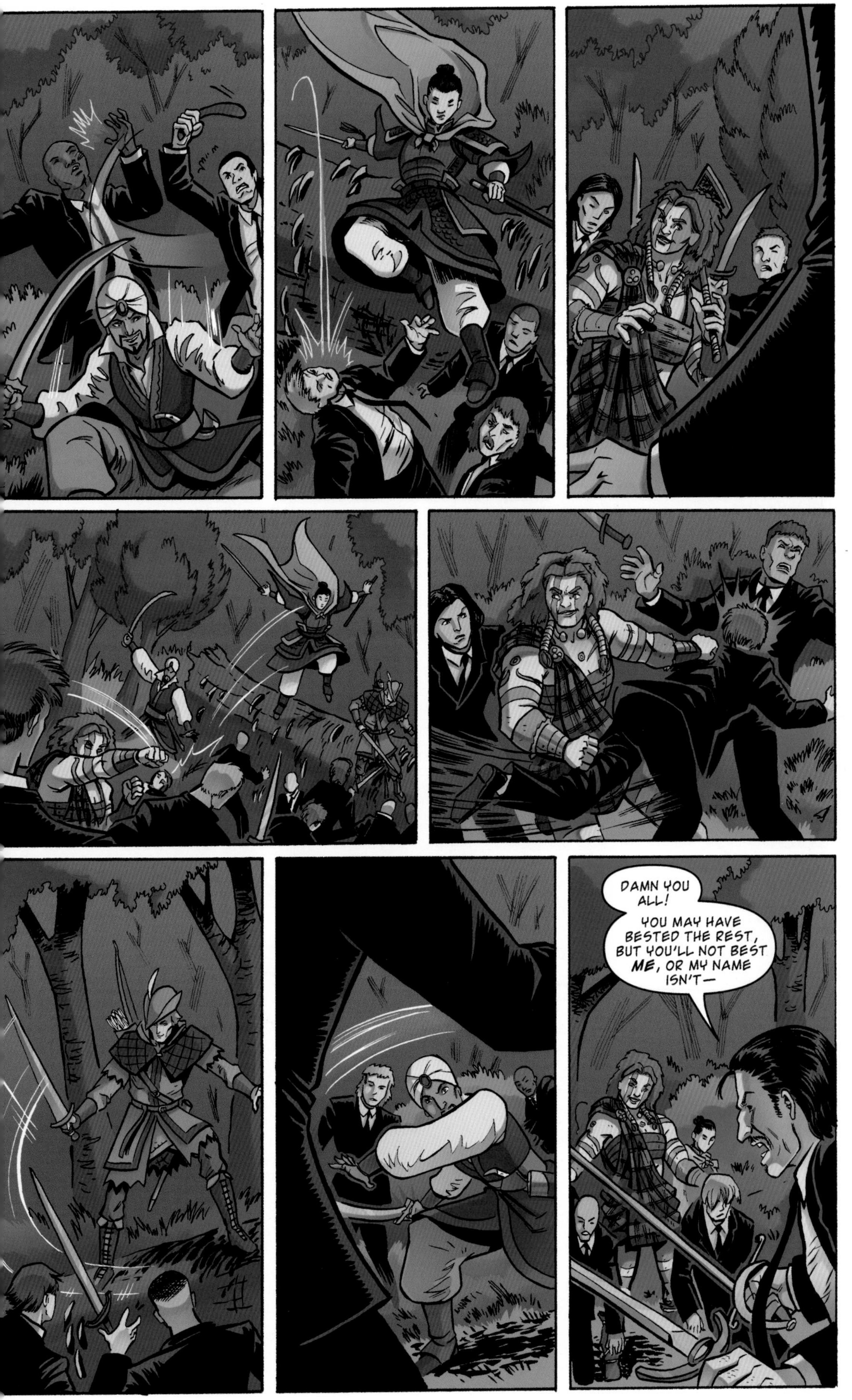
DAMN YOU ALL!
YOU MAY HAVE BESTED THE REST, BUT YOU'LL NOT BEST ***ME***, OR MY NAME ISN'T—

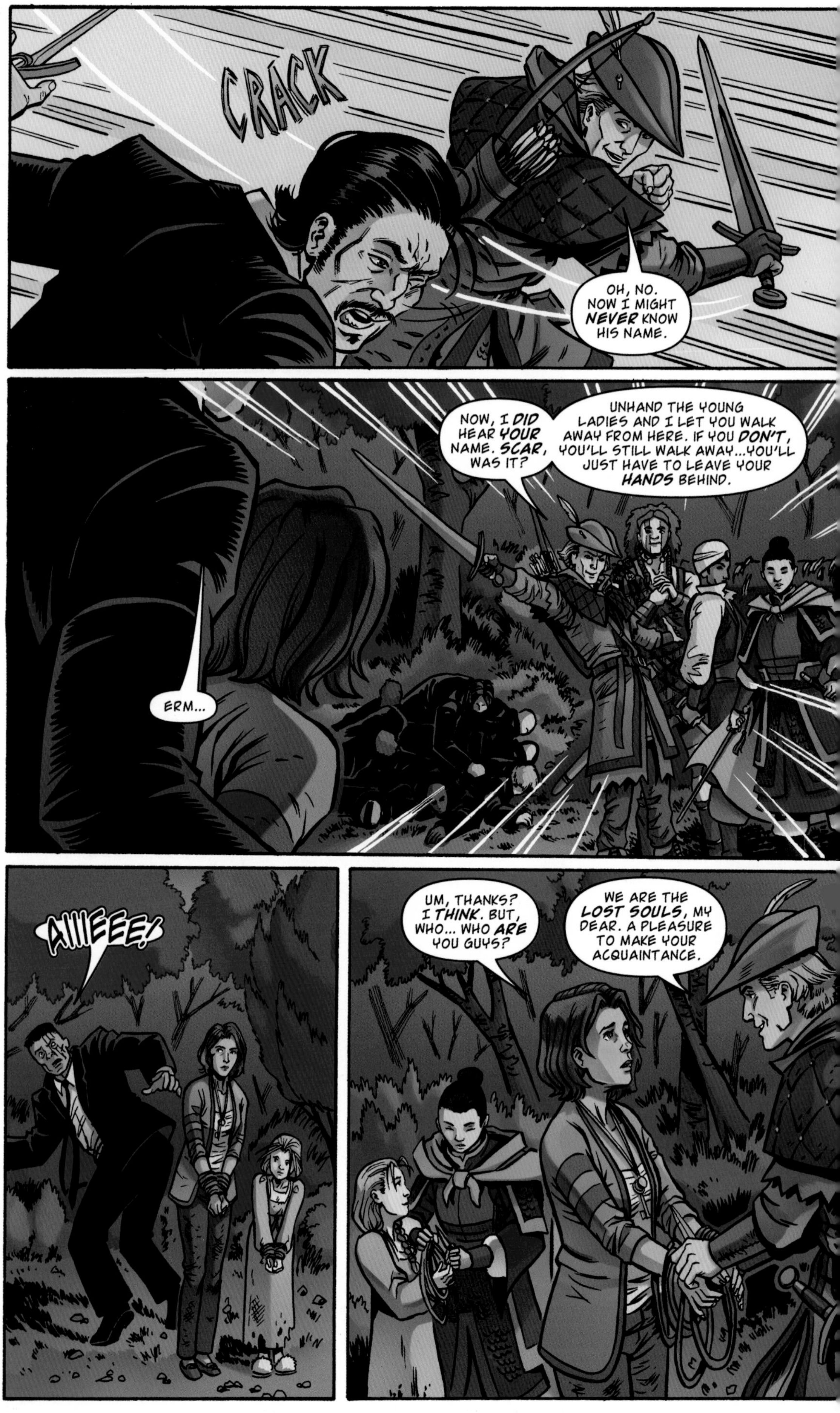
CRACK
OH, NO. NOW I MIGHT NEVER KNOW HIS NAME.
NOW, I DID HEAR YOUR NAME. SCAR, WAS IT?
UNHAND THE YOUNG LADIES AND I LET YOU WALK AWAY FROM HERE. IF YOU DON'T, YOU'LL STILL WALK AWAY...YOU'LL JUST HAVE TO LEAVE YOUR HANDS BEHIND.
ERM...
AIIIEEE!
UM, THANKS? I THINK. BUT, WHO... WHO ARE YOU GUYS?
WE ARE THE LOST SOULS, MY DEAR. A PLEASURE TO MAKE YOUR ACQUAINTANCE.

WITHIN THE IVORY TOWER, FAR ACROSS THE CURRENT SEA, ANOTHER BATTLE HAD ONLY RECENTLY CONCLUDED.

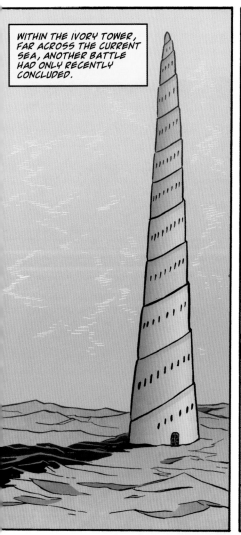

AND WITH THEIR SHADOW FOES FLED, THE LIBRARIANS TENDED TO THE AFTERMATH AS BEST THEY COULD, WHILE THEIR MISTRESS BABYLON ATTENDED TO THEIR RELUCTANT GUEST.

YOU ARE, OF COURSE, WELCOME TO REMAIN IN THE LIBRARY AS OUR GUEST FOR AS LONG AS YOU REQUIRE, SCHRODINGER.

YEAH, WELL, THANKS BUT *NO* THANKS. IF IT'S ALL THE SAME TO YOU, I THINK I'LL BE HEADING OUT.

NOT THAT I HAVE ANY IDEA WHERE I'M GOING...

IF YOU ARE UNSURE WHERE YOU MIGHT *GO*, PERHAPS YOU SHOULD PAUSE AND REFLECT ON WHERE YOU *ARE*.

HUH? OH, I GET IT. IT'S A *MAP*.

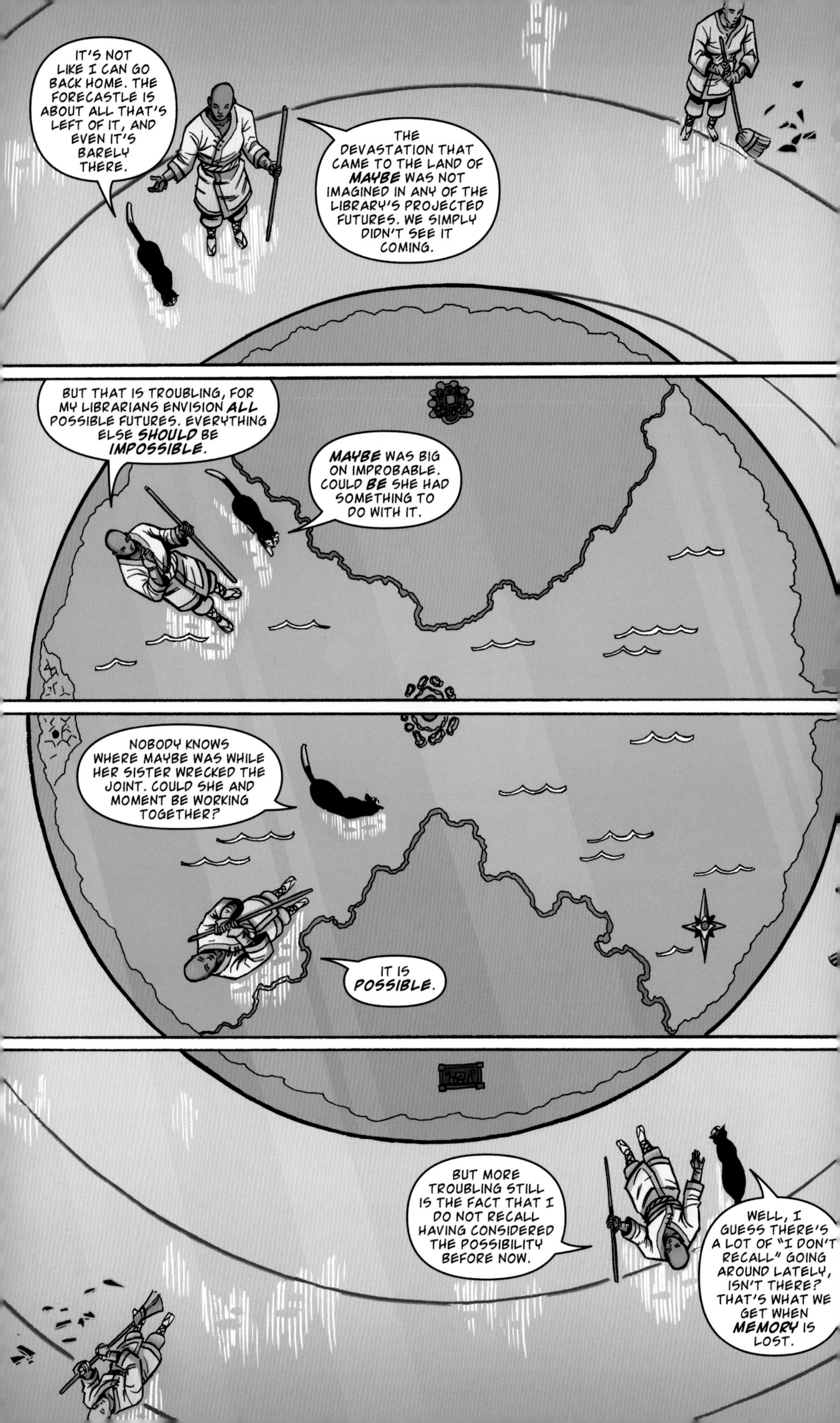
IT'S NOT LIKE I CAN GO BACK HOME. THE FORECASTLE IS ABOUT ALL THAT'S LEFT OF IT, AND EVEN IT'S BARELY THERE.
THE DEVASTATION THAT CAME TO THE LAND OF MAYBE WAS NOT IMAGINED IN ANY OF THE LIBRARY'S PROJECTED FUTURES. WE SIMPLY DIDN'T SEE IT COMING.
BUT THAT IS TROUBLING, FOR MY LIBRARIANS ENVISION ALL POSSIBLE FUTURES. EVERYTHING ELSE SHOULD BE IMPOSSIBLE.
MAYBE WAS BIG ON IMPROBABLE. COULD BE SHE HAD SOMETHING TO DO WITH IT.
NOBODY KNOWS WHERE MAYBE WAS WHILE HER SISTER WRECKED THE JOINT. COULD SHE AND MOMENT BE WORKING TOGETHER?
IT IS POSSIBLE.
BUT MORE TROUBLING STILL IS THE FACT THAT I DO NOT RECALL HAVING CONSIDERED THE POSSIBILITY BEFORE NOW.
WELL, I GUESS THERE'S A LOT OF "I DON'T RECALL" GOING AROUND LATELY, ISN'T THERE? THAT'S WHAT WE GET WHEN MEMORY IS LOST.

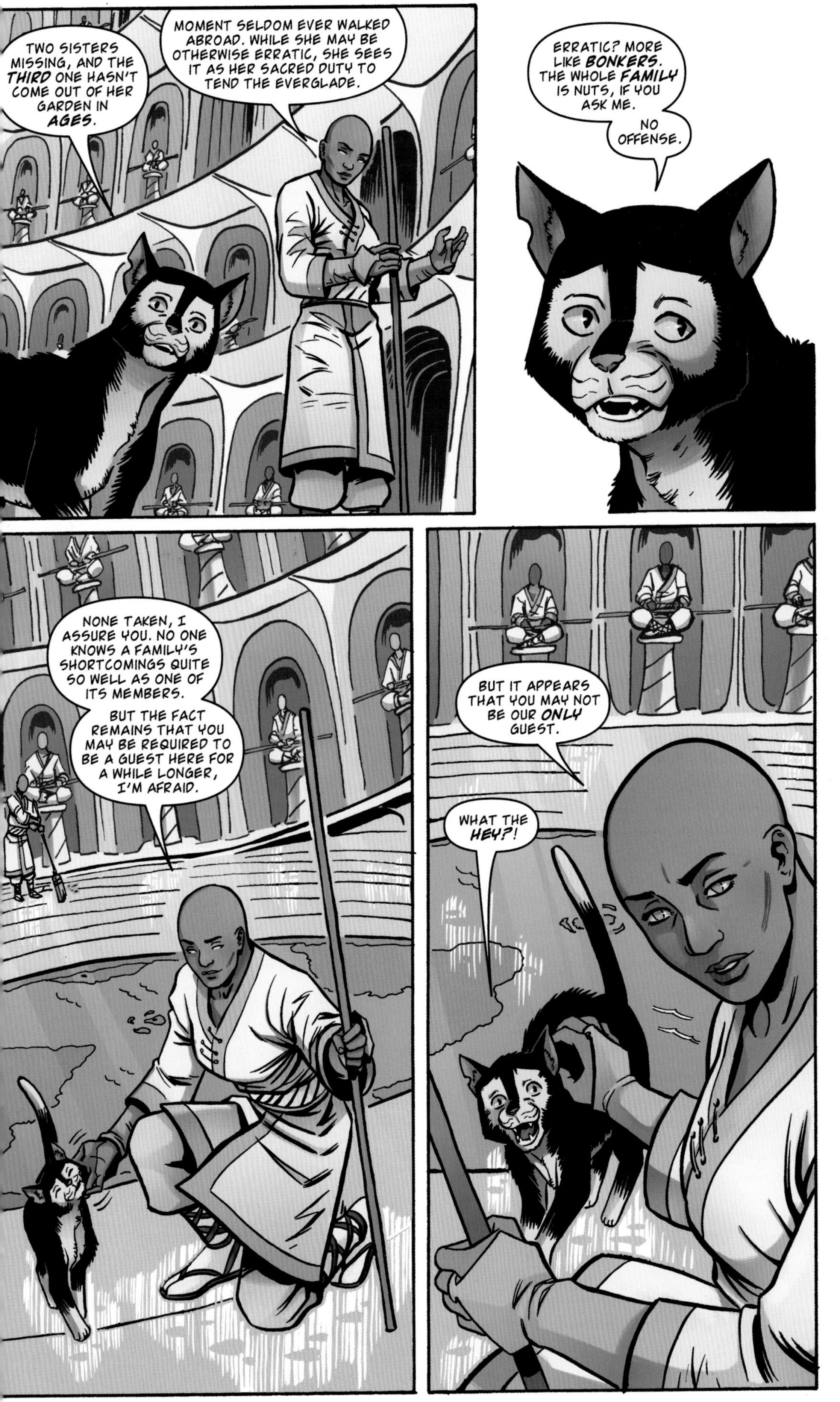
TWO SISTERS MISSING, AND THE THIRD ONE HASN'T COME OUT OF HER GARDEN IN AGES.
MOMENT SELDOM EVER WALKED ABROAD. WHILE SHE MAY BE OTHERWISE ERRATIC, SHE SEES IT AS HER SACRED DUTY TO TEND THE EVERGLADE.
ERRATIC? MORE LIKE BONKERS. THE WHOLE FAMILY IS NUTS, IF YOU ASK ME.
NO OFFENSE.
NONE TAKEN, I ASSURE YOU. NO ONE KNOWS A FAMILY'S SHORTCOMINGS QUITE SO WELL AS ONE OF ITS MEMBERS.
BUT THE FACT REMAINS THAT YOU MAY BE REQUIRED TO BE A GUEST HERE FOR A WHILE LONGER, I'M AFRAID.
BUT IT APPEARS THAT YOU MAY NOT BE OUR ONLY GUEST.
WHAT THE HEY?!

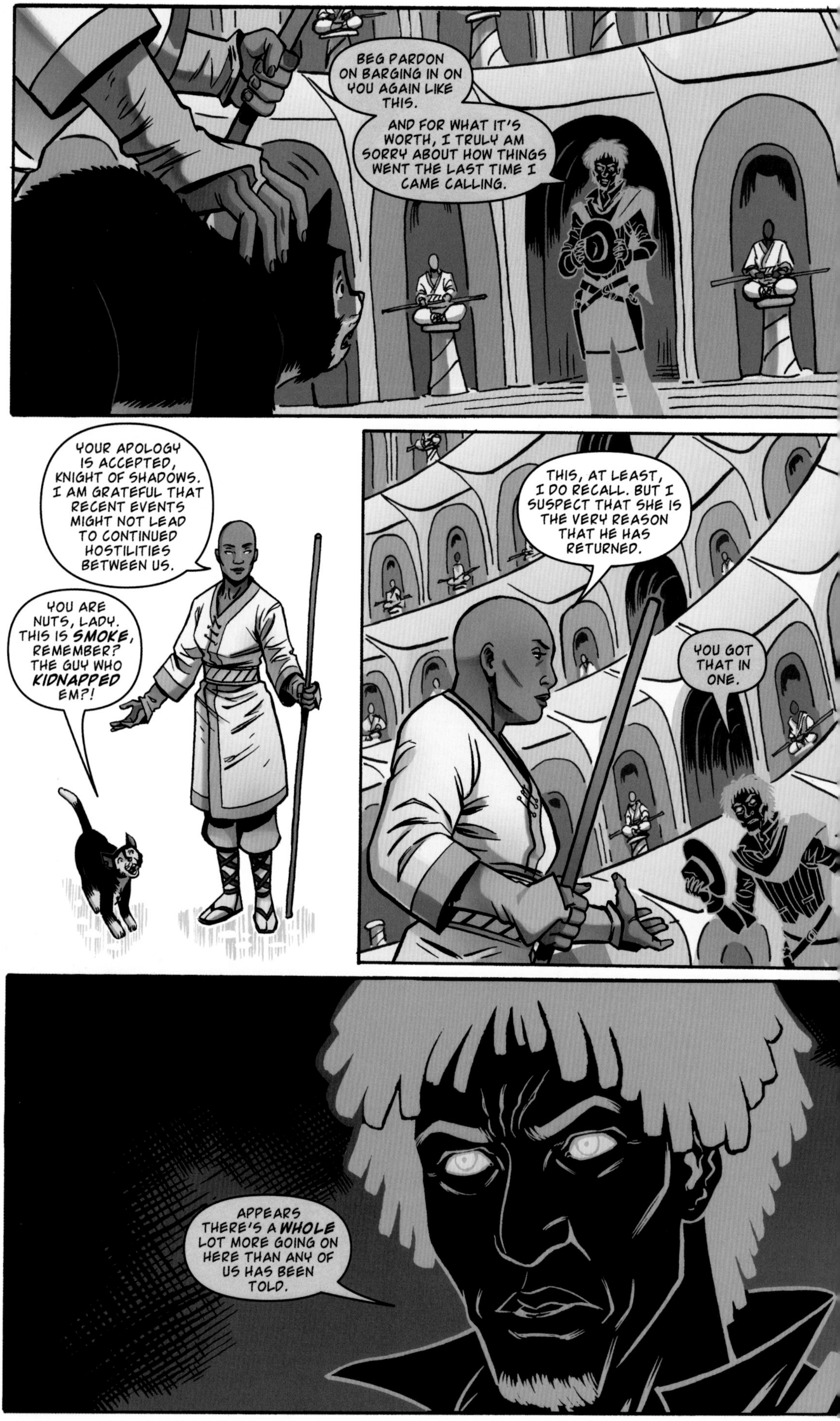
BEG PARDON ON BARGING IN ON YOU AGAIN LIKE THIS.
AND FOR WHAT IT'S WORTH, I TRULY AM SORRY ABOUT HOW THINGS WENT THE LAST TIME I CAME CALLING.
YOUR APOLOGY IS ACCEPTED, KNIGHT OF SHADOWS. I AM GRATEFUL THAT RECENT EVENTS MIGHT NOT LEAD TO CONTINUED HOSTILITIES BETWEEN US.
YOU ARE NUTS, LADY. THIS IS SMOKE, REMEMBER? THE GUY WHO KIDNAPPED EM?!
THIS, AT LEAST, I DO RECALL. BUT I SUSPECT THAT SHE IS THE VERY REASON THAT HE HAS RETURNED.
YOU GOT THAT IN ONE.
APPEARS THERE'S A WHOLE LOT MORE GOING ON HERE THAN ANY OF US HAS BEEN TOLD.

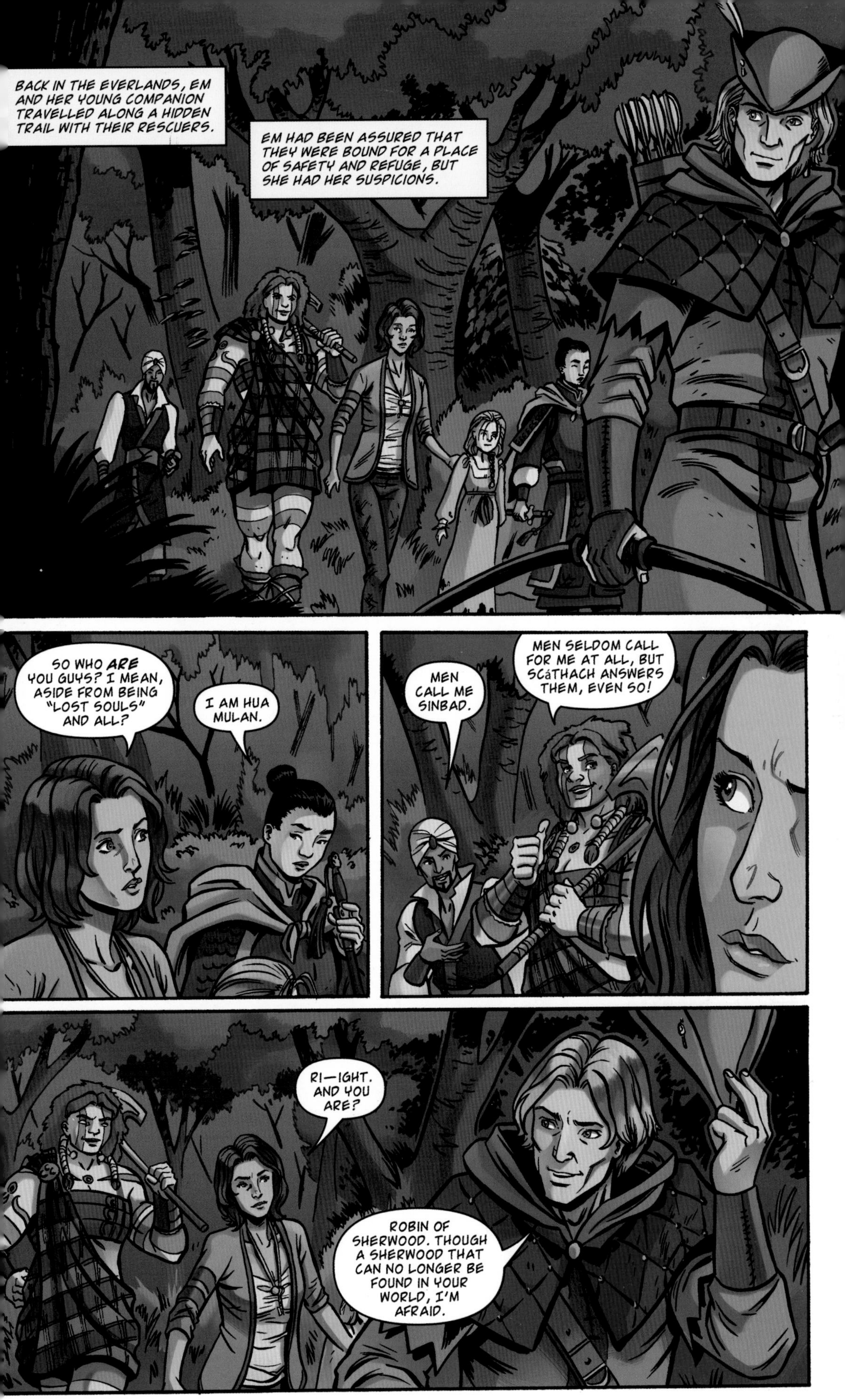
BACK IN THE EVERLANDS, EM AND HER YOUNG COMPANION TRAVELLED ALONG A HIDDEN TRAIL WITH THEIR RESCUERS.
EM HAD BEEN ASSURED THAT THEY WERE BOUND FOR A PLACE OF SAFETY AND REFUGE, BUT SHE HAD HER SUSPICIONS.
SO WHO ARE YOU GUYS? I MEAN, ASIDE FROM BEING "LOST SOULS" AND ALL?
I AM HUA MULAN.
MEN CALL ME SINBAD.
MEN SELDOM CALL FOR ME AT ALL, BUT SCáTHACH ANSWERS THEM, EVEN SO!
RI—IGHT. AND YOU ARE?
ROBIN OF SHERWOOD. THOUGH A SHERWOOD THAT CAN NO LONGER BE FOUND IN YOUR WORLD, I'M AFRAID.

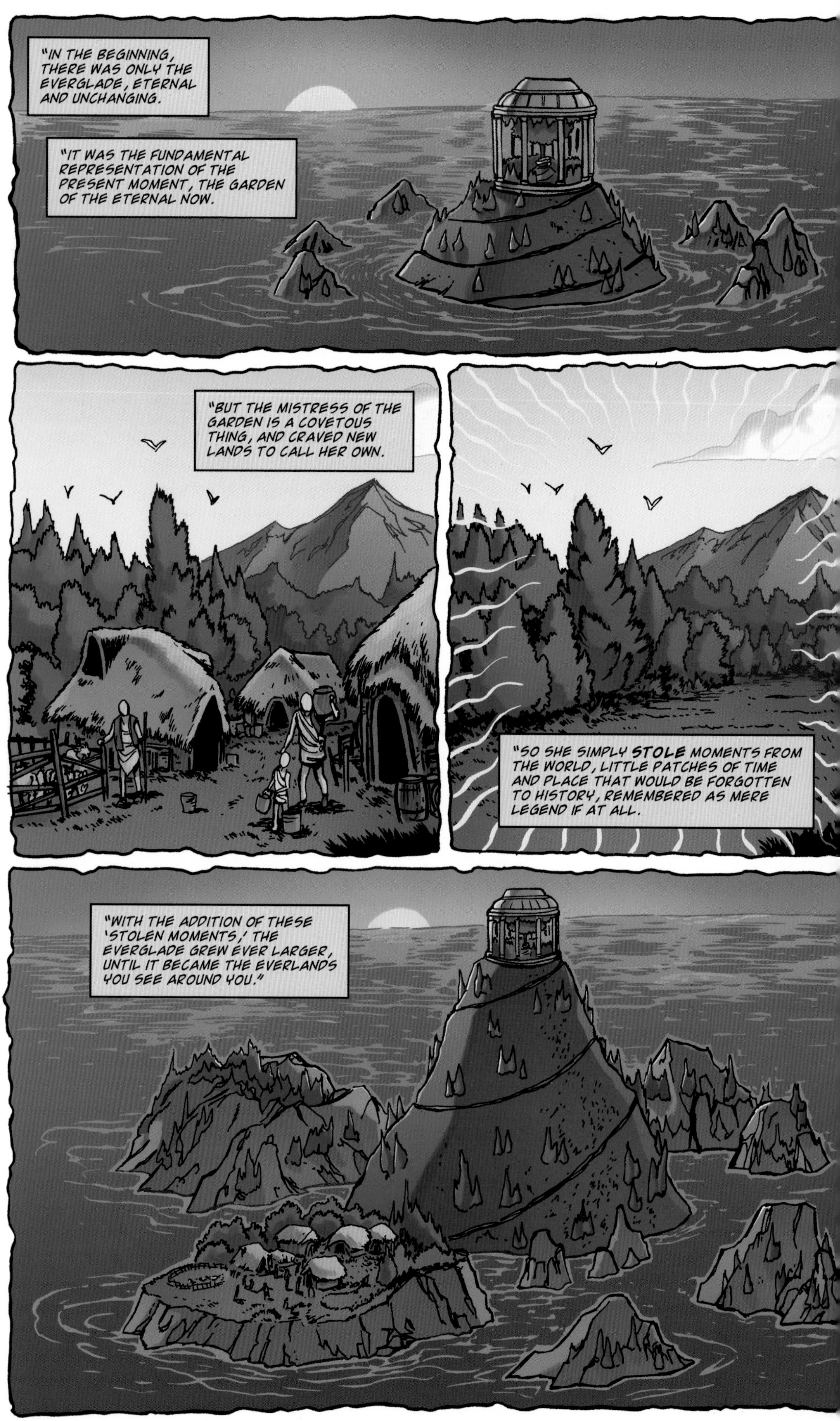
"IN THE BEGINNING, THERE WAS ONLY THE EVERGLADE, ETERNAL AND UNCHANGING.
"IT WAS THE FUNDAMENTAL REPRESENTATION OF THE PRESENT MOMENT, THE GARDEN OF THE ETERNAL NOW.
"BUT THE MISTRESS OF THE GARDEN IS A COVETOUS THING, AND CRAVED NEW LANDS TO CALL HER OWN.
"SO SHE SIMPLY STOLE MOMENTS FROM THE WORLD, LITTLE PATCHES OF TIME AND PLACE THAT WOULD BE FORGOTTEN TO HISTORY, REMEMBERED AS MERE LEGEND IF AT ALL.
"WITH THE ADDITION OF THESE 'STOLEN MOMENTS,' THE EVERGLADE GREW EVER LARGER, UNTIL IT BECAME THE EVERLANDS YOU SEE AROUND YOU."

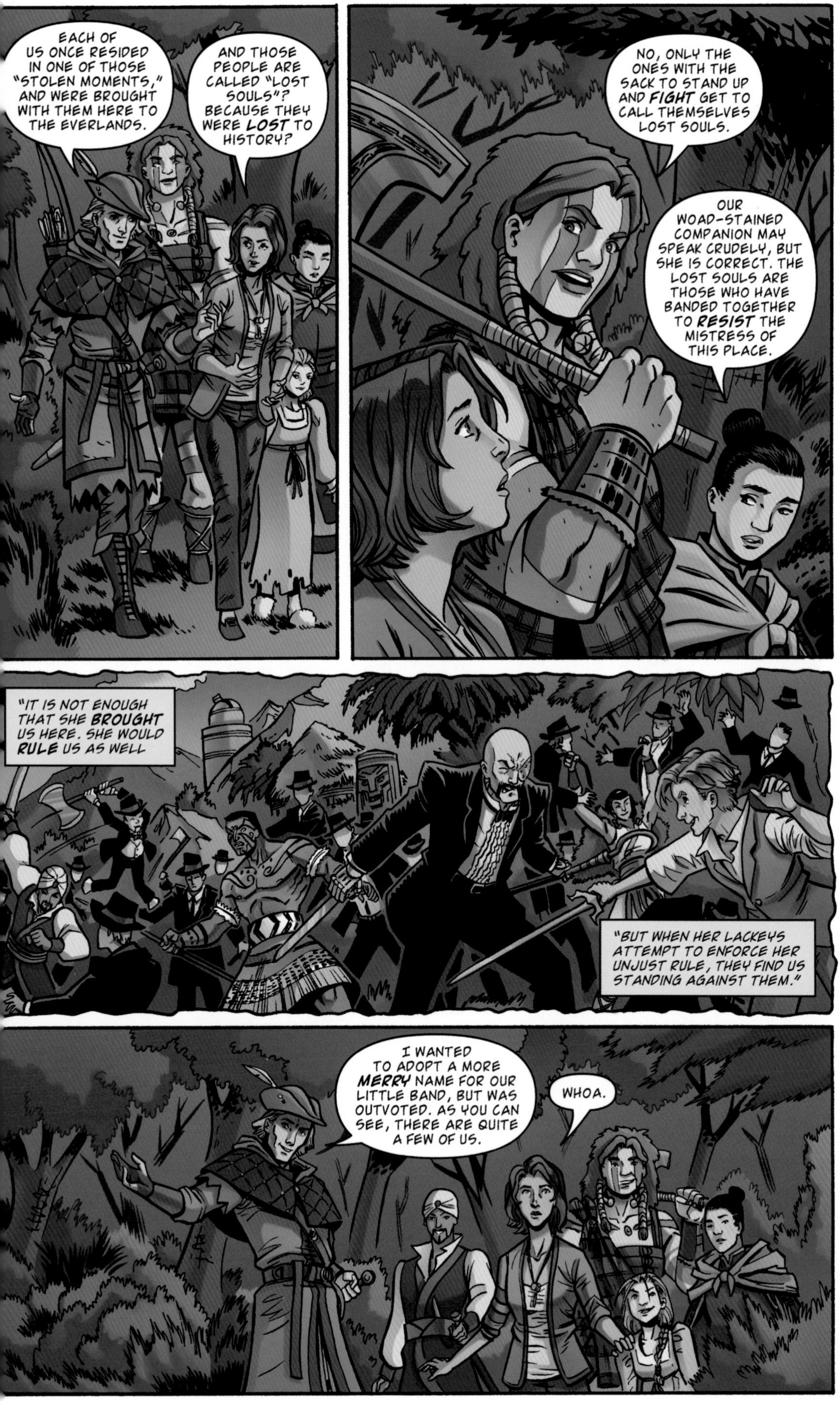
EACH OF US ONCE RESIDED IN ONE OF THOSE "STOLEN MOMENTS," AND WERE BROUGHT WITH THEM HERE TO THE EVERLANDS.
AND THOSE PEOPLE ARE CALLED "LOST SOULS"? BECAUSE THEY WERE **LOST** TO HISTORY?
NO, ONLY THE ONES WITH THE SACK TO STAND UP AND **FIGHT** GET TO CALL THEMSELVES LOST SOULS.
OUR WOAD-STAINED COMPANION MAY SPEAK CRUDELY, BUT SHE IS CORRECT. THE LOST SOULS ARE THOSE WHO HAVE BANDED TOGETHER TO **RESIST** THE MISTRESS OF THIS PLACE.
"IT IS NOT ENOUGH THAT SHE **BROUGHT** US HERE. SHE WOULD **RULE** US AS WELL
"BUT WHEN HER LACKEYS ATTEMPT TO ENFORCE HER UNJUST RULE, THEY FIND US STANDING AGAINST THEM."
I WANTED TO ADOPT A MORE **MERRY** NAME FOR OUR LITTLE BAND, BUT WAS OUTVOTED. AS YOU CAN SEE, THERE ARE QUITE A FEW OF US.
WHOA.

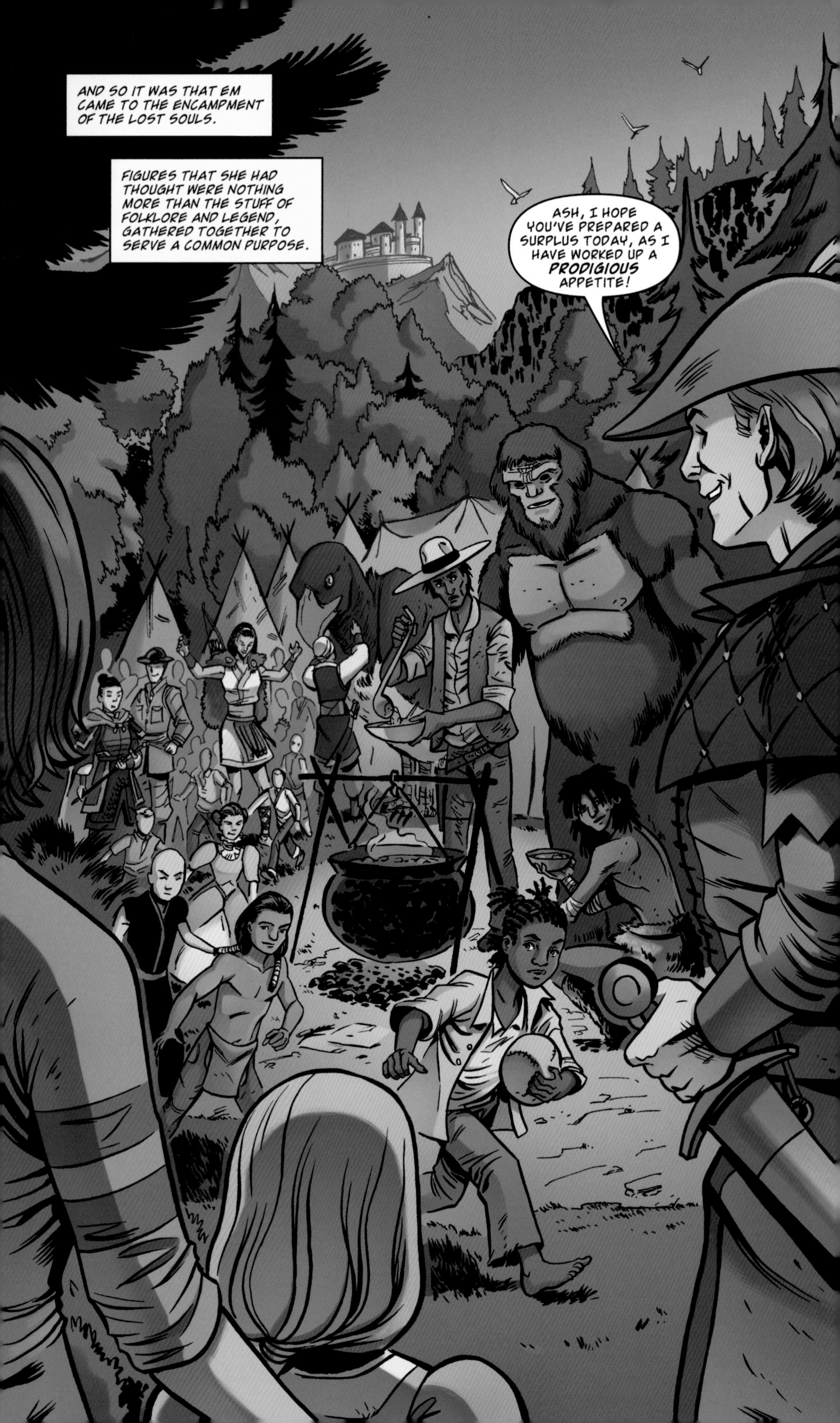
AND SO IT WAS THAT EM CAME TO THE ENCAMPMENT OF THE LOST SOULS.
FIGURES THAT SHE HAD THOUGHT WERE NOTHING MORE THAN THE STUFF OF FOLKLORE AND LEGEND, GATHERED TOGETHER TO SERVE A COMMON PURPOSE.
ASH, I HOPE YOU'VE PREPARED A SURPLUS TODAY, AS I HAVE WORKED UP A **PRODIGIOUS** APPETITE!

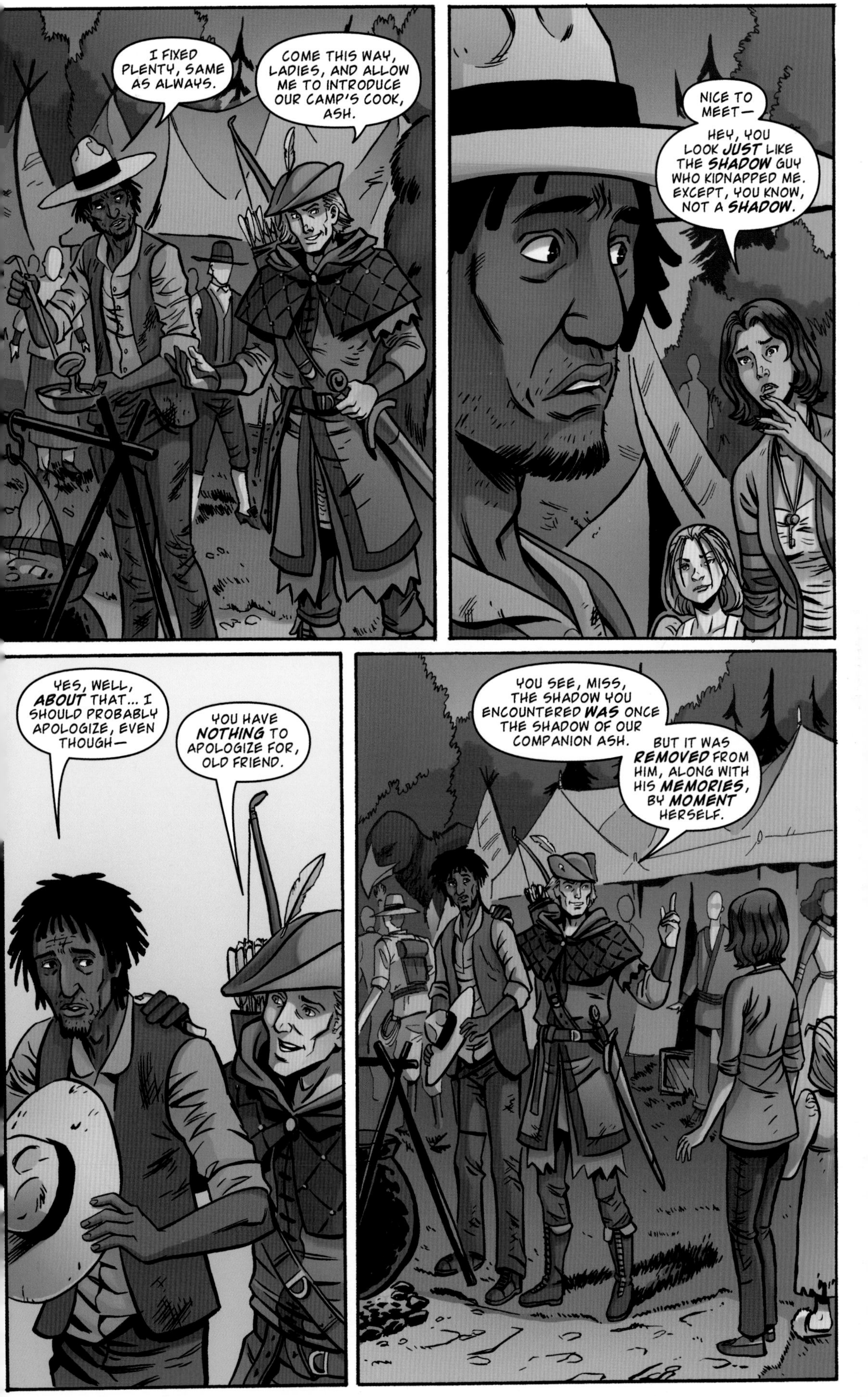

I FIXED PLENTY, SAME AS ALWAYS.
COME THIS WAY, LADIES, AND ALLOW ME TO INTRODUCE OUR CAMP'S COOK, ASH.
NICE TO MEET—
HEY, YOU LOOK JUST LIKE THE SHADOW GUY WHO KIDNAPPED ME. EXCEPT, YOU KNOW, NOT A SHADOW.
YES, WELL, ABOUT THAT... I SHOULD PROBABLY APOLOGIZE, EVEN THOUGH—
YOU HAVE NOTHING TO APOLOGIZE FOR, OLD FRIEND.
YOU SEE, MISS, THE SHADOW YOU ENCOUNTERED WAS ONCE THE SHADOW OF OUR COMPANION ASH.
BUT IT WAS REMOVED FROM HIM, ALONG WITH HIS MEMORIES, BY MOMENT HERSELF.

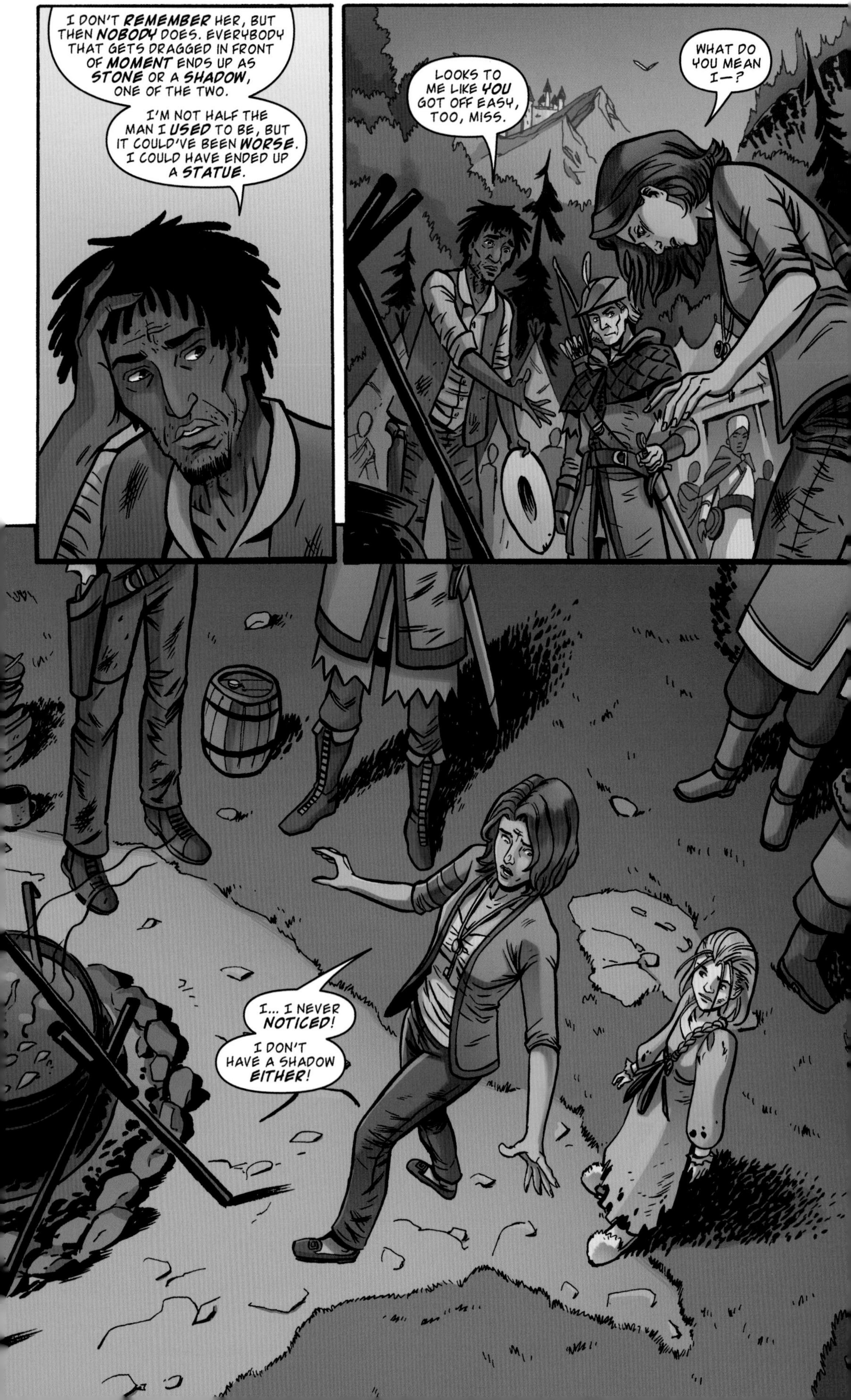
I DON'T REMEMBER HER, BUT THEN NOBODY DOES. EVERYBODY THAT GETS DRAGGED IN FRONT OF MOMENT ENDS UP AS STONE OR A SHADOW, ONE OF THE TWO.
I'M NOT HALF THE MAN I USED TO BE, BUT IT COULD'VE BEEN WORSE. I COULD HAVE ENDED UP A STATUE.
LOOKS TO ME LIKE YOU GOT OFF EASY, TOO, MISS.
WHAT DO YOU MEAN I—?
I... I NEVER NOTICED!
I DON'T HAVE A SHADOW EITHER!

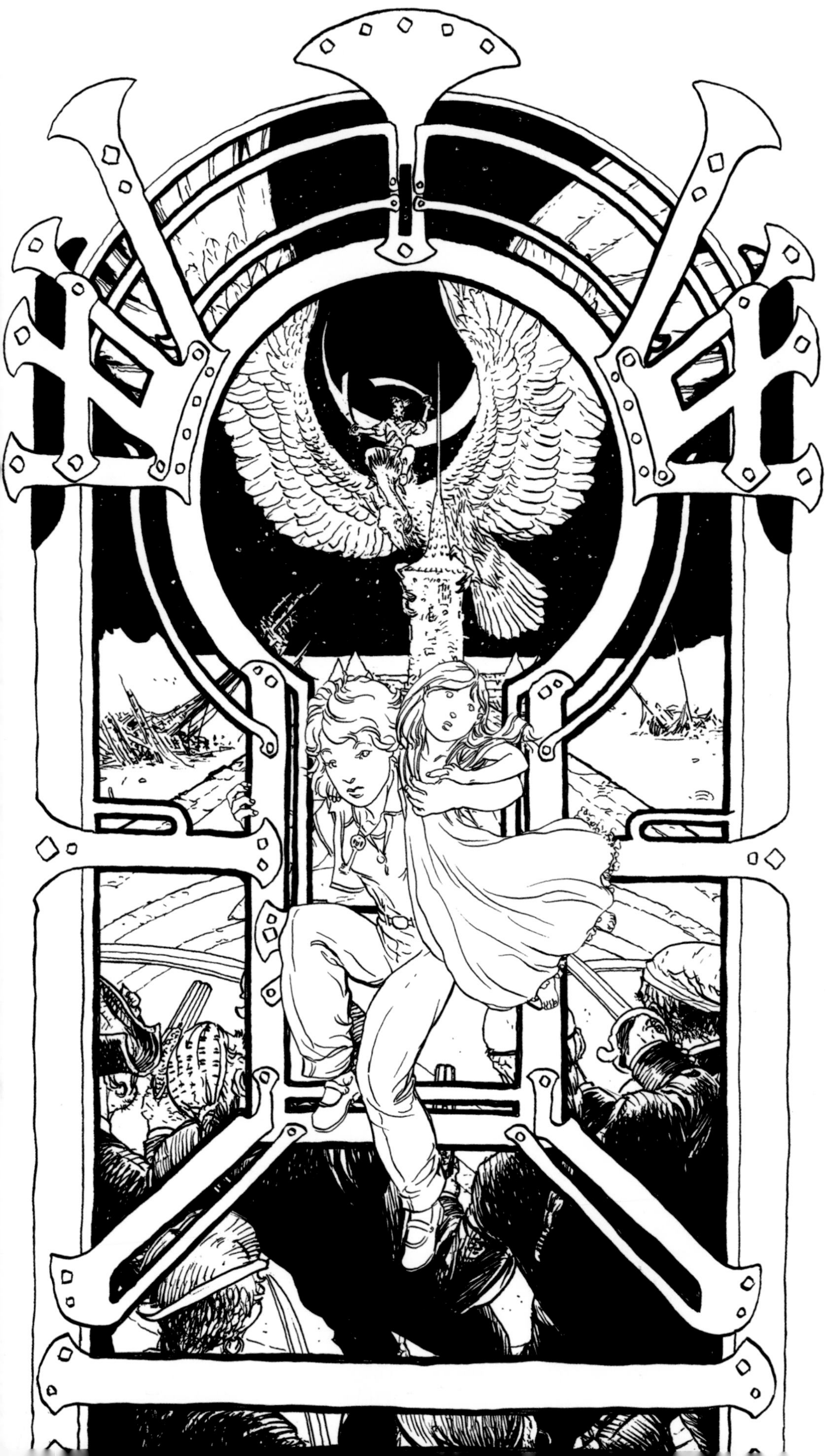

Chapter Five

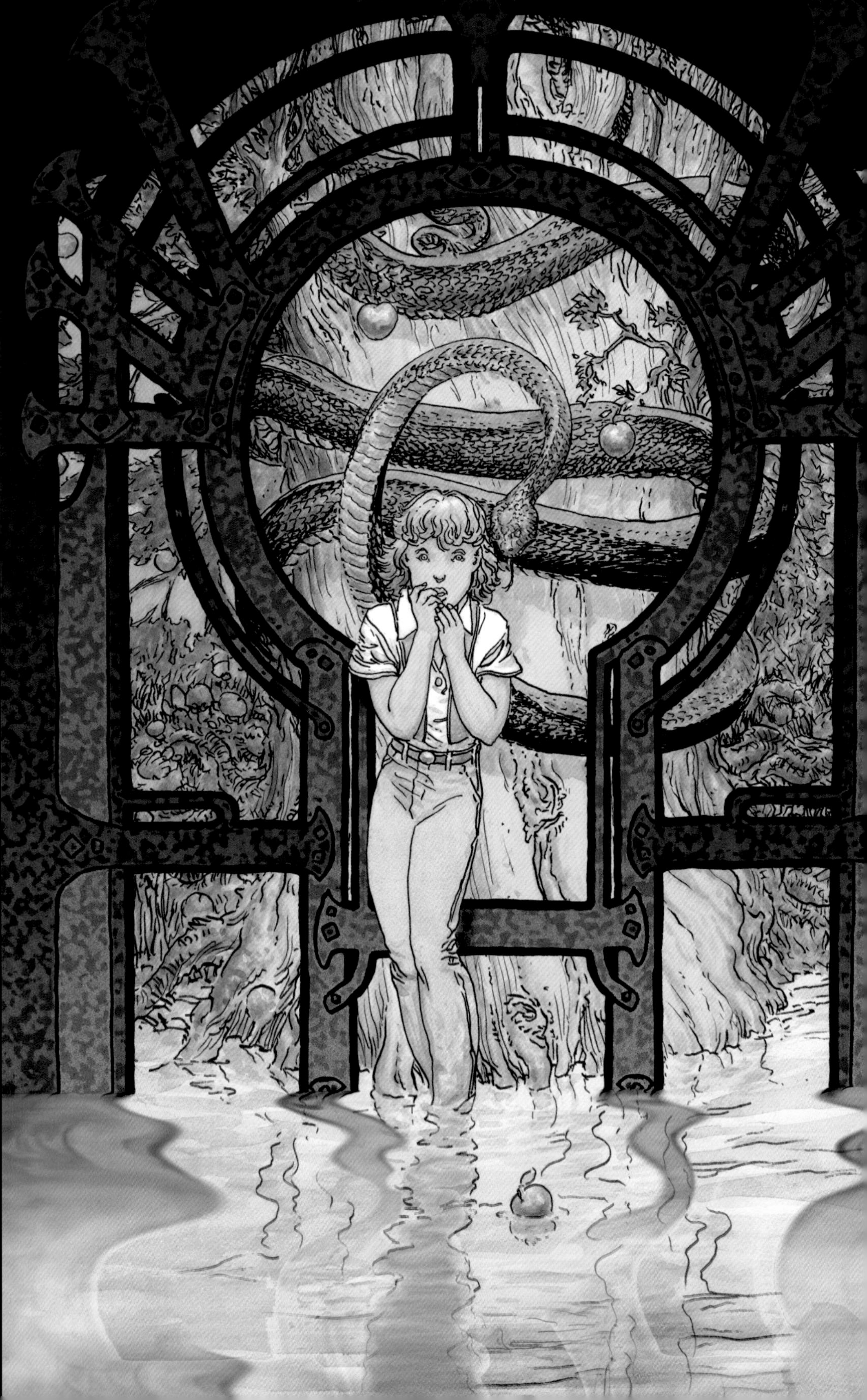

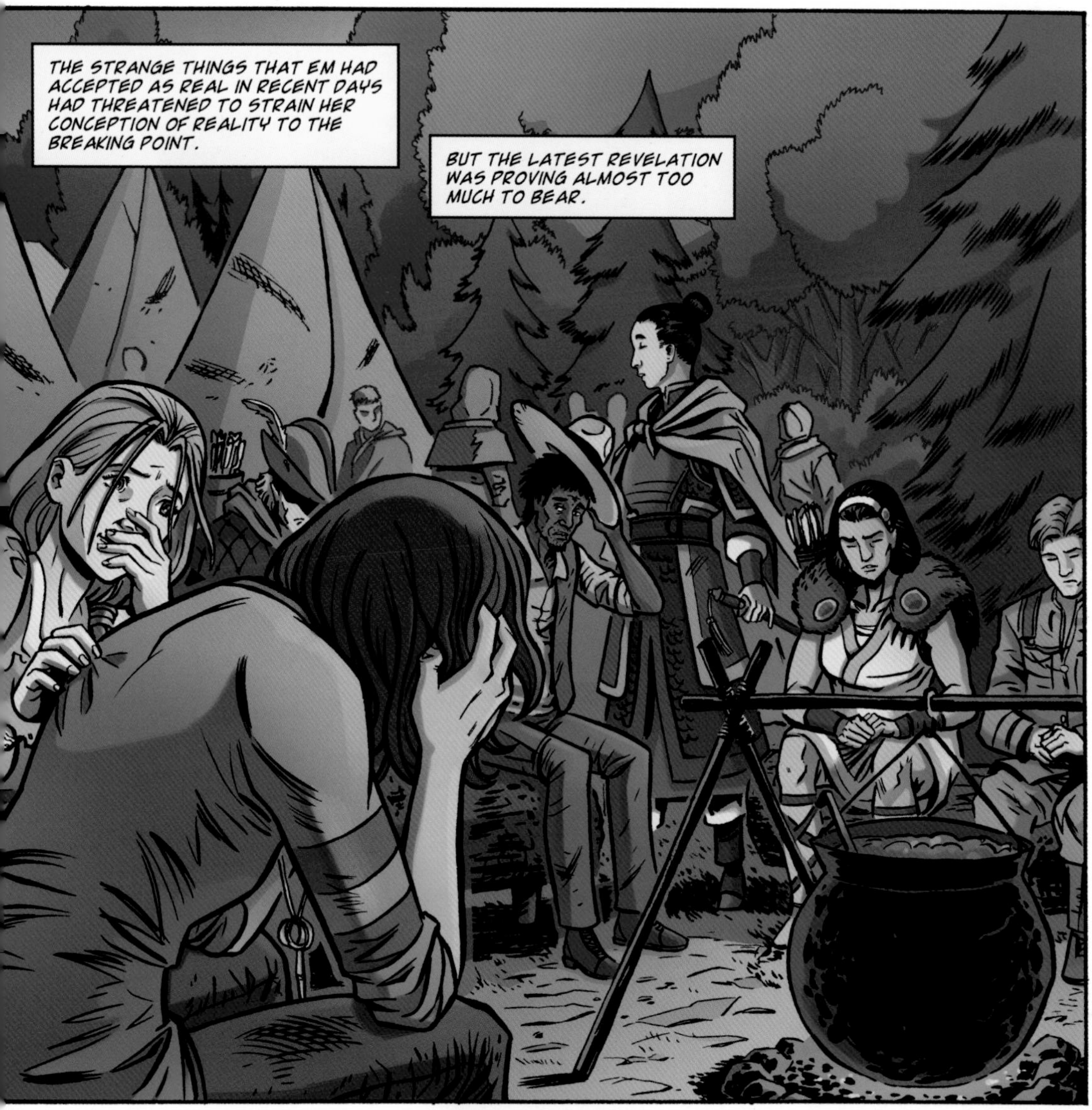
THE STRANGE THINGS THAT EM HAD ACCEPTED AS REAL IN RECENT DAYS HAD THREATENED TO STRAIN HER CONCEPTION OF REALITY TO THE BREAKING POINT.
BUT THE LATEST REVELATION WAS PROVING ALMOST TOO MUCH TO BEAR.

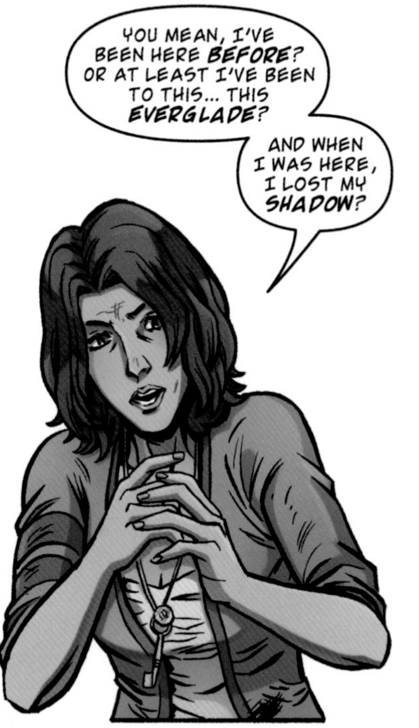
YOU MEAN, I'VE BEEN HERE **BEFORE**? OR AT LEAST I'VE BEEN TO THIS... THIS **EVERGLADE**?
AND WHEN I WAS HERE, I LOST MY **SHADOW**?

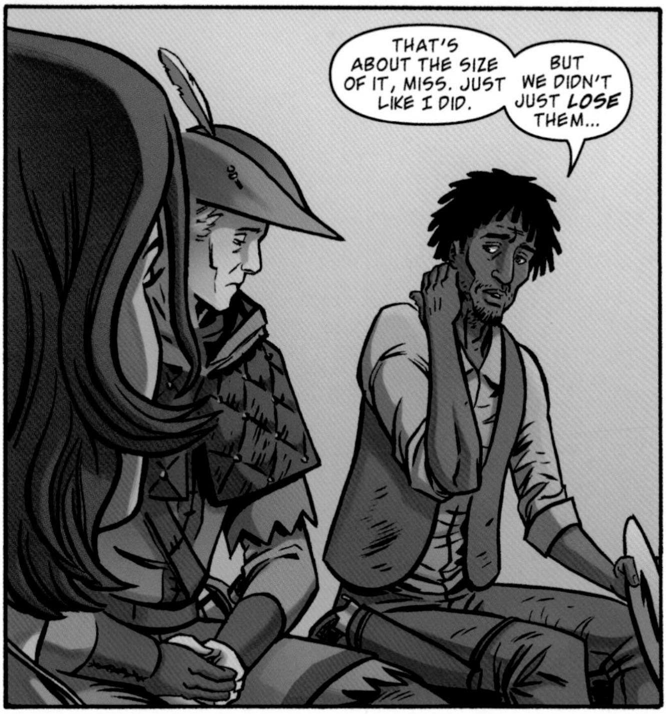
THAT'S ABOUT THE SIZE OF IT, MISS. JUST LIKE I DID.
BUT WE DIDN'T JUST **LOSE** THEM...

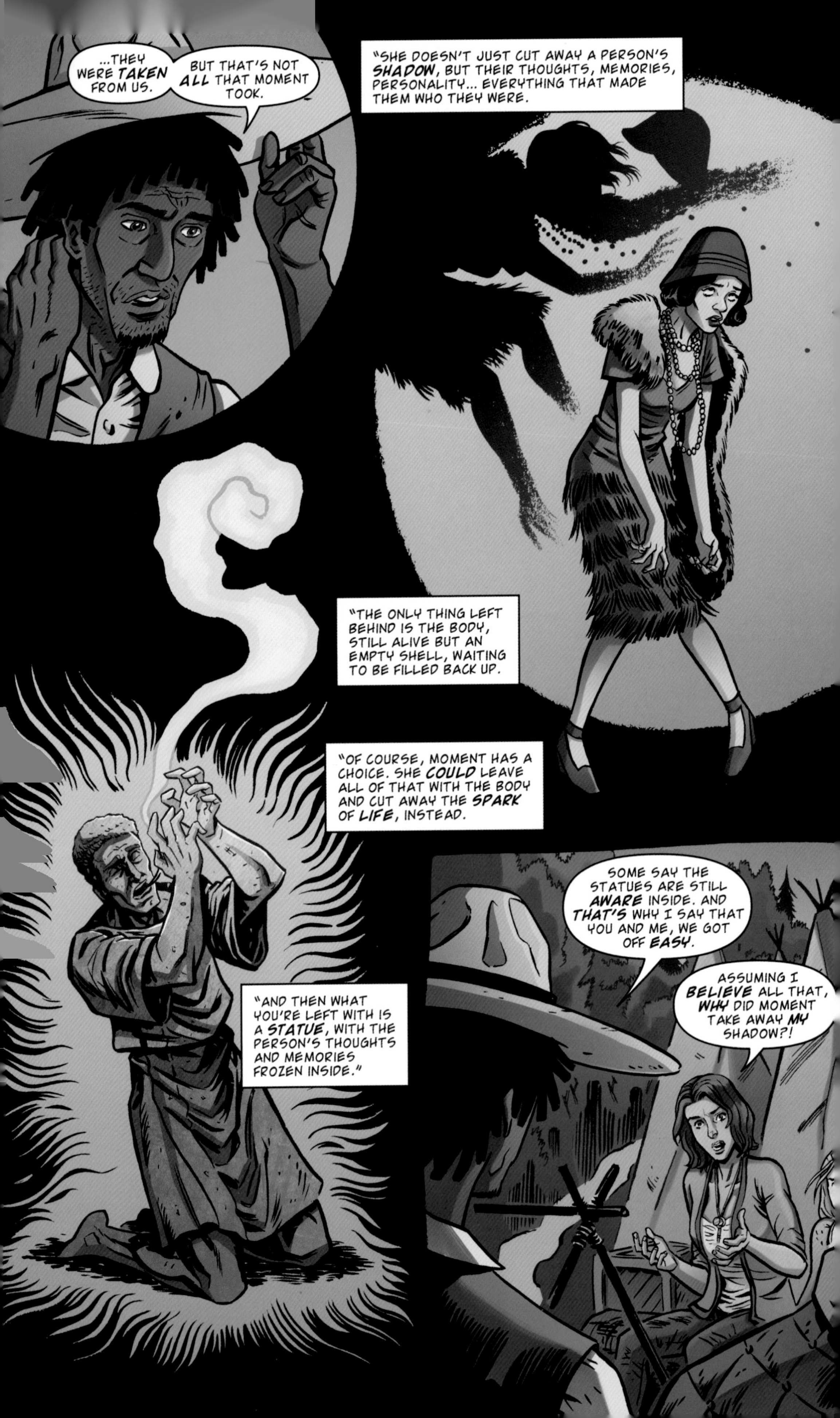
...THEY WERE TAKEN FROM US.
BUT THAT'S NOT ALL THAT MOMENT TOOK.
"SHE DOESN'T JUST CUT AWAY A PERSON'S SHADOW, BUT THEIR THOUGHTS, MEMORIES, PERSONALITY... EVERYTHING THAT MADE THEM WHO THEY WERE.
"THE ONLY THING LEFT BEHIND IS THE BODY, STILL ALIVE BUT AN EMPTY SHELL, WAITING TO BE FILLED BACK UP.
"OF COURSE, MOMENT HAS A CHOICE. SHE COULD LEAVE ALL OF THAT WITH THE BODY AND CUT AWAY THE SPARK OF LIFE, INSTEAD.
"AND THEN WHAT YOU'RE LEFT WITH IS A STATUE, WITH THE PERSON'S THOUGHTS AND MEMORIES FROZEN INSIDE."
SOME SAY THE STATUES ARE STILL AWARE INSIDE. AND THAT'S WHY I SAY THAT YOU AND ME, WE GOT OFF EASY.
ASSUMING I BELIEVE ALL THAT, WHY DID MOMENT TAKE AWAY MY SHADOW?!

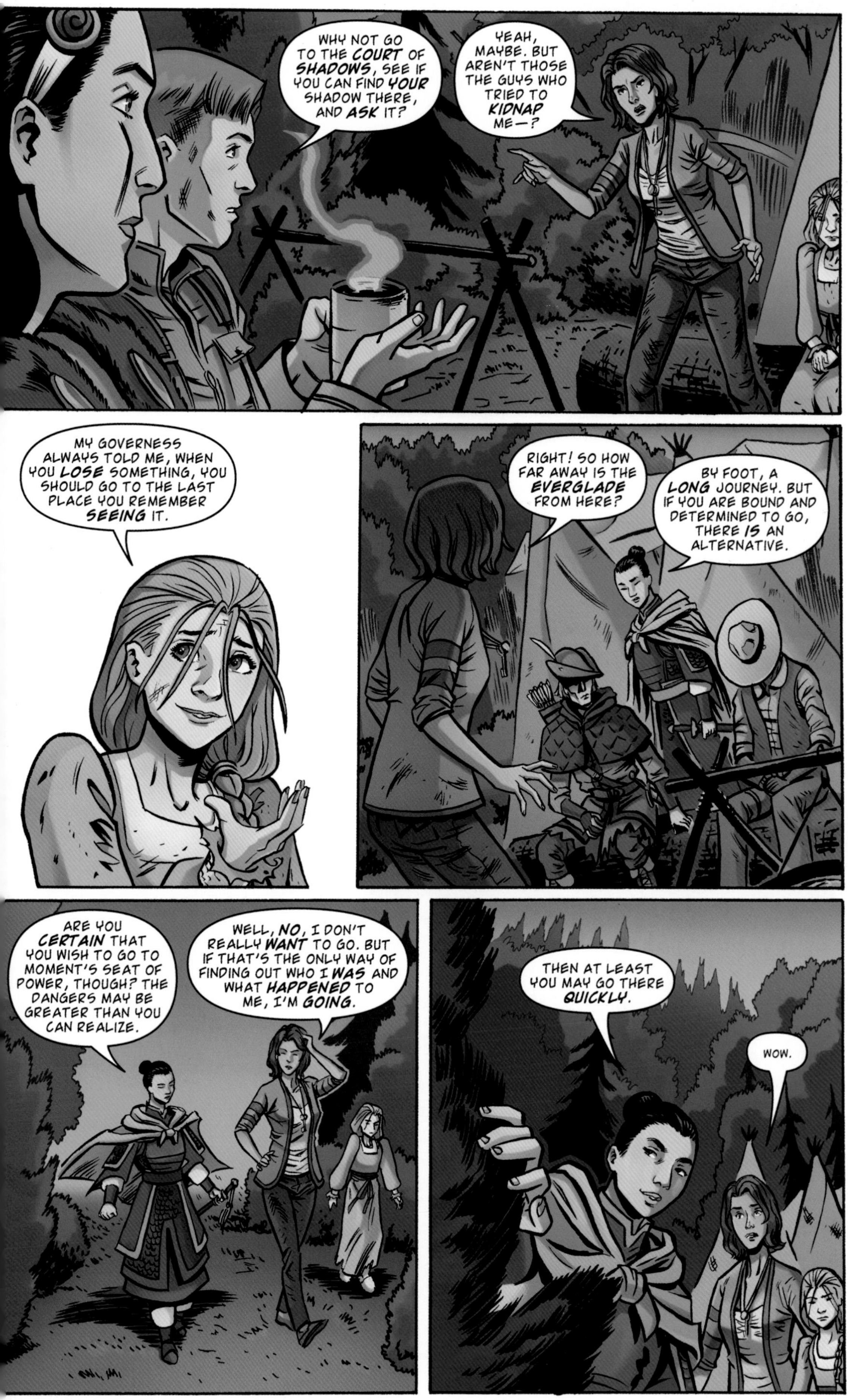
WHY NOT GO TO THE COURT OF SHADOWS, SEE IF YOU CAN FIND YOUR SHADOW THERE, AND ASK IT?
YEAH, MAYBE. BUT AREN'T THOSE THE GUYS WHO TRIED TO KIDNAP ME—?
MY GOVERNESS ALWAYS TOLD ME, WHEN YOU LOSE SOMETHING, YOU SHOULD GO TO THE LAST PLACE YOU REMEMBER SEEING IT.
RIGHT! SO HOW FAR AWAY IS THE EVERGLADE FROM HERE?
BY FOOT, A LONG JOURNEY. BUT IF YOU ARE BOUND AND DETERMINED TO GO, THERE IS AN ALTERNATIVE.
ARE YOU CERTAIN THAT YOU WISH TO GO TO MOMENT'S SEAT OF POWER, THOUGH? THE DANGERS MAY BE GREATER THAN YOU CAN REALIZE.
WELL, NO, I DON'T REALLY WANT TO GO. BUT IF THAT'S THE ONLY WAY OF FINDING OUT WHO I WAS AND WHAT HAPPENED TO ME, I'M GOING.
THEN AT LEAST YOU MAY GO THERE QUICKLY.
WOW.

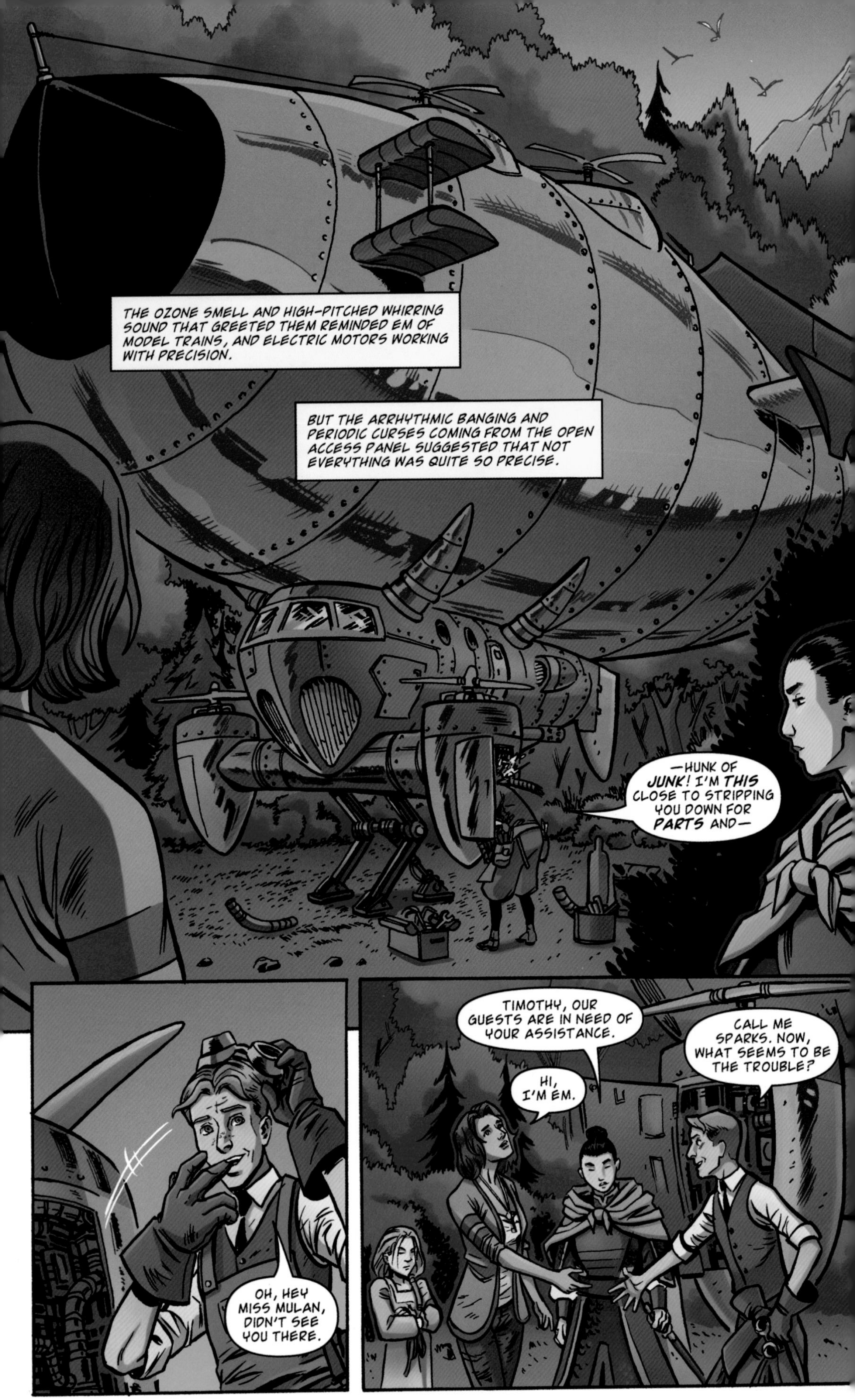
THE OZONE SMELL AND HIGH-PITCHED WHIRRING SOUND THAT GREETED THEM REMINDED EM OF MODEL TRAINS, AND ELECTRIC MOTORS WORKING WITH PRECISION.
BUT THE ARRHYTHMIC BANGING AND PERIODIC CURSES COMING FROM THE OPEN ACCESS PANEL SUGGESTED THAT NOT EVERYTHING WAS QUITE SO PRECISE.
—HUNK OF JUNK! I'M THIS CLOSE TO STRIPPING YOU DOWN FOR PARTS AND—
OH, HEY MISS MULAN, DIDN'T SEE YOU THERE.
TIMOTHY, OUR GUESTS ARE IN NEED OF YOUR ASSISTANCE.
HI, I'M EM.
CALL ME SPARKS. NOW, WHAT SEEMS TO BE THE TROUBLE?

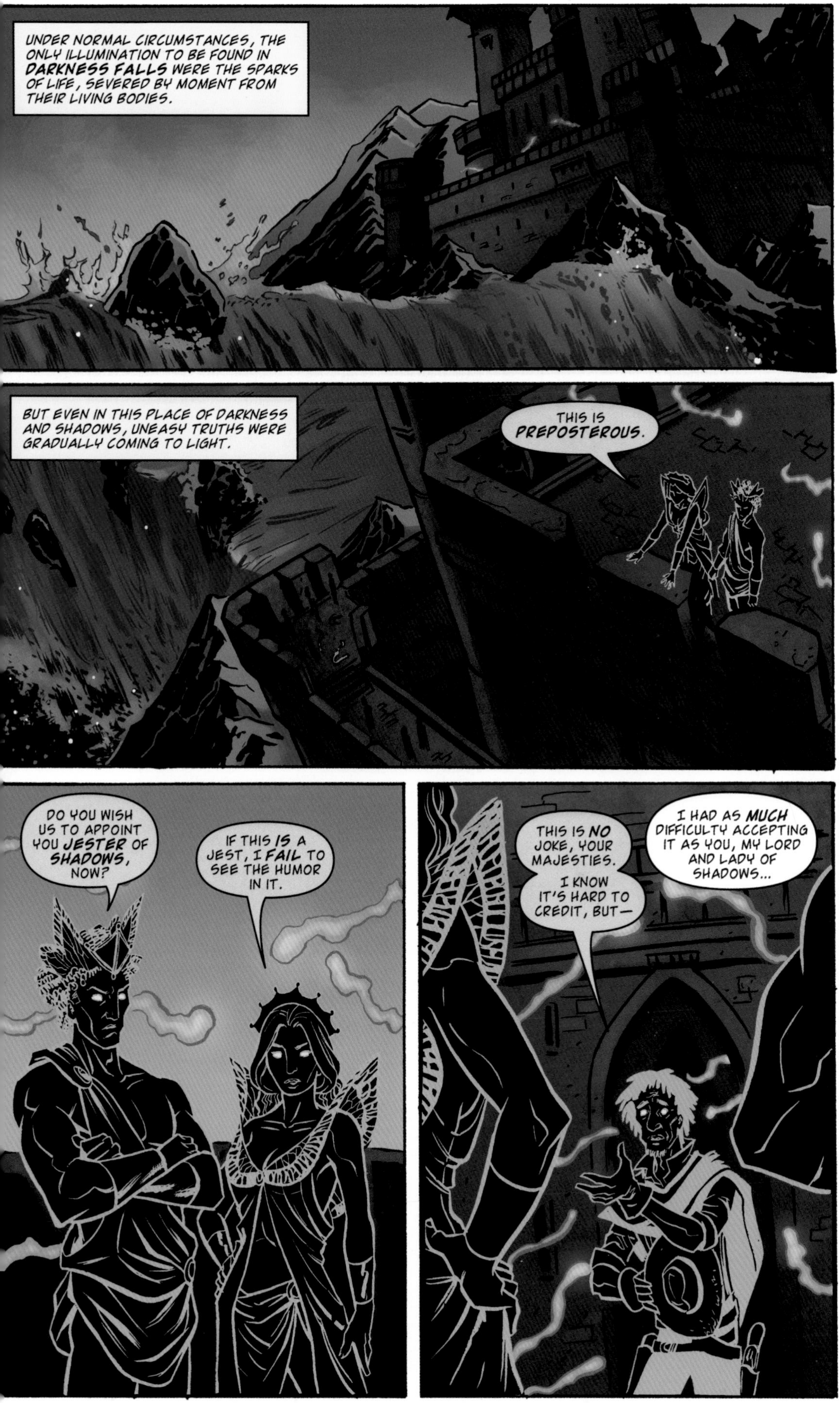
UNDER NORMAL CIRCUMSTANCES, THE ONLY ILLUMINATION TO BE FOUND IN DARKNESS FALLS WERE THE SPARKS OF LIFE, SEVERED BY MOMENT FROM THEIR LIVING BODIES.
BUT EVEN IN THIS PLACE OF DARKNESS AND SHADOWS, UNEASY TRUTHS WERE GRADUALLY COMING TO LIGHT.
THIS IS PREPOSTEROUS.
DO YOU WISH US TO APPOINT YOU JESTER OF SHADOWS, NOW?
IF THIS IS A JEST, I FAIL TO SEE THE HUMOR IN IT.
THIS IS NO JOKE, YOUR MAJESTIES.
I KNOW IT'S HARD TO CREDIT, BUT—
I HAD AS MUCH DIFFICULTY ACCEPTING IT AS YOU, MY LORD AND LADY OF SHADOWS...

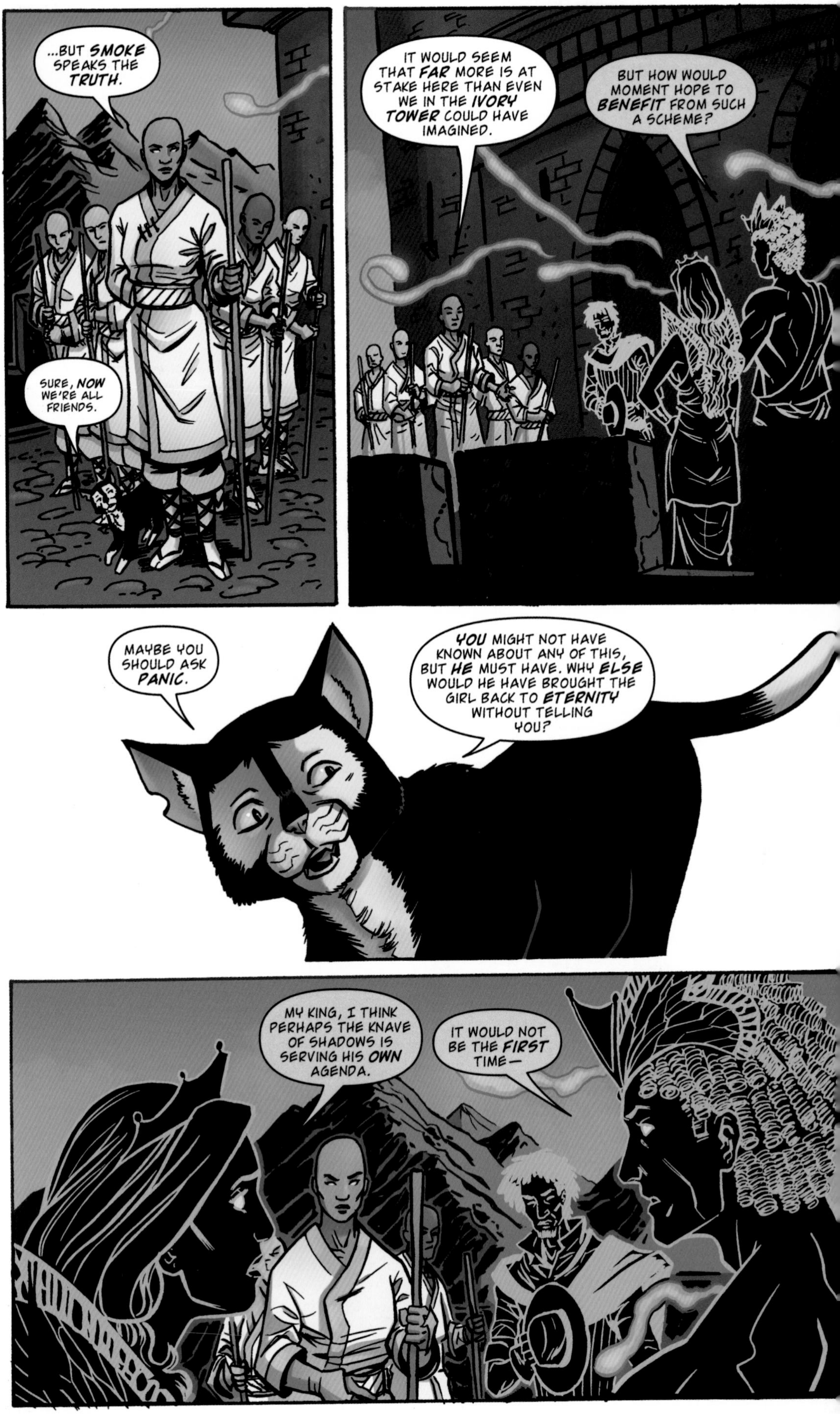
...BUT SMOKE SPEAKS THE TRUTH.
SURE, NOW WE'RE ALL FRIENDS.
IT WOULD SEEM THAT FAR MORE IS AT STAKE HERE THAN EVEN WE IN THE IVORY TOWER COULD HAVE IMAGINED.
BUT HOW WOULD MOMENT HOPE TO BENEFIT FROM SUCH A SCHEME?
MAYBE YOU SHOULD ASK PANIC.
YOU MIGHT NOT HAVE KNOWN ABOUT ANY OF THIS, BUT HE MUST HAVE. WHY ELSE WOULD HE HAVE BROUGHT THE GIRL BACK TO ETERNITY WITHOUT TELLING YOU?
MY KING, I THINK PERHAPS THE KNAVE OF SHADOWS IS SERVING HIS OWN AGENDA.
IT WOULD NOT BE THE FIRST TIME—

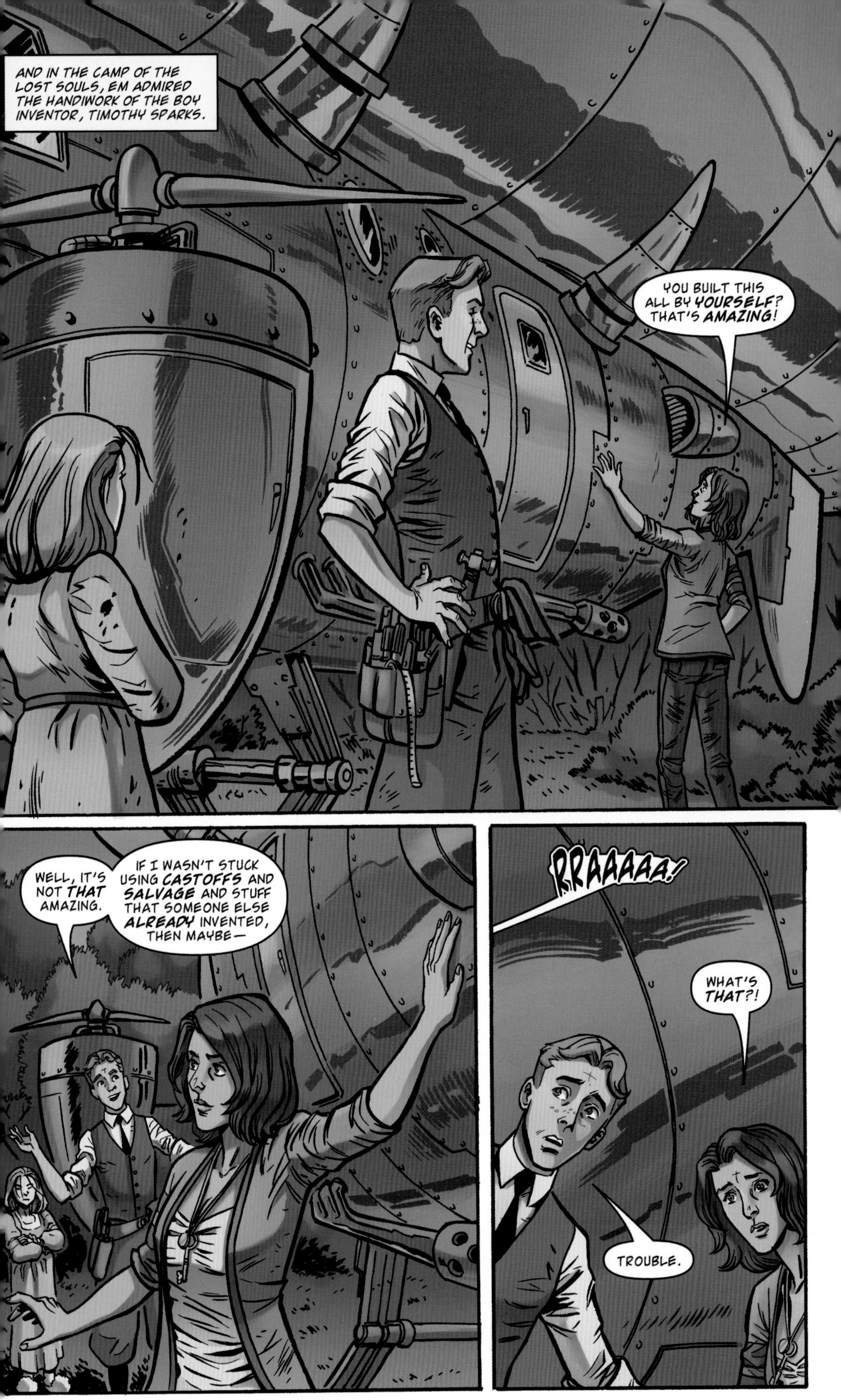
AND IN THE CAMP OF THE LOST SOULS, EM ADMIRED THE HANDIWORK OF THE BOY INVENTOR, TIMOTHY SPARKS.
YOU BUILT THIS ALL BY YOURSELF? THAT'S AMAZING!
WELL, IT'S NOT THAT AMAZING.
IF I WASN'T STUCK USING CASTOFFS AND SALVAGE AND STUFF THAT SOMEONE ELSE ALREADY INVENTED, THEN MAYBE—
RRAAAAA!
WHAT'S THAT?!
TROUBLE.

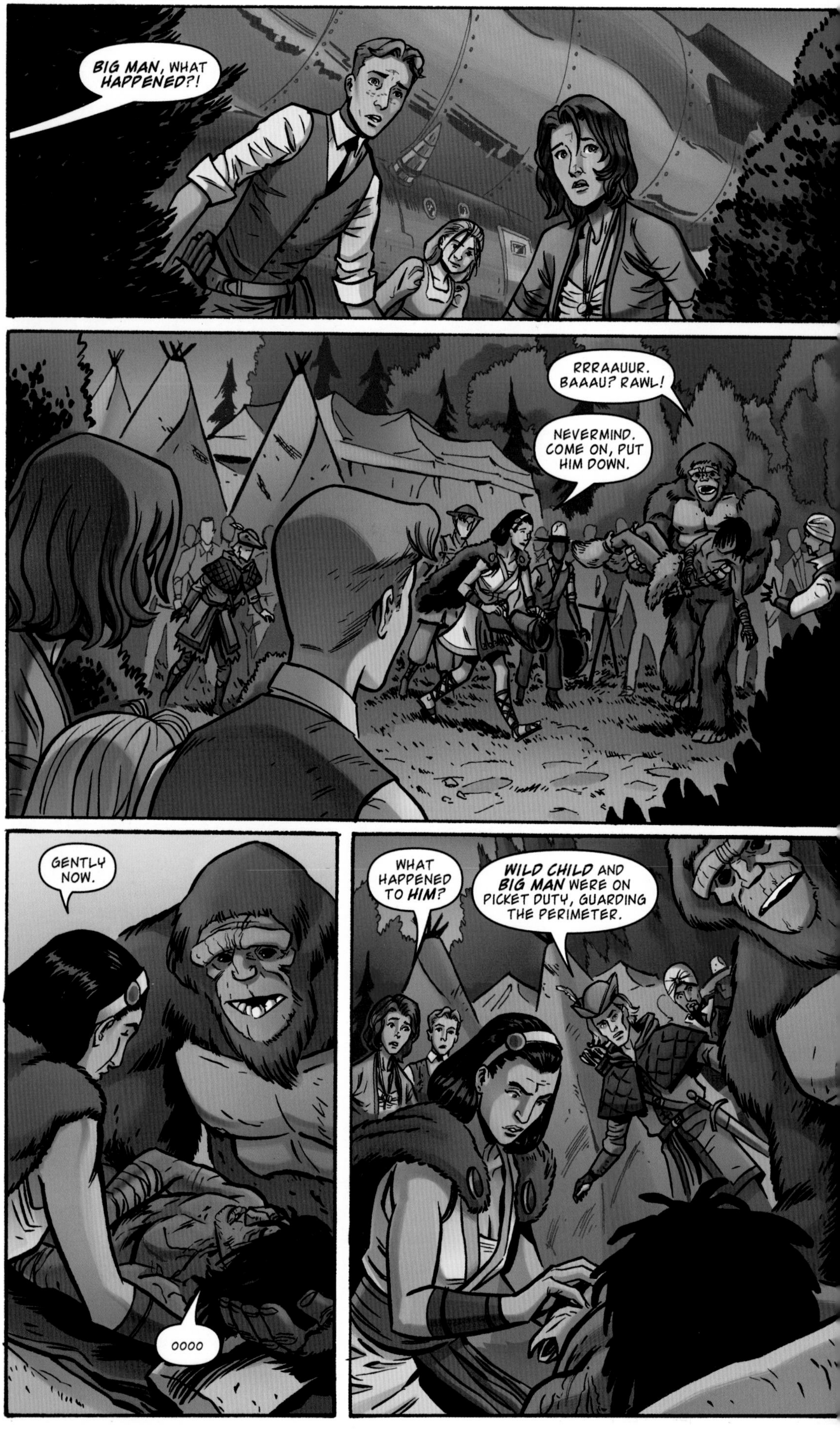

BIG MAN, WHAT HAPPENED?!
RRRAAUUR. BAAAU? RAWL!
NEVERMIND. COME ON, PUT HIM DOWN.
GENTLY NOW.
OOOO
WHAT HAPPENED TO HIM?
WILD CHILD AND BIG MAN WERE ON PICKET DUTY, GUARDING THE PERIMETER.

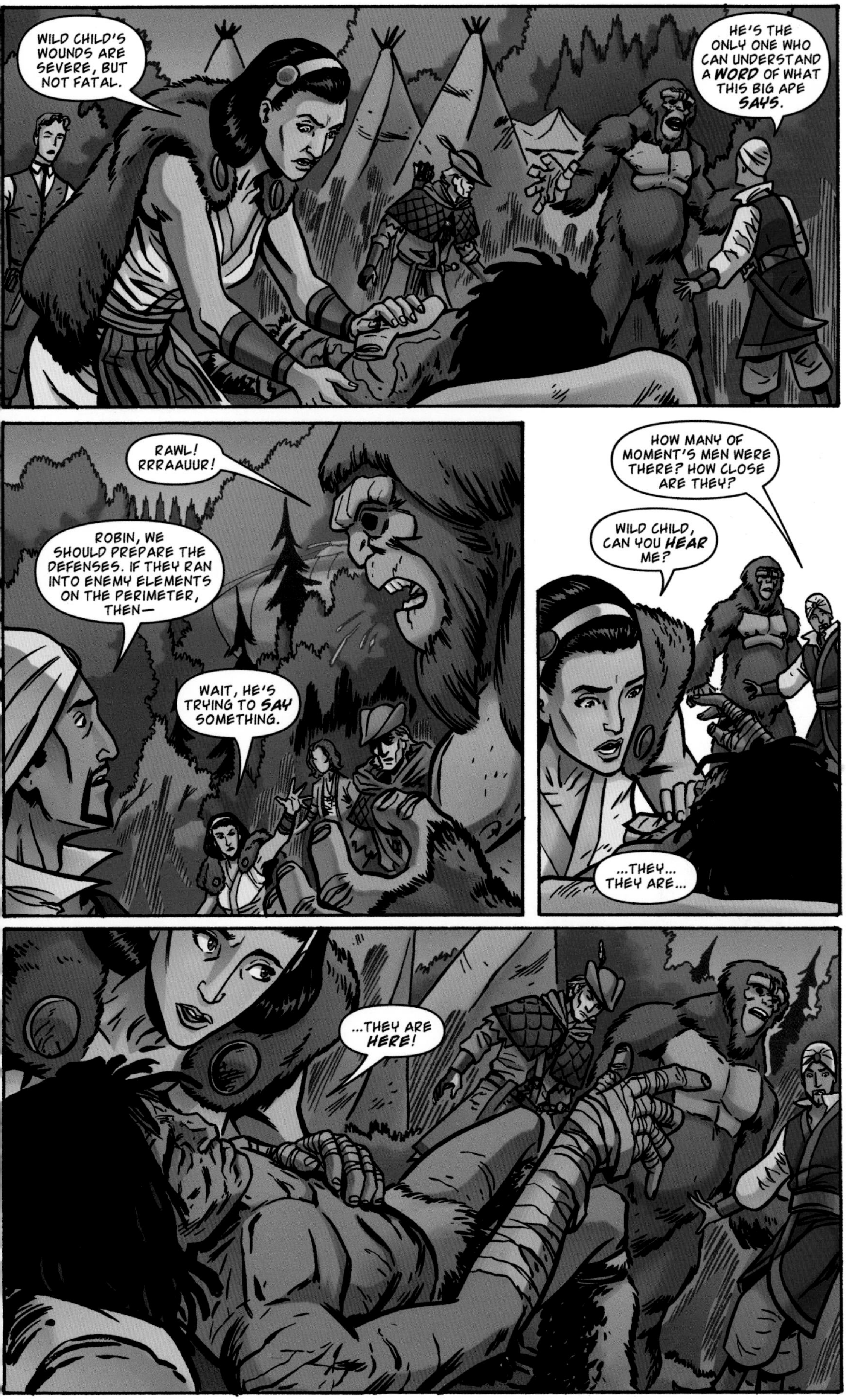
WILD CHILD'S WOUNDS ARE SEVERE, BUT NOT FATAL.
HE'S THE ONLY ONE WHO CAN UNDERSTAND A WORD OF WHAT THIS BIG APE SAYS.
RAWL! RRRAAUUR!
ROBIN, WE SHOULD PREPARE THE DEFENSES. IF THEY RAN INTO ENEMY ELEMENTS ON THE PERIMETER, THEN—
WAIT, HE'S TRYING TO SAY SOMETHING.
HOW MANY OF MOMENT'S MEN WERE THERE? HOW CLOSE ARE THEY?
WILD CHILD, CAN YOU HEAR ME?
...THEY... THEY ARE...
...THEY ARE HERE!

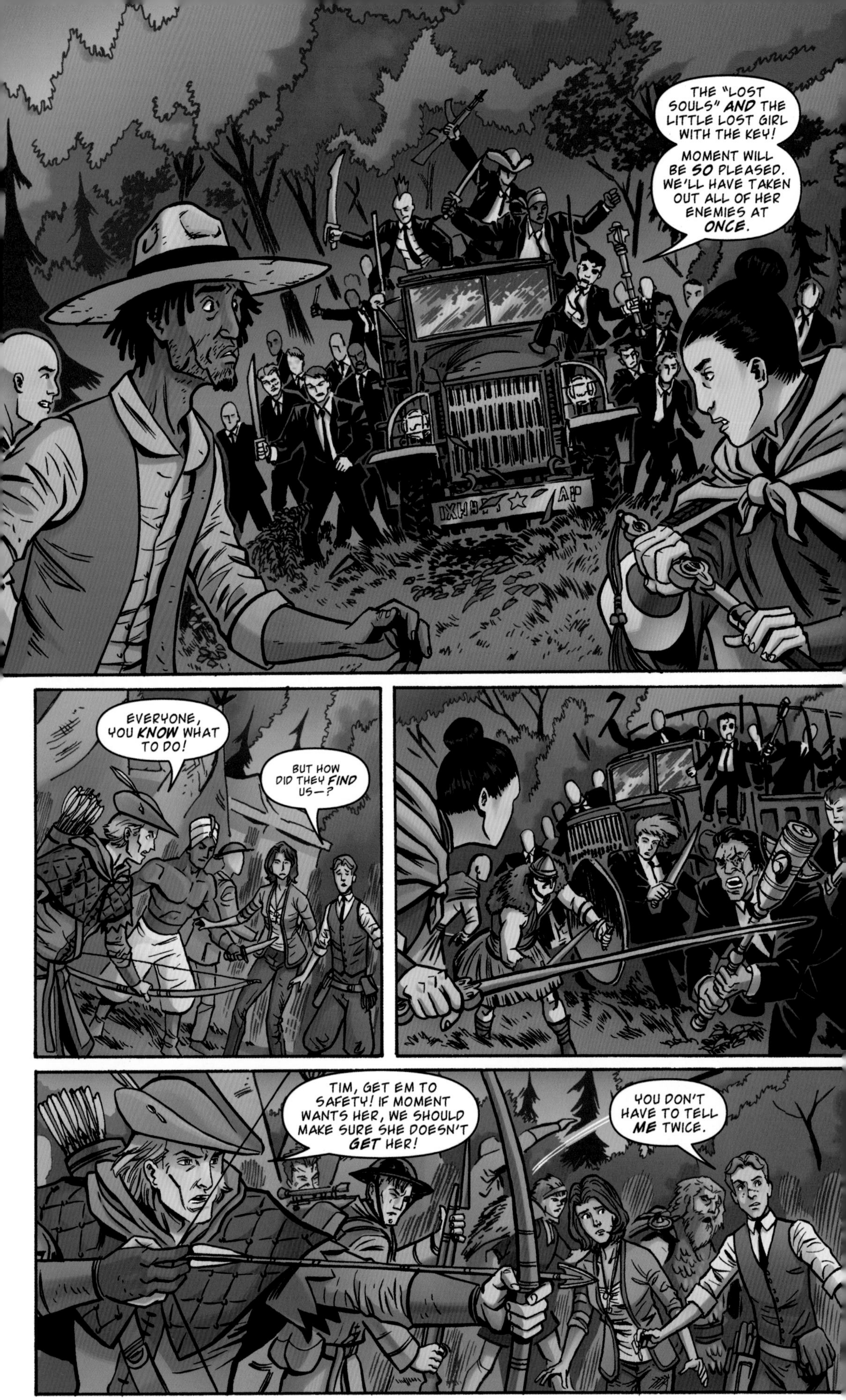
THE "LOST SOULS" AND THE LITTLE LOST GIRL WITH THE KEY!
MOMENT WILL BE SO PLEASED. WE'LL HAVE TAKEN OUT ALL OF HER ENEMIES AT ONCE.
EVERYONE, YOU KNOW WHAT TO DO!
BUT HOW DID THEY FIND US—?
TIM, GET EM TO SAFETY! IF MOMENT WANTS HER, WE SHOULD MAKE SURE SHE DOESN'T GET HER!
YOU DON'T HAVE TO TELL ME TWICE.

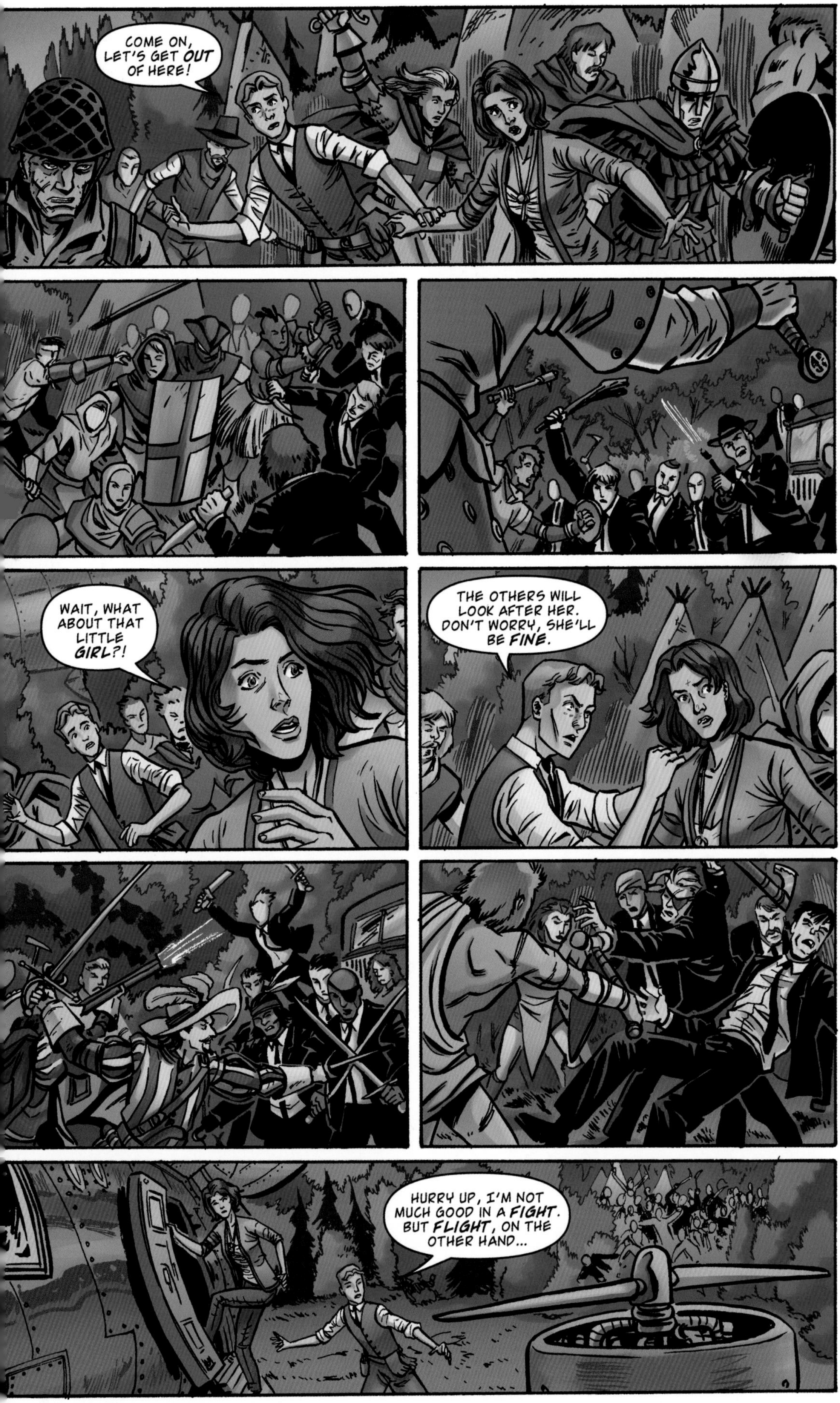
COME ON, LET'S GET OUT OF HERE!
WAIT, WHAT ABOUT THAT LITTLE GIRL?!
THE OTHERS WILL LOOK AFTER HER. DON'T WORRY, SHE'LL BE FINE.
HURRY UP, I'M NOT MUCH GOOD IN A FIGHT. BUT FLIGHT, ON THE OTHER HAND...

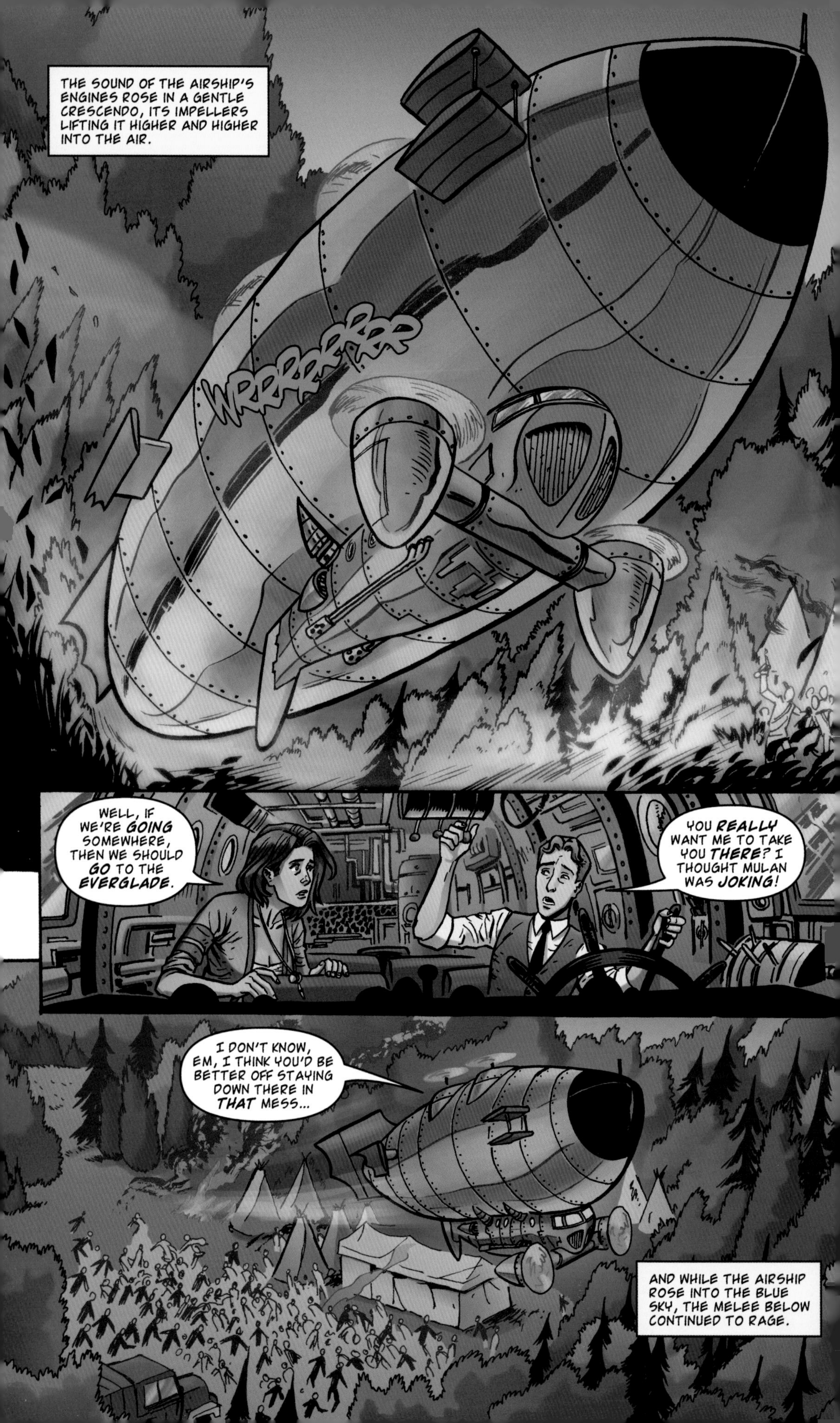
THE SOUND OF THE AIRSHIP'S ENGINES ROSE IN A GENTLE CRESCENDO, ITS IMPELLERS LIFTING IT HIGHER AND HIGHER INTO THE AIR.
WRRRRRRRR
WELL, IF WE'RE GOING SOMEWHERE, THEN WE SHOULD GO TO THE EVERGLADE.
YOU REALLY WANT ME TO TAKE YOU THERE? I THOUGHT MULAN WAS JOKING!
I DON'T KNOW, EM, I THINK YOU'D BE BETTER OFF STAYING DOWN THERE IN THAT MESS...
AND WHILE THE AIRSHIP ROSE INTO THE BLUE SKY, THE MELEE BELOW CONTINUED TO RAGE.

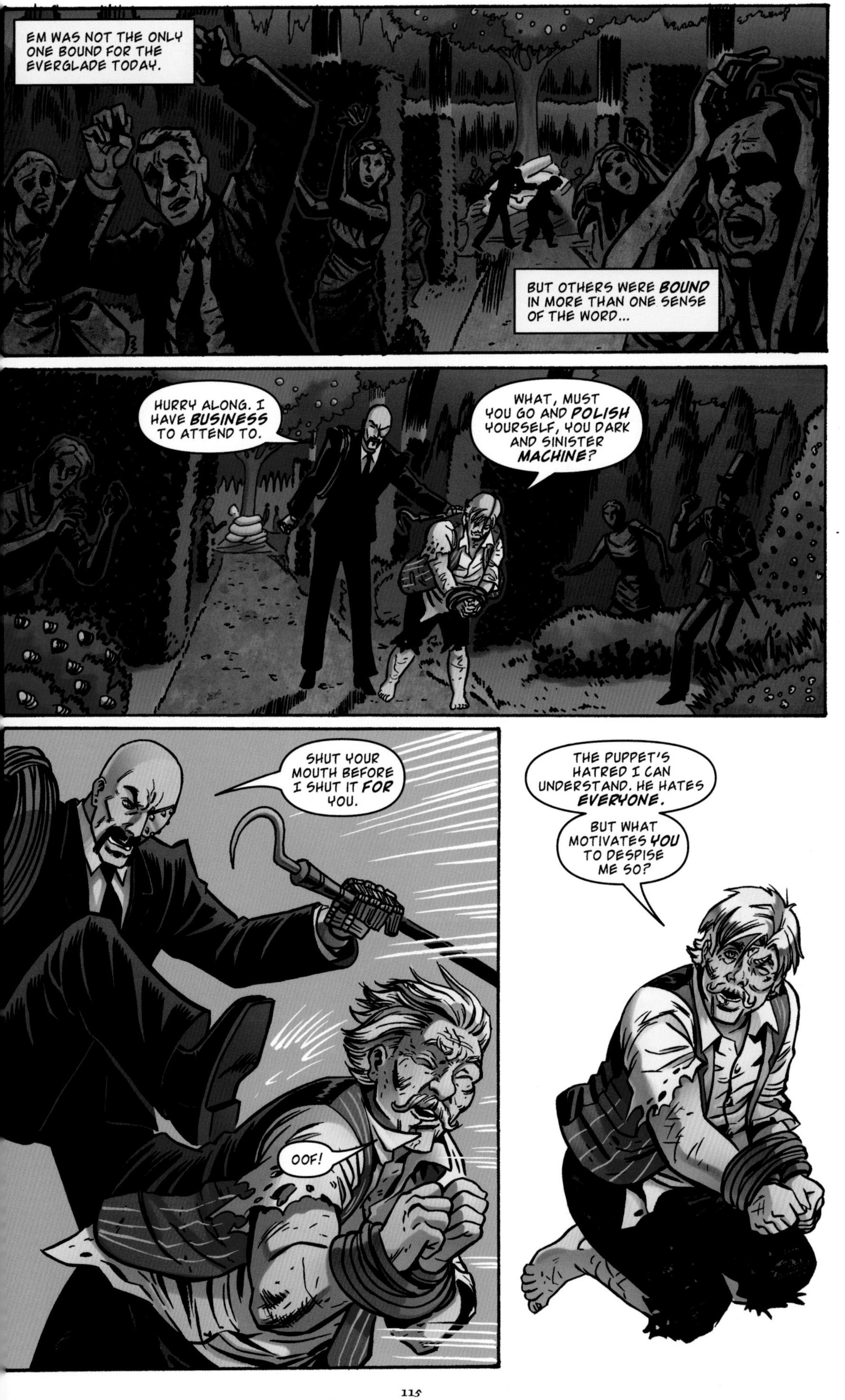
EM WAS NOT THE ONLY ONE BOUND FOR THE EVERGLADE TODAY.
BUT OTHERS WERE BOUND IN MORE THAN ONE SENSE OF THE WORD...
HURRY ALONG. I HAVE BUSINESS TO ATTEND TO.
WHAT, MUST YOU GO AND POLISH YOURSELF, YOU DARK AND SINISTER MACHINE?
SHUT YOUR MOUTH BEFORE I SHUT IT FOR YOU.
OOF!
THE PUPPET'S HATRED I CAN UNDERSTAND. HE HATES EVERYONE.
BUT WHAT MOTIVATES YOU TO DESPISE ME SO?

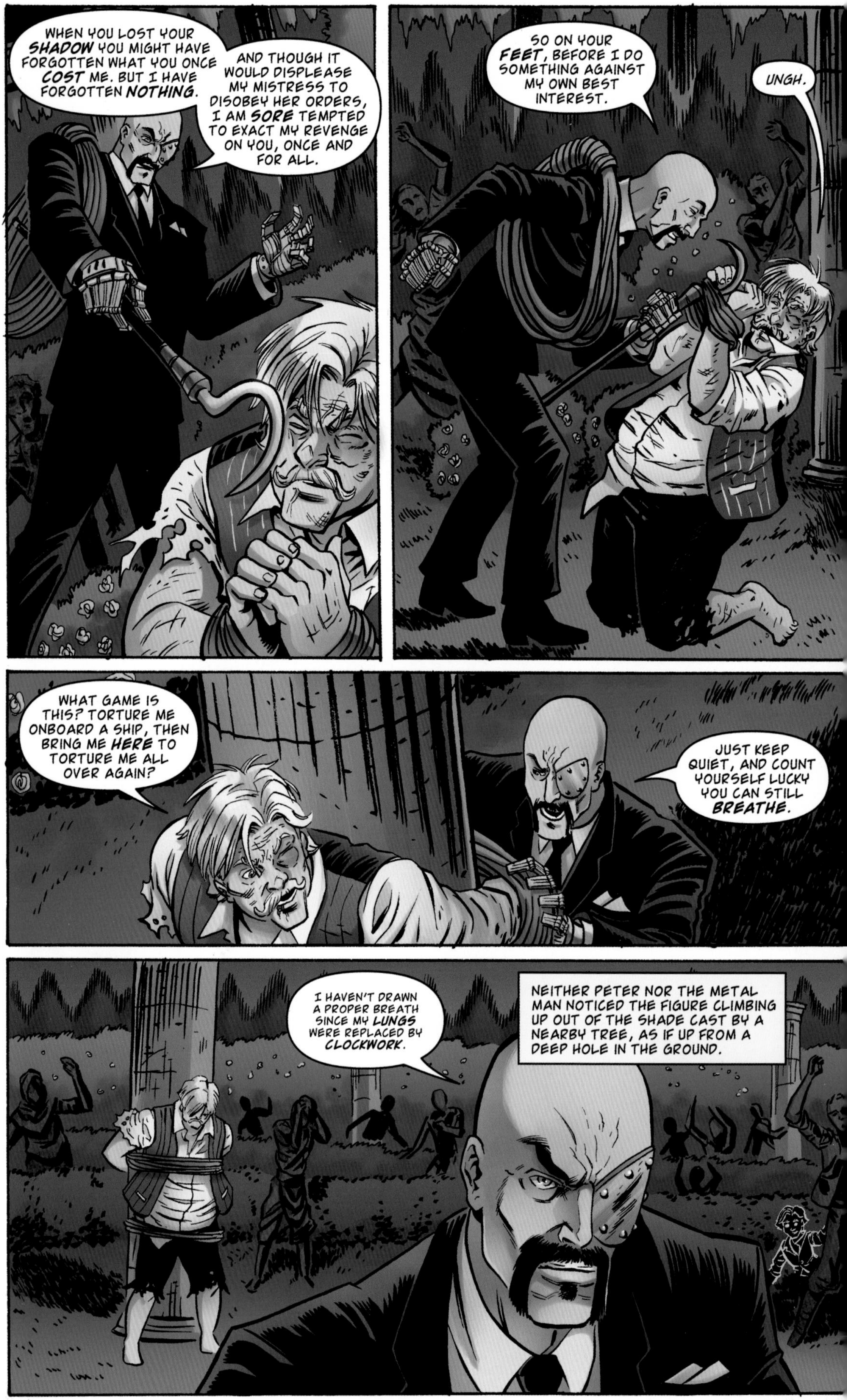
WHEN YOU LOST YOUR SHADOW YOU MIGHT HAVE FORGOTTEN WHAT YOU ONCE COST ME. BUT I HAVE FORGOTTEN NOTHING.
AND THOUGH IT WOULD DISPLEASE MY MISTRESS TO DISOBEY HER ORDERS, I AM SORE TEMPTED TO EXACT MY REVENGE ON YOU, ONCE AND FOR ALL.
SO ON YOUR FEET, BEFORE I DO SOMETHING AGAINST MY OWN BEST INTEREST.
UNGH.
WHAT GAME IS THIS? TORTURE ME ONBOARD A SHIP, THEN BRING ME HERE TO TORTURE ME ALL OVER AGAIN?
JUST KEEP QUIET, AND COUNT YOURSELF LUCKY YOU CAN STILL BREATHE.
I HAVEN'T DRAWN A PROPER BREATH SINCE MY LUNGS WERE REPLACED BY CLOCKWORK.
NEITHER PETER NOR THE METAL MAN NOTICED THE FIGURE CLIMBING UP OUT OF THE SHADE CAST BY A NEARBY TREE, AS IF UP FROM A DEEP HOLE IN THE GROUND.

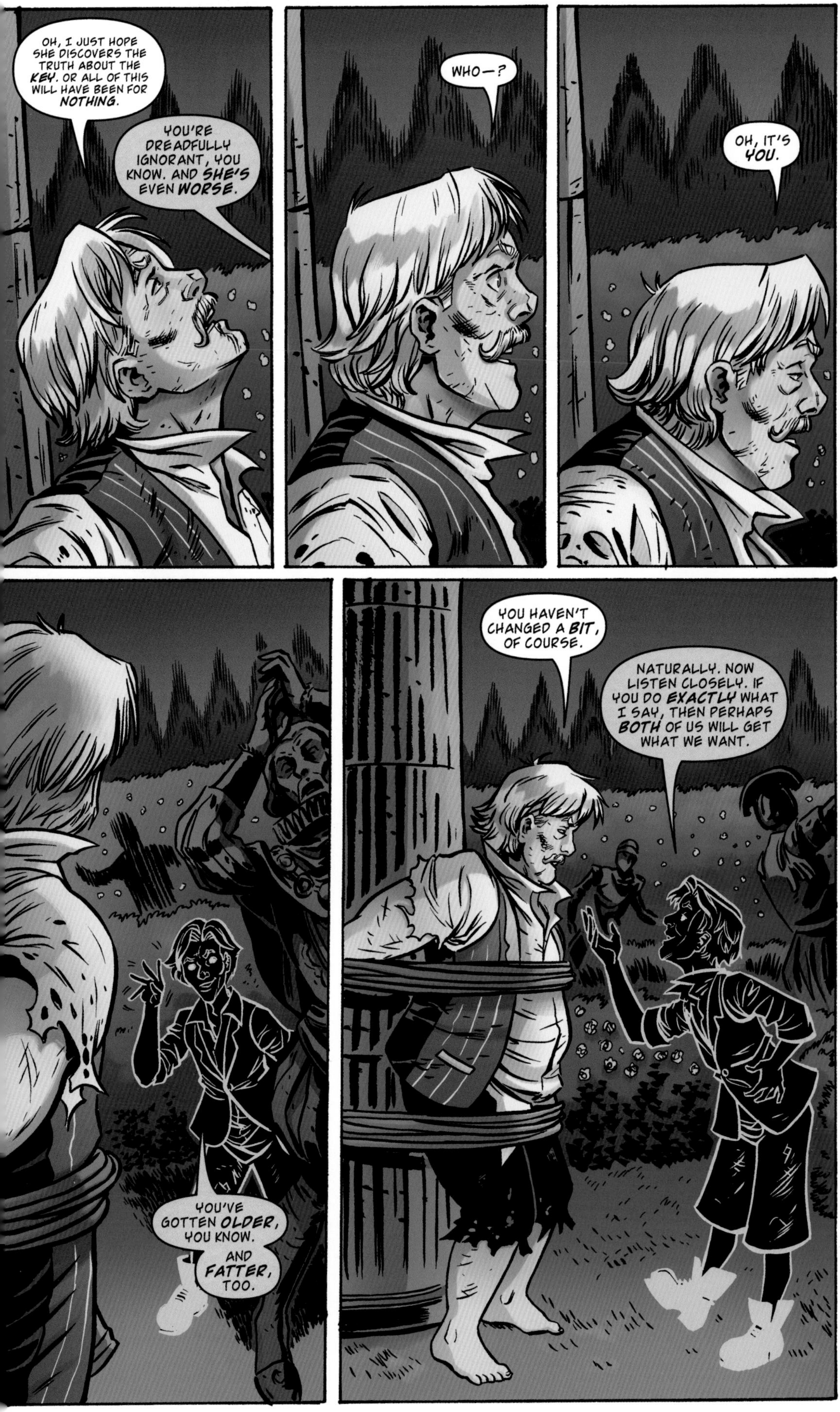
OH, I JUST HOPE SHE DISCOVERS THE TRUTH ABOUT THE KEY. OR ALL OF THIS WILL HAVE BEEN FOR NOTHING.
YOU'RE DREADFULLY IGNORANT, YOU KNOW. AND SHE'S EVEN WORSE.
WHO—?
OH, IT'S YOU.
YOU'VE GOTTEN OLDER, YOU KNOW.
AND FATTER, TOO.
YOU HAVEN'T CHANGED A BIT, OF COURSE.
NATURALLY. NOW LISTEN CLOSELY. IF YOU DO EXACTLY WHAT I SAY, THEN PERHAPS BOTH OF US WILL GET WHAT WE WANT.

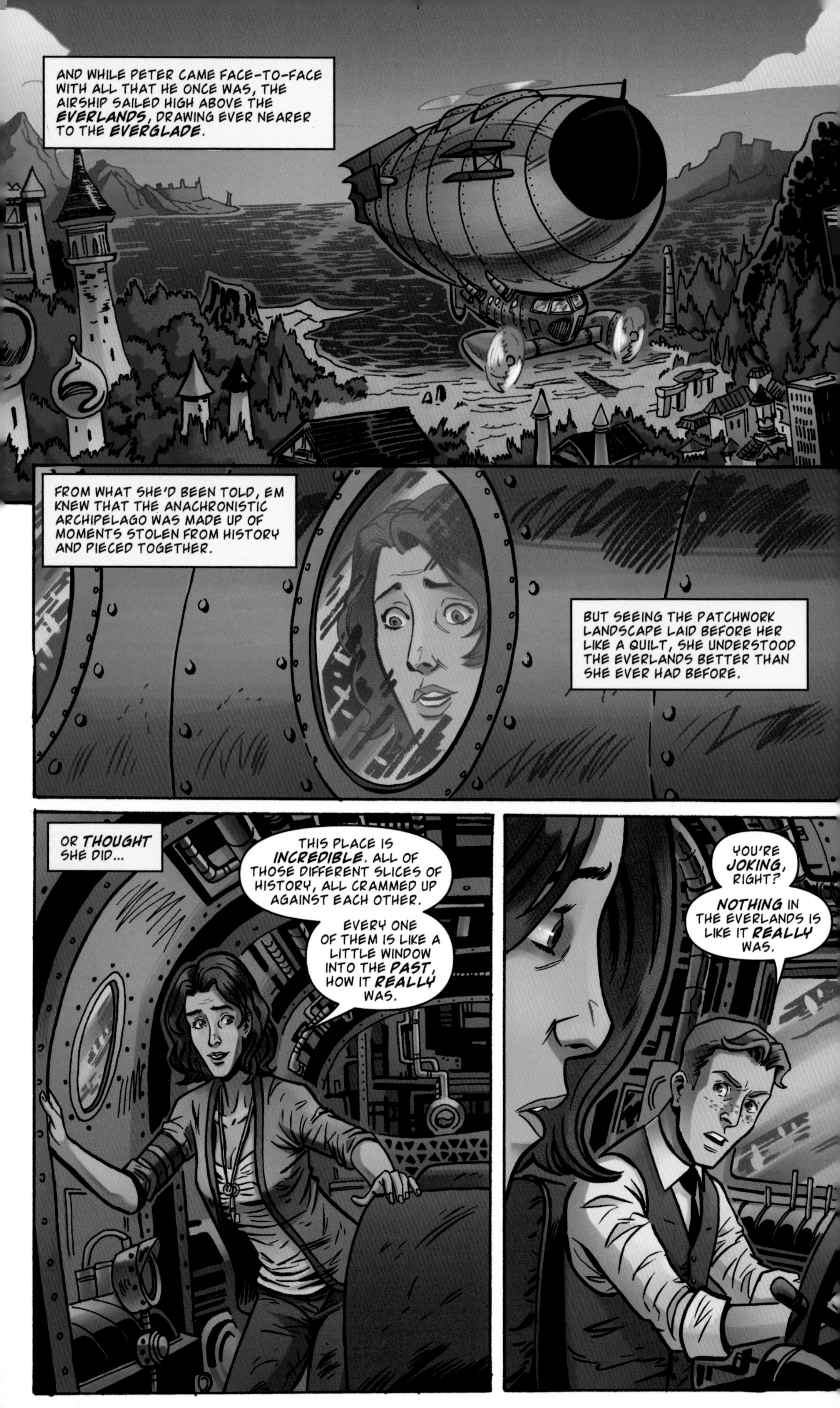
AND WHILE PETER CAME FACE-TO-FACE WITH ALL THAT HE ONCE WAS, THE AIRSHIP SAILED HIGH ABOVE THE EVERLANDS, DRAWING EVER NEARER TO THE EVERGLADE.
FROM WHAT SHE'D BEEN TOLD, EM KNEW THAT THE ANACHRONISTIC ARCHIPELAGO WAS MADE UP OF MOMENTS STOLEN FROM HISTORY AND PIECED TOGETHER.
BUT SEEING THE PATCHWORK LANDSCAPE LAID BEFORE HER LIKE A QUILT, SHE UNDERSTOOD THE EVERLANDS BETTER THAN SHE EVER HAD BEFORE.
OR THOUGHT SHE DID...
THIS PLACE IS INCREDIBLE. ALL OF THOSE DIFFERENT SLICES OF HISTORY, ALL CRAMMED UP AGAINST EACH OTHER.
EVERY ONE OF THEM IS LIKE A LITTLE WINDOW INTO THE PAST, HOW IT REALLY WAS.
YOU'RE JOKING, RIGHT?
NOTHING IN THE EVERLANDS IS LIKE IT REALLY WAS.

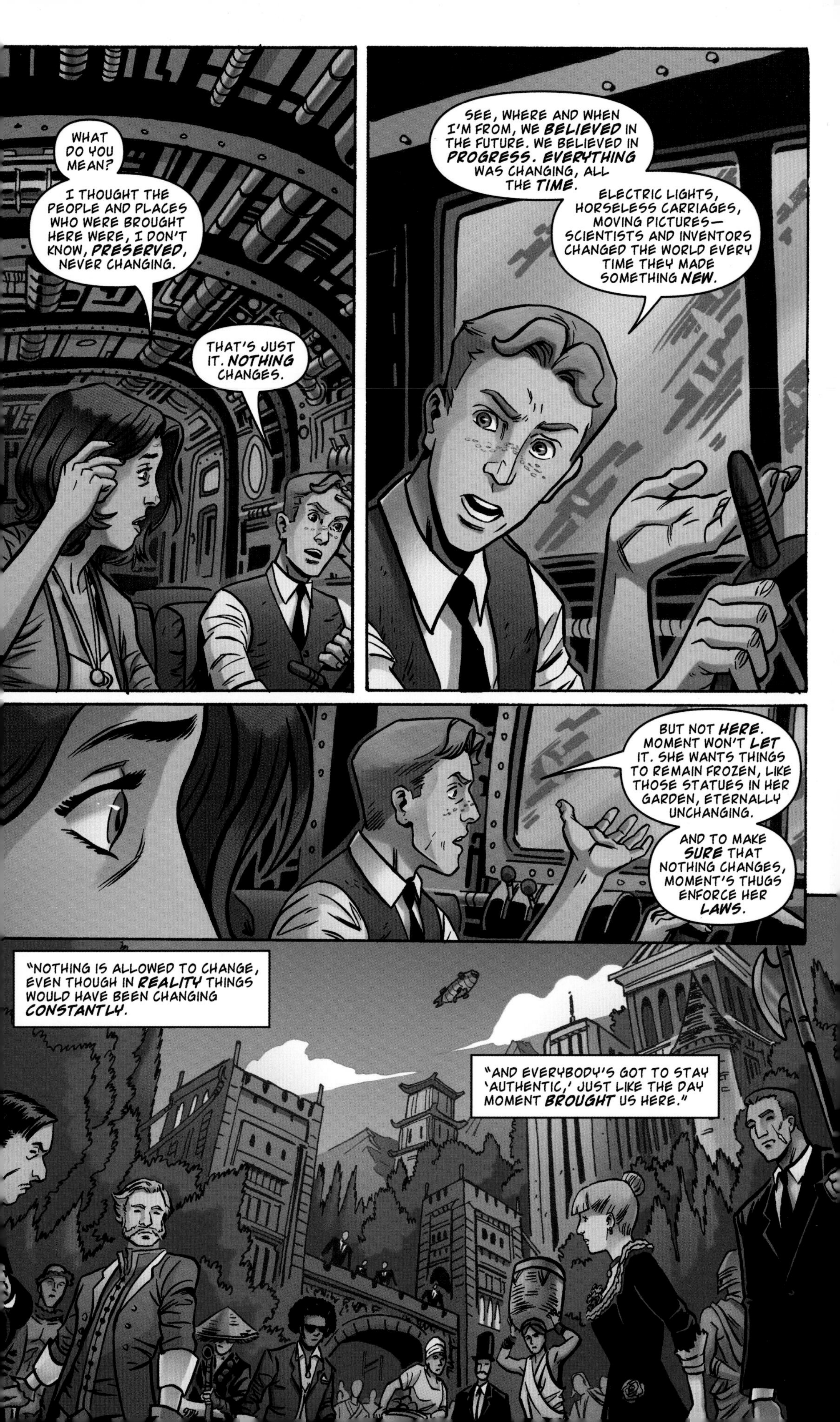
WHAT DO YOU MEAN?
I THOUGHT THE PEOPLE AND PLACES WHO WERE BROUGHT HERE WERE, I DON'T KNOW, PRESERVED, NEVER CHANGING.
THAT'S JUST IT. NOTHING CHANGES.
SEE, WHERE AND WHEN I'M FROM, WE BELIEVED IN THE FUTURE. WE BELIEVED IN PROGRESS. EVERYTHING WAS CHANGING, ALL THE TIME.
ELECTRIC LIGHTS, HORSELESS CARRIAGES, MOVING PICTURES—SCIENTISTS AND INVENTORS CHANGED THE WORLD EVERY TIME THEY MADE SOMETHING NEW.
BUT NOT HERE. MOMENT WON'T LET IT. SHE WANTS THINGS TO REMAIN FROZEN, LIKE THOSE STATUES IN HER GARDEN, ETERNALLY UNCHANGING.
AND TO MAKE SURE THAT NOTHING CHANGES, MOMENT'S THUGS ENFORCE HER LAWS.
"NOTHING IS ALLOWED TO CHANGE, EVEN THOUGH IN REALITY THINGS WOULD HAVE BEEN CHANGING CONSTANTLY.
"AND EVERYBODY'S GOT TO STAY 'AUTHENTIC,' JUST LIKE THE DAY MOMENT BROUGHT US HERE."

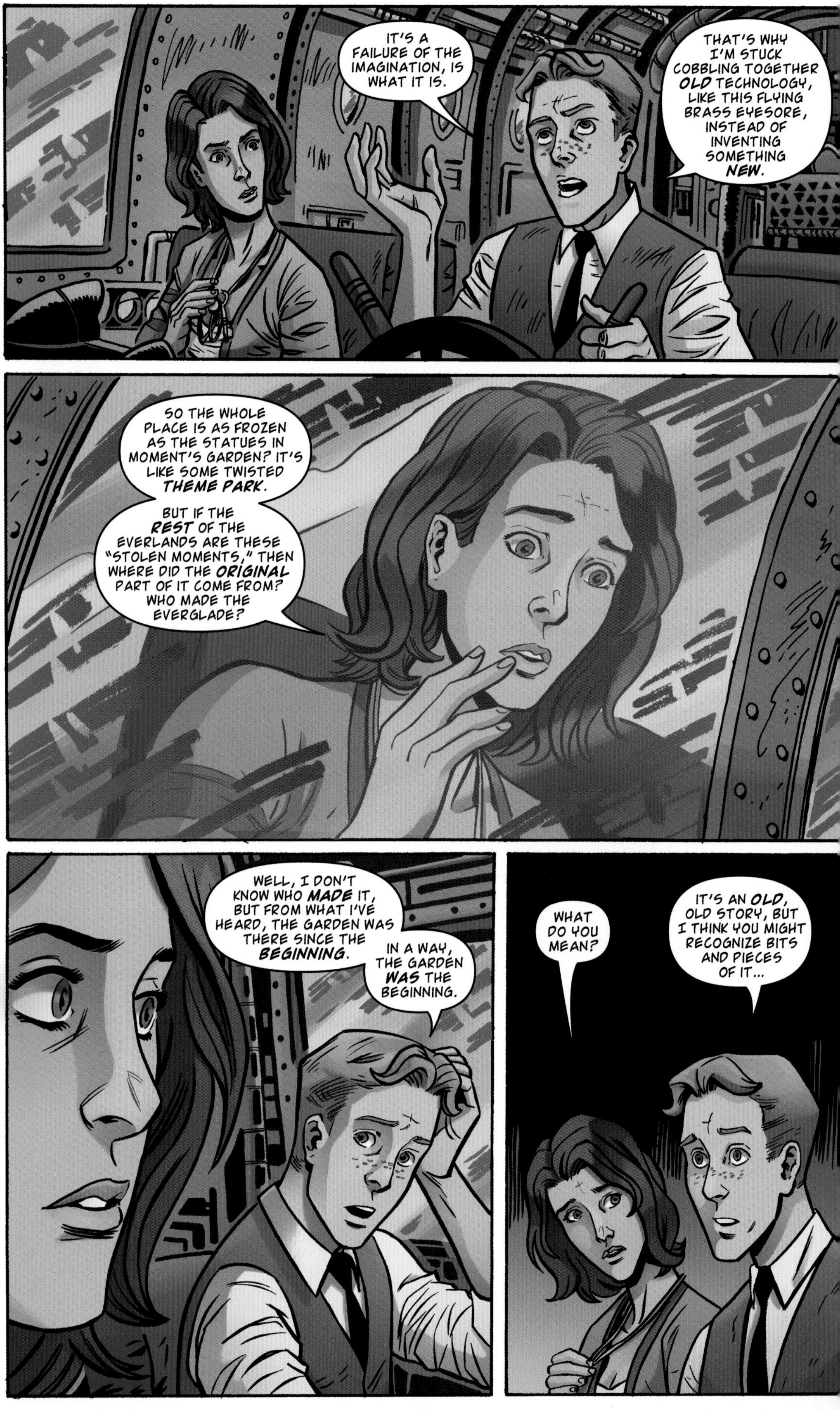
IT'S A FAILURE OF THE IMAGINATION, IS WHAT IT IS.
THAT'S WHY I'M STUCK COBBLING TOGETHER ***OLD*** TECHNOLOGY, LIKE THIS FLYING BRASS EYESORE, INSTEAD OF INVENTING SOMETHING ***NEW***.
SO THE WHOLE PLACE IS AS FROZEN AS THE STATUES IN MOMENT'S GARDEN? IT'S LIKE SOME TWISTED ***THEME PARK***.
BUT IF THE ***REST*** OF THE EVERLANDS ARE THESE "STOLEN MOMENTS," THEN WHERE DID THE ***ORIGINAL*** PART OF IT COME FROM? WHO MADE THE EVERGLADE?
WELL, I DON'T KNOW WHO ***MADE*** IT, BUT FROM WHAT I'VE HEARD, THE GARDEN WAS THERE SINCE THE ***BEGINNING***.
IN A WAY, THE GARDEN ***WAS*** THE BEGINNING.
WHAT DO YOU MEAN?
IT'S AN ***OLD***, OLD STORY, BUT I THINK YOU MIGHT RECOGNIZE BITS AND PIECES OF IT...

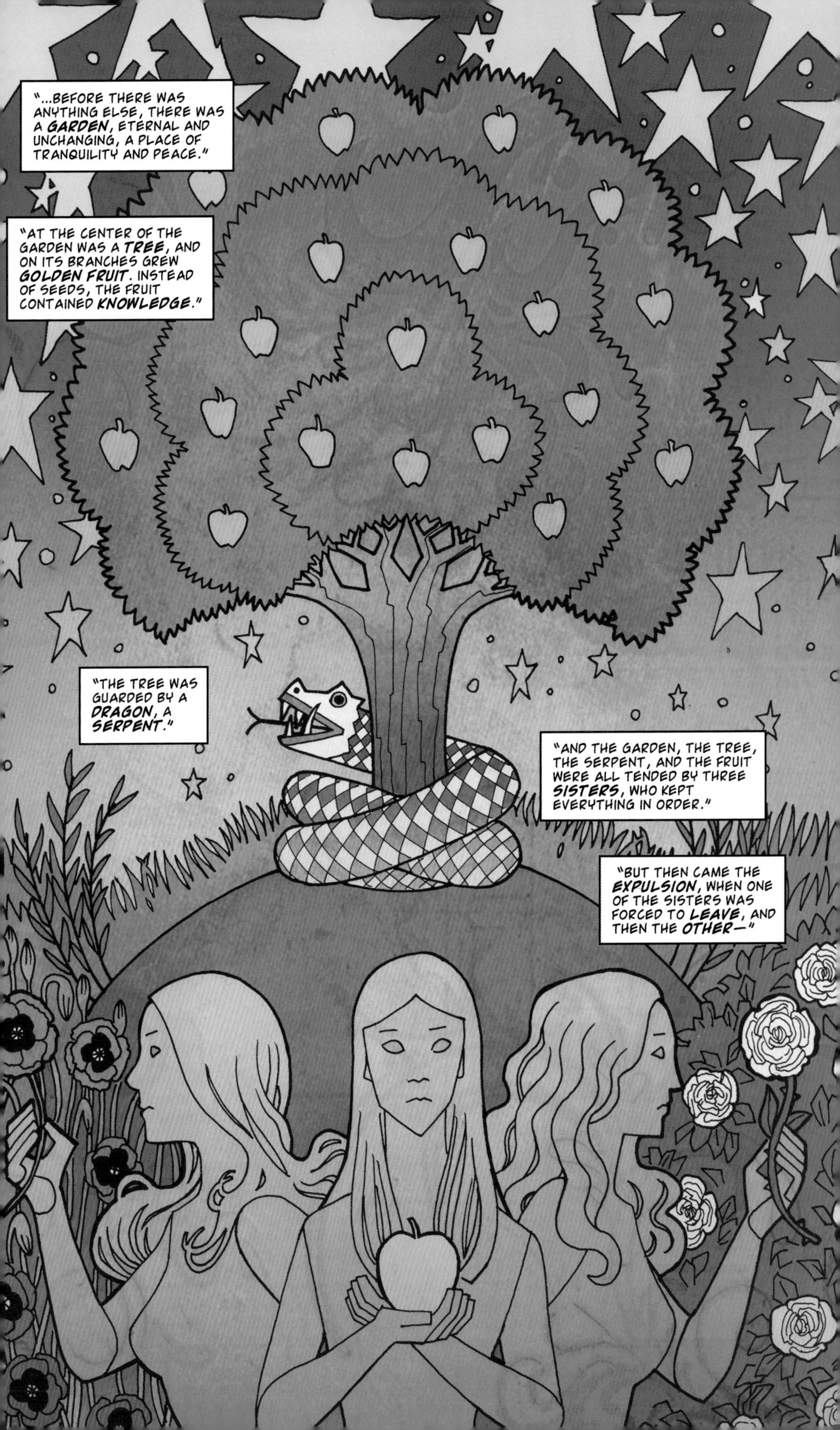
"...BEFORE THERE WAS ANYTHING ELSE, THERE WAS A GARDEN, ETERNAL AND UNCHANGING, A PLACE OF TRANQUILITY AND PEACE."
"AT THE CENTER OF THE GARDEN WAS A TREE, AND ON ITS BRANCHES GREW GOLDEN FRUIT. INSTEAD OF SEEDS, THE FRUIT CONTAINED KNOWLEDGE."
"THE TREE WAS GUARDED BY A DRAGON, A SERPENT."
"AND THE GARDEN, THE TREE, THE SERPENT, AND THE FRUIT WERE ALL TENDED BY THREE SISTERS, WHO KEPT EVERYTHING IN ORDER."
"BUT THEN CAME THE EXPULSION, WHEN ONE OF THE SISTERS WAS FORCED TO LEAVE, AND THEN THE OTHER—"

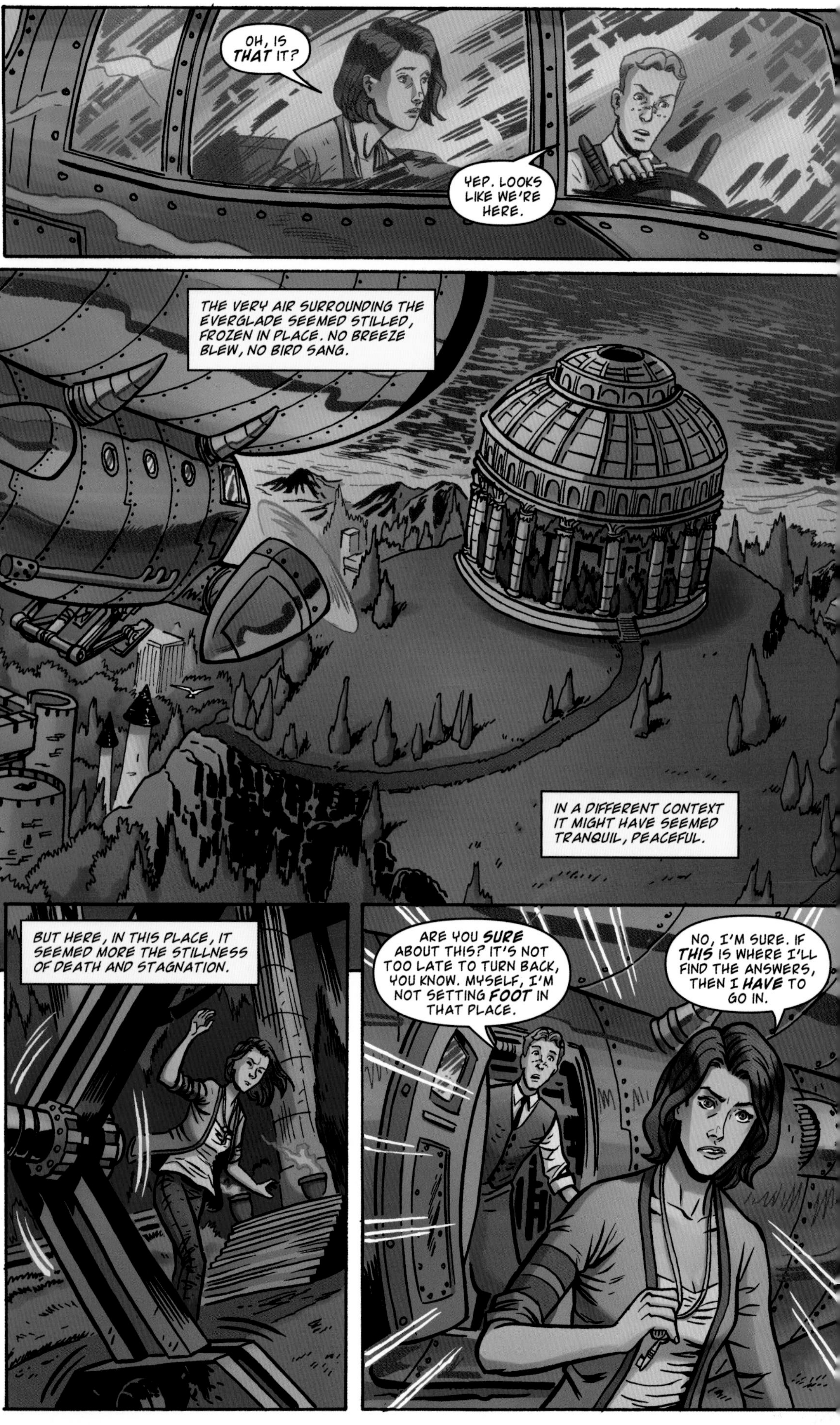

OH, IS THAT IT?
YEP. LOOKS LIKE WE'RE HERE.
THE VERY AIR SURROUNDING THE EVERGLADE SEEMED STILLED, FROZEN IN PLACE. NO BREEZE BLEW, NO BIRD SANG.
IN A DIFFERENT CONTEXT IT MIGHT HAVE SEEMED TRANQUIL, PEACEFUL.
BUT HERE, IN THIS PLACE, IT SEEMED MORE THE STILLNESS OF DEATH AND STAGNATION.
ARE YOU SURE ABOUT THIS? IT'S NOT TOO LATE TO TURN BACK, YOU KNOW. MYSELF, I'M NOT SETTING FOOT IN THAT PLACE.
NO, I'M SURE. IF THIS IS WHERE I'LL FIND THE ANSWERS, THEN I HAVE TO GO IN.

SEEING THE GARDEN, EM COULD SCARCELY IMAGINE HOW SHE COULD FORGET HAVING SEEN IT BEFORE.

I AM SURE, RIGHT...?

UM, WOW.

BUT IF IT WERE POSSIBLE TO FORGET A PLACE SUCH AS THIS, SHE WONDERED WHAT **ELSE** HAD SHE LOST.

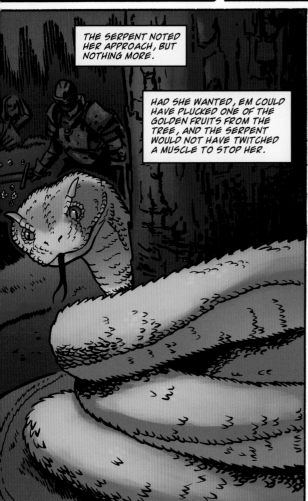

THE SERPENT NOTED HER APPROACH, BUT NOTHING MORE.

HAD SHE WANTED, EM COULD HAVE PLUCKED ONE OF THE GOLDEN FRUITS FROM THE TREE, AND THE SERPENT WOULD NOT HAVE TWITCHED A MUSCLE TO STOP HER.

FINALLY. I WAS BEGINNING TO THINK YOU'D **NEVER** GET HERE.

YOU?!

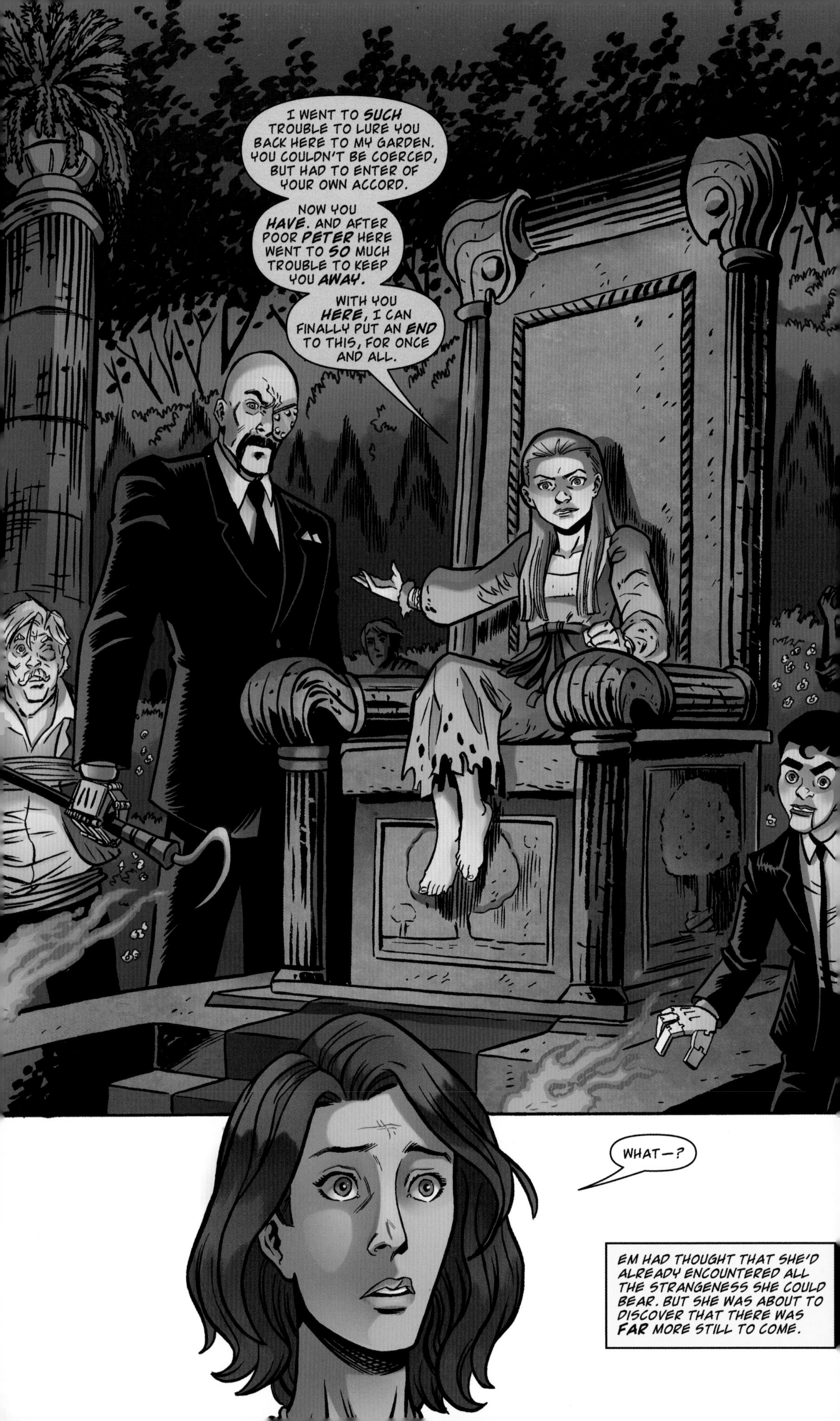
I WENT TO SUCH TROUBLE TO LURE YOU BACK HERE TO MY GARDEN. YOU COULDN'T BE COERCED, BUT HAD TO ENTER OF YOUR OWN ACCORD.
NOW YOU HAVE. AND AFTER POOR PETER HERE WENT TO SO MUCH TROUBLE TO KEEP YOU AWAY.
WITH YOU HERE, I CAN FINALLY PUT AN END TO THIS, FOR ONCE AND ALL.
WHAT—?
EM HAD THOUGHT THAT SHE'D ALREADY ENCOUNTERED ALL THE STRANGENESS SHE COULD BEAR. BUT SHE WAS ABOUT TO DISCOVER THAT THERE WAS FAR MORE STILL TO COME.

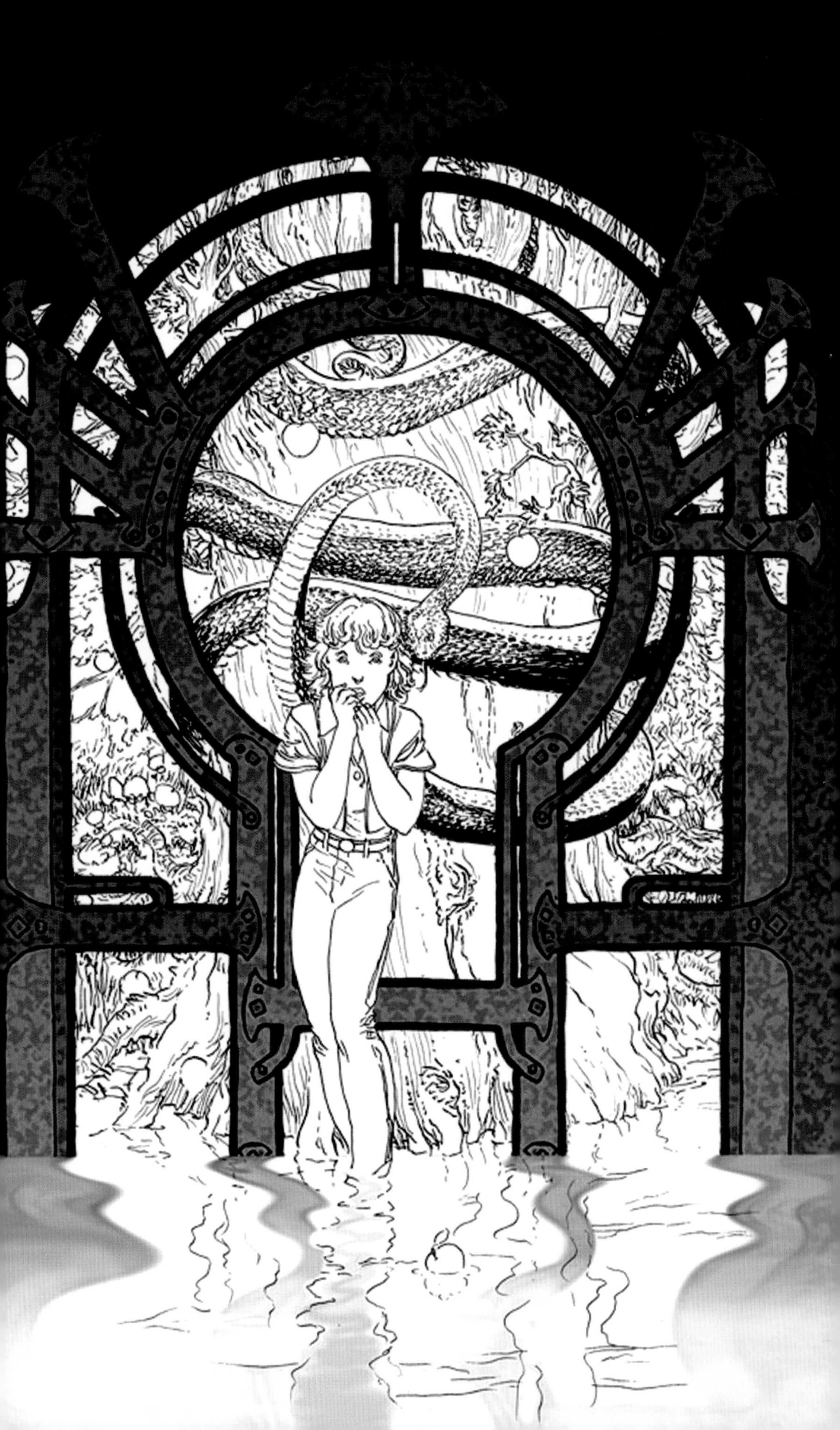

Chapter Six

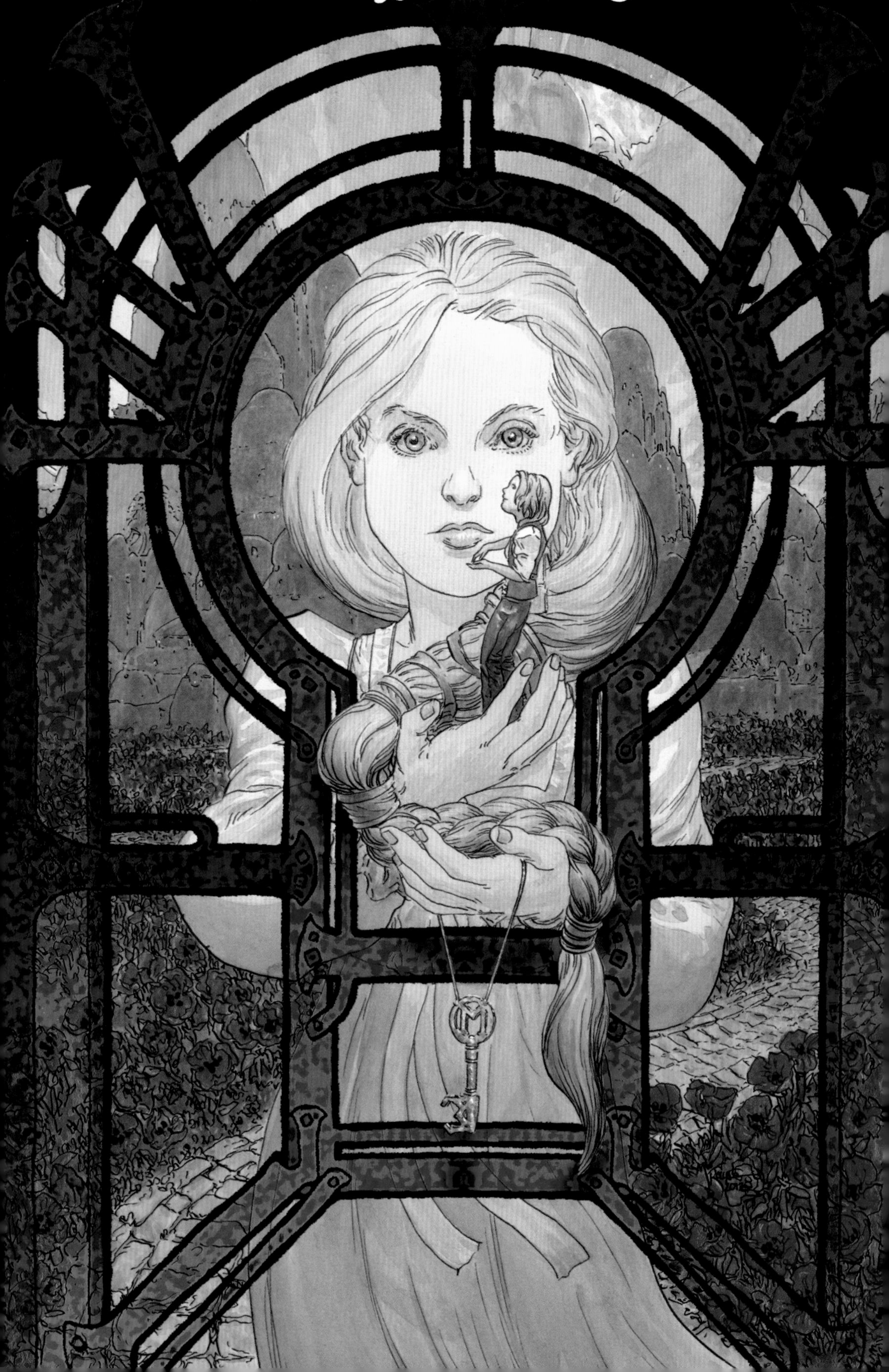

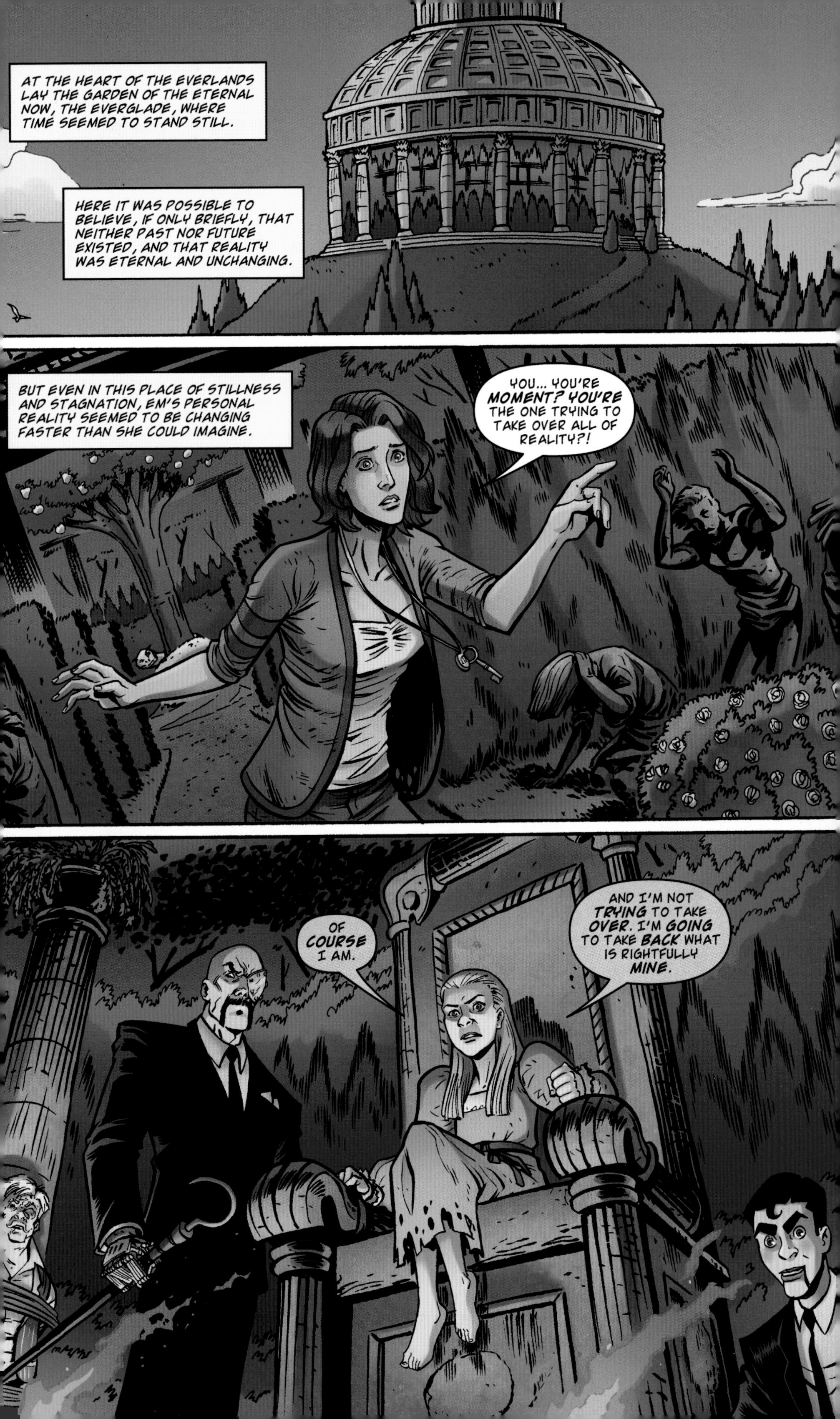
AT THE HEART OF THE EVERLANDS LAY THE GARDEN OF THE ETERNAL NOW, THE EVERGLADE, WHERE TIME SEEMED TO STAND STILL.
HERE IT WAS POSSIBLE TO BELIEVE, IF ONLY BRIEFLY, THAT NEITHER PAST NOR FUTURE EXISTED, AND THAT REALITY WAS ETERNAL AND UNCHANGING.
BUT EVEN IN THIS PLACE OF STILLNESS AND STAGNATION, EM'S PERSONAL REALITY SEEMED TO BE CHANGING FASTER THAN SHE COULD IMAGINE.
YOU... YOU'RE MOMENT? YOU'RE THE ONE TRYING TO TAKE OVER ALL OF REALITY?!
OF COURSE I AM.
AND I'M NOT TRYING TO TAKE OVER. I'M GOING TO TAKE BACK WHAT IS RIGHTFULLY MINE.

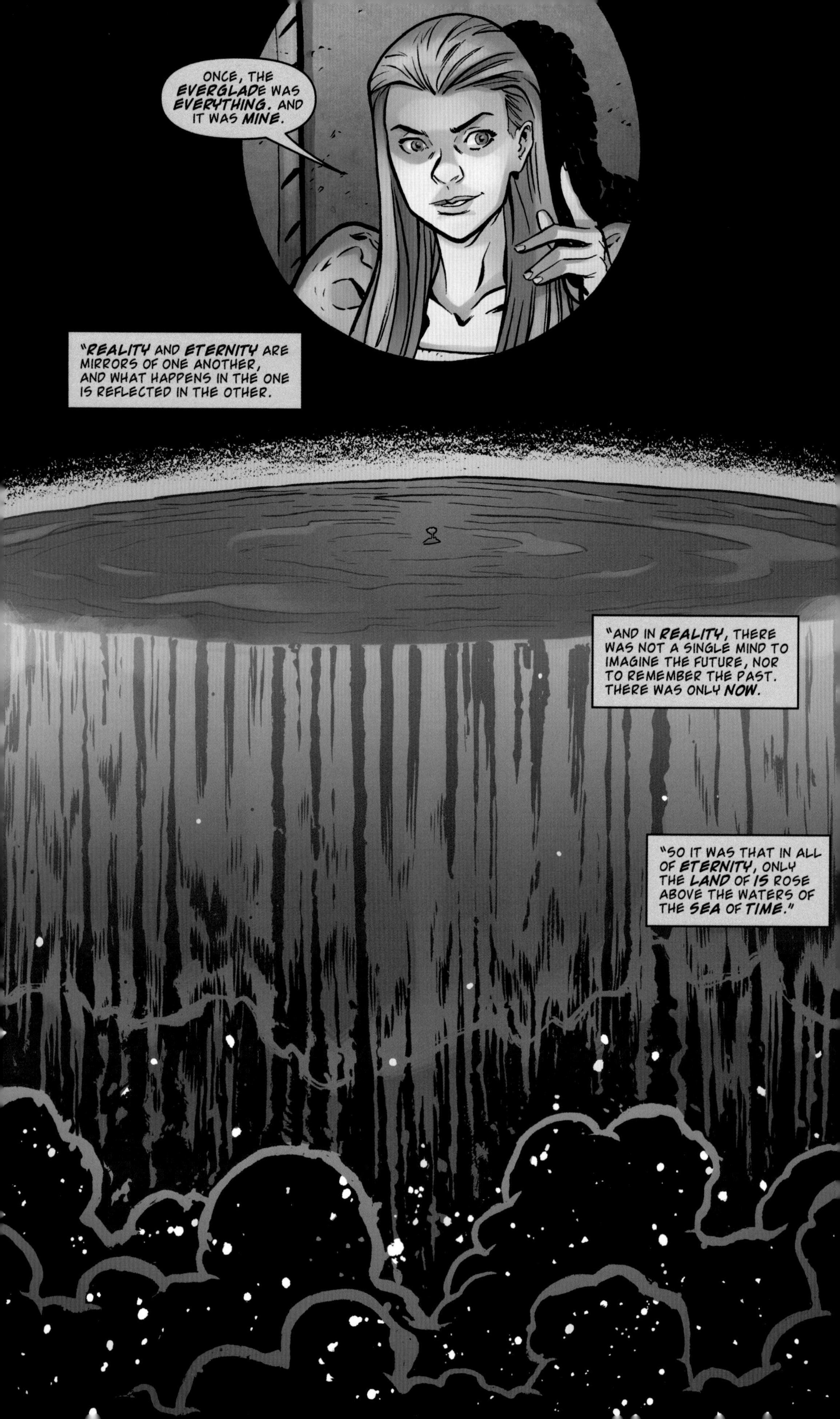
ONCE, THE EVERGLADE WAS EVERYTHING. AND IT WAS MINE.
"REALITY AND ETERNITY ARE MIRRORS OF ONE ANOTHER, AND WHAT HAPPENS IN THE ONE IS REFLECTED IN THE OTHER.
"AND IN REALITY, THERE WAS NOT A SINGLE MIND TO IMAGINE THE FUTURE, NOR TO REMEMBER THE PAST. THERE WAS ONLY NOW.
"SO IT WAS THAT IN ALL OF ETERNITY, ONLY THE LAND OF IS ROSE ABOVE THE WATERS OF THE SEA OF TIME."

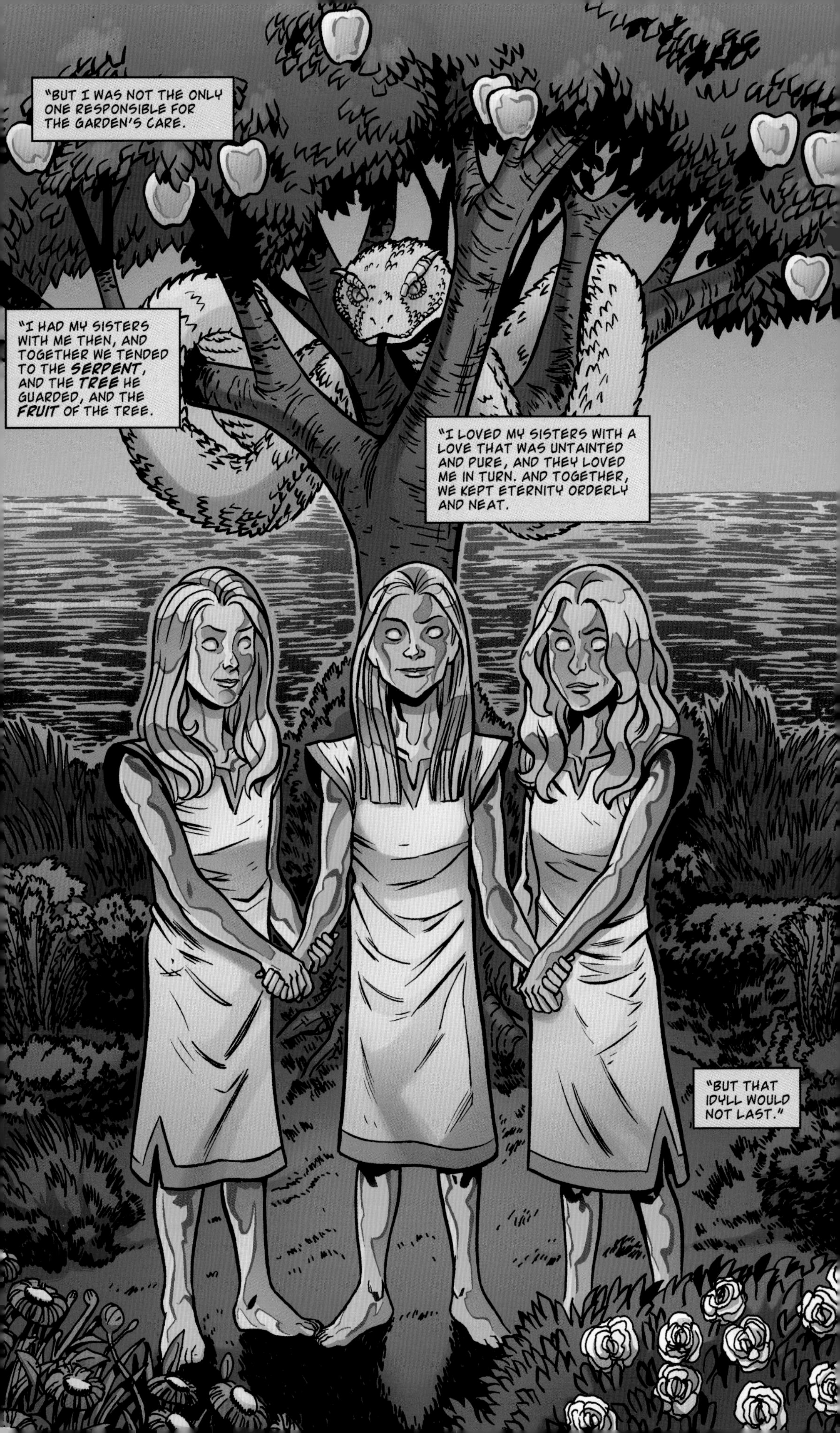
"BUT I WAS NOT THE ONLY ONE RESPONSIBLE FOR THE GARDEN'S CARE.
"I HAD MY SISTERS WITH ME THEN, AND TOGETHER WE TENDED TO THE ***SERPENT***, AND THE ***TREE*** HE GUARDED, AND THE ***FRUIT*** OF THE TREE.
"I LOVED MY SISTERS WITH A LOVE THAT WAS UNTAINTED AND PURE, AND THEY LOVED ME IN TURN. AND TOGETHER, WE KEPT ETERNITY ORDERLY AND NEAT.
"BUT THAT IDYLL WOULD NOT LAST."

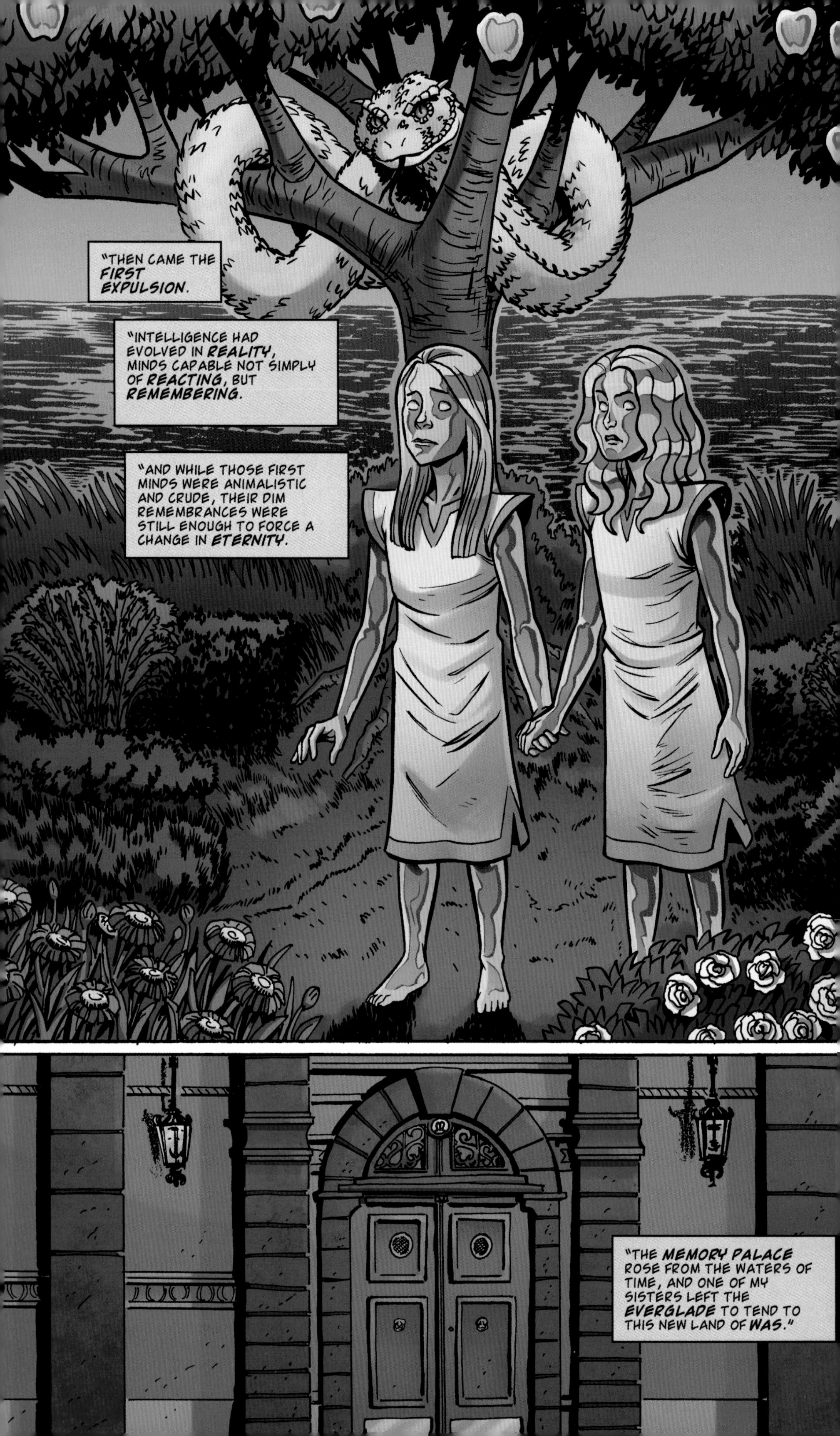
"THEN CAME THE FIRST EXPULSION.
"INTELLIGENCE HAD EVOLVED IN REALITY, MINDS CAPABLE NOT SIMPLY OF REACTING, BUT REMEMBERING.
"AND WHILE THOSE FIRST MINDS WERE ANIMALISTIC AND CRUDE, THEIR DIM REMEMBRANCES WERE STILL ENOUGH TO FORCE A CHANGE IN ETERNITY.
"THE MEMORY PALACE ROSE FROM THE WATERS OF TIME, AND ONE OF MY SISTERS LEFT THE EVERGLADE TO TEND TO THIS NEW LAND OF WAS."

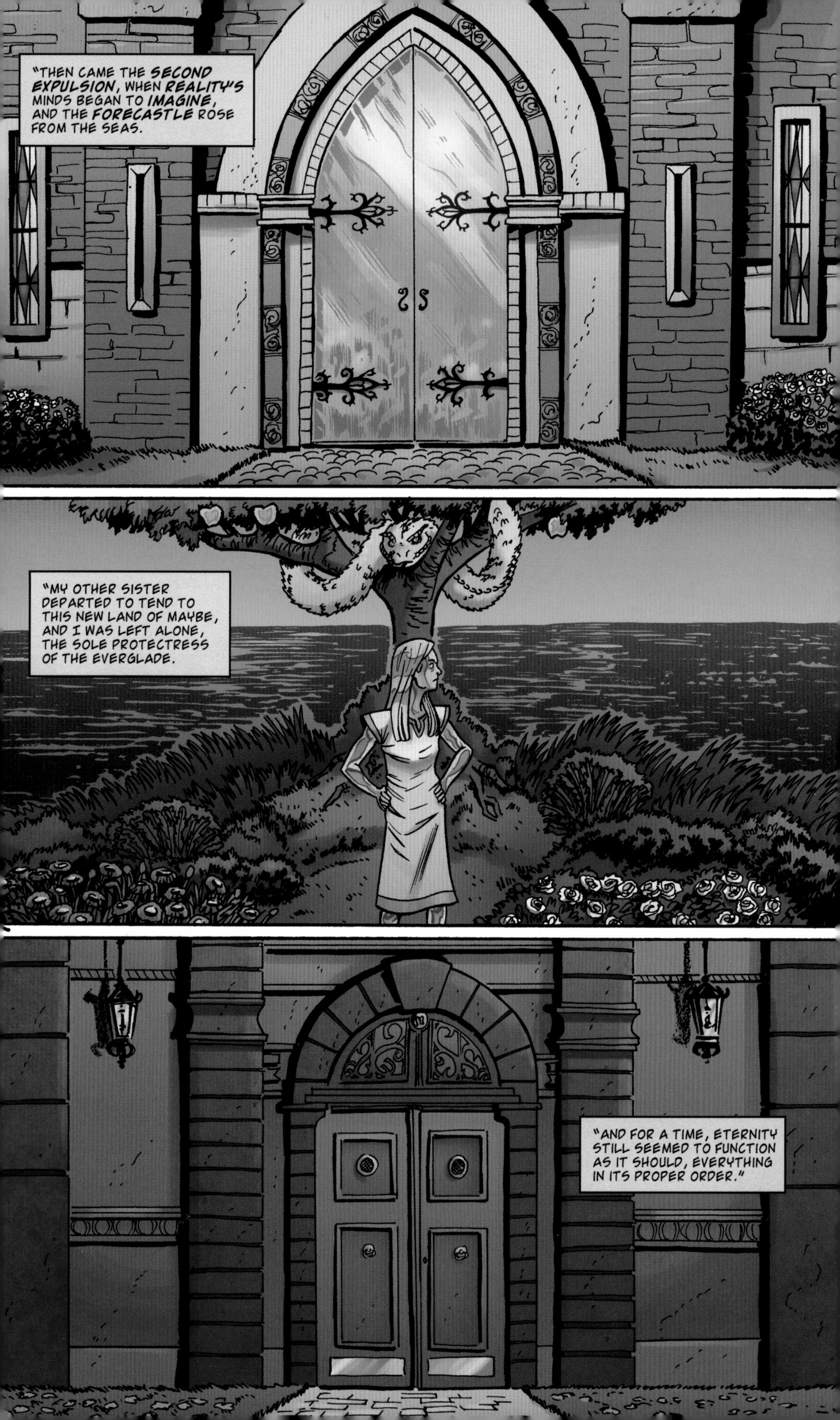
"THEN CAME THE SECOND EXPULSION, WHEN REALITY'S MINDS BEGAN TO IMAGINE, AND THE FORECASTLE ROSE FROM THE SEAS.
"MY OTHER SISTER DEPARTED TO TEND TO THIS NEW LAND OF MAYBE, AND I WAS LEFT ALONE, THE SOLE PROTECTRESS OF THE EVERGLADE.
"AND FOR A TIME, ETERNITY STILL SEEMED TO FUNCTION AS IT SHOULD, EVERYTHING IN ITS PROPER ORDER."

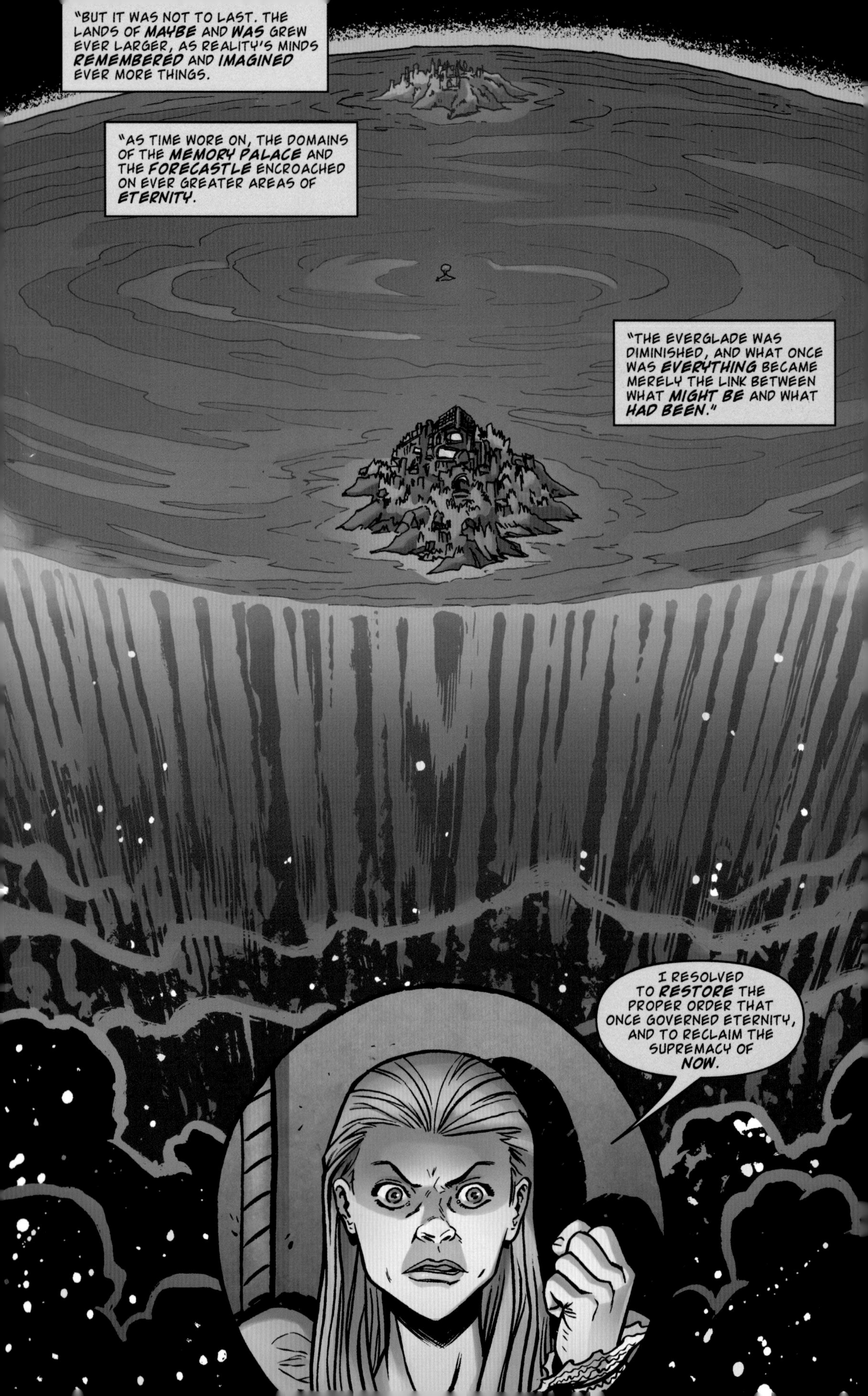
"BUT IT WAS NOT TO LAST. THE LANDS OF MAYBE AND WAS GREW EVER LARGER, AS REALITY'S MINDS REMEMBERED AND IMAGINED EVER MORE THINGS.
"AS TIME WORE ON, THE DOMAINS OF THE MEMORY PALACE AND THE FORECASTLE ENCROACHED ON EVER GREATER AREAS OF ETERNITY.
"THE EVERGLADE WAS DIMINISHED, AND WHAT ONCE WAS EVERYTHING BECAME MERELY THE LINK BETWEEN WHAT MIGHT BE AND WHAT HAD BEEN."
I RESOLVED TO RESTORE THE PROPER ORDER THAT ONCE GOVERNED ETERNITY, AND TO RECLAIM THE SUPREMACY OF NOW.

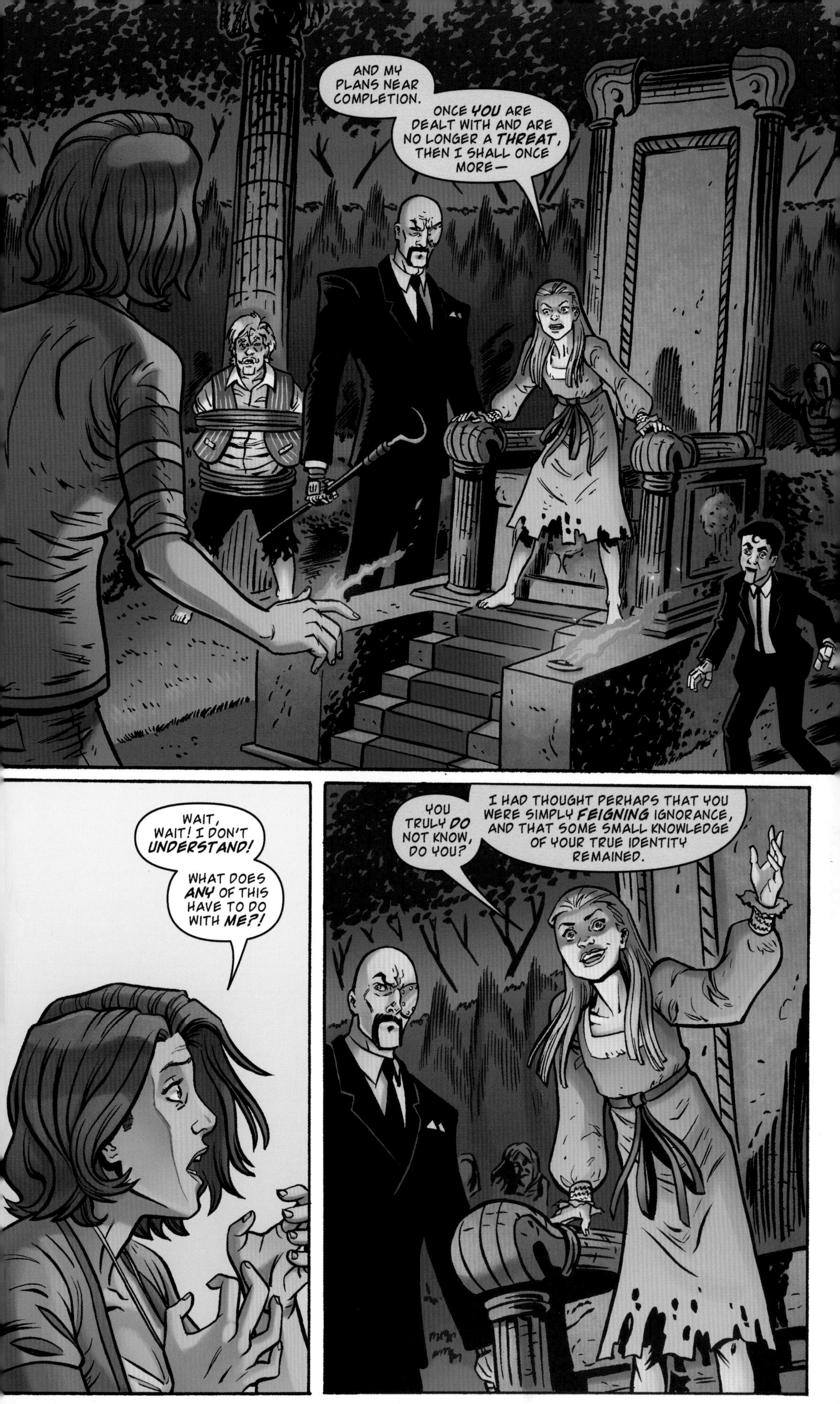
AND MY PLANS NEAR COMPLETION.
ONCE YOU ARE DEALT WITH AND ARE NO LONGER A THREAT, THEN I SHALL ONCE MORE—
WAIT, WAIT! I DON'T UNDERSTAND!
WHAT DOES ANY OF THIS HAVE TO DO WITH ME?!
YOU TRULY DO NOT KNOW, DO YOU?
I HAD THOUGHT PERHAPS THAT YOU WERE SIMPLY FEIGNING IGNORANCE, AND THAT SOME SMALL KNOWLEDGE OF YOUR TRUE IDENTITY REMAINED.

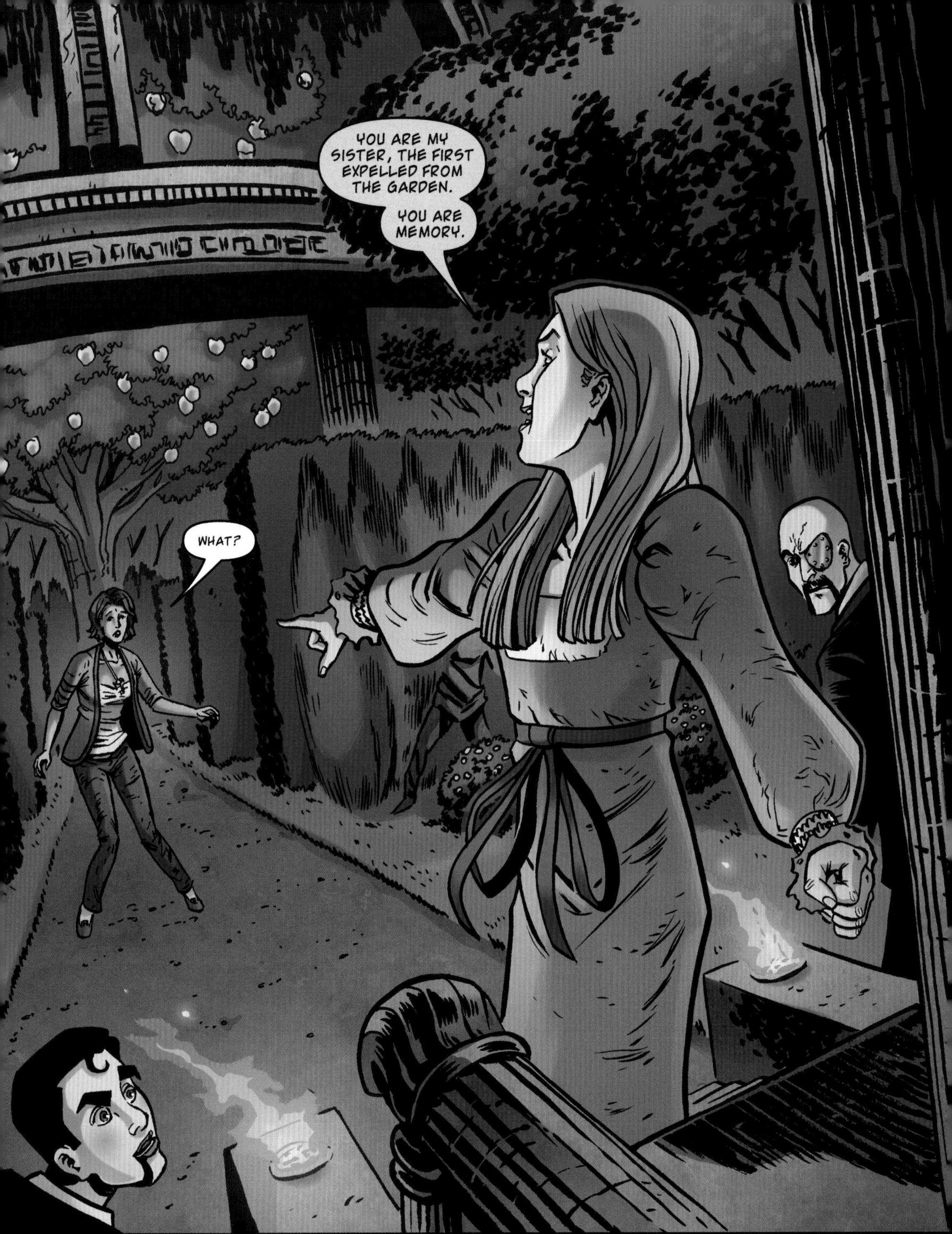
YOU ARE MY SISTER, THE FIRST EXPELLED FROM THE GARDEN.
YOU ARE MEMORY.
WHAT?

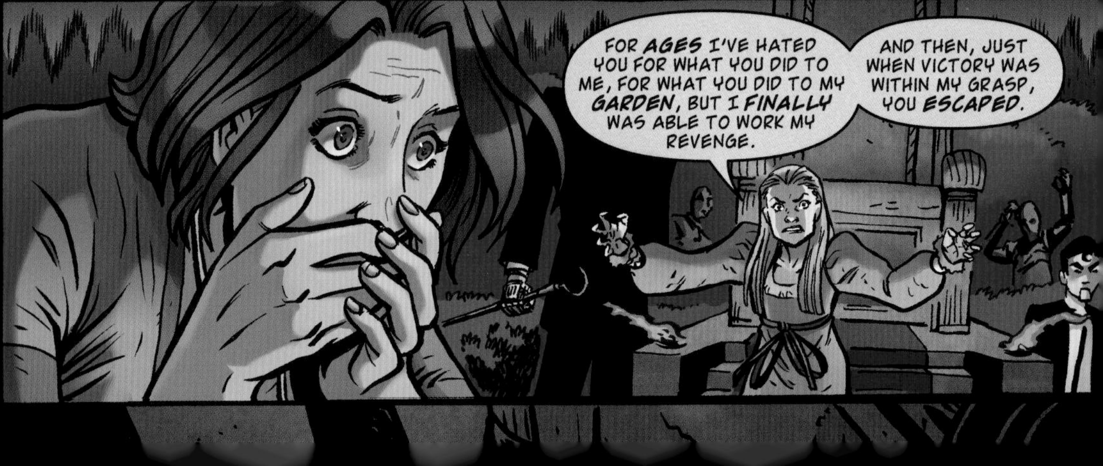
FOR AGES I'VE HATED YOU FOR WHAT YOU DID TO ME, FOR WHAT YOU DID TO MY GARDEN, BUT I FINALLY WAS ABLE TO WORK MY REVENGE.
AND THEN, JUST WHEN VICTORY WAS WITHIN MY GRASP, YOU ESCAPED.

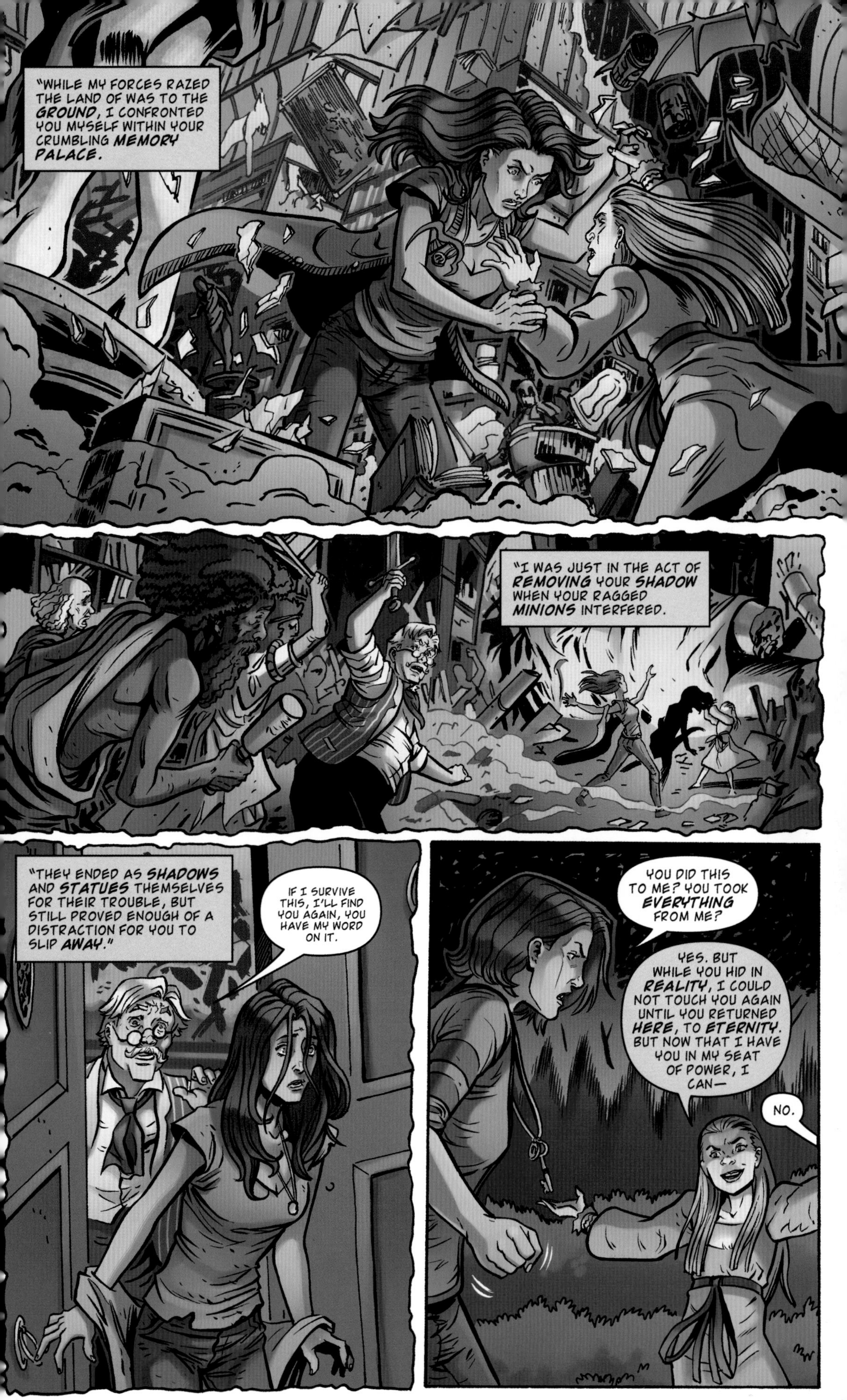
"WHILE MY FORCES RAZED THE LAND OF WAS TO THE GROUND, I CONFRONTED YOU MYSELF WITHIN YOUR CRUMBLING MEMORY PALACE.
"I WAS JUST IN THE ACT OF REMOVING YOUR SHADOW WHEN YOUR RAGGED MINIONS INTERFERED.
"THEY ENDED AS SHADOWS AND STATUES THEMSELVES FOR THEIR TROUBLE, BUT STILL PROVED ENOUGH OF A DISTRACTION FOR YOU TO SLIP AWAY."
IF I SURVIVE THIS, I'LL FIND YOU AGAIN, YOU HAVE MY WORD ON IT.
YOU DID THIS TO ME? YOU TOOK EVERYTHING FROM ME?
YES. BUT WHILE YOU HID IN REALITY, I COULD NOT TOUCH YOU AGAIN UNTIL YOU RETURNED HERE, TO ETERNITY. BUT NOW THAT I HAVE YOU IN MY SEAT OF POWER, I CAN—
NO.

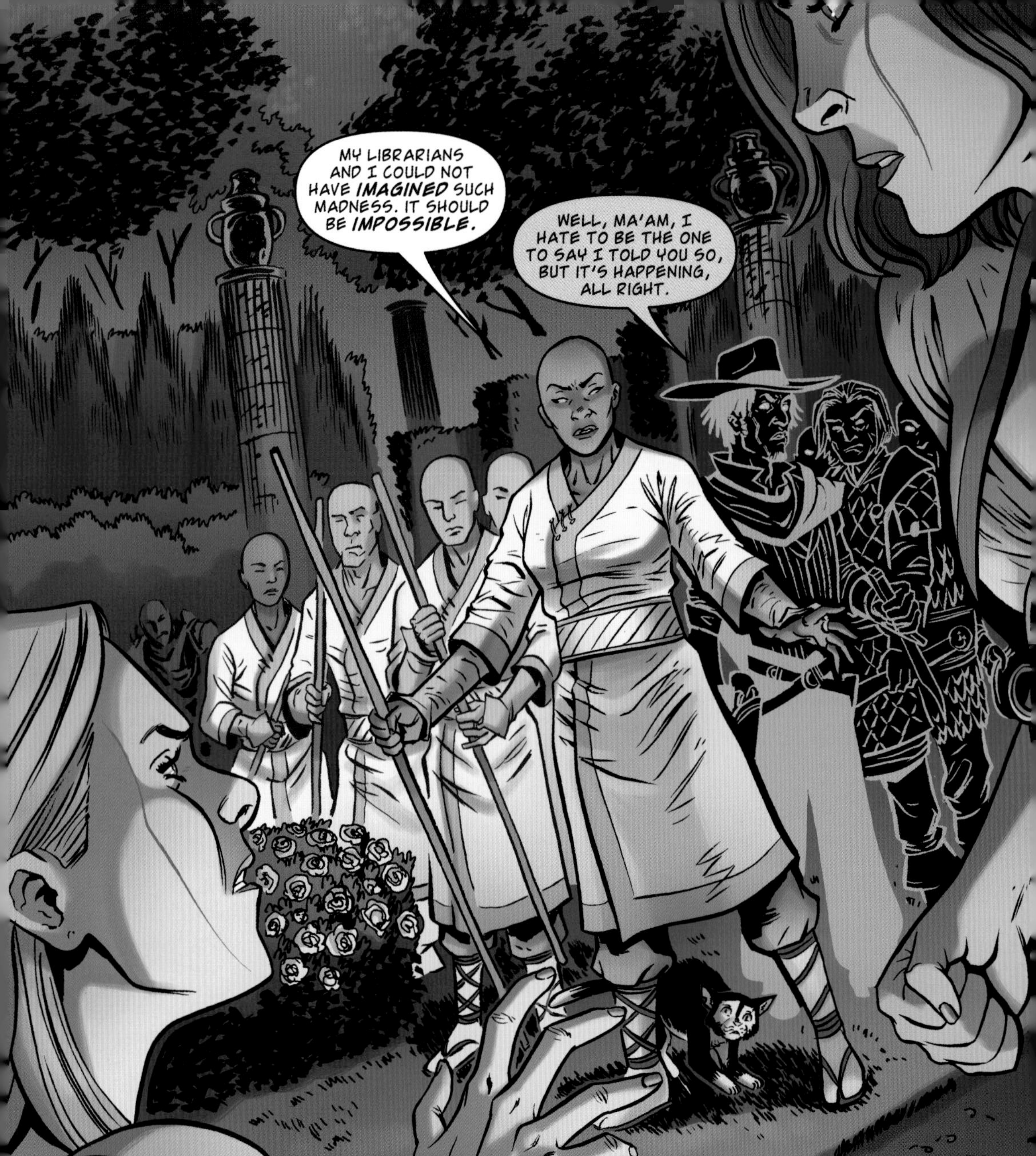
MY LIBRARIANS AND I COULD NOT HAVE IMAGINED SUCH MADNESS. IT SHOULD BE IMPOSSIBLE.
WELL, MA'AM, I HATE TO BE THE ONE TO SAY I TOLD YOU SO, BUT IT'S HAPPENING, ALL RIGHT.

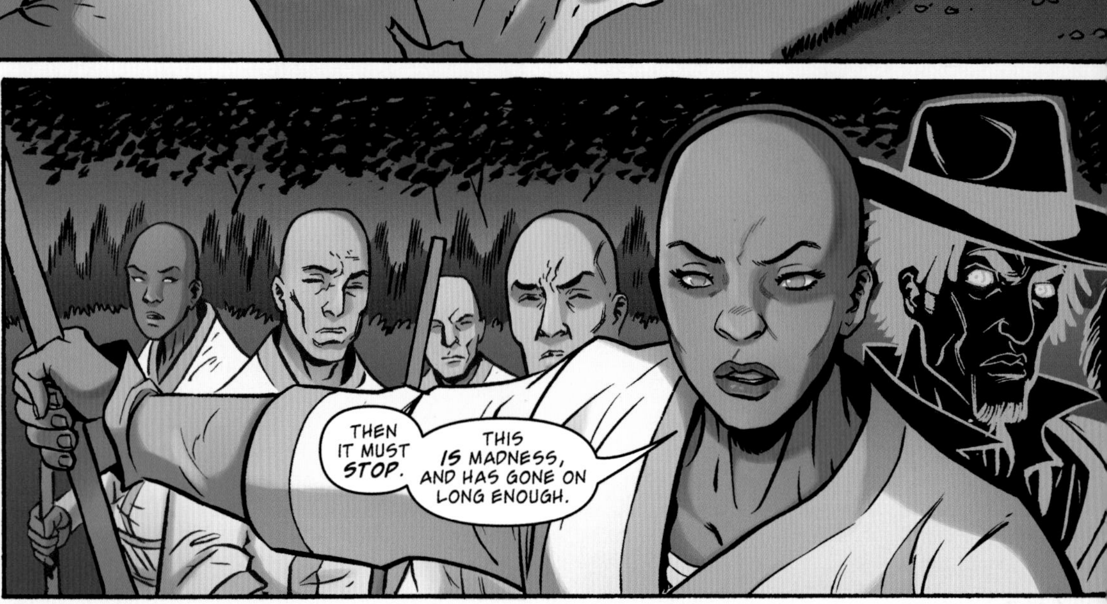
THEN IT MUST STOP.
THIS IS MADNESS, AND HAS GONE ON LONG ENOUGH.

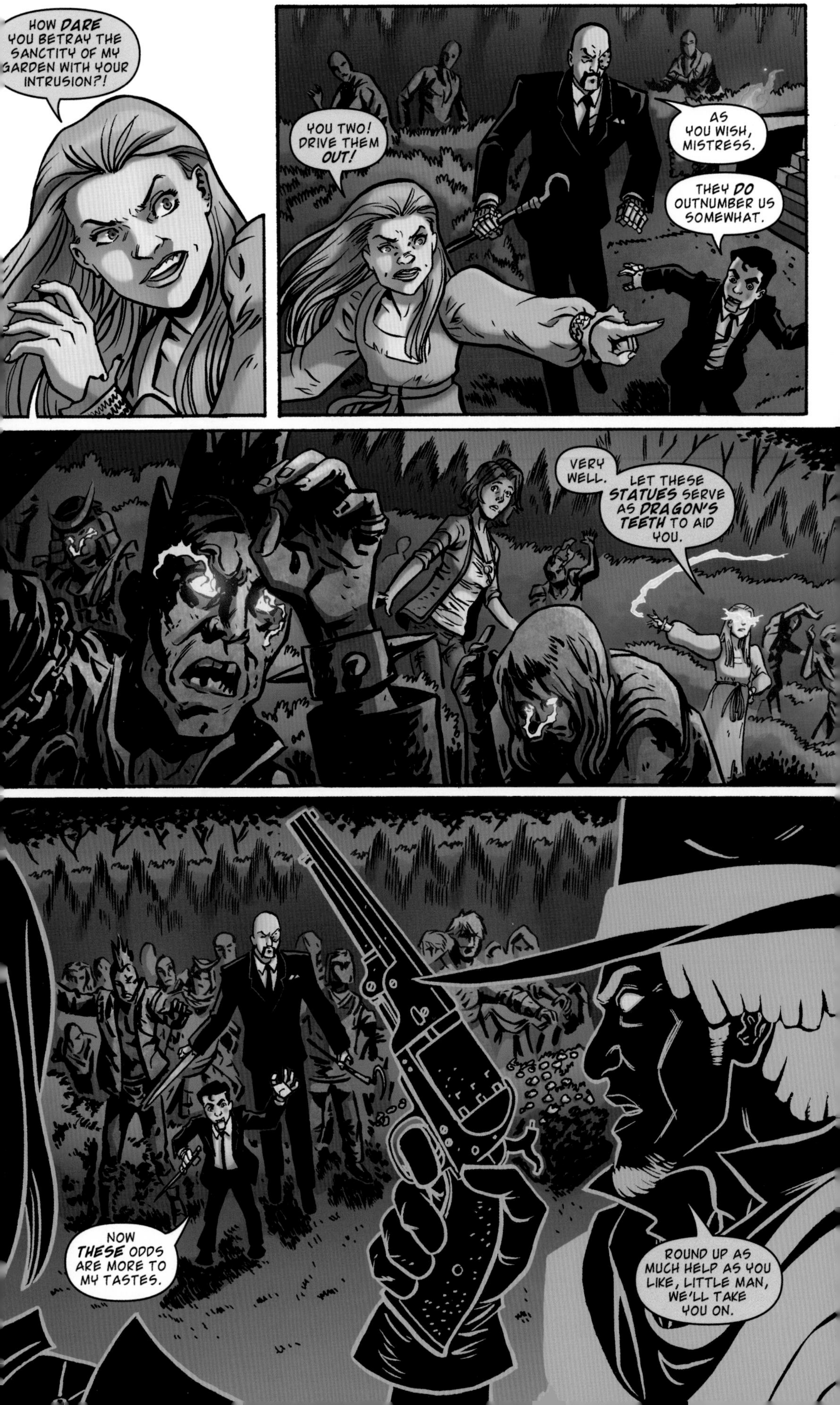
HOW DARE YOU BETRAY THE SANCTITY OF MY GARDEN WITH YOUR INTRUSION?!
YOU TWO! DRIVE THEM OUT!
AS YOU WISH, MISTRESS.
THEY DO OUTNUMBER US SOMEWHAT.
VERY WELL.
LET THESE STATUES SERVE AS DRAGON'S TEETH TO AID YOU.
NOW THESE ODDS ARE MORE TO MY TASTES.
ROUND UP AS MUCH HELP AS YOU LIKE, LITTLE MAN, WE'LL TAKE YOU ON.

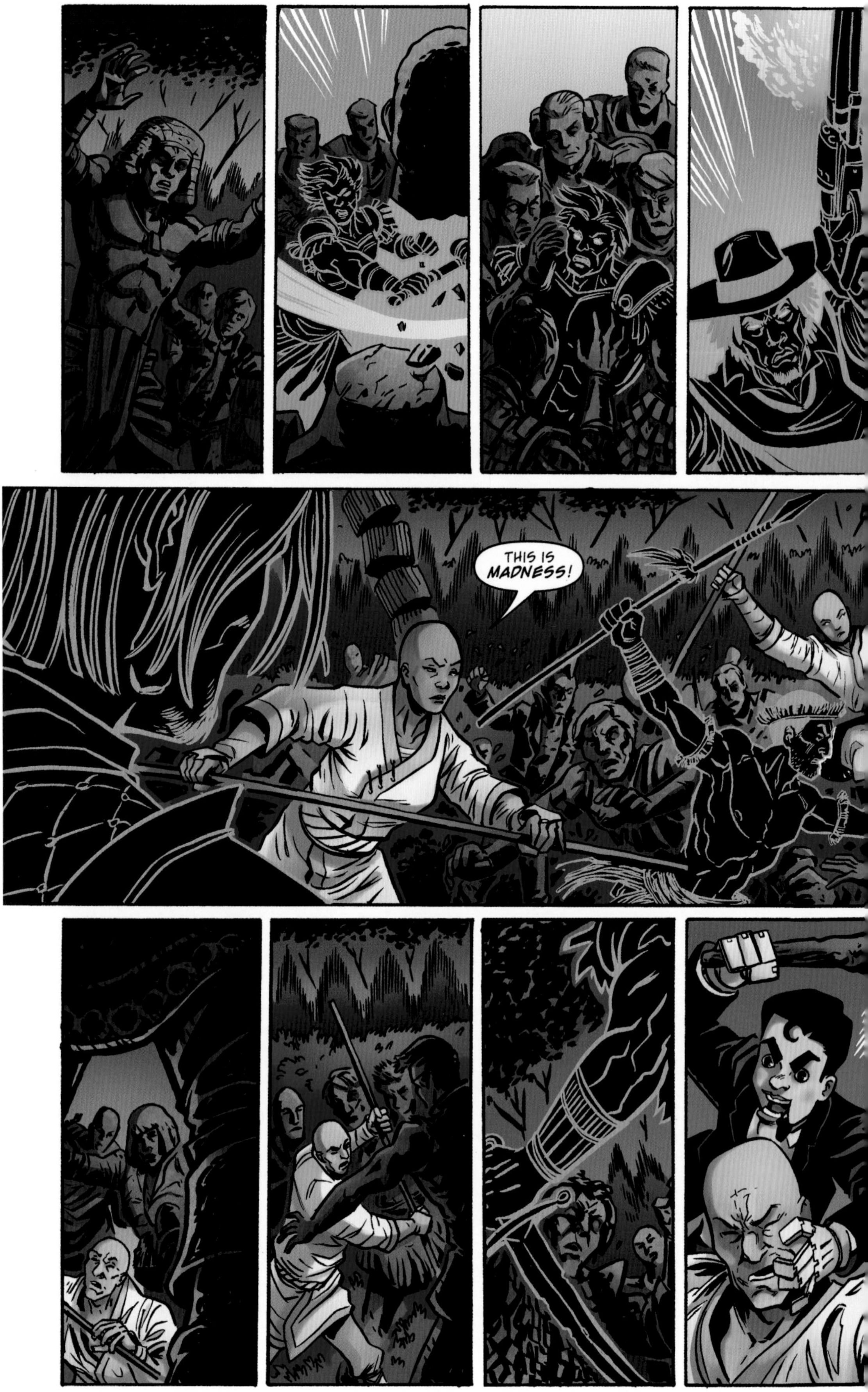
THIS IS MADNESS!

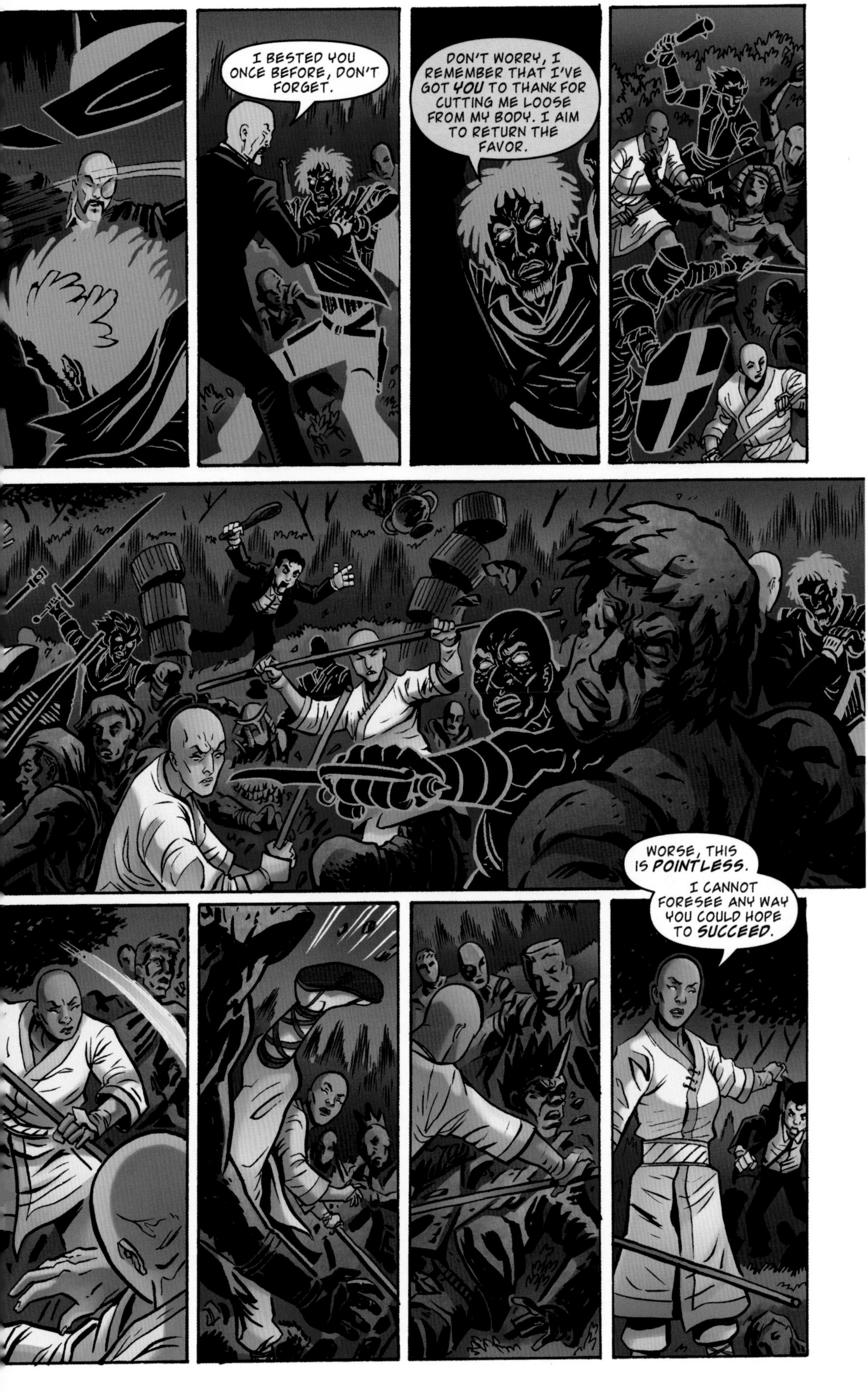
I BESTED YOU ONCE BEFORE, DON'T FORGET.
DON'T WORRY, I REMEMBER THAT I'VE GOT *YOU* TO THANK FOR CUTTING ME LOOSE FROM MY BODY. I AIM TO RETURN THE FAVOR.
WORSE, THIS IS ***POINTLESS***.
I CANNOT FORESEE ANY WAY YOU COULD HOPE TO ***SUCCEED***.

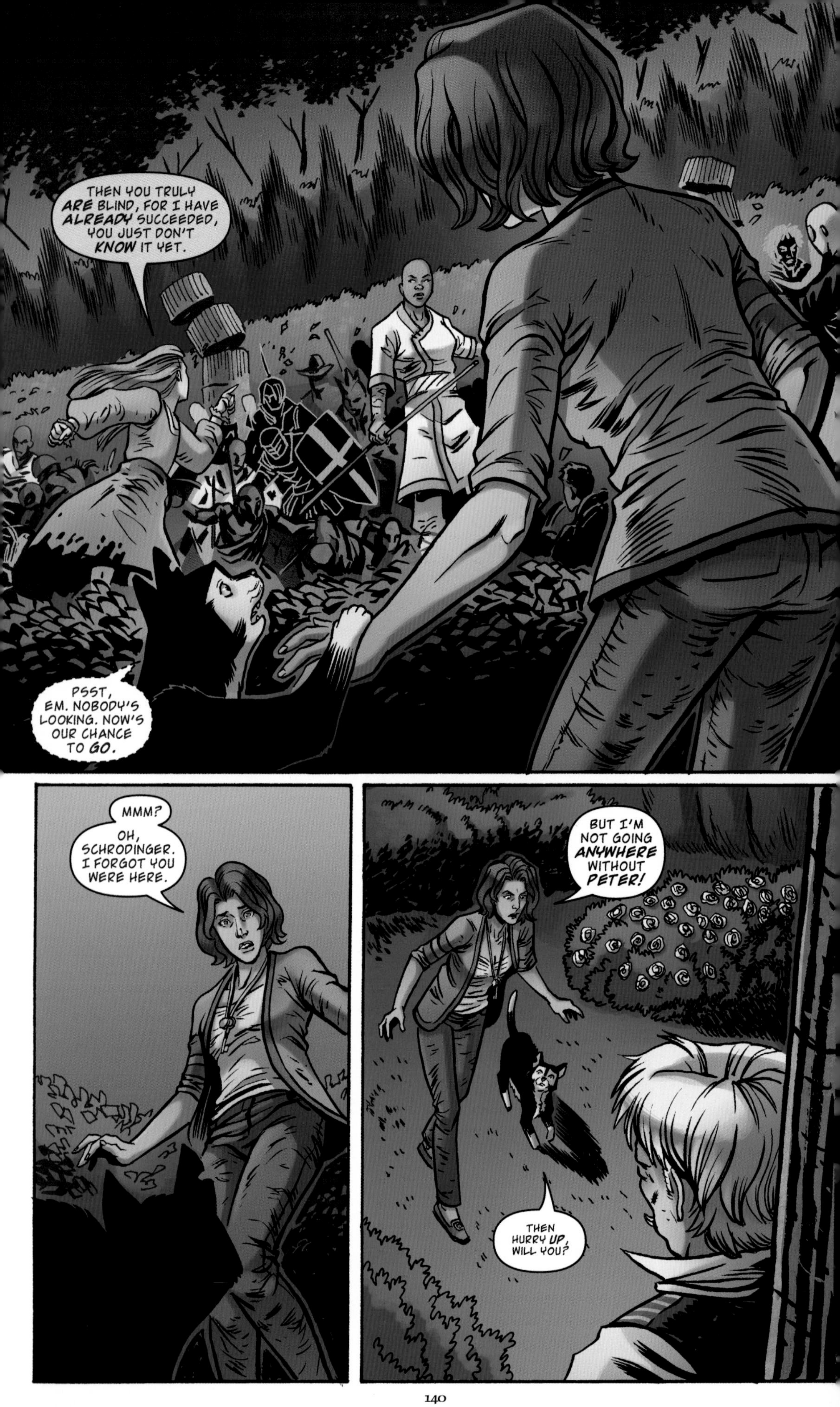
THEN YOU TRULY ARE BLIND, FOR I HAVE ALREADY SUCCEEDED, YOU JUST DON'T KNOW IT YET.
PSST, EM. NOBODY'S LOOKING. NOW'S OUR CHANCE TO GO.
MMM?
OH, SCHRODINGER. I FORGOT YOU WERE HERE.
BUT I'M NOT GOING ANYWHERE WITHOUT PETER!
THEN HURRY UP, WILL YOU?

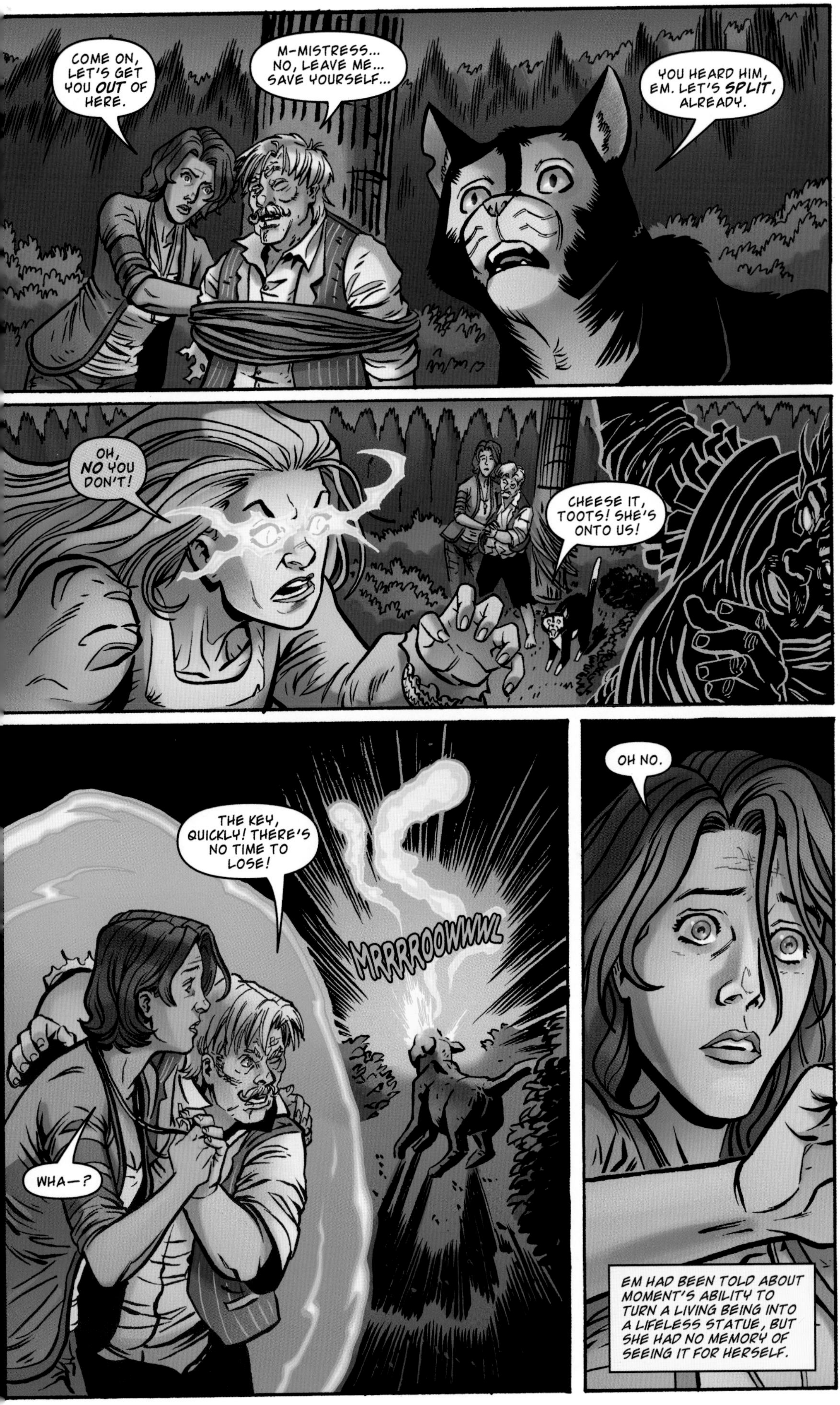
COME ON, LET'S GET YOU OUT OF HERE.
M-MISTRESS... NO, LEAVE ME... SAVE YOURSELF...
YOU HEARD HIM, EM. LET'S SPLIT, ALREADY.
OH, NO YOU DON'T!
CHEESE IT, TOOTS! SHE'S ONTO US!
THE KEY, QUICKLY! THERE'S NO TIME TO LOSE!
MRRRROOWWWL
WHA—?
OH NO.
EM HAD BEEN TOLD ABOUT MOMENT'S ABILITY TO TURN A LIVING BEING INTO A LIFELESS STATUE, BUT SHE HAD NO MEMORY OF SEEING IT FOR HERSELF.

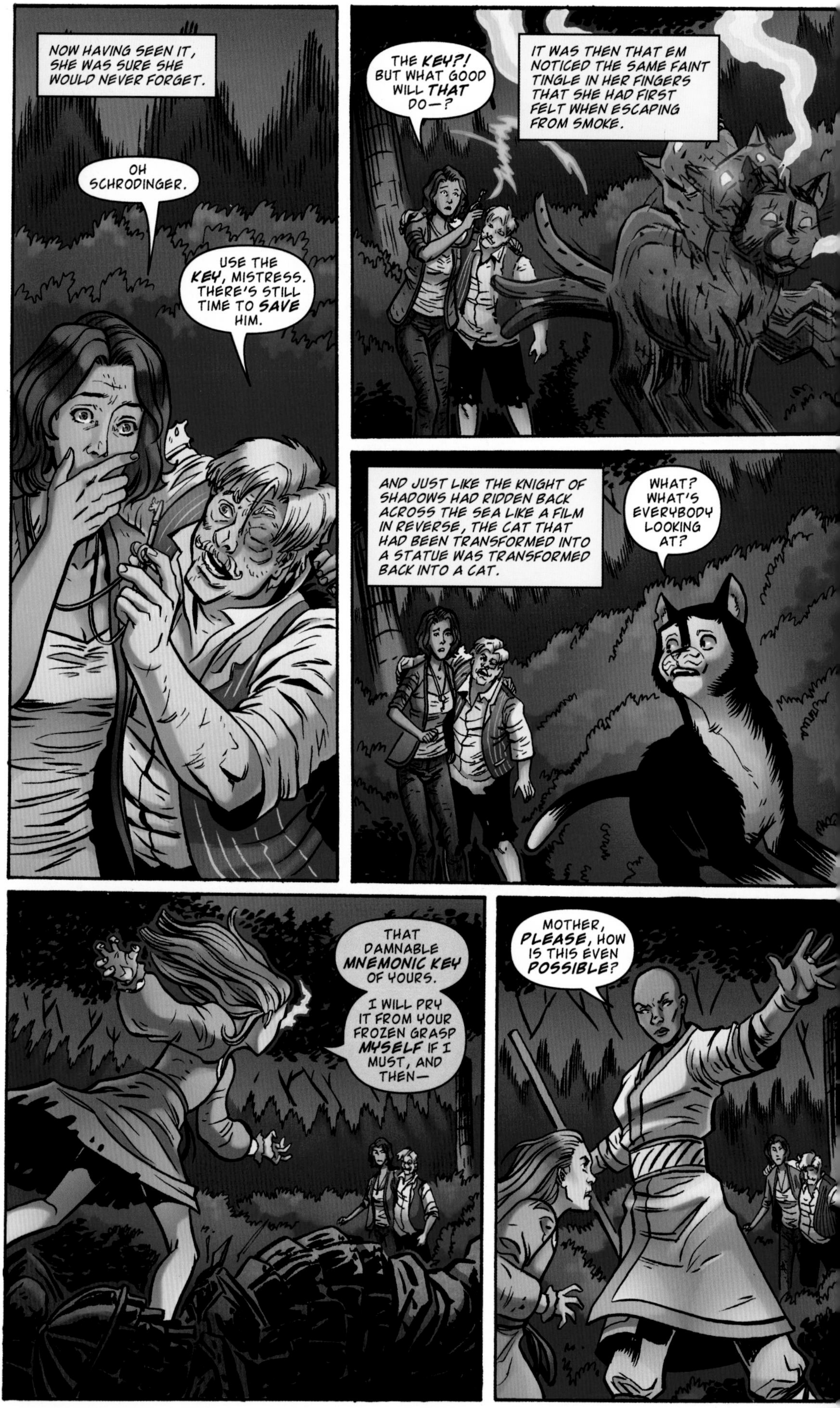
NOW HAVING SEEN IT, SHE WAS SURE SHE WOULD NEVER FORGET.
OH SCHRODINGER.
USE THE KEY, MISTRESS. THERE'S STILL TIME TO SAVE HIM.
THE KEY?! BUT WHAT GOOD WILL THAT DO—?
IT WAS THEN THAT EM NOTICED THE SAME FAINT TINGLE IN HER FINGERS THAT SHE HAD FIRST FELT WHEN ESCAPING FROM SMOKE.
AND JUST LIKE THE KNIGHT OF SHADOWS HAD RIDDEN BACK ACROSS THE SEA LIKE A FILM IN REVERSE, THE CAT THAT HAD BEEN TRANSFORMED INTO A STATUE WAS TRANSFORMED BACK INTO A CAT.
WHAT? WHAT'S EVERYBODY LOOKING AT?
THAT DAMNABLE MNEMONIC KEY OF YOURS.
I WILL PRY IT FROM YOUR FROZEN GRASP MYSELF IF I MUST, AND THEN—
MOTHER, PLEASE, HOW IS THIS EVEN POSSIBLE?

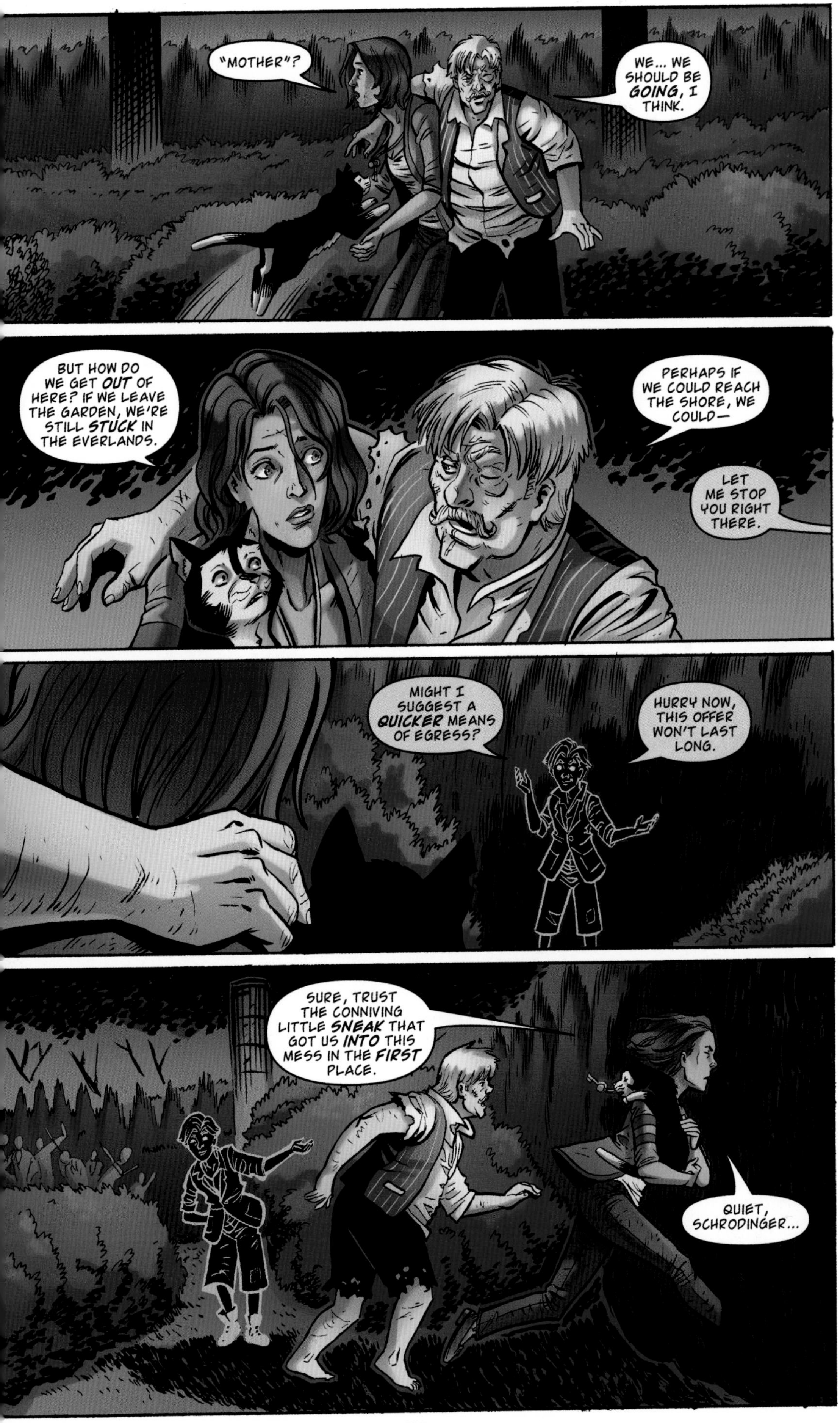
"MOTHER"?
WE... WE SHOULD BE GOING, I THINK.
BUT HOW DO WE GET OUT OF HERE? IF WE LEAVE THE GARDEN, WE'RE STILL STUCK IN THE EVERLANDS.
PERHAPS IF WE COULD REACH THE SHORE, WE COULD—
LET ME STOP YOU RIGHT THERE.
MIGHT I SUGGEST A QUICKER MEANS OF EGRESS?
HURRY NOW, THIS OFFER WON'T LAST LONG.
SURE, TRUST THE CONNIVING LITTLE SNEAK THAT GOT US INTO THIS MESS IN THE FIRST PLACE.
QUIET, SCHRODINGER...

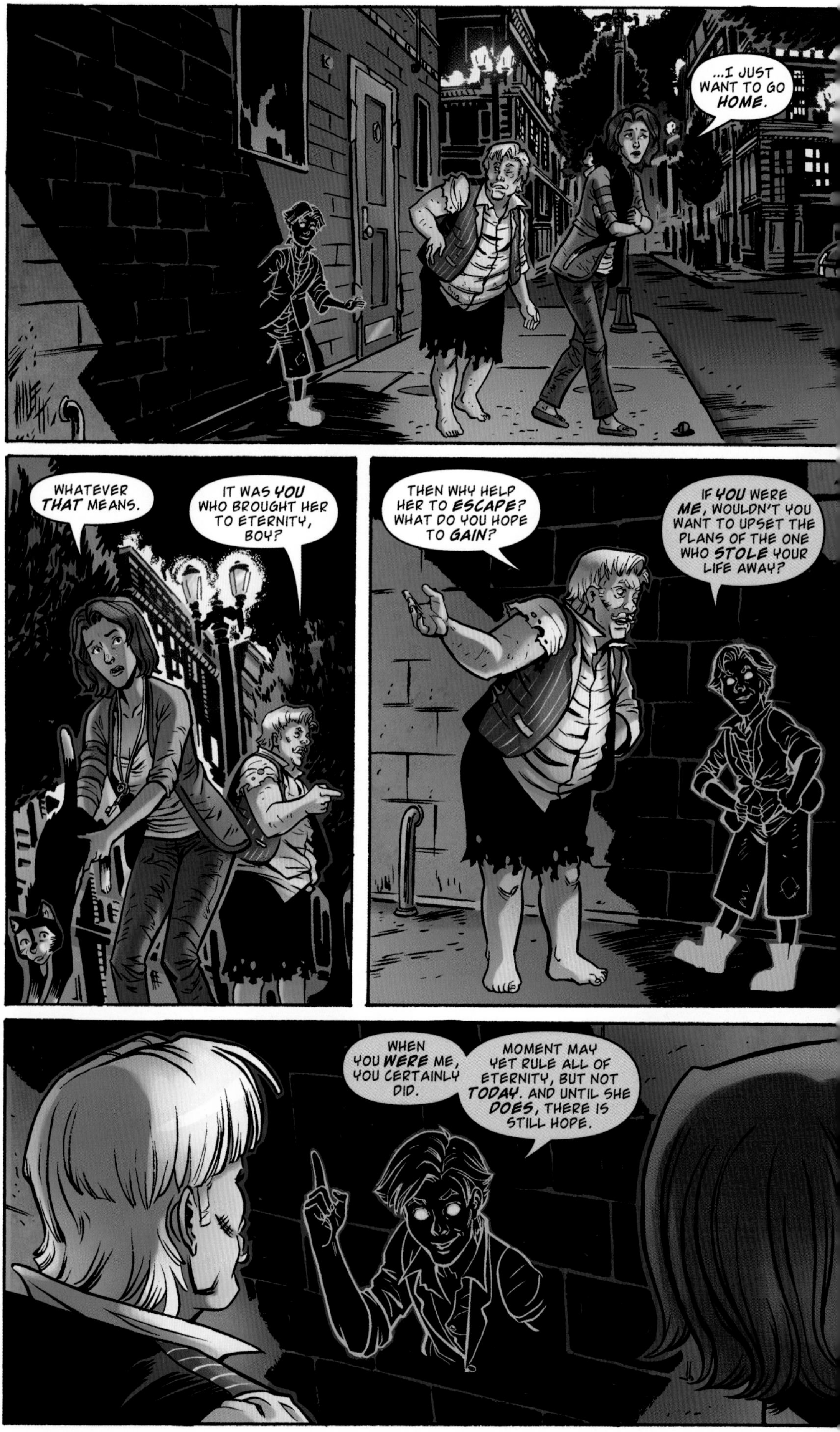
...I JUST WANT TO GO HOME.
WHATEVER THAT MEANS.
IT WAS YOU WHO BROUGHT HER TO ETERNITY, BOY?
THEN WHY HELP HER TO ESCAPE? WHAT DO YOU HOPE TO GAIN?
IF YOU WERE ME, WOULDN'T YOU WANT TO UPSET THE PLANS OF THE ONE WHO STOLE YOUR LIFE AWAY?
WHEN YOU WERE ME, YOU CERTAINLY DID.
MOMENT MAY YET RULE ALL OF ETERNITY, BUT NOT TODAY. AND UNTIL SHE DOES, THERE IS STILL HOPE.

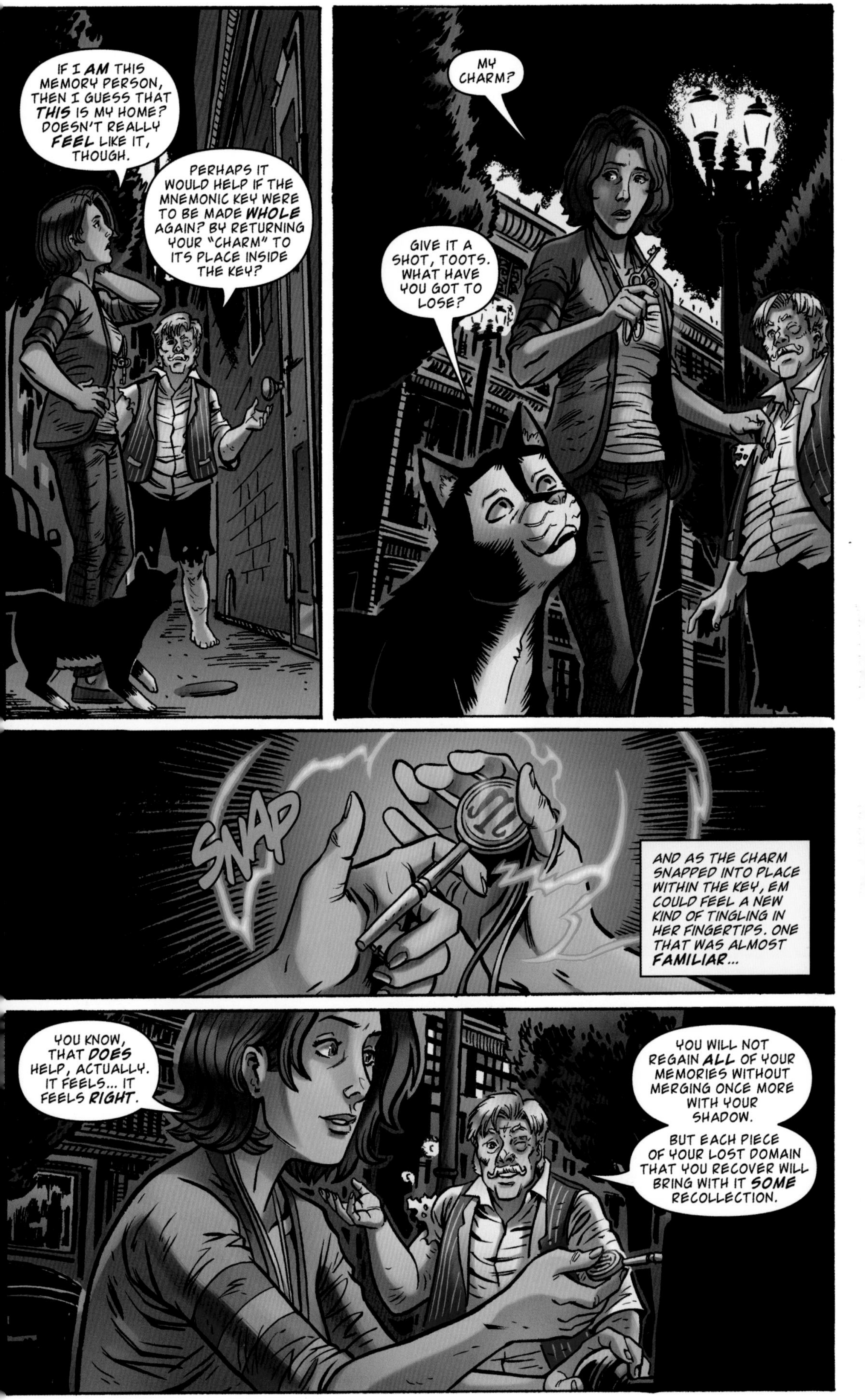
IF I AM THIS MEMORY PERSON, THEN I GUESS THAT THIS IS MY HOME? DOESN'T REALLY FEEL LIKE IT, THOUGH.
PERHAPS IT WOULD HELP IF THE MNEMONIC KEY WERE TO BE MADE WHOLE AGAIN? BY RETURNING YOUR "CHARM" TO ITS PLACE INSIDE THE KEY?
MY CHARM?
GIVE IT A SHOT, TOOTS. WHAT HAVE YOU GOT TO LOSE?
SNAP
AND AS THE CHARM SNAPPED INTO PLACE WITHIN THE KEY, EM COULD FEEL A NEW KIND OF TINGLING IN HER FINGERTIPS. ONE THAT WAS ALMOST FAMILIAR...
YOU KNOW, THAT DOES HELP, ACTUALLY. IT FEELS... IT FEELS RIGHT.
YOU WILL NOT REGAIN ALL OF YOUR MEMORIES WITHOUT MERGING ONCE MORE WITH YOUR SHADOW.
BUT EACH PIECE OF YOUR LOST DOMAIN THAT YOU RECOVER WILL BRING WITH IT SOME RECOLLECTION.

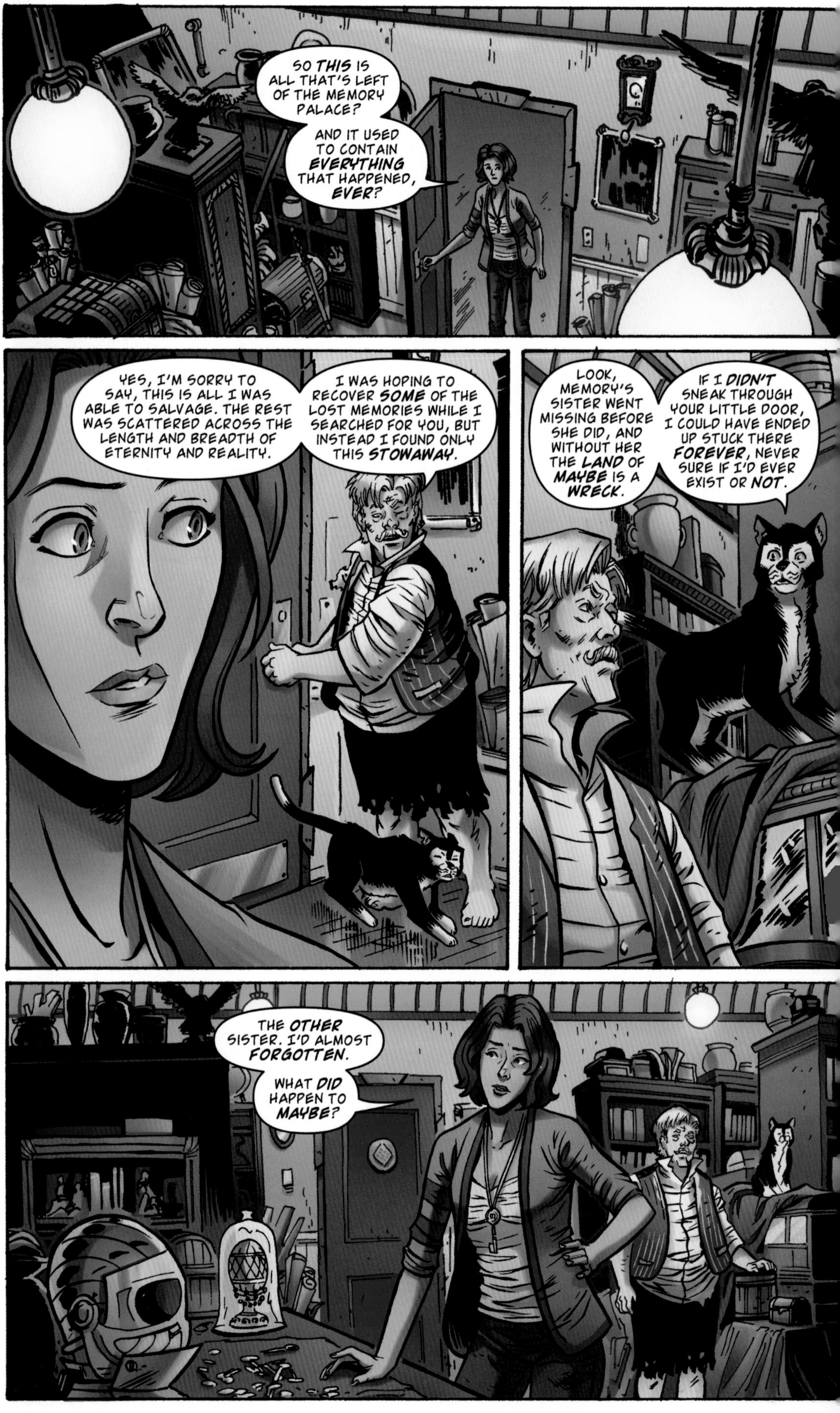
SO THIS IS ALL THAT'S LEFT OF THE MEMORY PALACE?
AND IT USED TO CONTAIN EVERYTHING THAT HAPPENED, EVER?
YES, I'M SORRY TO SAY, THIS IS ALL I WAS ABLE TO SALVAGE. THE REST WAS SCATTERED ACROSS THE LENGTH AND BREADTH OF ETERNITY AND REALITY.
I WAS HOPING TO RECOVER SOME OF THE LOST MEMORIES WHILE I SEARCHED FOR YOU, BUT INSTEAD I FOUND ONLY THIS STOWAWAY.
LOOK, MEMORY'S SISTER WENT MISSING BEFORE SHE DID, AND WITHOUT HER THE LAND OF MAYBE IS A WRECK.
IF I DIDN'T SNEAK THROUGH YOUR LITTLE DOOR, I COULD HAVE ENDED UP STUCK THERE FOREVER, NEVER SURE IF I'D EVER EXIST OR NOT.
THE OTHER SISTER. I'D ALMOST FORGOTTEN.
WHAT DID HAPPEN TO MAYBE?

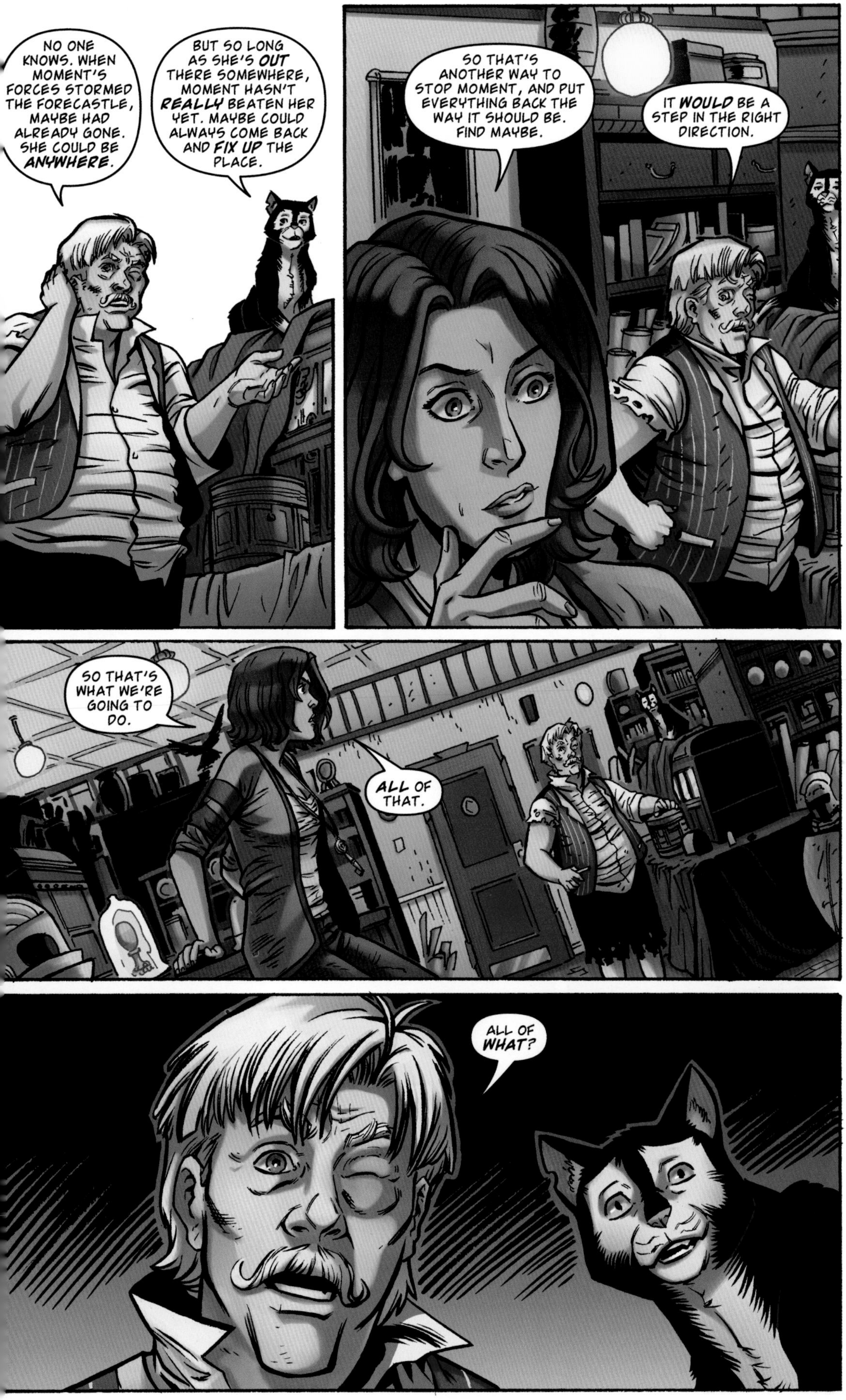
NO ONE KNOWS. WHEN MOMENT'S FORCES STORMED THE FORECASTLE, MAYBE HAD ALREADY GONE. SHE COULD BE ANYWHERE.
BUT SO LONG AS SHE'S OUT THERE SOMEWHERE, MOMENT HASN'T REALLY BEATEN HER YET. MAYBE COULD ALWAYS COME BACK AND FIX UP THE PLACE.
SO THAT'S ANOTHER WAY TO STOP MOMENT, AND PUT EVERYTHING BACK THE WAY IT SHOULD BE. FIND MAYBE.
IT WOULD BE A STEP IN THE RIGHT DIRECTION.
SO THAT'S WHAT WE'RE GOING TO DO.
ALL OF THAT.
ALL OF WHAT?

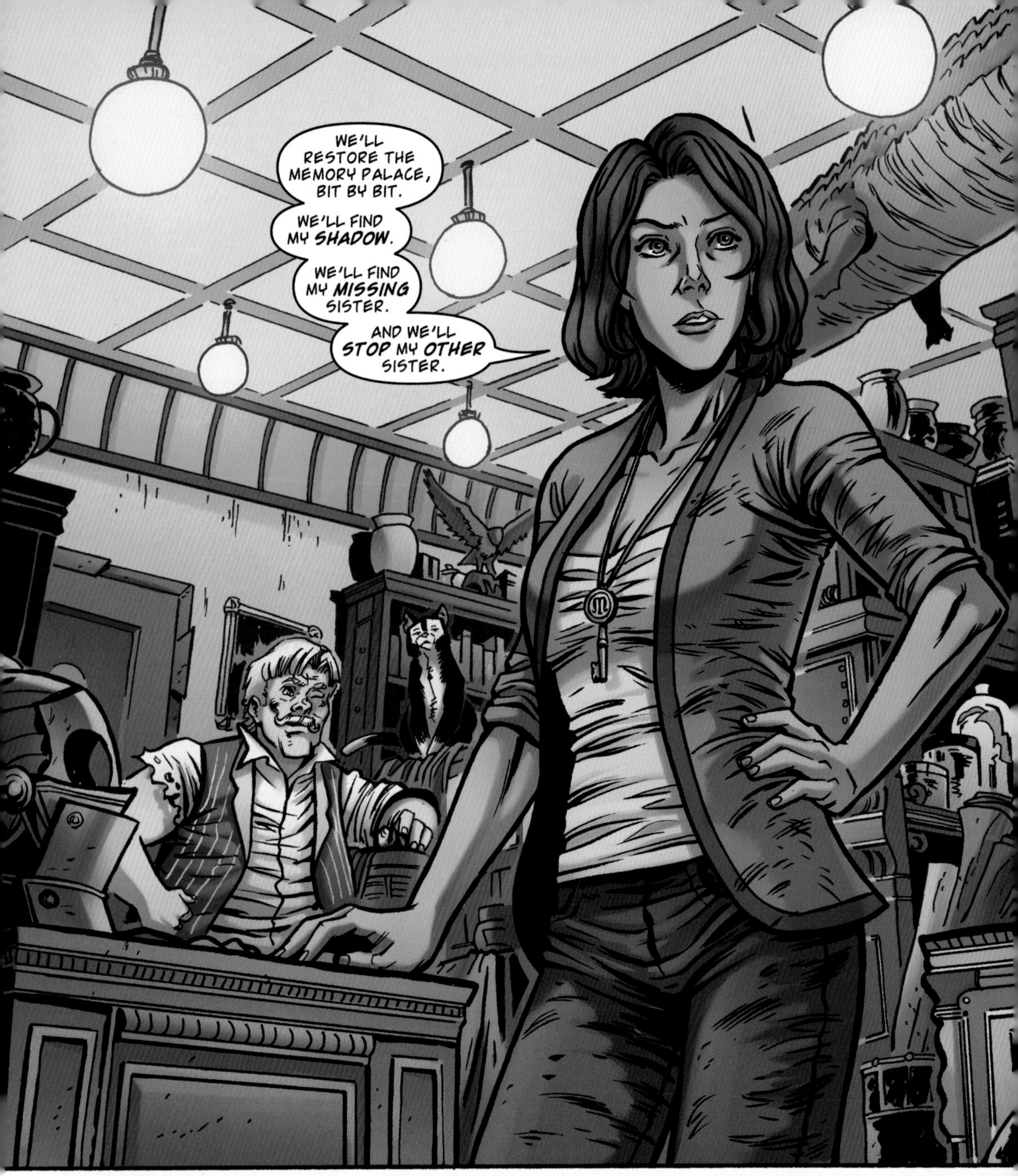
WE'LL RESTORE THE MEMORY PALACE, BIT BY BIT.
WE'LL FIND MY **SHADOW**.
WE'LL FIND MY **MISSING** SISTER.
AND WE'LL **STOP** MY **OTHER** SISTER.

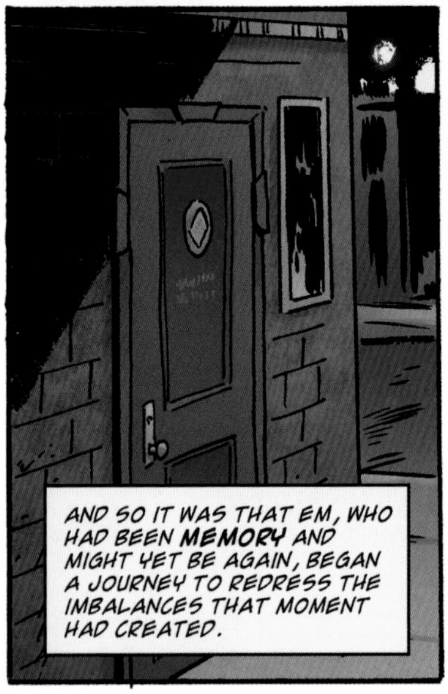
AND SO IT WAS THAT EM, WHO HAD BEEN **MEMORY** AND MIGHT YET BE AGAIN, BEGAN A JOURNEY TO REDRESS THE IMBALANCES THAT MOMENT HAD CREATED.

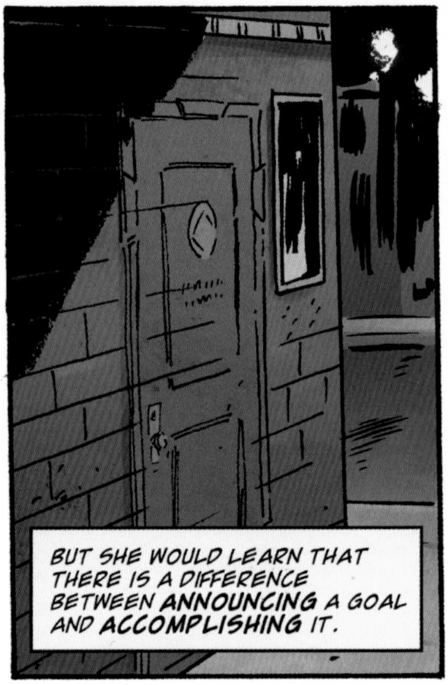
BUT SHE WOULD LEARN THAT THERE IS A DIFFERENCE BETWEEN **ANNOUNCING** A GOAL AND **ACCOMPLISHING** IT.

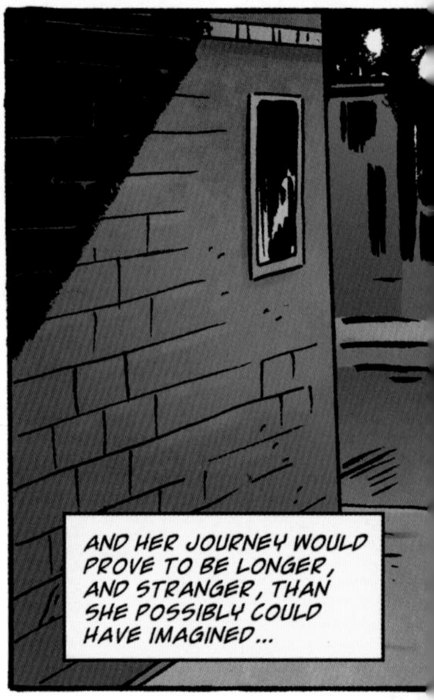
AND HER JOURNEY WOULD PROVE TO BE LONGER, AND STRANGER, THAN SHE POSSIBLY COULD HAVE IMAGINED...

Art & Design Gallery

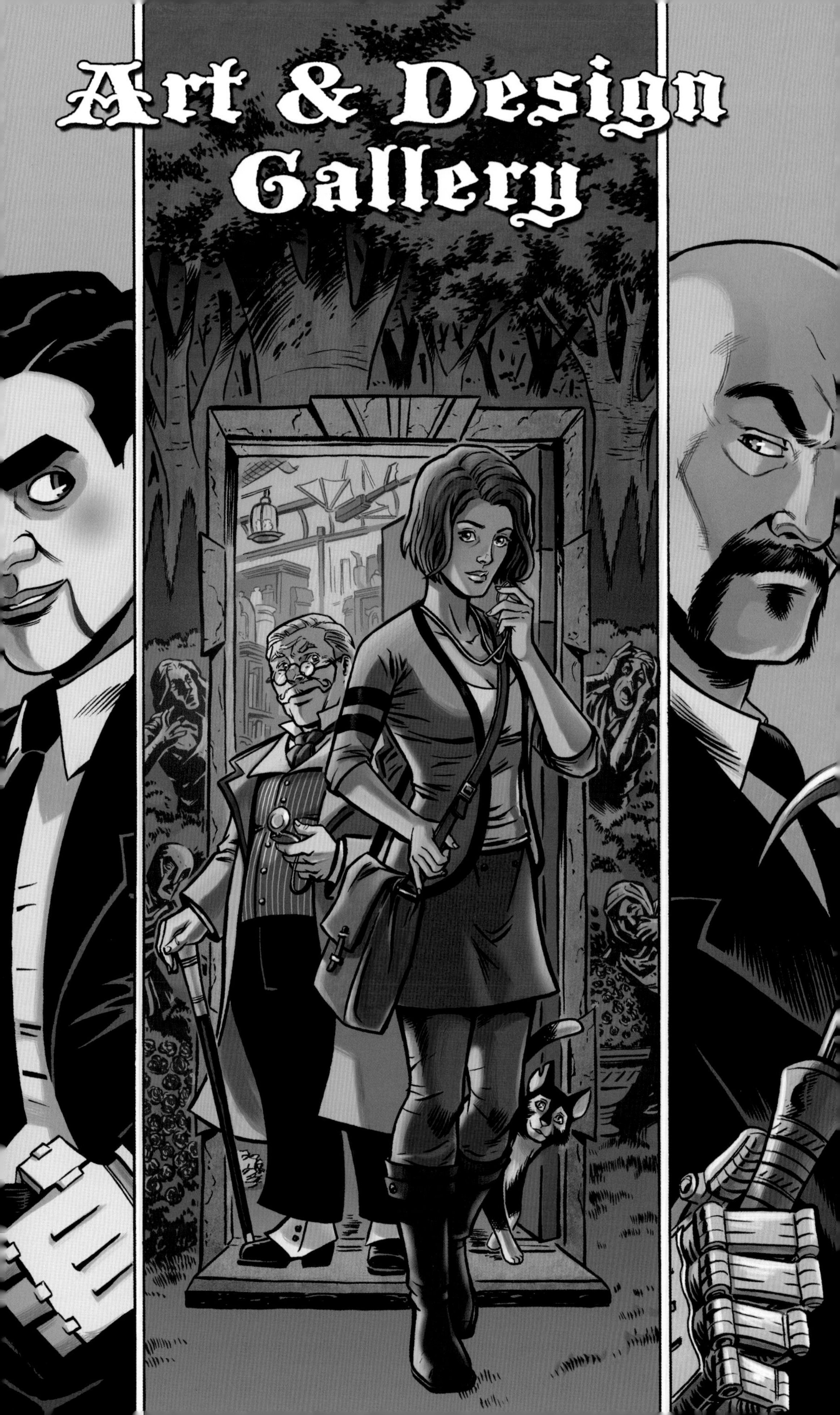

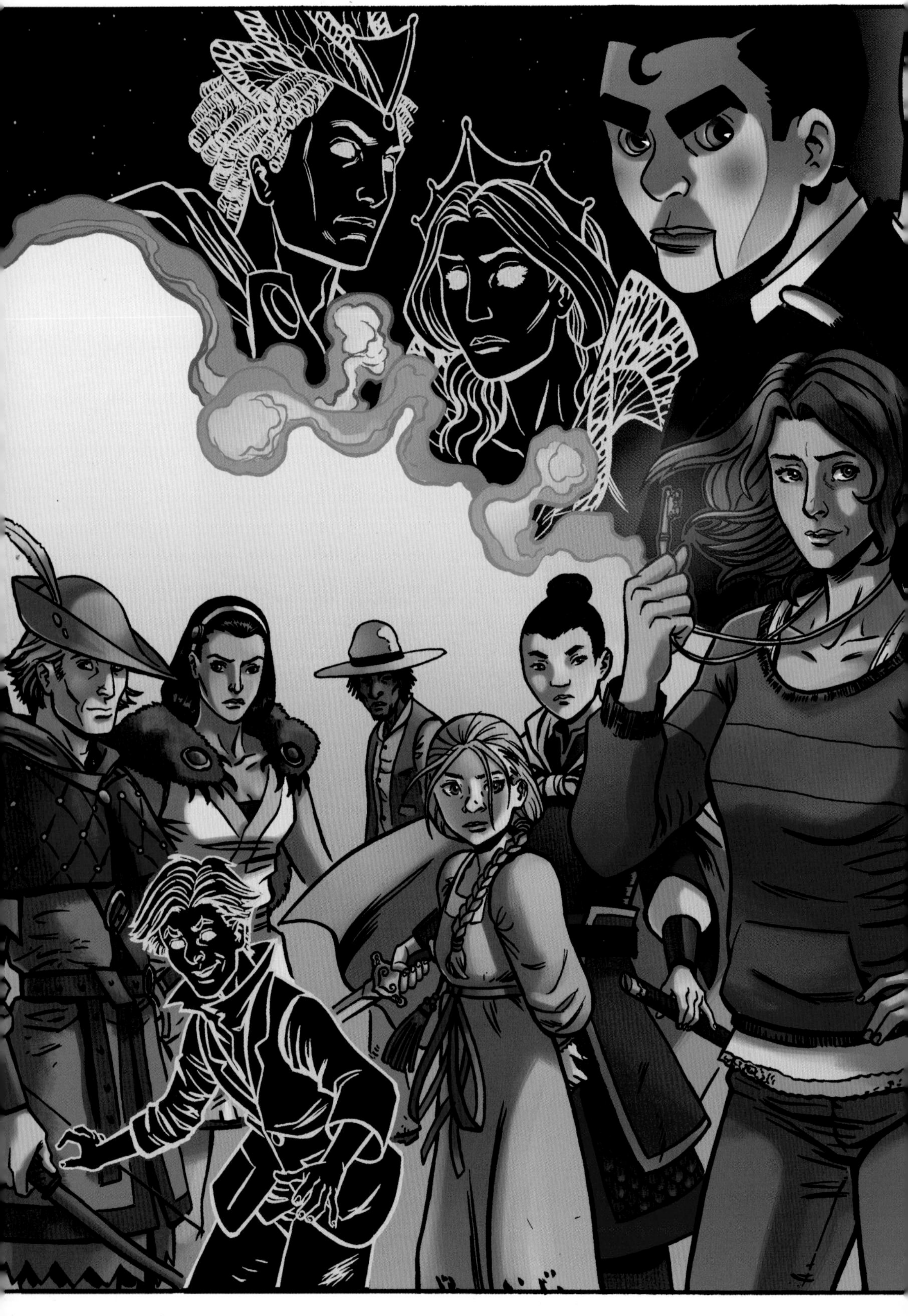

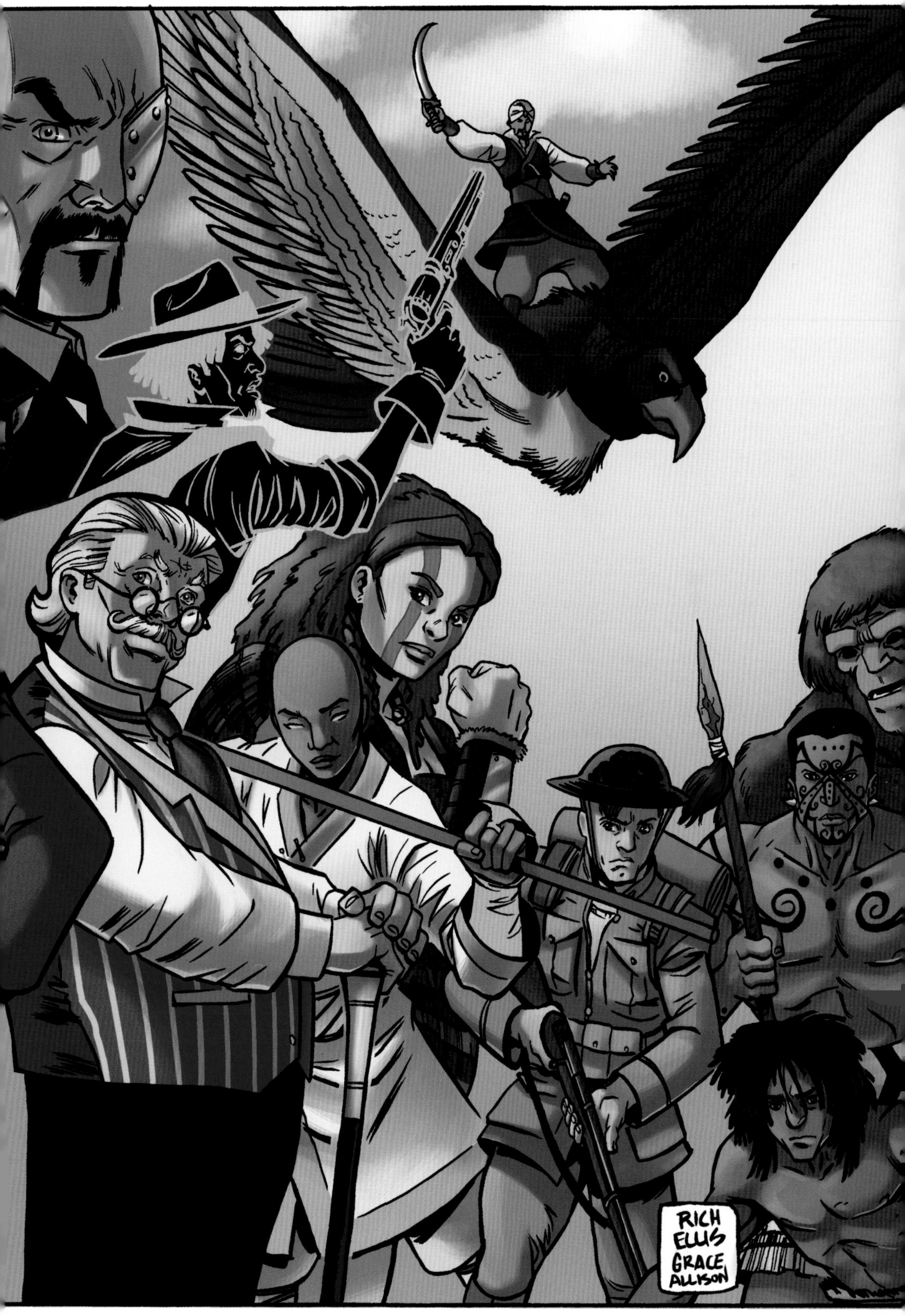
RICH
ELLIS
GRACE
ALLISON

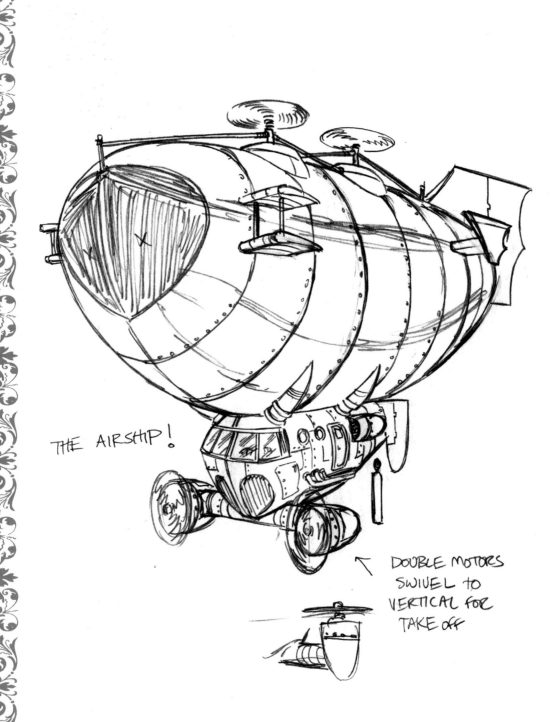

THE AIRSHIP!

DOUBLE MOTORS
SWIVEL to
VERTICAL FOR
TAKE OFF

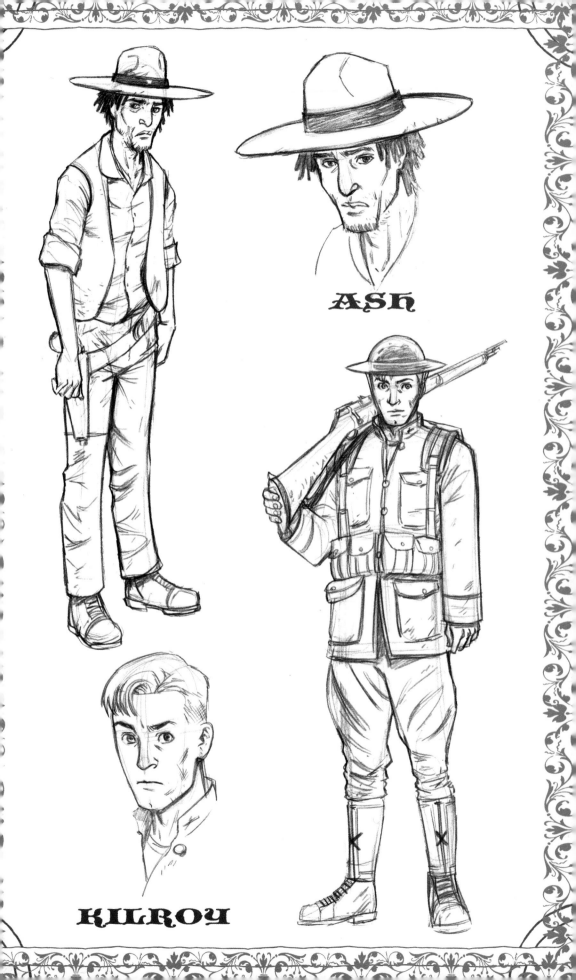

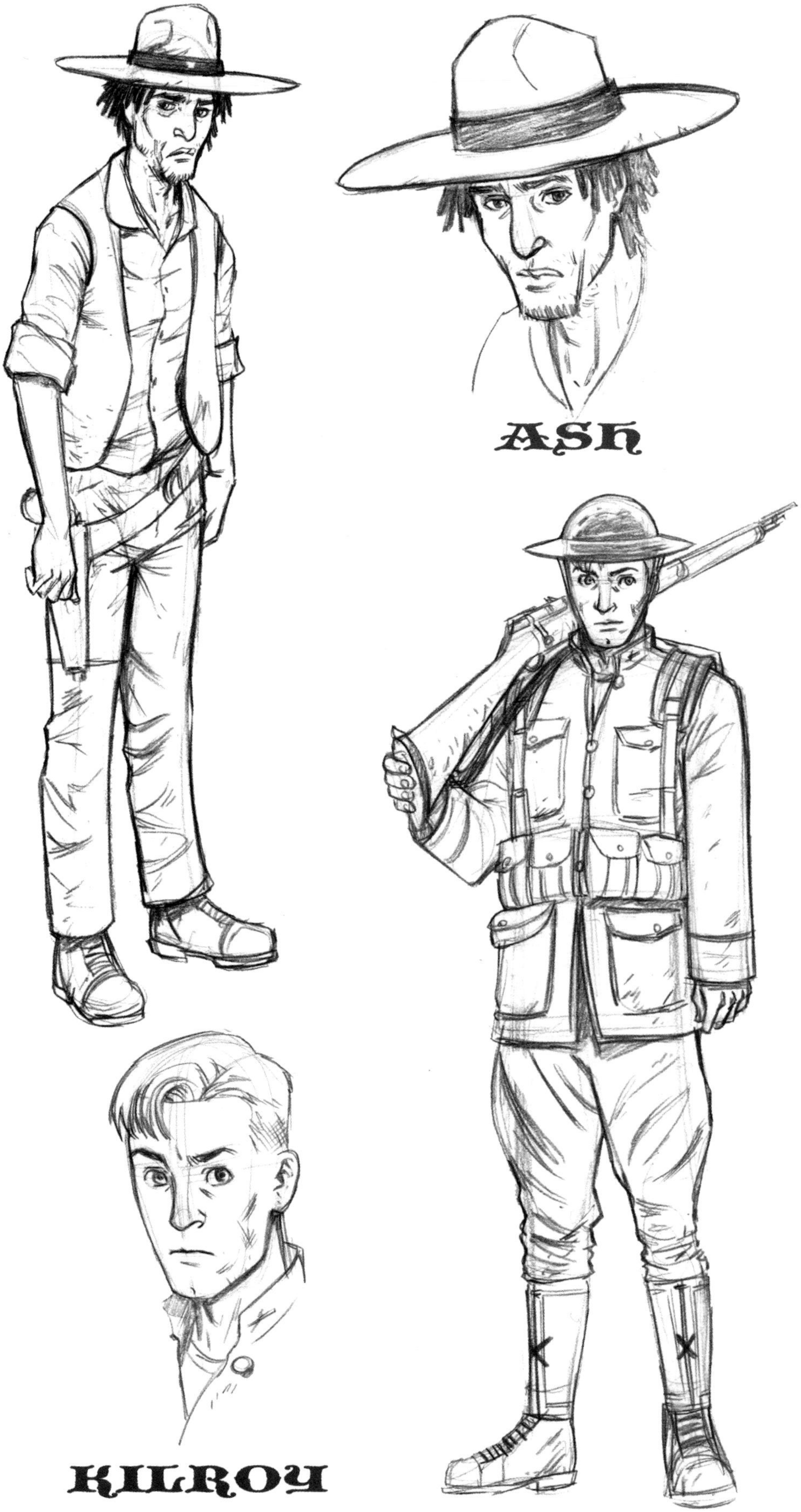
ASH
KILROY

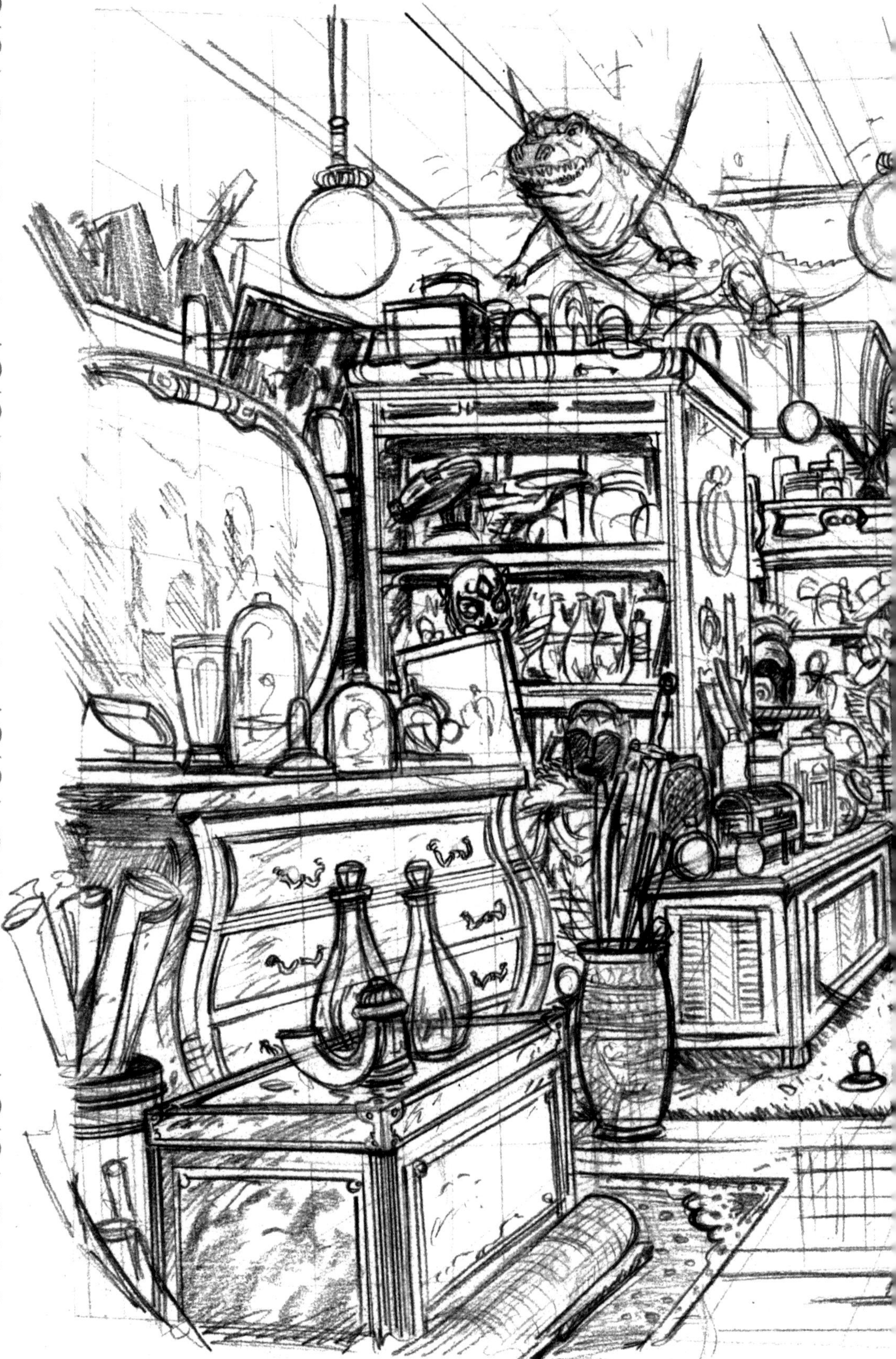

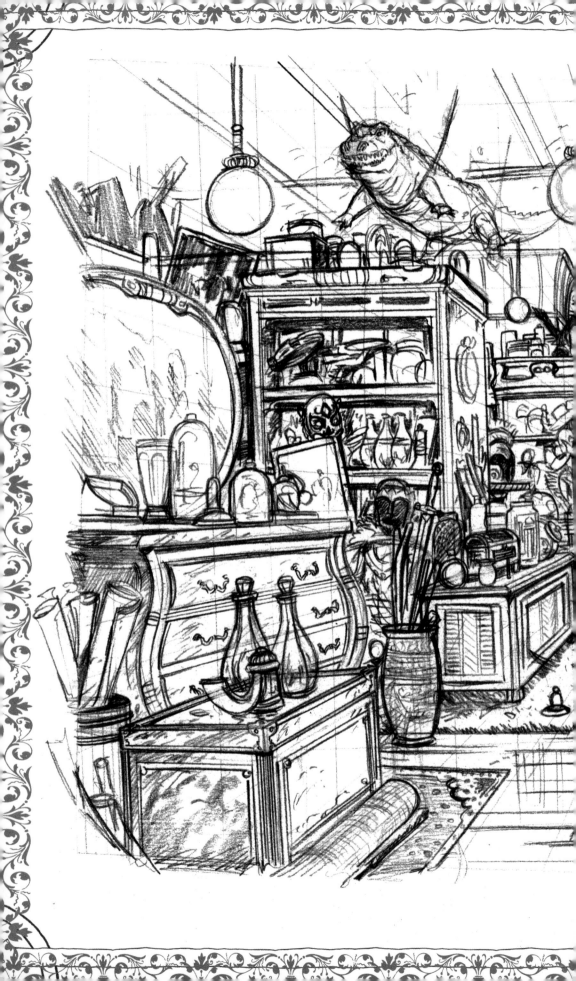

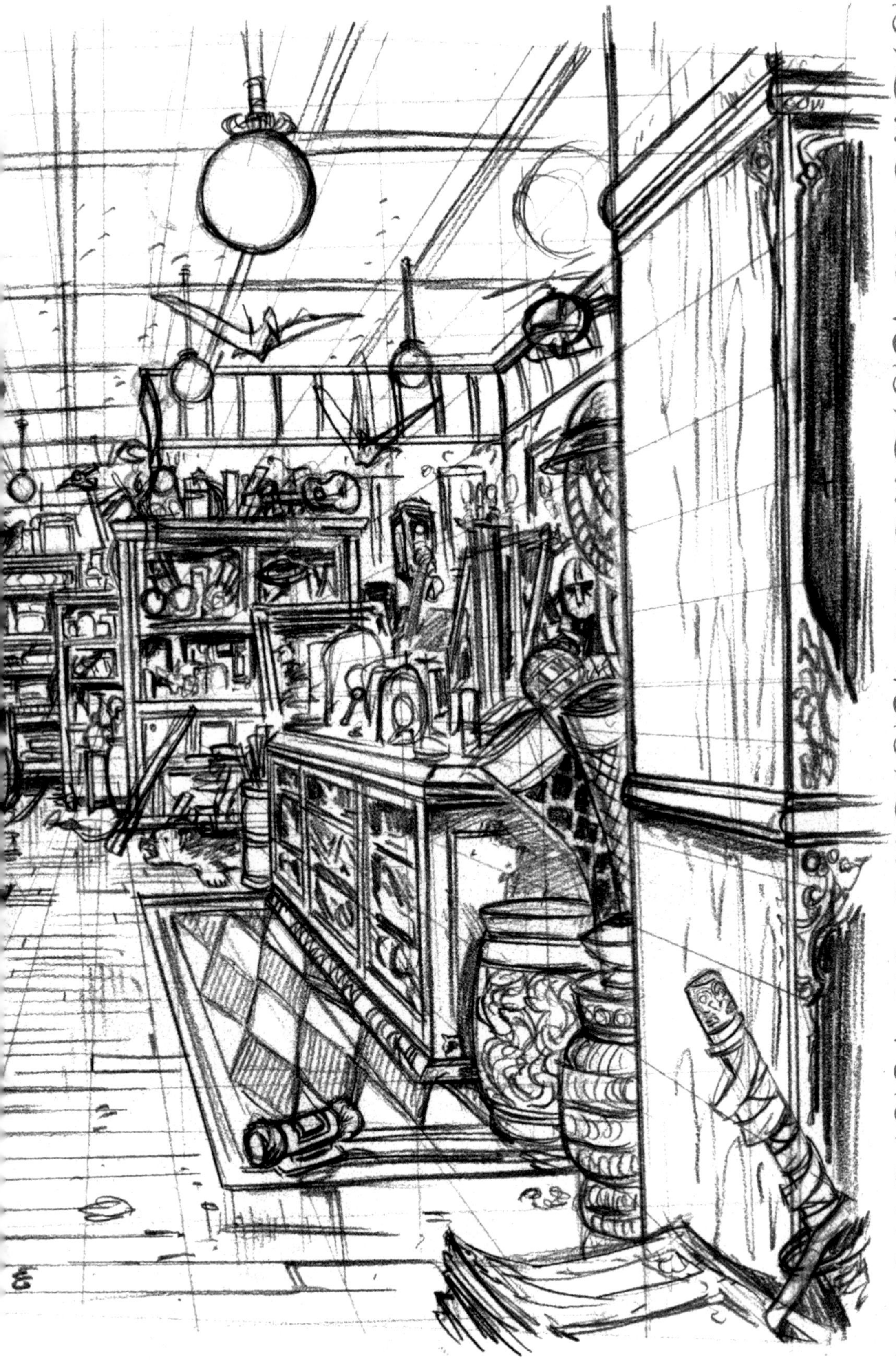
MEMORIAL CURIOSITIES & ANTIQUES

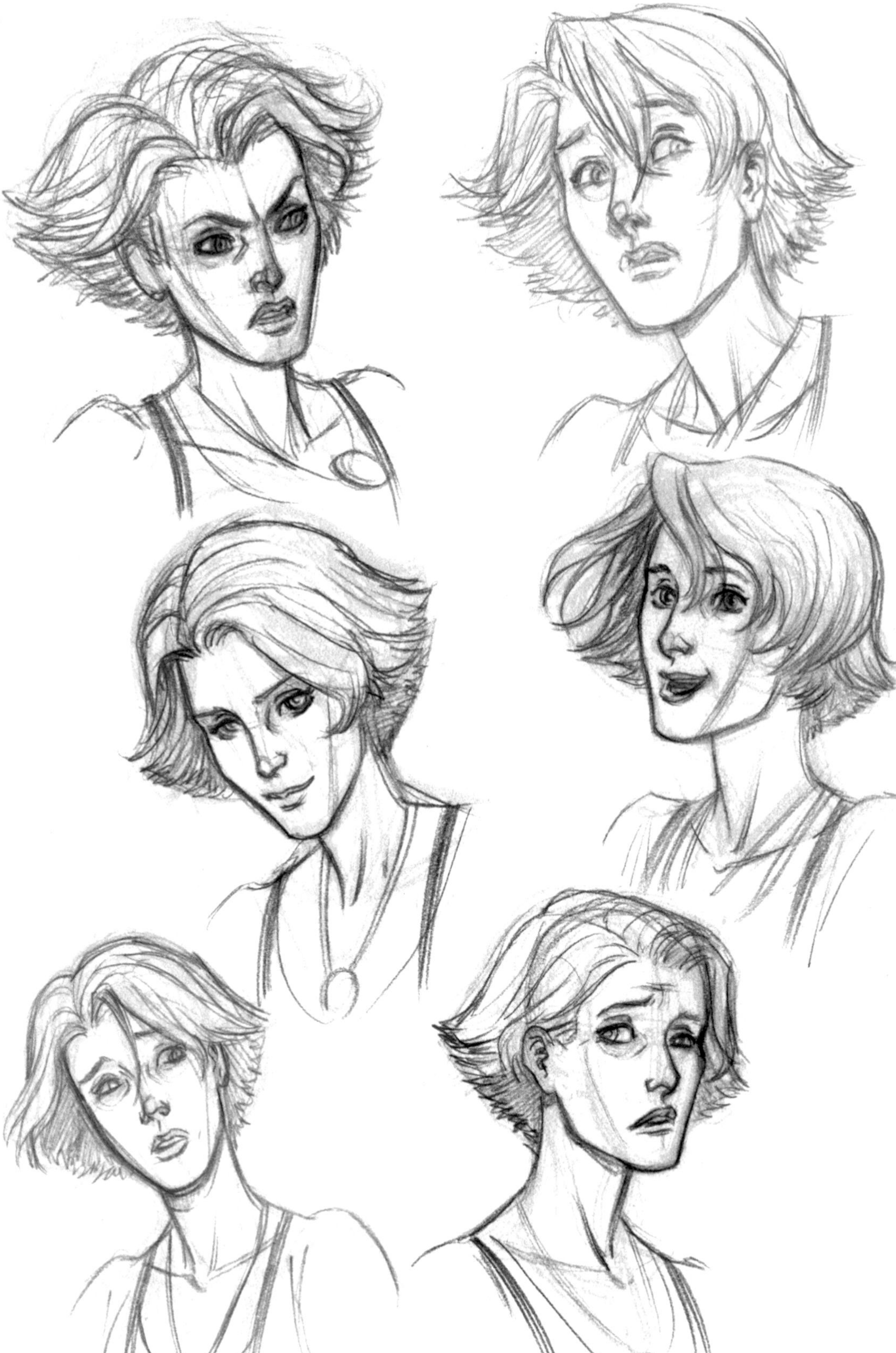

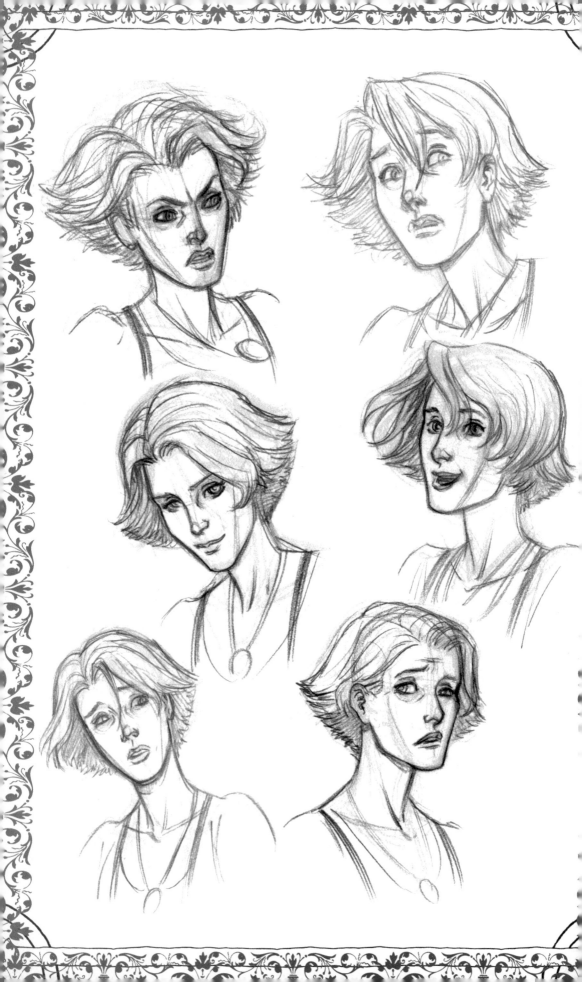

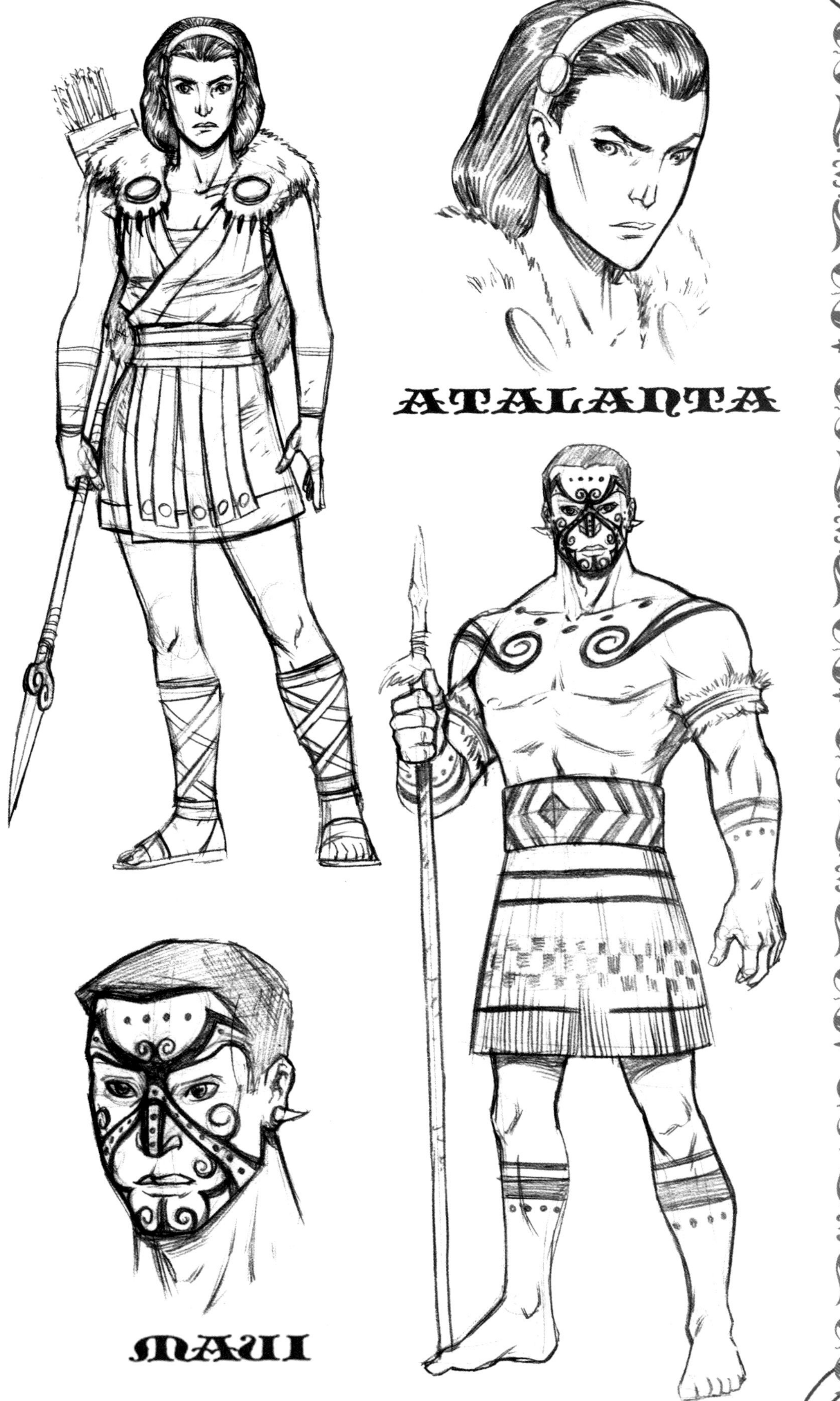
ATALANTA
MAUI

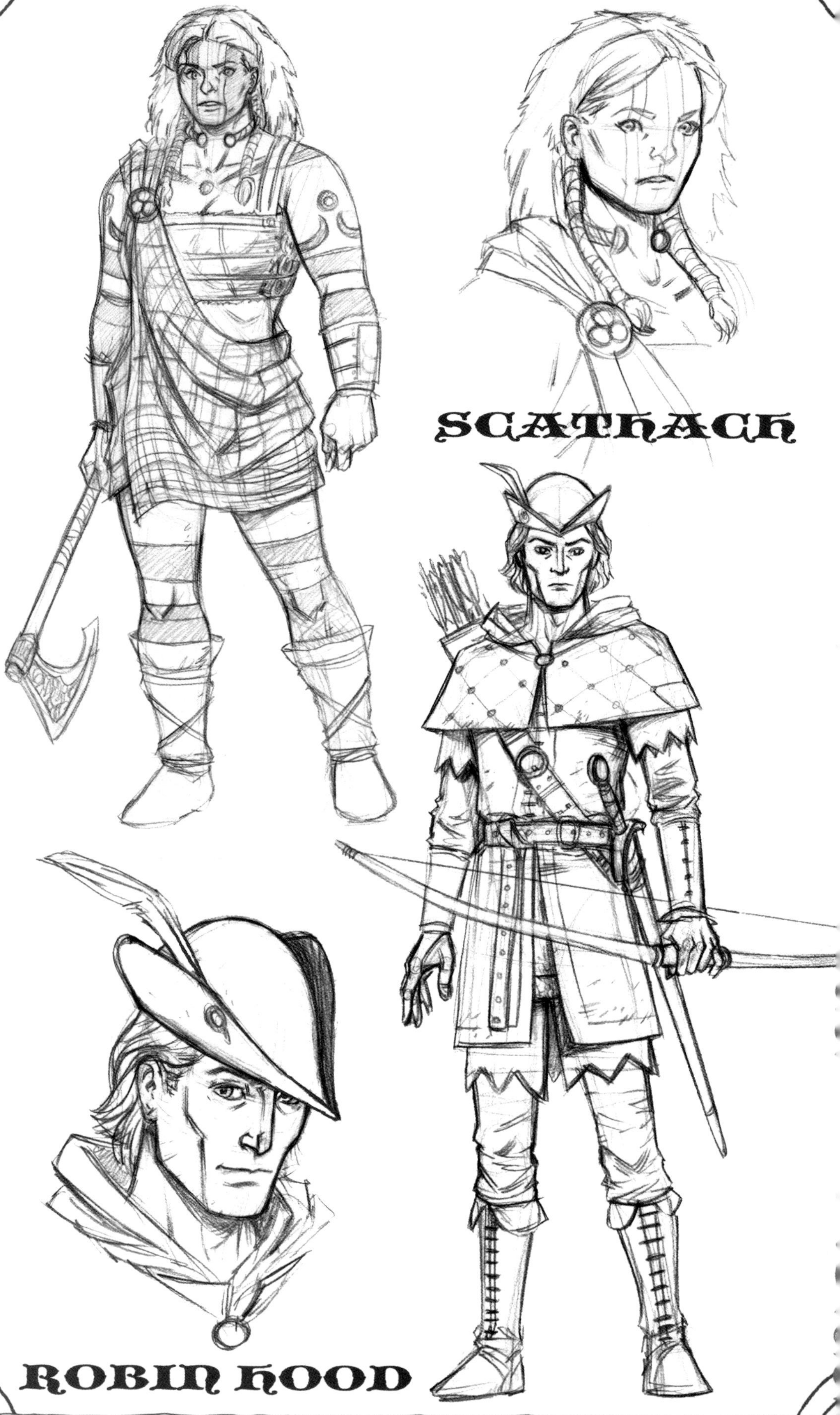
SCATHACH
ROBIN HOOD